A Merry Xmas
1993

To
Ruth
From
Mary & Bill
xxx

THE
FARMHOUSE KITCHEN
COOKBOOK

Edited by Mary Watts

MULBERRY EDITIONS

© Yorkshire Television Enterprises Ltd, 1992

This omnibus edition published in 1992
by Cresset Press for Mulberry Editions

Front cover illustration: Mary Evans Picture Library

Incorporating

Farmhouse Kitchen Book 3
First published in 1982 by
Yorkshire Television Enterprises Ltd
© Yorkshire Television Enterprises Ltd, 1982
Text illustrations: Mary Evans Picture Library, pages
28, 61, 84, 94, 145, 148, 180, 187; The Mansell
Collection, page 13; Peter Newark's Historical
Pictures, page 117; John Topham Picture Library,
page 101

Farmhouse Kitchen Cooking for One & Two
First published in 1988 by
Yorkshire Television Enterprises Ltd
© Yorkshire Television Enterprises Ltd, 1988
Text illustrations: Mary Evans Picture Library, 'Food
and Drink Collection' and '1800 Woodcuts' both
published by Dover Publications

ISBN 1–85813–011–5

Printed and bound in Great Britain

The Farmhouse Kitchen television series was
presented for 12 years by Dorothy Sleightholme and
subsequently by her successor Grace Mulligan

THE
FARMHOUSE KITCHEN
RECIPES

ACKNOWLEDGMENTS

In this third collection of recipes, which will be used in our television programmes for the next 4 or 5 years, I have once again been delighted to receive contributions from all over the British Isles and some from abroad. Many viewers have sent in their family favourites, many others have written with requests for traditional county fare, for vegetarian recipes, for oriental dishes.

It has given Grace Mulligan, Graham Watts and me much pleasure to visit the Women's Institute of Cornwall, Devon, Dorset, Gloucestershire, Gwent, East and West Kent, Somerset, West Sussex and Worcestershire. Each of these federations presented a wonderful array of local delicacies and traditional dishes and many of their recipes have been selected for this book. Through the Dorset W.I. I discovered The Piddle Valley Cookbook and I am indebted to the Piddletrenthide Parochial Church Council for permission to print John Firrell's version of Mackerel with Gooseberries, known to him as Portland-style Mackerel. The work of individual W.I. members in seeking out old recipes, bringing them up to date and preparing them for us to taste was remarkable and is greatly appreciated.

Sarah Brown, who began the Terrace Project in Scarborough 4 years ago, which numbers amongst its activities a wholefood restaurant and shop, has offered me many of her successful dishes and will demonstrate them in the programmes. Some of the other wholefood recipes have been contributed by Janet Horsley, who has recently published through Prism Press a book of her own called Bean Cuisine. Permission to use Elizabeth Shears' recipe has been granted by the Nutrition Science Research Institute, Brookthorpe, Gloucester.

Priya Wickramasinghe is Sri Lankan, is much travelled and has lived in this country for 15 years (her 3 young children are all English-born). She was introduced to me by Messrs. J. M. Dent & Sons Ltd with whom she has published Spicy and Delicious and Oriental Cookbook. Her recipes, which are examples of everyday and special-occasion oriental cookery, are written with the western cook in mind and will allow you to make at home many dishes which you may hitherto have only tried at Indian, Sri Lankan, Indonesian or Chinese restaurants.

Without the help of some of our old friends and programme participants I could not present this book to you confident that every recipe has been tried and tested. The recipes do work and have been tried out on husbands, families and friends of Judith Adshead, Margaret Heywood, Liz Mickery, Sybil Norcott, Dennis Rouston and Anne Wallace, who have also given us many of their own recipes.

I am indebted also for much help and advice to the Home Food Science Section (M.A.F.F.) Long Ashton Research Station; the Prestige Group p.l.c., for information concerning pressure cooking; and last but not least to Joyce Town who has organised the typing of every recipe and typed many herself two or three times over.

Mary Watts
Summer 1982

CONTENTS

INTRODUCTION

Compiling a cookery book brings one face to face with the need to make cooking not just an everyday necessity but an exciting challenge to stimulate all the senses. There is no point in having a highly nutritious meal if it looks and tastes dull.

Dorothy and I have tried very hard to show that good food is not necessarily expensive food. We want to encourage you to experiment with wholewheat flours, raw vegetables and fruit, herbs, spices, pulses and grains so that you eat for your health's sake too.

Traditional cooking has not been forgotten and we have many recipes from counties north and south. From the East there are recipes with exciting aromatic ingredients to tempt you. Superb cakes, buns, fruit breads, preserves and drinks are all here.

With four children of my own I know well the need for substantial, filling and nutritious dishes for bleak winter days but we have also tried to remember those of you who live alone and your need for an elegant, light but nutritious meal.

We hope this book, with its contributions from many others besides Dorothy and myself, will convey to you our enthusiam for cooking of all kinds so that it becomes a pleasure for you too.

We also hope you will take one or two steps in other directions, away from your regular old standby recipes, and possibly find some things which in time will become new firm favourites.

Grace Mulligan   *Dorothy Sleightholme*

Yorkshire Television's Farmhouse Kitchen series is produced and directed by Mary and Graham Watts.

Chapter 1

Soups
and
Starters

Stock from a piece of meat or a whole chicken has the most flavour. The following recipe uses an excellent broth derived from cooking a piece of lamb or beef which is removed after about 2 hours and served as a main course with vegetables. Remember to start the night before.

DUNDEE BROTH

50 g/2 oz dried green peas
50 g/2 oz barley
2·8 litres/5 pints cold water
675 g/1½ lb piece of beef or lamb, tied with string
225 g/8 oz diced carrots
125 g/4 oz diced turnip
125 g/4 oz chopped cabbage
2 whole leeks, chopped
Extra carrot and turnip cut in chunks to serve with the boiled meat
1 tablespoon chopped parsley
Salt and pepper

1. Wash and soak the dried peas overnight.
2. Put peas and barley on to cook in a large pan with the water.
3. Tie meat with string so that it can be carved as a joint. Put it into pan when water is hot.
4. Add diced and chopped vegetables. Put lid on pan.
5. Cook steadily for about 2 hours.
6. 30 minutes before the soup is to be served add the extra vegetables.
7. When the time is up and the meat and vegetables cooked, lift out meat and vegetables. Lift out vegetables. Keep hot.
8. Add salt and pepper to soup as required. Add parsley and serve.

Mrs Grace McGlinn
Dundee, Scotland

CLEAR BEEF SOUP

25 g/1 oz dripping or more
1 large onion, chopped
A clove of garlic, chopped
1 teaspoon sugar
225 to 350 g/8 to 12 oz shin of beef, cut small
225 g/8 oz ox liver, cut small
1 pig's trotter or calf's foot
1 small carrot, scrubbed and chopped
1 large tomato, halved and grilled
A bouquet garni (a sprig of thyme, parsley and 1 bay leaf tied together)
1·7 litres/3 pints water
Salt and pepper
1 large egg-white
2 to 3 tablespoons sherry or madeira (optional)

1. Melt dripping in a frying pan. Fry onion and garlic until soft. Sprinkle with sugar and stir. Leave to cook without stirring until sugar caramelises (i.e., browns) but do not allow onion to burn.
2. Lift onion and garlic out of frying pan into a large saucepan or flame-proof casserole.
3. Now brown beef and liver in frying pan, adding a little more fat if necessary.
4. Put beef, liver, trotter, carrot, tomato and herbs into the saucepan with onion and garlic. Pour in water.
5. Bring to the boil, season with salt and pepper, put on lid and simmer for about 2 hours either on top of stove or in a moderate oven, Gas 3, 325°F, 160°C.
6. Strain off liquid and leave overnight so that fat can rise.
7. Next day scrape off the fat and put jellied stock into a large saucepan over gentle heat.
8. When it is liquid and warm but *not* hot, add egg-white. Start to whisk with a hand rotary egg-beater or an electric whisk so that surface of soup is covered in a white froth. Allow to boil for 2 or 3 minutes.
9. Turn off heat and leave for 10 minutes. A brownish scum will cling to the egg-white, thus clearing the soup underneath.
10. Now pour contents of pan very gently through a sieve lined with muslin or thin cloth.

11. Re-heat soup and adjust seasoning. Taste it and if flavour is not strong enough boil it uncovered, reducing water content and so increasing flavour.

12. Take pan from heat and add wine just before serving. Although it is given as optional there is no doubt that this traditional ingredient adds to the flavour.

Serve with Sippets (*see page 12*) or some cooked pasta, or parsley.

Also delicious served chilled as a jelly. It will set in a jelly if the pig's trotter or calf's foot has been well cooked.

Freezes well.

Potted Meat

Using the remaining cooked shin of beef and pig's trotter, strip away fat and gristle. Mince the meat, beat into it enough softened butter to give a thick, creamy, spreading consistency. Season to taste. A little of the clear jelly may be added at this time to help the consistency. Press into pots and pour on a covering of melted butter.

Keeps for 3 or 4 days in a fridge, or a month in a freezer.

HAM SHANK

There are many ways to use an inexpensive shank. A smoked bacon or ham shank can also be used.

From 1 shank you should get 2·25 litres/4 pints of rich stock, 225 g/8 oz ham pieces and some ham fat

To cook shank and make stock

1. Put shank in a large saucepan with 2·7 to 3 litres/4½ to 5½ pints of water. Cover pan, bring to boil and simmer 1½ hours until meat and fat is falling off bones. Or, pressure cook for ¾ hour adding only the maximum quantity of water indicated in your pressure cooker manual.

2. Strain liquid into jugs. Allow to cool. Then put in refrigerator or wait until fat has risen and stock is set to a firm jelly.

3. When shank has cooled remove meat and separate fatty bits, skin and bones.

4. Lift fat off jellied stock to use for frying, etc.

Skin and fatty bits from meat can be rendered down to produce more dripping. Put them into a small pan, cover with water and put on lid. Simmer for 1 hour, then pour into a small bowl. As it cools fat will rise and when set can be lifted off liquid beneath.

Stock freezes well.

Ham may be chopped into white sauce and used on toast or in Vol-au-vents (*see page 112*), or pancakes (*see page 93*).

Try these dishes too: Ham Soup (*below*), Ham, Egg and Onion Flan (*page 108*), Ham Rissoles (*page 31*).

HAM SOUP

For 6 or more people

Using stock from ham shank take care to taste before using. It may be very salty and require diluting with water.

175 to 225 g/6 to 8 oz yellow split peas
2 medium-sized carrots
2 medium-sized onions
1·7 litres/3 pints ham stock

Other vegetables can be used— e.g., cabbage, leek, parsnips, turnips—400 to 450 g/14 to 16 oz vegetables is about right.

To serve

A little finely-chopped ham
2 tablespoons chopped, fresh parsley

1. Soak split peas in water for 3 hours. Then drain. If pressure cooking it is not necessary to soak first.

2. Scrub and chop carrots. Peel and chop onions.

3. Put split peas, vegetables and stock in a saucepan with a lid and simmer for 1 hour. Or pressure cook for 30

minutes taking care not to exceed maximum quantity of liquid indicated in your pressure cooker manual.

4. Add ham, parsley and seasoning if necessary and cook for 5 minutes.

Serve very hot.

This soup can be liquidised before parsley is added. It is then particularly delicious served with Sippets fried in ham fat (*see page 12*).

HOT BEETROOT SOUP

This soup freezes well.
A liquidiser is needed.

450 g/1 lb raw beetroot
450 g/1 lb potatoes
2 onions
50 g/2 oz butter or margarine
1·5 to 1·75 litres/2½ to 3 pints strong chicken stock
Salt
Freshly ground pepper

To garnish: yoghurt or soured cream

1. Peel and dice beetroot and potatoes. Peel and chop onions.
2. Melt butter in a large saucepan and cook vegetables gently with lid on pan for about 5 minutes.
3. Stir in the stock, bring to the boil and simmer until beetroot is cooked.
4. Cool the soup and reduce it to a purée in liquidiser. Return to pan. Adjust seasoning.
5. Just before serving, bring soup to boiling point and serve with a swirl of yoghurt or soured cream in each bowl.

Freeze before yoghurt or soured cream is added.

CARROT SOUP

2 onions
40 g/1½ oz butter
1 clove of garlic
A pinch of salt
450 g/1 lb carrots
Pepper

1 dessertspoon coriander seeds
1 glass of sherry
600 ml/1 pint chicken stock
600 ml/1 pint milk
To garnish: chopped parsley

1. Peel and slice onions and cook carefully in butter in a large pan until transparent.
2. Crush garlic with salt and add to onions.
3. Scrub carrots, slice thinly and add to pan.
4. Season with salt and pepper. Add coriander seeds and sherry. Cover and cook gently until vegetables are soft, about 10 to 15 minutes.
5. Add stock and cook a further 15 to 20 minutes. Allow to cool.
6. Liquidise or sieve the soup, then strain into a clean pan.
7. Add milk when ready to serve. Reheat carefully. Adjust seasoning.
8. Sprinkle parsley in each bowl of soup.

CREAM OF LEEK AND POTATO SOUP

4 medium-sized leeks
50 g/2 oz butter
4 small potatoes
150 ml/¼ pint water
600 ml/1 pint chicken stock
Salt and pepper
150 ml/¼ pint thick cream

1. Wash and trim leeks and chop into small pieces, using both white and green parts.
2. Melt butter in a saucepan and add leeks. Cover pan and reduce heat so that leeks cook slowly without browning, for about 5 minutes. Shake pan occasionally.
3. Meanwhile, peel potatoes and cut into small cubes.
4. Add potatoes to leeks with water and stock. Season to taste.
5. Bring to boil, cover pan and simmer soup for 25 minutes.
6. Sieve or liquidise soup and return it to the pan.
7. Add cream. Heat, but do not boil.

Mrs Eileen Trumper
Llanvair Kilgeddin, Gwent

SPICED RED LENTIL SOUP

This soup is a flaming orange colour.

4 large or 6 good helpings. Easy to make less.

1 medium-sized onion
1 red pepper
2 sticks of celery
225 g/8 oz marrow or courgettes
125 g/4 oz red lentils
1 tablespoon oil
1 teaspoon paprika
1 teaspoon turmeric
A pinch of cinnamon
A pinch of cayenne pepper
A 400 g/14 oz can of tomatoes
1 teaspoon basil
1 bay leaf
About 750 ml/1¼ pints water or vegetable stock
Salt and pepper
1 tablespoon shoyu (*see page 80*)

1. Chop vegetables finely.
2. Wash lentils and pick them over for stones.
3. Heat oil and fry spices—i.e., paprika, turmeric, cinnamon and cayenne.
4. Add vegetables and lentils. Stir well so that oil and spices coat the vegetables. Cook about 5 minutes, stirring occasionally.
5. Cut up tomatoes, put them in a measuring jug and add enough water or stock to make 1·1 litres/2 pints.
6. Add this with basil and bay leaf to pan of vegetables. Bring to boil and simmer for 40 minutes or until lentils are cooked.
7. Add salt and pepper to taste. Add the shoyu. Add more water or stock if necessary.

Sarah Brown
Scarborough, Yorkshire

MINTY GREEN SOUP

For this you need a liquidiser.

At least enough for 6 but freezes well

175 g/6 oz green split peas
1 medium-sized onion
225 g/8 oz carrots
2 small potatoes
2 sticks celery
1 small parsnip
1 tablespoon oil
1·1 litres/2 pints light stock or water
¼ to 1 tablespoon dried mint or chopped fresh mint to taste
Salt and pepper
1 tablespoon shoyu (*see page 80*)
Milk (optional)

To garnish: 2 tablespoons cream, sprigs of fresh mint

1. Wash the split peas.
2. Peel and finely chop onion.
3. Scrub and finely chop carrots, potatoes, celery and parsnip.
4. Gently fry onion in oil until translucent.
5. Add other vegetables and fry gently for 5 minutes, mixing well so that oil coats vegetables and seals in flavour.
6. Add green split peas and stock or water. Bring to boil and simmer for about 40 minutes until peas are cooked.
7. Put soup through liquidiser, adding mint, seasoning and shoyu as it blends. Return to pan.
8. If soup is too thick either stock, water or milk may be added. Heat gently, check seasoning.

Serve with a swirl of cream and sprigs of mint floating on surface.

Sarah Brown
Scarborough, Yorkshire

SIMPLE ONION SOUP

For 4 people

4 large onions, about 675 g/1½ lb
40 g/1½ oz butter or margarine
900 ml/1½ pints well-flavoured chicken stock
Salt and Pepper Mix (*see page 44*)

1. Cut up onions very fine.
2. Melt butter or margarine in a saucepan. Add onion, stir well and put on lid.
3. Turn heat down very low and allow onion to sweat for 10 minutes. Shake

pan from time to time but avoid taking off lid.

4. Add stock, season to taste, bring to the boil and simmer for 3 minutes or until onion is tender.

CREAM OF TOMATO SOUP

Freezes well, but do so before milk or cream is added.

1 medium-sized carrot, scrubbed
1 onion, peeled
2 sticks of celery, washed
75 g/3 oz butter or margarine
A 400 g/14 oz tin of tomatoes
1 teaspoon sugar
600 ml/1 pint light stock
Salt and Pepper Mix (see page 44)
25 g/1 oz plain flour
1 tablespoon tomato paste or purée*
150 ml/¼ pint top-of-milk or single cream

To garnish: chopped parsley

(*See: To keep tomato purée fresh, page 45)

1. Slice carrot, onion and celery finely.
2. Soften 40 g/1½ oz of the butter or margarine in a large saucepan. Add vegetables, put on lid and cook gently until soft, shaking pan occasionally.
3. Add tomatoes with their juice, sugar, 300 ml/½ pint of the stock, salt and pepper to taste. Simmer for 5 minutes.
4. Sieve contents of pan into a bowl. Rinse out pan.
5. Melt remaining 40 g/1½ oz butter or margarine in pan. Stir in flour and cook for 1 minute. Stir in rest of stock and tomato paste. Cook for 1 minute. Stir until boiling and simmer for 1 minute.
6. Add tomato mixture from bowl, and the milk or cream. Check seasoning. Heat to nearly boiling point, but do not actually boil or the soup may curdle.

Serve sprinkled with chopped parsley.

WHITE FOAM SOUP

Enough for 6 but easy to make half quantity

1 onion
1 stick of celery
A clove of garlic
40 g/1½ oz butter
25 g/1 oz flour
1·1 litres/2 pints of milk
A blade of mace
2 eggs
Salt and pepper
50 g/2 oz finely-grated cheese
1 tablespoon chopped parsley

Serve with tiny cubes of bread fried in butter or margarine. (See Sippets, below)

1. Chop onion and celery very fine. Crush garlic.
2. Melt butter in a 2 litre/3 pint saucepan. Stir in flour, then add milk slowly, stirring thoroughly till smooth. Bring to the boil and cook for 2 minutes.
3. Add onion, celery, garlic and mace. Let the soup barely simmer for 20 to 30 minutes until it is well flavoured.
4. Cool slightly, then add beaten yolks of the eggs.
5. Reheat without boiling. Then add salt and pepper to taste, and grated cheese. Do not allow to boil.
6. Beat egg-whites to a stiff froth. Fold half into the soup. Pour the rest into a hot tureen and pour soup over. Sprinkle with chopped parsley.

Mrs Irene Mills
For Leckhampton W.I., Glos.

SIPPETS

Fry cubes or small triangles of bread in hot bacon, or ham fat, or butter until brown and crisp, turning often.

Delicious if a clove of garlic, chopped into 2 or 3 pieces, is first fried in the fat. Try these also cold surrounding salads with soft ingredients.

SOUP NUTS

To accompany soup, 12 to 15 portions

Using half the quantity of choux pastry given on *page 106*, bake tiny raisin-sized pieces of the paste on a greased baking tray in a moderately hot oven, Gas 6, 400°F, 200°C, for 10 to 12 minutes until pale golden brown and dry.

Store in an airtight container. Or freeze.

Anne Wallace,
Stewarton, Ayrshire

MELBA TOAST

1. Cut slices of bread for toast—not too thick.
2. Toast lightly brown on both sides.
3. Cut in half diagonally to make triangles. Then slice the bread through the centre between the toasted sides to make two pieces from one.
4. Place in a large roasting tin and dry off at the bottom of the oven until crisp.

5. Store in an airtight tin.

Goes well with hot or cold soup.

MARINATED SMOKED MACKEREL

For 4 people

Buy two 125 g/4 oz fillets of smoked mackerel, cooked

Marinade

1 small onion, finely-chopped
2 tablespoons salad oil
1 tablespoon wine vinegar or lemon juice
¼ teaspoon dry mustard

To serve: chopped fresh parsley

1. Skin mackerel and divide into portions in a shallow dish.
2. Mix marinade ingredients and pour over mackerel.
3. Cover with a lid or greaseproof paper and foil and put in refrigerator or a cool place for about 3 hours.
4. Lift mackerel on to separate plates. Sprinkle with parsley.

Delicious with crusty French bread.

13

FRESH MUSSELS WITH PARSLEY

For 2 people

450 g/1 lb fresh mussels in the shells*
15 g/½ oz butter
½ a large clove of garlic, crushed
1 dessertspoon parsley

*Try to buy mussels on the day you mean to use them. If it is necessary to keep them overnight put them in a flat dish in a cool place with a sprinkling of water, or cover with a wet cloth.

1. Wash and scrub mussels, pull off the beards. Using the back of an old knife knock off any barnacles. Discard any open mussels.
2. Put mussels in a large pan with the other ingredients. Put on lid and cook over a high heat. Shake pan from time to time. Cook for only enough time to open the mussel shells. Shake again so that the liquor gets into the mussels. Not more than five minutes in all.
3. Serve immediately with crusty French bread to mop up the delicious soup.

AVOCADO AND SALMON MOUSSE

Best eaten the day it is made.

225 g/8 oz tinned salmon
15 g/½ oz gelatine
3 tablespoons water
2 avocado pears
¼ teaspoon salt
A dash of pepper
2 teaspoons anchovy essence
3 tablespoons single cream
2 or 3 drops of green food-colouring
2 egg-whites

To garnish: 1 stuffed green olive, chopped fresh parsley

1. Drain salmon. Reserve juice. Remove bones, skin and flake the flesh finely.
2. Put gelatine in 3 tablespoons water in a cup or small bowl. Set the cup in a pan of hot water and heat gently until the gelatine is completely dissolved. Stir well.
3. Split, stone, skin and cut up the avocados. Scrape as much pulp as possible from skin as this will give the mousse a deep green colour.
4. Liquidise the avocados, salt, pepper, anchovy essence and salmon juice. Or, if you do not have a liquidiser or food processor, mash thoroughly and beat until smooth.
5. Place in a large bowl, strain in the dissolved gelatine. Stir in cream and flaked salmon adding green colouring if needed.
6. Whisk egg-whites until they will stand up in peaks. Then fold into salmon mixture.
7. Turn into a fish or ring mould which has been rinsed in cold water and leave to set.
8. Turn out into a serving dish. Garnish with the stuffed olive, for eyes, and parsley.

This recipe would make excellent individual ramekins too.

SMOKED COD'S ROE PÂTÉ

225 g/8 oz smoked cod's roe
Juice of 1 lemon
150 ml/¼ pint double cream or 75 g/3 oz soft butter mixed with milk made up to 150 ml/¼ pint
A pinch each of ground ginger, cayenne pepper and paprika

Do not use an electric mixer or blender for this as it would break up the tiny eggs.

1. Remove skin from the cod's roe and empty into a bowl.
2. Put in half of the lemon juice and mash well with a fork. Add rest of lemon juice and beat again.
3. Gradually beat in cream, or the butter and milk.
4. Season to taste with the ginger and cayenne pepper.

5. Transfer to serving dish. Sprinkle with paprika and refrigerate.

Serve with hot buttered toast.

SMOKED MACKEREL PÂTÉ

For this you need a liquidiser or food processor.

350 g/12 oz smoked mackerel
2 thick slices wholemeal or brown bread
45 ml/3 tablespoons wine or cider vinegar
Half a tart eating apple, about 100 g/4 oz peeled and cored
Black pepper to taste

1. If using home-smoked mackerel proceed straight to step 2. Otherwise proceed as follows. Soak fish in water for an hour or two to relieve strong smoky taste. Wash thoroughly and cook in water just to cover, simmering for 5 minutes. Drain.
2. Remove bones and skin from fish.
3. Soak bread with vinegar.
4. Place all ingredients in liquidiser or food processor and switch on until all is blended and smooth.
5. Press into a ½ kg/1 lb loaf tin or a 13 cm/5 inch round tin or a soufflé dish. Chill.
6. Turn out on an attractive plate to serve.

Serve with Melba Toast (*see page 13*) and butter, a nice salad or plain water-cress.

Anne Wallace
Stewarton, Ayrshire

LIVER PÂTÉ

For this you need a liquidiser or a food processor.

As a lunch or supper dish, enough for 5 people. As a starter, 10 portions.

150 ml/¼ pint thick white sauce made with 20 g/¾ oz butter, 20 g/¾ oz flour, 150 ml/¼ pint milk, salt and pepper
250 g/8 oz chicken, calf or lamb liver

15 g/½ oz butter
A clove of garlic, crushed
125 g/4 oz fat bacon pieces
Half a sour apple, peeled, cored and sliced
4 anchovy fillets
1 egg
125 g/4 oz streaky bacon rashers
1 bay leaf

1. Make white sauce. Melt butter, stir in flour and cook 1 minute. Add milk gradually, stirring till it is thick, and boil gently for 2 minutes. Season with salt and pepper.
2. Trim skin and gristle from liver if necessary and cut it into 2·5 cm/1 inch pieces.
3. Fry it quickly in butter, just to set it. Put into liquidiser.
4. Add garlic, bacon pieces, apple, anchovy, egg and sauce to liver in liquidiser with salt and pepper to taste. Switch on and blend till mixture is smooth.
5. Line a ½ kg/1 lb loaf tin or oven dish with streaky bacon.
6. Pour in liver mixture and lay bay leaf on top.
7. Cover closely (greaseproof paper and foil will do) and put it in a roasting tin half filled with water.
8. Cook in middle of a moderate oven, Gas 4, 350°F, 180°C, for 2 hours.
9. Remove from oven and roasting tin. Press the pâté with a weight on top until it is cold.
10. Turn out on a plate and serve in slices with salad, Melba Toast (*see page 13*) or hot toast and butter.

Can be kept in refrigerator for a week or in freezer for 6 weeks, but long freezing is not suitable because garlic flavour tends to get a bit strong.

Anne Wallace
Stewarton, Ayrshire

SUSSEX FARMHOUSE PÂTÉ

Freezes well.

450 g/1 lb belly pork
225 g/8 oz bacon pieces

225 g/8 oz pig's liver
1 medium sized onion
2 teaspoons chopped fresh
herbs, such as parsley, thyme,
sage, marjoram, etc., or 1
teaspoon mixed dried herbs
Salt and black pepper
125 g/4 oz wholewheat
breadcrumbs

1. Remove all skin, white bones, etc.,
from pork and bacon and any pipes
from liver.
2. Put meat through mincer twice
with onion, herbs, seasoning and
breadcrumbs.
3. Put the mixture into a greased
½ kg/1 lb loaf tin. Cover with greaseproof paper and foil and place in a
baking tin with enough water to come
halfway up sides.
4. Bake in the centre of a slow oven,
Gas 2, 300°F, 150°C for 1½ to 1¾ hours.
5. Do not strain fat or juices off but
leave to get cold in tin with a weight
on top.

Mrs Janice Langley
Shoreham-by-Sea, West Sussex

PORK SPARE RIBS IN A BARBECUE SAUCE

*This recipe makes a good first
course with, say, 3 ribs per person.
There is enough sauce for 4 people.*

About 1 dozen meaty spare ribs
of pork, split into singles

Sauce
300 ml/½ pint dry cider or dry
home-made white wine
1 dessertspoon cornflour
2 tablespoons cold water
1 large teaspoon dry mustard
1 tablespoon soya sauce
1 level tablespoon brown sugar
125 g/4 oz tinned pineapple
pieces, drained and cut in half

1. Cook the spare ribs. Either roast in
a moderately hot oven, Gas 6, 400°F,
200°C, for 30 minutes until brown and
crisp. Or put them in a saucepan,
cover with water and boil until meat is
tender. Drain well and put ribs into a
roasting tin or oven dish.

2. Heat cider. Slake cornflour with
the water and add to pan. Stir as it
thickens and cook for 2 minutes.
3. Mix mustard into soya sauce and
add to pan with sugar and pineapple.
4. Pour sauce over spare ribs and put
in oven to heat through, reducing
temperature to moderate, Gas 4, 350°F,
180°C, for 15 minutes.

Best eaten with your fingers.

APRICOT AND ORANGE

A simple and refreshing starter to a
meal, or a sweet, or even for breakfast.

125 g/4 oz dried apricots
Boiling water
3 oranges
A sprig of mint, for decoration

1. Cut apricots into small pieces. Easy
with kitchen scissors. Put them in a
bowl or jar and cover with boiling
water.
2. Squeeze oranges. Add juice and
pulp to apricots.
3. Leave in a cool place or refrigerator
overnight or longer so that flavours
blend and apricots are really plump.

Serve in separate glasses or little
bowls with a mint leaf to decorate.

Anne Wallace
Stewarton, Ayrshire

CUCUMBER AND GRAPEFRUIT SALAD

Nice as a starter or a salad.

2 grapefruit
¼ cucumber
50 g/2 oz diced Cheddar cheese
150 ml/5 fl oz natural yoghurt

1. Cut grapefruit in half and remove
segments. Discard all pith and chop up
the fruit.
2. Dice the cucumber.
3. Mix all ingredients together with
the yoghurt and fill the halved
grapefruit shells.
4. Serve chilled.

Judith Adshead
Mottram St. Andrew, Cheshire

CHEESE STRUDEL SLICES

For 6 people

A 225 g/8 oz packet of frozen
puff pastry or use home-made
rough puff pastry (*see page 106*)

Filling

1 large beaten egg
125 g/4 oz Cheddar cheese,
finely-grated
225 g/8 oz curd or single cream
cheese
1 level tablespoon chopped
parsley or chives, or a mixture
A pinch of garlic salt
Pepper and salt

To decorate: sesame seeds

1. Roll out pastry on a floured board
to a rectangle about 31 by 23 cm/12 by
9 inches.
2. Prepare filling. Keep aside 1 tablespoon of the egg and mix all other
ingredients together.
3. Spread filling over pastry to within
2·5 cm/1 inch of edges.
4. Turn edges in to hold filling in
place and then fold three times to
make a flattened Swiss-roll shape
about 8 cm/3 inches deep.
5. Lift roll on to a baking sheet, brush
with remaining egg and scatter sesame
seeds over top. Cut six shallow slits
through pastry top.
6. Bake near top of a hot oven, Gas 7,
425°F, 220°C for 10 minutes. Then
reduce heat to moderately hot, Gas 5,
375°F, 190°C for a further 15 minutes.
7. Cut into slices and serve hot.

Judith Adshead
Mottram St. Andrew, Cheshire

HUMUS

A dish from the eastern
Mediterranean and the Middle East.

*Enough for 8 people—easy to make
in small quantities*

225 g/8 oz dry chick peas
150 ml/¼ pint stock (use cooking
water from chick peas)

4 to 5 tablespoons tahini*, white
if possible
Juice of 1½ lemons
A teaspoon shoyu (*see page 80*) or
soya sauce
A clove of garlic, crushed, or 1
teaspoon garlic powder
½ teaspoon salt
¼ teaspoon paprika
Black pepper

*Tahini is a paste made from
crushed sesame seeds, similar in
texture to creamy peanut butter.
It's purpose is to thicken the chick
pea paste as well as to add flavour.
White tahini is made from hulled
sesame seeds, brown tahini is from
whole seed. Both have a nutty
flavour, but the brown type has a
much stronger flavour.

To serve

Slices of lemon
Parsley
Wholemeal bread or pitta (*see
page 139*)

1. Soak chick peas in water overnight.
2. Next day drain them, discarding
water. Rinse, re-cover with about 1·5
litres/3 pints water, put on lid and boil
hard for 25 minutes. Then reduce heat
and simmer until soft but not mushy.
3. Meanwhile prepare other
ingredients.
4. Drain chick peas, reserving liquid
for stock and grind them to a fine
powder. This can be done in a food
processor or through a mincer or
mouli-grater. If chick peas are cooked
for about 2 hours until really soft they
can be mashed by hand.
5. Add enough of the reserved liquid
to make a stiff paste. Mix in all other
ingredients.
6. Put humus in a shallow dish
garnished with lemon slices and
parsley.

Serve with bread. Traditionally
served with Pitta bread (*see page 139*).

Will keep 4 or 5 days in refrigerator.

Sarah Brown
Scarborough, Yorkshire

17

STUFFED RINGS OF RED AND GREEN PEPPERS

For 6 or more people

A very pretty and delicious dish.
For this you need a liquidiser or food
processor.

**2 small red peppers
2 small green peppers**

Stuffing

This is a pâté of chicken livers which
can be made in larger quantities to
serve on its own. Can be frozen, but
only for 1 or 2 weeks.

**125 g/4 oz chicken livers
25 g/1 oz butter
1 tablespoon oil
1 onion, finely-chopped
A clove of garlic, finely-chopped
½ level teaspoon chopped fresh
thyme, or ¼ level teaspoon dried**

**2 tablespoons medium-sweet
sherry
125 g/4 oz cream cheese
Salt and pepper**

To serve: hot buttered toast

1. Cut a lid off each pepper with its
stalk and hollow out by removing core,
seeds and white membrane.
2. Prepare chicken livers by scraping
out core and cutting away any part
tinged with green. Chop, but not
small.
3. Melt butter with oil and fry liver,
onion, garlic and thyme, gently
turning all the time, about 5 minutes.
Cool.
4. Add sherry to the pan. Then blend
in a liquidiser or food processor.
5. Add cream cheese, salt and pepper.
Continue processing until well
combined.
6. Fill this mixture into the hollowed-
out peppers. Chill.
7. Just before serving, cut in 1 cm/½
inch rings.

Serve with hot buttered toast.

Chapter 2

Fish

COCKLE CAKES

A recipe from Gwent where they are called Teisen Gocos.

Enough for 4

4 dozen cockles in their shells, or 350 g/12 oz shelled cockles, fresh or frozen
Salt
A little oatmeal
Deep oil for cooking

For the batter

225 g/8 oz flour
A pinch of salt
2 tablespoons oil
1 egg, separated
300 ml/½ pint tepid water

To serve: brown bread and butter, lemon wedges

1. If the cockles are in shells try to use them the day they are bought or gathered. Scrub well, rinse and put in a saucepan with 1 teaspoon salt. Pour boiling water over to cover and boil cockles for 3 minutes. Then drain and leave to cool.
2. If using shelled cockles, wash very well to remove grit and soak for 1 hour in cold water.
3. Meanwhile, start the batter. Put flour and salt in a basin, add oil, beaten egg-yolk and water. Beat well and leave in a cool place.
4. Remove cockles from shells.
5. Beat egg-white stiffly and fold it into batter.
6. Take 3 or 4 cockles at a time on a dessertspoon. Fill spoon with batter and drop into hot oil. Fry until golden.
7. Drain on kitchen paper.

Serve with brown bread and butter and lemon wedges.

Mrs Eileen Trumper
Llanvair Kilgeddin, Gwent

SPANISH COD

A delicious dish for a special occasion.

For 4 people

4 cod steaks, allow 150 to 175 g/5 to 6 oz per person

Sauce

25 g/1 oz butter or good margarine
25 g/1 oz plain flour
150 ml/¼ pint white wine
150 ml/¼ pint water
Pepper and salt

Topping

50 g/2 oz chopped onion
1 tablespoon olive oil
50 g/2 oz sliced mushrooms
1 tablespoon chopped green pepper
2 tomatoes, peeled (*see page 72*) sliced and seeds removed
50 g/2 oz prawns
1 tablespoon chopped parsley
Pepper and salt

1. Prepare a moderately hot oven—Gas 6, 400°F, 200°C.
2. Start with sauce. Melt butter or margarine over low heat, stir in flour and let it sizzle for a minute. Pour in wine and water gradually, stirring as it thickens and let it boil gently for 3 minutes. Season with pepper and salt.
3. Pour sauce into an oven dish. Use a dish in which cod steaks will fit side by side.
4. Wash and dry fish and place on top of sauce.
5. Fry onion in oil till soft but not brown.
6. Add mushrooms and green pepper and continue cooking for a moment longer until pepper starts to soften.
7. Stir in tomato, prawns, parsley, pepper and salt. Spread this topping over fish steaks.
8. Cover with a piece of greased paper and bake for about 30 minutes. Test fish by using the point of a knife in the centre of steaks. Fish loses its translucent appearance when cooked.

Anne Wallace
Stewarton, Ayrshire

COLEY WITH A HOT CUCUMBER SAUCE

Coley is very like haddock but is dark in appearance when raw. It cooks easily and turns very white.

4 small fillets of fresh coley, skinned
About 300 ml/½ pint milk
A little lemon juice

Sauce

1 small unskinned cucumber
Salt
A 142 ml/5 fl oz carton of single cream
142ml/5 fl oz plain yoghurt
1 teaspoon castor sugar
Pepper

1. Put coley in a shallow pan, barely cover with milk and poach gently either under grill or on top of stove for 15 to 20 minutes until done.
2. Drain off milk and keep fish hot in a serving dish.
3. Meanwhile make sauce. Grate the entire cucumber coarsely. Spread out the pulp in a flat shallow dish. Sprinkle with salt and leave for 20 minutes. Strain.
4. Turn pulp into a small saucepan. Stir in cream and yoghurt. Add sugar and pepper.
5. When mixture starts to bubble turn it into a jug to serve separately with the fish.
6. Sprinkle chopped parsley and a squeeze of lemon over fish.

FISH AND MUSHROOM PIE

Makes about 6 portions

275 g/10 oz rich pie pastry (*see page 105*)
125 g/4 oz mushrooms
150 ml/¼ pint water
450 g/1 lb white fish—e.g., cod, coley, haddock, whiting, etc.

Basic white sauce

50 g/2 oz butter or good margarine
50 g/2 oz flour
About 300 ml/½ pint milk
1 teaspoon chopped fresh tarragon, or ¼ teaspoon dried
Salt and pepper

1. Roll out two thirds of pastry to fit an 18 cm/7 inch pie plate and roll out the rest to fit top.

2. Stew mushrooms gently in the water in a covered pan for 5 minutes.
3. Drain liquid into a measuring jug. Slice mushrooms.
4. Meanwhile remove and discard skin and any bones from fish and cut it up into small pieces.
5. Now make the sauce. Melt butter or margarine over low heat, stir in flour and let it sizzle for a minute.
6. Add milk to mushroom liquid to make 450 ml/¾ pint. Add to pan gradually, stirring as it thickens and comes to boil. Let it bubble for 3 minutes.
7. Season sauce well with tarragon, salt and pepper.
8. Add fish and mushrooms to sauce. Allow to cool.
9. Fill the prepared pastry case. Damp edges and fit on lid pressing to seal. Do not make holes in top yet or filling may boil over and spoil top.
10. Bake near top of a moderately hot oven, Gas 6, 400°F, 200°C, for 45 minutes, moving pie to middle as it begins to brown. When it is done remove from oven and cut slits in top in one or two places, to let out steam and keep pastry crisp.

Serve hot or cold. Nice with green peas or beans.

Anne Wallace
Stewarton, Ayrshire

HADDOCK AND TOMATOES

With a crisp cheese topping

For 4 people

450 g/1 lb haddock fillets
Salt and Pepper Mix (*see page 44*)
2 teaspoons lemon juice
1 small onion, finely-chopped
4 tomatoes, skinned (*see page 72*) and sliced
2 tablespoons finely-grated cheese
4 tablespoons fresh breadcrumbs

1. Wipe and trim fillets, cutting into portions if too large, and arrange them in a shallow oven dish.

2. Sprinkle fish with salt, pepper and lemon juice.
3. Scatter onions on top and then make a layer of sliced tomatoes.
4. Mix together cheese and bread-crumbs. Sprinkle over tomatoes.
5. Cook at top of a moderate oven, Gas 4, 350°F, 180°C, for 30 minutes.

HADDOCK PUFFS

A Devonshire recipe. Very light and especially tasty with smoked fish. An economical alternative to scampi.

Enough for 4 as a starter, 3 as a main course

225 g/8 oz haddock, fresh or smoked
150 ml/¼ pint milk
50 g/2 oz self-raising flour*
1 tablespoon chopped fresh parsley, 1 teaspoon dried
Cayenne pepper
Salt
2 beaten eggs
Deep fat for frying

*Wholewheat flour can be used. If you cannot get self-raising wholewheat mix in ¼ level teaspoon baking powder.

1. Poach fish in milk almost to cover. It will take 10 to 15 minutes depending on thickness of fish. Then drain fish, saving the liquid.
2. Flake fish in a basin with 2 table-spoons of the liquid. Mix in flour, parsley, cayenne pepper and salt to taste. Salt will not be necessary with smoked haddock.
3. Mix in beaten egg and 2 to 3 table-spoons of the cooking liquid to make a soft consistency.
4. Deep-fry in hot fat, dropping mixture in a teaspoon at a time. Fry until golden brown, turning from time to time, about 3 to 4 minutes.

Serve very hot with brown bread and butter and tartare sauce (*see below*).

Mrs Becky Blackmore
Exeter, Devon

TARTARE SAUCE

300 ml/½ pint mayonnaise (*see page 64*)
1 tablespoon chopped capers
1 tablespoon chopped cucumber
1 teaspoon chopped parsley
½ teaspoon chopped onion
1 teaspoon vinegar

Prepare mayonnaise then mix into it all the other ingredients.

SMOKED HADDOCK IN SCALLOP SHELLS

Or in a fish pie.

1 kg/2 lb boiled and creamed potatoes
700 g/1½ lb smoked haddock
700 ml/1¼ pints milk
50 g/2 oz butter or margarine
50g/2 oz flour
75 g/3 oz grated cheese, Parmesan and Cheddar mixed
Pepper and salt
125 g/4 oz lightly-cooked green peas

1. Prepare potatoes.
2. Cook haddock gently in the milk. Strain, saving milk for the thick white sauce.
3. Melt 40 g/1½ oz of the butter, stir in flour and sizzle for 1 minute.
4. Gradually add milk, stirring as sauce thickens. Cook 3 minutes.
5. Stir in 50 g/2 oz of the grated cheese. Remove from heat.
6. Meanwhile flake the haddock, removing skin and any bones.
7. Fold the haddock and peas into the thick white sauce and adjust the seasoning.

To make a fish pie
Pour the fish mixture into a greased pie dish and top with the creamed potato. Smooth the potato then score across in a rough pattern. Dot with remaining 15 g/½ oz butter. Sprinkle on remaining cheese and brown under the grill.

Reheat when required in a moderate oven, Gas 4, 350°F, 180°C, for about 30 minutes.

To serve in scallop shells

Using a piping bag with a large star nozzle, put in the potato and decorate the border of each shell generously with stars. Fill centre of shells with haddock mixture. Sprinkle on remaining cheese and dot potato with last 15 g/½ oz of butter.

Reheat near top of a moderate oven, Gas 4, 350°F, 180°C, for about 20 minutes.

PILAFF OF SMOKED HADDOCK

For 4 people

350 g/12 oz smoked haddock
1 tablespoon oil
25 g/1 oz butter
1 onion, chopped
175 g/6 oz brown rice
1 green pepper, chopped
2 tomatoes, skinned (*see page 72*) **and chopped**
1 pint chicken stock
1 teaspoon turmeric
Pepper
Chopped parsley

1. Trim fish, removing any skin and bone. Cut it into bite-sized pieces.
2. Melt butter in oil and fry onion lightly. When soft but not brown stir in rice and dry for a minute.
3. Add fish, green pepper, tomatoes, stock, turmeric and pepper.
4. Bring to boil, cover pan, lower heat and cook gently until rice is almost tender—about 20 minutes.
5. Sprinkle liberally with chopped parsley just before serving.

Anne Wallace
Stewarton, Ayrshire

SMOKED FISH AND EGG ON TOAST

A snack for 4 people but a smaller quantity could easily be made

350 g/12 oz smoked fish fillet
150 ml /¼ pint milk
150 ml/¼ pint water

2 eggs
25 g/1 oz butter or margarine
25 g/1 oz wholemeal or white flour
Black pepper
2 tablespoons chopped parsley
Pieces of freshly-toasted crisp wholemeal bread
Mustard and cress

1. Put fish in a saucepan, pour over it the milk and water. Bring to the boil, cover pan and simmer for 10 minutes.
2. Put eggs in water to boil for 10 minutes.
3. When fish is done, remove from liquid and flake into largish pieces. Save the liquid.
4. When eggs are done, plunge them into cold water and remove the shells. (Held under running cold tap the eggs will not burn your fingers while you shell them.)
5. Roughly chop eggs and put them with flaked fish.
6. Melt butter or margarine in a pan, add flour and let it sizzle for a minute without browning.
7. Stir in 150 to 300 ml/¼ to ½ pint of the fish liquid. Stir over low heat until sauce is thick and let it simmer 2 or 3 minutes.
8. Add fish, egg, a grating of black pepper and the parsley and heat gently.

Serve on or with crisply-toasted wholemeal bread and have mustard and cress with it.

SAVOURY PUFFS

These are light and crisp with a moist centre. Good as a supper dish for 4 or 5 people or on cocktail sticks as hot savouries for a party.

Makes 40 bite-sized puffs

Can be frozen.

Choux pastry, quantity given on page 106
About 175 g/6 oz flaked smoked fish or any canned fish
Deep fat to fry
Chopped parsley
Paprika pepper

1. Prepare choux pastry paste and mix fish into it.
2. Have fat heated and drop small teaspoons of mixture into it, turning if necessary, so that they brown evenly. They puff up as they cook.
3. When golden brown, remove with a draining spoon on to kitchen paper. Keep hot while cooking rest of puffs.
4. Pile on a hot dish, sprinkle with parsley and paprika pepper.

Anne Wallace
Stewarton, Ayrshire

MUSTARD HERRINGS

For 4 people

4 fresh herrings
Salt and freshly-ground black pepper
40 g/1½ oz butter
50 g/2 oz onion, finely-chopped

Mustard sauce

15 g/½ oz butter
15 g/½ oz flour
1 large teaspoon made English mustard
A pinch of sugar
300 ml/½ pint water
4 tablespoons milk
25 g/1 oz grated cheese

1. Scale, gut, wash and trim heads, tails and fins from herrings. Cut each one open from belly to tail. Press out flat, skin side uppermost, and press along backbone. Turn fish over and lift out backbone from tail to head.
2. Lay in a large flat oven dish, season with salt and pepper. Cover with foil or a lid.
3. Bake in a moderately hot oven Gas 6, 400°F, 200°C, for 15 to 20 minutes.
4. Meanwhile melt butter in a small pan and cook onions until tender. Lay aside.
5. Take another pan to make the sauce. Melt butter, remove from the heat and beat in the flour and mustard.
6. Add sugar and blend in water gradually.

7. Return to heat and bring to boiling point. Simmer for 4 to 5 minutes, stirring often. Remove from the heat.
8. Add milk and half of the cheese.
9. Take dish out of oven, scatter cooked onion over herrings. Pour sauce over. Sprinkle with rest of cheese and brown under a hot grill.

FRESH MACKEREL SPICED IN CIDER

6 small mackerel
Wholewheat flour seasoned with salt and pepper (*see page 44*)
300 ml/½ pint apple juice, sparkling or still, or cider
½ level teaspoon pickling spice
2 bay leaves
1 medium-sized onion

1. To fillet the fish, follow instructions in Portland-style Mackerel (*see below*).
2. Sprinkle inside fish with a little seasoned flour.
3. Roll up fish loosely from tail to head and place them close together in a fairly deep oven dish.
4. Pour over apple juice or cider. Then sprinkle with pickling spice and add bay leaves. Peel and slice onion and spread over fish.
5. Cover dish with a lid or greaseproof paper and foil and put in a cool oven, Gas 1, 275°F, 140°C, for 1½ hours.
6. Remove from oven and allow to cool in the liquid.

Serve with boiled potatoes or brown bread and butter.

Sybil Norcott
Irlam, Nr. Manchester

PORTLAND-STYLE MACKEREL

For 4 people

4 fresh mackerel
Wholewheat flour, seasoned with salt and pepper (*see page 44*)

Gooseberry Sauce

225 g/8 oz gooseberries, fresh or frozen

30 ml/2 tablespoons water
50 g/2 oz sugar
25 g/1 oz butter
A pinch of nutmeg

1. If you have to bone mackerel yourself this is the way to do it. Gut and clean, removing head and tail. Cut open to backbone from belly to tail. Open out slightly and place on a board, cut side down. Bang hard with a rolling pin along the backbone until mackerel is flat. Turn fish over and backbone just pulls out, bringing most of the other bones as well. Pull out any long rib bones remaining. Trim off fins and tiny spines. Wash fish and pat dry.
2. Simmer gooseberries in the water until tender.
3. Put gooseberries through a sieve and then return purée to the pan.
4. Add sugar and stir well over gentle heat till it is dissolved.
5. Add butter and nutmeg and simmer for 5 minutes.
6. Dust mackerel with seasoned wholewheat flour.
7. Grill until golden brown, 4 to 5 minutes each side. Time varies according to size of fish.

Serve sauce separately.

John Firrell
Piddletrenthide, Dorset

SALMON MOUSSE

It is nice to use a fish-shaped mould for this.

A 212 g/7½ oz tin of salmon
1 dessertspoon tomato purée*
15 g/½ oz gelatine
2 tablespoons water
1 tablespoon vinegar
1 egg-white
A 175 g/6 oz tin of evaporated milk, refrigerated for 1 hour before using
1 teaspoon lemon juice

Decoration

A little paprika pepper
1 stuffed olive
2 gherkins

*See To keep tomato purée fresh, p. 45

1. Lightly oil a suitable 850 ml/1½ pint mould.
2. Flake salmon, removing bones and dark skin. Mash it with tomato purée.
3. Using a small basin which will fit over a pan of very hot but not boiling water, put gelatine to dissolve in the water and vinegar. Stir once and leave until it becomes clear.
4. Whisk egg-white until firm.
5. In another bowl whisk cold evaporated milk until thick, adding lemon juice to help it thicken.
6. Stir gelatine into salmon. Fold in whisked milk, and then egg-white. Mix all together gently.
7. Pour into mould and leave 3 to 4 hours to set in a cool place. Goes a bit tough if it sets too quickly.
8. Turn out on to a flat dish. Sprinkle a little paprika pepper down the centre, place half a stuffed olive for the eye, and gherkins, sliced part-way and fanned out for fins.

A GOOD IMITATION ASPIC JELLY

Gives a shining finish to pieces of cold chicken set out for a salad. Can also be used to top a savoury mousse by decorating with slices of cucumber and tomato and then covering with jelly to a depth of 7 mm/¼ inch. Spectacular used to coat a large salmon or ham for a special meal. Try it for Avocado and Salmon Mousse (*see page 14*), or Salmon Mousse (*see above*), Fresh Trout with Herb Mayonnaise (*see page 26*), Poached Chicken (*see page 38*).

For this you need 1 or 2 refrigerator trays of ice-cubes.

25 g/1 oz gelatine
25 ml/1 fl oz water
A 300 g/11 oz tin of consommé
3 tablespoons sherry
Juice of half a lemon
425 ml/¾ pint water

1. Put the 25 ml/1 fl oz of water in a cup or small bowl, sprinkle the gelatine over the surface.

2. Set the cup or bowl in a pan of warm water. Heat gently, stirring all the time until the gelatine dissolves.
3. In a pan mix consommé, sherry, lemon juice and 425 ml/¾ pint water. Stir over low heat until it is liquid.
4. Strain in the gelatine and stir.
5. Now stand pan on a baking tin full of ice. Stir until the aspic is syrupy. It is now ready to use.

SOLE ON A BED OF PASTA SHELLS WITH PRAWNS AND CREAM SAUCE

For 4 people
100 g/4 oz butter
Salt and pepper
8 small fillets of sole
½ litre/¾ pint milk
175 g/6 oz pasta shells
50 g/2 oz flour
4 tablespoons dry sherry
150 ml/5 fl oz single cream
1 teaspoon anchovy essence or sauce
50 to 100 g/2 to 4 oz frozen prawns
To garnish: 2 tomatoes, lemon slices

1. Use 50 g/2 oz of the butter and divide it into 8 little pieces.
2. Shake a little salt and pepper on each fish fillet and roll it up around a piece of butter.
3. Place fish in an oven dish. Pour round 150 ml/¼ pint of the milk. Cover dish with greased paper or foil.
4. Cook in middle of a moderate oven, Gas 4, 350°F, 180°C for about 20 minutes until fish is cooked.
5. Meanwhile, put pasta on to cook in slightly salted water, allowing for it to be done when fish comes out of oven.
6. Then make a roux of remaining butter and flour. This means melting butter in a pan, stirring in flour and allowing it to sizzle for 1 minute without browning.
7. Stir in remaining milk and then liquid from fish. Stir over low heat until thick, and boil for 2 minutes.

8. When fish is done lift it carefully out of dish on to a plate for a moment.
9. Drain pasta and put it in fish dish. Set fish on top and keep it warm.
10. Return to the sauce. Add sherry, cream, anchovy essence and prawns. Bring it back to boiling point so that prawns are well heated.
11. Pour sauce over fish and garnish with slices of tomato and lemon.

Anne Wallace
Stewarton, Ayrshire

FRESH TROUT WITH HERB MAYONNAISE

A liquidiser is needed.
4 fresh trout, about 275 g/10 oz each
Wine vinegar
Salt

Mayonnaise
A bundle of fresh herbs, parsley, chervil (or fennel), chives, tarragon, spinach and watercress (or sorrel), about 50 g/2 oz herbs altogether
1 very small onion or small shallot, very finely chopped
2 anchovy fillets
1 dessertspoon capers
1 small pickled gherkin
1 hard boiled egg-yolk
1 fresh egg-yolk
1 teaspoon lemon juice
25 ml to 50 ml/1 to 2 fl oz sunflower oil
Salt and freshly-ground pepper
To garnish: lettuce, cucumber slices

1. Leave heads and tails on trout, gut them, wash and wipe out with salt and kitchen paper.
2. Take a large pan, big enough to lay trout out flat. Try them for size and cover with water.
3. To each pint of water add 1 tablespoon vinegar and ½ teaspoon salt. Now remove trout.
4. Bring water to the boil, then slip in each trout. Bring back to the boil and at once remove pan from heat. Allow

the trout to get quite cold in the pan of stock.

5. Now for the mayonnaise.
Wash herbs.

6. Chop the onion or shallot very finely and put it in a pan of boiling water. Boil for 1 minute. Drain into a sieve and run under tap.

7. Put herbs, onion, anchovy fillets, capers, gherkin, both egg-yolks and lemon juice into a liquidiser.

8. Liquidise for 10 seconds at high speed. Then start to dribble in the oil, a little at a time until the mixture thickens and emulsifies.

9. Season with salt and pepper and more lemon juice if necessary.

10. Lift cold trout out of stock. Pat dry and lay it on a nice dish with lettuce and cucumber.

11. Serve mayonnaise separately, giving each person a little pot.

TUNA FISH CASSEROLE

For 2 people, or can be served in ramekins as a starter for 6 people.

1·2 litres/2 pints water
Salt
125 g/4 oz wholewheat pasta
A 100 g/3½ oz can of tuna fish
1 tin of condensed cream of mushroom soup
50 g/2 oz butter
Pepper
A squeeze of lemon juice (optional)
1 tablespoon chopped parsley

1. Bring the water to the boil. Add a little salt, then the pasta, and bring back to simmering point. Stir to make sure pasta is not sticking together then partly cover the pan and simmer for 7 minutes or more. Cooking time will depend on the type of pasta you use. It should be not quite done when you drain it.

2. Meanwhile, remove bones from the fish and flake it.

3. Drain the pasta and add to it the fish with the soup, butter, pepper and lemon juice. Mix well. Taste for seasoning and return pan to heat.

4. As soon as it is hot stir in most of the chopped parsley. Turn the mixture into a warmed oven dish and brown it under the grill.

Sprinkle the rest of the parsley on top just before serving.

Anne Wallace
Stewarton, Ayrshire

TUNA TART

225 g/8 oz self-raising flour
½ level teaspoon salt
40 g/1½ oz butter or margarine
150 ml/¼ pint milk
200 g/7 oz can of tuna fish
2 teaspoons vinegar
225 g/8 oz tomatoes, fresh or tinned
75 g/3 oz grated Lancashire cheese
Stuffed olives (optional)

1. Sift the flour and salt into a bowl.

2. Rub in the butter or margarine until mixture is like fine breadcrumbs.

3. Mix to a soft dough with the milk.

4. Roll out on a floured board to 25·4 cm/10 inch round and lay this on a lightly-greased baking sheet, or use a loose-based flan tin of the same size. However, as this is like a pizza, roll dough to fit bottom only, not sides.

5. Drain oil from tuna, break it up and mix in vinegar.

6. Skin tomatoes (*see page 72*) and slice. If using tinned tomatoes, drain well before slicing.

7. Arrange the tomato slices on top of dough. Then cover with tuna.

8. Sprinkle on the cheese and decorate the top with sliced, stuffed olives.

9. Bake in a moderately hot oven, Gas 6, 400°F, 200°C for 30 minutes.

Eat hot.

Sybil Norcott
Irlam, Nr. Manchester

27

WHITING WITH MUSHROOMS

Enough for 2 or 3, but can be made in any quantity

Quick to make.

40 g/1½ oz butter
3 or 4 fillets of whiting
50 g/2 oz mushrooms, sliced
1 tablespoon chopped fresh parsley
25 to 50 g/1 to 2 oz fresh bread-crumbs

White sauce

15 g/½ oz butter or margarine
15 g/½ oz flour
150 ml/¼ pint milk
Salt and pepper

1. Start with sauce. Melt the 15 g/½ oz butter or margarine, stir in the flour and let it sizzle for 1 minute.
2. Gradually add milk, stirring as it thickens. Then cook for 2 minutes. Season to taste with salt and pepper.
3. Use some of the 40 g/1½ oz butter to grease an oven dish. Melt rest of butter in a pan.
4. Spread white sauce in dish.
5. Lay whiting fillets on sauce. Cover with mushrooms, and pour over melted butter.
6. Sprinkle parsley over mushrooms and finish with a layer of bread-crumbs.
7. Bake in a moderately hot oven, Gas 5, 375°F, 190°C for 15 to 18 minutes.

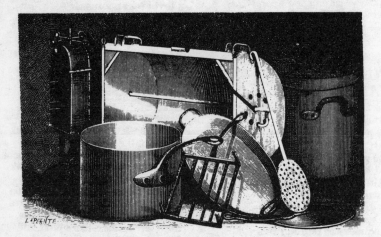

Chapter 3

Poultry, Game and Rabbit

BONED AND STUFFED ROAST TURKEY

For 5 to 6 people

The thought of carving a boned and stuffed turkey or chicken is very appealing, especially if you are doing it with a hungry family watching. Boning isn't really as difficult as it sounds. All you need is an extremely sharp, short-bladed knife, a steel to keep it sharp and some nimble finger work.

A 1·8 to 2·3 kg/4 to 5 lb turkey, with giblets

Stuffing

200 g/7 oz prunes, soaked overnight
75 g/3 oz butter
1 large onion, finely-chopped
125 g/4 oz fresh wholewheat breadcrumbs
50 g/2 oz sultanas
50 g/2 oz chopped walnuts
Grated rind and juice of 1 lemon
2 tablespoons chopped fresh parsley
Salt and pepper
1 beaten egg

To roast

75 g/3 oz bacon fat or good dripping
225 g/8 oz streaky bacon, cut off rinds

Gravy

Giblets
A piece of onion
A piece of carrot
1 bay leaf and 4 peppercorns
600 ml/1 pint water
25 g/1 oz flour

To bone the bird

1. Lay it breast down on a board. Cut right down the back from neck to tail, or parson's nose.
2. Now start cutting the flesh from the carcass, working down and completing one side at a time. Very short cutting movements are needed. In some places by careful manipulation with the fingers the flesh can be pushed off the bone. Continue cutting, keeping close to the bones all the time and taking care not to puncture the skin.
3. Cut through wing and thigh joints and continue cutting to release flesh up to the breast-bone.
4. Do not work on thigh bones or wings yet.
5. Now work round other side of carcass.
6. When both sides are clear, cut up and along the breast bone. Take care not to break the skin as the flesh is very thin along the ridge.
7. The whole carcass should now be free. Pull it out gently (and be sure to boil it later for a good full-bodied stock for soup).
8. Working from inside, remove thigh bones cutting carefully between bones where drumstick joins.

For this recipe leave the bones in the drumsticks and wings as this will give the stuffed bird a better shape. However, they can be removed and the cavity stuffed but it may be necessary to cut through the skin and flesh on the inner side—i.e., breast side.

Stuffing

1. Remove stones from prunes and chop flesh.
2. Melt 25 g/1 oz of the butter and fry onion until soft but not brown.
3. Combine prunes, onions, breadcrumbs, sultanas, walnuts, lemon rind and juice, a little of the parsley, salt and pepper. Mix with beaten egg.
4. Now cream remaining 50 g/2 oz butter with parsley, salt and pepper and use half of it to rub inside of bird.
5. Pack stuffing into all the corners of the bird and make the rest into a large wide sausage for the middle.
6. Using a large needle threaded with fine string, sew up the skin, with large overcasting stitches, reshaping the bird as well as possible. For safety, tie bird up with 2 strings around its middle.
7. Rub remaining parsley-butter over outside of bird.

To roast

1. Melt fat in a roasting tin. Put in the bird and baste it before it goes in oven. Cover with foil.
2. Roast in a moderately hot oven, Gas 6, 400°F, 200°C, for 1¼ to 1½ hours, or until done. 15 minutes before end of cooking time remove foil and spread bacon across bird.

To test if it is cooked, pierce thigh with a skewer. If juice is pink then it needs further cooking. If juice is clear it is done.

Cooking time is calculated at 15 minutes to the ½ kg/1 lb plus 15 minutes. Weigh bird after stuffing.

3. Meanwhile put giblets, onion, carrot, bay leaf, peppercorns and water in a pan. Put on lid and simmer for 40 minutes.
4. Remove bird from oven on to a warm serving dish and keep hot. Make gravy in roasting tin.
5. Pour off as much fat as possible from tin, leaving the residue of turkey juices.
6. Work flour into juices. Put tin on top of stove over low heat.
7. Gradually stir in strained giblet stock and extra water if necessary. Stir until gravy thickens. Let it boil for 1 minute.
8. Pour into a warm jug or serving boat and keep hot.

Try Cranberry and Orange Preserve (*see page 171*) with this.

AUNT POLLY'S PIE

A way to use left-over turkey, chicken, stuffing and stock.

225 g/8 oz bacon rashers
225 g/8 oz left-over chicken or turkey
225 g/8 oz pork sausage-meat
50 ml/2 fl oz stock from boiling chicken carcass
Left-over stuffing

1. De-rind bacon, lay rashers on a board and, using a knife with a wide blade, press out rashers to stretch and widen them.
2. Line a deep pie-dish with bacon rashers, saving 1 or 2 for later.

3. Add chicken or turkey cut up into bite-sized pieces.
4. Cover with a layer of sausage-meat.
5. Pour over the stock.
6. Bake in a warm oven, Gas 3, 325°F, 160°C for 10 to 15 minutes. Then remove pie from oven and press stuffing over top. Cover with remaining bacon. Bake a further 20 minutes.

Can be eaten hot from the dish or cold, turned out and sliced.

Sybil Norcott
Irlam, Nr. Manchester

RISSOLES

Chicken or Turkey and Bacon

125 g/4 oz cooked chicken or turkey, finely-minced
1 rasher of bacon
50 g/2 oz fresh brown bread-crumbs (*see page 33*)
Salt and pepper
1 tablespoon basic white sauce (*see page 94*) or 1 egg-yolk
1 beaten egg
Dried breadcrumbs to coat rissoles (*see page 33*)
Deep fat or oil to fry

1. Prepare chicken.
2. De-rind bacon, fry it until really crisp, then crush into small pieces.
3. Mix chicken, bacon and fresh breadcrumbs with enough white sauce or egg-yolk to bind it together.
4. With floured hands, shape mixture into short fat sausages. Leave aside to firm up.
5. Dip rissoles in beaten egg, then in breadcrumbs. Leave aside to firm up.
6. Heat fat or oil until really smoking. Fry rissoles until golden. Drain on kitchen paper.

Ham

125 g/4 oz cooked ham, finely-minced
50 g/2 oz fresh brown bread-crumbs
1 teaspoon chopped fresh parsley
Salt and pepper

1 tablespoon basic white sauce
(*see page 94*) or 1 egg-yolk
1 beaten egg
Dried breadcrumbs to coat
rissoles
Deep fat or oil to fry

1. Mix ham, fresh breadcrumbs and
parsley. Season well with salt and
pepper.
2. Bind mixture with sauce or egg-
yolk.
3. With floured hands, shape mixture
into short fat sausages. Leave in
refrigerator to firm up.
4. Dip sausages in beaten egg, then in
dried breadcrumbs. Refrigerate for 1
hour.
5. Heat fat or oil until nearly smoking
hot. Fry rissoles until golden and
crisp. Drain on kitchen paper.

ROAST DUCKLING WITH WALNUT SAUCE
For 4 people
A 2 kg/4 to 4½ lb duckling
Salt

Sauce

2 tablespoons duckling dripping
1 medium-sized onion, chopped
50 g/2 oz walnuts, chopped
1 level tablespoon plain flour
300 ml/½ pint duckling stock
Grated rind and juice of 1
orange
2 tablespoons sherry
2 teaspoons chopped parsley

To serve and garnish

1 tablespoon duckling dripping
25 g/1 oz walnut halves
Watercress
1 orange, cut into slices

1. Wipe duckling dry inside and out.
Place on a rack in a shallow roasting
tin. Prick the skin all over with a fork.
This allows the fat to flow out during
cooking and bastes the bird without
any attention. Sprinkle well with salt.
2. Place in a hot oven, Gas 7, 425°F,
220°C and immediately reduce heat to
a moderate, Gas 4, 350°F, 180°C. Roast

for 1½ to 1¾ hours or until tender and
well browned, and the juices run clear
when the thickest part of the leg is
pierced with a skewer.
3. **To prepare sauce.** Heat duckling
dripping in a pan, add chopped onion
and walnuts and cook gently until
lightly browned.
4. Stir in flour and cook 1 minute.
5. Gradually blend in stock, orange
rind and juice and simmer gently for 2
minutes, stirring throughout.
6. Stir in sherry and chopped parsley
and season to taste.
7. **To serve.** (a) Gently fry walnut
halves in duckling dripping then drain
well on kitchen paper.
(b) Put duckling on a hot serving dish
and garnish with watercress, fried
walnuts and orange slices. Serve
walnut sauce in a separate bowl.

For a party
ROAST DUCKLING WITH 3 SAUCES

Apricot
A 425 g/15 oz tin of apricot
halves in syrup

Apple

2 large cooking apples
1 tablespoon lemon juice
2 tablespoons water
15 g/½ oz butter
1 tablespoon sugar

Redcurrant Jelly Sauce

3 to 4 tablespoons redcurrant
jelly
1 tablespoon water
Finely-grated rind and juice of ½
lemon
A good pinch of nutmeg

To serve and garnish

2 to 3 teaspoons redcurrant jelly
1 rosy dessert apple
A little lemon juice
Watercress

Apricot Sauce

1. Reserve 8 apricot halves for
decoration and heat through in oven
10 minutes before end of cooking time.

2. Press remaining fruit and syrup through a sieve, or liquidise. Heat through in small pan.

Apple Sauce
1. Peel and core apples then slice into a saucepan.
2. Add lemon juice and water and simmer gently until soft and pulpy.
3. Beat in butter and sugar.

Redcurrant Jelly Sauce
Place all ingredients in a small saucepan and stir over gentle heat until jelly has dissolved. Simmer 2 minutes.

To serve
Fill apricot halves with a little redcurrant jelly. Cut fine slices of unpeeled apple and sprinkle with lemon juice. Arrange these on a warm serving dish around the duckling and decorate with sprigs of watercress.

Serve the three sauces in similar containers so that guests may help themselves.

Any remaining sauces may be mixed together to make a tasty sauce to serve with grilled sausages or cold meats.

Audrey Hundy
Abbots Morton, Worcestershire

BASIC STUFFING FOR POULTRY AND MEAT

This can be made in bulk and frozen without its main seasoning or flavouring ingredients.

700 g/1½ lb onions
350 g/12 oz fresh breadcrumbs, wholewheat or white
50 g/2 oz butter or margarine
50 g/2 oz shredded suet
2 lemons
1 beaten egg
Salt and pepper

A *variety of flavourings*, some of which combine well with each other:
Chopped prunes, soaked in water overnight
Chopped apricots, soaked overnight
Chopped apples
Chopped celery
Chopped herbs like sage, parsley, marjoram, thyme, etc.
Chopped nuts

1. Peel and finely chop onions, fry in butter until soft.
2. Cool, mix with the rest of the ingredients. Season well.
3. Divide into four: freeze in separate bags.
4. To use, defrost and add the selected flavouring ingredients. The stuffing is then ready to use.

TO MAKE DRIED BREADCRUMBS

1. Lay slices of stale bread in a dry roasting tin and place in the bottom of the oven while something else is cooking. Remove when dry and brittle.
2. Now crush, using a rolling pin.

If really well dried they should keep in airtight jars for months.
Use for coating fish, chicken, rissoles, etc., before either shallow or deep frying.

Fresh breadcrumbs are made from semi-fresh bread using an electric coffee grinder, blender or food processor. Or by hand with a grater. Most sliced bread is unsuitable because of its foam plastic nature.

Keep in a fridge for a few days. Freezes well.

For stuffings, treacle tart, etc.

CHICKEN KEBABS
For 2 people

This makes a very nice main course when served with Yoghurt and Tahini Dip (*see page 65*), Stir-fried Vegetables (*see page 77*) and hot Greek Pitta Bread (*see page 139*).

2 chicken portions, breast and wing pieces

It is cheaper to buy the chicken this way, although only the boned breasts are required for this recipe. Cut off the wings and with a sharp-pointed knife cut bones away from breast flesh. The butcher will do this for you. Save the wings for another meal, like Chicken and Honey (see below).

Marinade

3 tablespoons corn oil
2 tablespoons soya sauce
2 heaped teaspoons coriander seeds or 2 level teaspoons ground coriander
A clove of garlic, crushed
1 tablespoon lemon juice
1 teaspoon brown sugar
½ teaspoon ground ginger
Salt and pepper

1. Start this the night before it is to be eaten. Prepare the chicken breasts, cutting flesh into bite-sized pieces.
2. Mix all the marinade ingredients, grinding the coriander seeds in a mortar or a mill.
3. Mix chicken into marinade and leave it overnight in refrigerator.
4. Next day Yoghurt and Tahini Dip can be made. (It is best made without garlic when accompanying this dish.) Vegetables for stir-frying should be prepared close to the time of the meal.
5. Finally, preheat grill to hot.
6. Thread chicken pieces on to skewers and grill about 5 minutes on each side until browning a little and cooked through. Any remaining marinade can be used to baste chicken as it cooks.

If serving with hot pitta bread cut each piece in half and open it like a pocket. Put in a little of the stir-fried vegetables, then some kebabs and finally the cold dip. Eat it like a sandwich.

Can also be served with well-flavoured brown rice.

Elizabeth Mickery
Pudsey, West Yorkshire

CHICKEN AND HONEY

For 3 people
Delicious with cold Yoghurt and Tahini Dip (see page 65).

6 chicken wings, thighs or legs
50 g/2 oz melted butter
2 tablespoons oil
2 teaspoons soya sauce
A little clear honey
Salt

1. Preheat grill to high.
2. Trim chicken, but leave skin on.
3. Mix butter, oil and soya sauce and brush this all over chicken. Put under grill.
4. Turn grill down to moderate heat and cook chicken for 15 minutes, turning several times.
5. Brush with any remaining oil mixture. Smear each wing with honey and sprinkle with salt.
6. Return to grill for another 10 minutes until cooked and the skin is dark brown and crisp.

Elizabeth Mickery
Pudsey, West Yorkshire

CHICKEN COOKED IN WHITE WINE WITH TOMATOES

This is the well-known Poulet Chasseur.

1 chicken, jointed, or 6 chicken pieces
2 tablespoons seasoned flour (see page 44)
50 g/2 oz butter or 2 tablespoons oil
1 large onion, chopped small
A clove of garlic, crushed
450 ml/¾ pint chicken stock
Salt and pepper
A 400 g/14 oz tin of tomatoes
1 tablespoon tomato purée*
1 teaspoon soya sauce
A dash of Worcestershire sauce
A small glass of white wine, dry home-made wine is useful

*See page 45 for a tip on how to keep tomato purée fresh

1. Roll chicken pieces in seasoned flour and brown in the fat in a frying pan. Remove from the pan.
2. Fry onion and garlic and remove from the pan.

3. Add 1 tablespoon of remaining flour to pan, stir in the chicken stock carefully and allow to thicken on a low heat.

4. Add seasoning, tomatoes, purée, soya sauce, Worcestershire sauce and wine.

5. Lastly, add chicken pieces, put on lid and cook gently on top of the stove for 1 hour. Or, transfer to a covered casserole and cook for 1 hour in a moderate oven, Gas 4, 350°F, 180°C.

Mrs Patricia Chantry
Hook, Goole, N. Humberside

CHICKEN CASSEROLE

For 4 people

65 g/2½ oz butter or margarine
4 chicken joints
1 onion, finely-chopped
2 sticks celery, finely-chopped
225 g/8 oz long grain brown or white rice
A 400 g/14 oz tin of tomatoes
600 ml/1 pint stock
1 teaspoon mixed herbs
1 level teaspoon sugar
125 g/4 oz mushrooms, sliced

1. Heat 50 g/2 oz of the butter or margarine and brown the chicken joints. Lift them out of fat into a casserole.

2. Fry onion, celery and rice gently for 3 to 4 minutes.

3. Stir in tomatoes, stock, herbs and sugar. Bring to the boil, stirring.

4. Pour rice mixture over chicken. Cover the casserole and cook in a moderately hot oven, Gas 6, 400°F, 200°C, for 1 hour.

5. Heat remaining butter and fry mushrooms quite briskly for 2 minutes. Add to casserole.

Freezes well.

CEYLON CHICKEN CURRY

For 4 people

2 large onions
2 tablespoons ground coriander
2 teaspoons ground cumin
1 teaspoon chilli powder
½ teaspoon turmeric
¼ teaspoon cardamom powder
A 5 cm/2 inch piece of cinnamon bark, or ¼ teaspoon ground cinnamon
2 teaspoons salt
4 cloves of garlic, finely-chopped
4 tablespoons vegetable oil
A 1·4 kg/3 lb chicken, jointed
50 g/2 oz creamed coconut
350 ml/12 fl oz hot water
Juice of 1 lemon
2 tablespoons finely-chopped fresh coriander leaves, if you can get them

1. Grate one of the onions and mix with the spices and salt.

2. Finely-slice second onion and fry with garlic in the heated oil until golden brown.

3. Add grated onion and spice mixture and stir for about 5 minutes until heated through.

4. Add chicken joints and fry for another 5 minutes until well-coated in mixture in pan.

5. Dissolve creamed coconut in the hot water and add to chicken.

6. Bring to the boil, lower heat, cover pan and simmer for about 1 hour until chicken is cooked.

7. Before serving, add the lemon juice and garnish with the coriander leaves if available.

Serve with Boiled Rice (*see page 86*) or rice sticks or noodles.

Priya Wickramasinghe
Cardiff

FRIED TARRAGON CHICKEN

For 2 or 3 people

225 g/8 oz chicken pieces, breast, wings or legs
1 beaten egg
1 to 2 tablespoons dried breadcrumbs (*see page 33*)
20 g/¾ oz butter
20 g/¾ oz lard

Marinade (*see page 52*)

2 tablespoons oil
2 tablespoons white wine, or
cider vinegar, or lemon juice
1 large teaspoon finely-chopped
fresh tarragon or ½ teaspoon
dried
A clove of garlic, crushed
½ teaspoon dry mustard

Sauce

150 ml/¼ pint chicken stock
1 teaspoon cornflower
1 tablespoon water
Salt and pepper

1. Remove skin from chicken.
2. Mix marinade ingredients.
3. Lay chicken pieces in a flat dish.
Pour over marinade and leave for 2 or
3 hours. If you like tarragon flavour
leave overnight.
4. Remove chicken and pat dry. Save
marinade for the sauce.
5. Dip chicken pieces in beaten egg
and then in breadcrumbs.
6. Heat butter and lard and fry
chicken until crisp, brown and cooked.
7. Meanwhile, make sauce. Put
marinade in a pan with chicken stock.
8. Slake cornflour in water and add to
pan. Bring to the boil, stirring as
sauce thickens. Simmer 2 or 3 minutes.
Season to taste.
9. Put chicken on a warm dish. Serve
sauce separately.

HUFFED CHICKEN

In this old Sussex recipe a chicken was
stuffed, then wrapped in suet pastry
and probably a pudding cloth, and
boiled for several hours. This is an
updated and delicious adaptation.

4 chicken breasts

Stuffing

100 g/4 oz prunes, stoned and
chopped
100 g/4 oz cooking apples,
peeled, cored and chopped fine
1 large onion, finely-chopped
25 g/1 oz fresh wholewheat or
white breadcrumbs
Rind of half a lemon
Pepper and salt
1 small beaten egg

Suet Pastry

450 g/1 lb plain flour
½ level teaspoon salt
225 g/8 oz shredded suet
225 to 275 ml/8 to 10 fl oz cold
water
Beaten egg, to glaze

1. Remove skin from chicken and bone
it if necessary. Cut a pocket in each
breast.
2. Mix stuffing ingredients and fill the
pockets.
3. Prepare suet pastry. Mix flour, salt
and suet, then mix with water to make
a firm dough.
4. Using a floured board, roll out
about 7 mm/¼ inch thick.
5. Cut pastry to wrap around each
piece of chicken. Damp edges and press
together. Put on a greased baking tray
with pastry join underneath.
6. Make pastry leaves to decorate and
stick them on with water. Brush with
beaten egg.
7. Bake in a moderately hot oven, Gas
6, 400°F, 200°C, for 30 minutes, when
the pastry will be golden brown and
crisp.

Mrs Janice Langley
Shoreham-by-Sea, West Sussex

INDONESIAN CHICKEN SATE

For 4 people

A 2 kg/4 lb fresh chicken

Marinade

2 tablespoons soya sauce
2 tablespoons cooking oil
2 tablespoons hot water

Peanut Sate Sauce

175 g/6 oz roasted peanuts
4 dried red chillis
2 tablespoons shallots, chopped
2 tablespoons soya sauce
1 tablespoon brown sugar
1 teaspoon salt
1 tablespoon oil
125 ml/4 fl oz water

To garnish: lime wedges, if
possible, or lemon

1. Skin the chicken, remove flesh from bone and cut it into bite-sized pieces.
2. Take 8 skewers and thread a few pieces of meat on to each skewer.
3. In a shallow dish mix the marinade ingredients.
4. Lay skewered meat in this marinade for at least 3 hours, turning from time to time.
5. While the meat is marinating, prepare the peanut sate sauce.
6. Using an electric blender or a mortar and pestle, grind and blend all sauce ingredients except oil and water to form a smooth paste.
7. In a pan, heat oil and fry these ingredients until the oil separates.
8. Add a half cup of water and bring to the boil.
9. Reduce heat and simmer for 5 minutes.
10. While sauce is simmering, grill or barbecue the skewered chicken on a low flame, taking care to brown evenly on all sides.
11. Just before serving, arrange the skewered chicken pieces on a platter and pour the peanut sauce over them.
12. Garnish with lime wedges when available, or lemon.
This goes well with rice and salads.

Priya Wickramasinghe
Cardiff

SIMPLE BARBECUED CHICKEN

For 4 people

4 chicken joints
1 tablespoon oil
40 g/1½ oz butter
1 onion, chopped
2 dessertspoons tomato purée
2 level teaspoons barbados sugar
1 teaspoon prepared mustard
1 teaspoon Worcestershire sauce
1 level teaspoon salt
Black pepper
Juice of half a lemon
150 ml/¼ pint water

1. Dry the chicken joints and fry in oil and 25 g/1 oz of the butter until nicely browned. Lift out into a casserole.

2. Add remaining butter to pan and lightly fry onion until soft and golden.
3. Add all remaining ingredients and simmer for 5 minutes. Pour over chicken.
4. Cover casserole and cook in a moderate oven, Gas 4, 350°F, 180°C for 1 hour.

This dish freezes well.

Judith Adshead
Mottram St. Andrew, Cheshire

SPICY CHICKEN JOINTS

For 4 people

4 chicken joints
25 g/1 oz butter
1 tablespoon oil
2 large onions, finely-chopped
1 green pepper, de-seeded and chopped
A clove of garlic, finely-chopped
2 teaspoons dry mustard
2 tablespoons tomato purée*
300 ml/½ pint chicken stock
25 g/1 oz soft brown sugar
3 tablespoons vinegar
1 teaspoon Worcestershire sauce
½ teaspoon salt
1 large sprig fresh tarragon, or ½ teaspoon dried

*See how to keep tomato purée fresh, page 45.

1. Skin the chicken joints.
2. In a pan, combine butter and oil and fry chicken joints on all sides until brown.
3. Remove joints to a large casserole.
4. Now lightly fry onion, green pepper and garlic for 3 to 4 minutes.
5. Mix mustard into tomato purée and add stock, sugar, vinegar, Worcestershire sauce and salt. Lastly add the tarragon. Stir until sugar is dissolved.
6. Cover casserole and put it in a moderate oven, Gas 3, 325°F, 160°C, for about 2 hours or until chicken is tender.

TANDOURI CHICKEN

A recipe from the Punjab.
Traditionally a brilliant red, but
colouring is not necessary.

Serves 4 people

A fresh 1·6 kg/3½ lb chicken
1 medium-sized onion, minced
or finely-chopped
3 cloves of garlic, chopped
1 teaspoon fresh ginger,
chopped (*see opposite*)
1 cup natural yoghurt
Rind and juice of 1 lemon
2 tablespoons vinegar
1 tablespoon paprika powder
2 teaspoons garam masala (*see*
opposite)
2 teaspoons coriander powder
1 teaspoon cumin powder
½ teaspoon red food colouring
(optional)

To serve and garnish

2 tablespoons ghee (*see opposite*)
Lettuce leaves
Fresh onion rings
Cucumber slices
Lemon wedges

1. Skin the chicken, then cut it into 2
along breast bone and back bone.
2. Using a sharp knife, make slanting
incisions 2·5 cm/1 inch long in the
chicken on each limb and breast,
taking care not to cut through to the
bone.
3. In a non-metallic large bowl mix all
other ingredients except those listed
for serving and garnish. This will
make a brilliant red marinade.
4. Marinate the chicken in this spicy
yoghurt mixture for between 8 and 24
hours.
5. Turn the chicken occasionally in
the marinade to ensure that all sides
become uniformly soaked.
6. Heat oven to very hot, Gas 8, 450°F,
230°C.
7. Lift chicken out of marinade and
place on a greased wire rack over a
baking tray. Cover with foil.
8. Roast on top shelf of oven for 1
hour. Baste chicken with marinade
mixture once during the cooking.
9. Just before serving, heat ghee, pour
it over the chicken halves and ignite.

10. Serve the chicken on a bed of
lettuce garnished with onion rings,
cucumber slices and lemon wedges.
Serve with Pitta Bread (*see page 139*).

Serve with Pitta Bread (*see page 139*).

Priya Wickramasinghe
Cardiff

Oriental Recipes

The oriental recipes to be found in this
book have been devised using ingredients
readily available in Britain and the West
and it is to be hoped you will see Mrs
Wickramasinghe making some of the
dishes in the television programmes. A few
explanatory notes follow.

Curry leaves are used fresh if possible.
They are aromatic and slightly pungent
and although not like the bay leaf they are
used in a similar way. Available from
continental and oriental food shops.

Fresh ginger is infinitely preferable to
dried ginger powder. Sometimes called
green ginger, it can be bought in many
supermarkets and greengrocers, besides
the oriental food shops. Look for plump,
smooth roots. Avoid shrivelled pieces. It
freezes well.

Garam Masala, the Indian name for a
basic mixture of curry spices. Many people
prepare their own, grinding the whole
spices specially. It is obtainable ready-
prepared from Indian grocery shops and
some wholefood shops.

Ghee is much used in Indian cookery. It is
simply clarified unsalted butter. It can be
bought in oriental food shops. A cheaper
way is to make it at home. In a heavy-
bottomed pan heat 250 g/8 oz unsalted
butter on a very low heat for about 30
minutes. Do not allow it to smoke or burn.
Remove the floating scum. Strain through
a piece of muslin into a bowl. Allow to cool.
Store in refrigerator. Keeps for months.

Poppadoms are made with a special
blend of lentil flour. Buy them at oriental
food shops. They can either be grilled or
deep fried before serving.

POACHED CHICKEN

A way to prepare chicken when really
moist cooked chicken is required.
Provides also a delicious jellied stock.
(*See Chicken and Ham Pie below.*)

1 chicken
1 litre/1¾ pints water
1 onion, sliced

1 teaspoon mixed dried herbs
Salt and pepper

1. Put whole chicken into a pan which just contains it. *Or*, cut chicken into joints and put in a pan.
2. Add water, onion, herbs and seasoning. Cover pan.
3. Bring to the boil over gentle heat and cook until tender, 1½ to 2 hours.
4. Remove chicken from pan.
5. Boil stock to reduce quantity and so strengthen flavour and jelly properties.

Sybil Norcott
Irlam, Nr. Manchester

CHICKEN AND HAM PIE

A delicious pie to eat hot or cold. Can be made with left-over chicken but it needs to be moist, preferably poached, so that stock sets in a jelly when pie is cold (*see previous recipe*).

175 g/6 oz shortcrust pastry (*see page 104*)
350 g/12 oz cooked chicken, preferably poached
1 small onion, finely-chopped
15 g/½ oz butter
75 g/3 oz fresh breadcrumbs
75 to 125 g/3 to 4 oz cooked ham, minced or finely-chopped
1 teaspoon mixed herbs
Salt and pepper
A little beaten egg
300 ml/½ pint stock from poaching chicken or chicken bone stock

1. Make pastry and chill.
2. Remove skin and bones and cut chicken into pieces. Put them in a 1·2 litre/2 pint pie dish. A pie funnel may be useful.
3. Fry onion gently in butter for 3 minutes. Add to breadcrumbs with ham, herbs, seasoning and a little beaten egg to bind if needed.
4. Form into balls and place in dish with chicken. Pour in stock.
5. Roll out pastry to 1·5 cm/½ inch wider than needed to cover pie. Cut off a strip of this width.

6. Moisten edge of pie dish with water. Lay strip in place, moisten it, then cover pie with pastry, pressing to seal. Flute or fork the edge.
7. Brush with beaten egg or milk and decorate pie with the trimmings.
8. Bake near top of a moderately hot oven, Gas 6, 400°F, 200°C for 20 minutes.

Mrs Aileen Houghton
Kemsing, Nr. Sevenoaks, Kent

CHICKEN SALAD WITH AVOCADO

For 2 to 3 people as a main course, but served in lettuce leaves on small plates would make a starter for 4 people.

175 g/6 oz small macaroni, pasta shapes or noodles
Boiling water
1 teaspoon corn oil
Salt
2 chicken quarters, cooked*
1 tomato
1 avocado pear

*Chicken can be poached (*see previous page*)

Dressing

For this you need a liquidiser.

50 g/2 oz blue cheese
2 tablespoons mayonnaise (*see page 64*)
1 teaspoon lemon juice
A little milk
Salt and pepper

To serve: lettuce leaves

1. The dressing can be made in advance. Put cheese, mayonnaise and lemon juice in a liquidiser, switch on to blend until smooth.
2. As it blends, add milk a little at a time until a pouring consistency is made. Add salt and pepper to taste.
3. Boil macaroni, pasta or noodles in plenty of water with the oil and salt until it is cooked but firm to the bite. Then drain, run cold water through it and chill.

39

4. Meanwhile cut chicken and tomato into small pieces.

5. Skin the avocado, remove stone and dice flesh.

6. Toss all ingredients gently together with dressing and serve on lettuce leaves.

Elizabeth Mickery
Pudsey, West Yorkshire

PHEASANT CASSEROLE

Pheasant may be cooked whole or in joints.

50 g/2 oz seedless raisins
150 ml/¼ pint cider (or home-made white wine)
1 pheasant, about 1.1 kg/2½ lb
450 ml/¾ pint water
A small piece of carrot
1 medium-sized onion
2 sticks of celery
2 medium-sized cooking apples and 1 dessert apple
15 g/½ oz flour
Salt and pepper
A pinch of mixed spice
65 g/2½ oz butter
300 ml/½ pint stock (from giblets)
150 ml/5 fl oz yoghurt or cream

1. Put raisins to soak in cider or wine for 2 hours.

2. Remove giblets from pheasant and make stock by simmering them in the water for ¾ hour with the carrot, a quarter of the onion and a small piece of the celery. Then drain and reserve stock.

3. Chop remaining onion and celery finely. Peel, core and slice cooking apples.

4. Either truss pheasant by tying the legs, or joint it. Dust with flour seasoned with salt, pepper and spice.

5. Melt butter and turn pheasant in it to brown. Then lift it out on to a plate.

6. Fry onion gently until transparent. Then add celery and cooking apple and fry for a further 5 minutes.

7. Stir in any remaining flour and cook for 1 minute.

8. Add cider, raisins and stock and bring to the boil.

9. Put this and the pheasant into a pan which just contains it. Put on a tight-fitting lid and let it just simmer for about 1 to 1½ hours for a whole pheasant, 45 minutes to 1 hour for joints, or until tender. Cooking time will vary according to age of bird.

10. When tender, lift pheasant out into a warmed serving dish and keep it warm.

11. If the sauce is very runny, boil without lid to reduce and thicken. Then add yoghurt or cream, adjust seasoning and reheat but do not boil. Pour into a separate bowl if pheasant is served whole or around the joints in the serving dish.

12. Peel dessert apple, cut out core and slice into fine rings. Fry these lightly in remaining butter and set them on dish around the pheasant.

HARE CASSEROLE WITH MUSHROOMS

1 hare, weight about 1.1 kg/2½ lb, jointed into even-sized pieces

Marinade (*see page 52*)
1 tablespoon redcurrant jelly
75 ml/3 fl oz port or cream sherry
75 ml/3 fl oz wine vinegar
75 ml/3 fl oz mushroom ketchup
1 dessertspoon chopped mixed fresh thyme and marjoram or 1 level teaspoon of each dried
1 medium-sized onion, chopped

To cook hare
225 g/8 oz streaky bacon rashers
50 g/2 oz butter
2 medium-sized onions
50 g/2 oz plain flour
A clove of garlic, crushed
Salt and pepper
Nutmeg
1½ to 1¾ litres/2½ to 3 pints chicken stock
300 ml/½ pint red wine (home-made would be excellent)
225 g/8 oz button mushrooms

1. Melt redcurrant jelly and pour it into a dish. Mix in the other marinade ingredients.
2. Lay the pieces of hare in the marinade and leave for 3 hours.
3. Remove hare from marinade and pat dry. Strain the marinade, discarding onion, but keep liquid to add to gravy.
4. Cut up bacon, discarding rind.
5. Using a large pan, heat the butter, fry bacon gently for a few minutes, then remove to a dish.
6. Add chopped onion and fry gently until transparent. Remove to dish.
7. Sprinkle the flour into the pan and allow it to colour a rich brown.
8. Now put in pieces of hare, turning and shaking the pan to make sure that they are well browned, about 10 minutes. Remove hare.
9. To same pan add garlic, salt and pepper, nutmeg, onion, bacon, stock, wine and all the marinade. Stir well. Return the hare.
10. Put on lid, cook steadily for 1½ hours or until tender. This may be done on top of stove or in a warm oven, Gas 3, 325°F, 160°C.
11. Wash mushrooms and chop roughly.
12. When hare is tender, remove it on to a dish and keep warm. Strain the sauce, putting bacon with hare.
13. Add mushrooms to sauce, cover and simmer for 10 minutes. Then return hare and bacon to sauce and reheat for 10 minutes if necessary.

Serve with plain boiled potatoes and a green vegetable.

RABBIT CASSEROLE WITH DUMPLINGS

Can be done in oven or on top of stove.

700 g/1½ lb rabbit, jointed
1 tablespoon vinegar
Water
25 g/1 oz flour, seasoned with salt and pepper
40 g/1½ oz dripping
2 onions, sliced

2 apples, sliced
A 400 g/14 oz can of tomatoes, or 450 g/1 lb fresh ripe tomatoes, skinned and sliced (see page 72)
450 ml/¾ pint stock
1 tablespoon redcurrant jelly
1 slice of dry bread, without crusts
½ teaspoon made mustard
½ teaspoon mixed herbs

Dumplings*

125 g/4 oz self-raising flour
¼ teaspoon salt
50 g/2 oz grated suet
1 tablespoon freshly-chopped parsley or ½ teaspoon dried mixed herbs
3 to 4 tablespoons water

*See also Sussex Swimmers, page 54.

1. Soak rabbit joints for 1 hour in vinegar and water. Then drain, pat dry and roll them in seasoned flour.
2. Melt dripping in a pan. Fry rabbit for a few minutes, turning pieces over in hot fat to brown a little. Lift joints out into a casserole or large saucepan.
3. Fry onions and apples for just 1 minute. Then put them with rabbit.
4. Add the tomatoes to rabbit.
5. Stir stock into residue in pan. Add redcurrant jelly.
6. Spread mustard on dry bread, sprinkle on the herbs and put it into the stock. Allow to soak, then beat in. Pour over rabbit.
7. Cover the casserole and cook in a moderate oven, Gas 4, 350°F, 180°C, for 1½ hours. If using a saucepan, put on the lid, bring gently to the boil and simmer for 1½ hours.
8. Meanwhile, prepare dumplings. Mix flour, salt, suet and herbs. Mix to a softish dough with water.
9. Turn on to a well-floured board, cut into 8 pieces and roll them into balls.
10. 20 to 25 minutes before rabbit is done drop dumplings into casserole or pan and replace lid. Keep rabbit simmering as dumplings cook. In casserole allow 25 minutes. In saucepan allow 20 minutes.

SOMERSET RABBIT

Enough for 4 but easy to cut down for 1 or 2. Or, as it freezes well, cook quantity given, divide it into portions to suit your household and freeze for future use.

Goes well under a pie crust or cobbler or with dumplings.

1 rabbit
2 tablespoons flour, seasoned with salt and pepper
50 g/2 oz lard or oil
1 onion, chopped
450 g/1 lb mixed root vegetables, scrubbed and cut into chunks
1 tablespoon tomato purée or ketchup
1 teaspoon yeast extract such as Marmite
½ teaspoon mixed herbs
300 ml/½ pint cider
300 ml/½ pint light chicken stock
Salt and pepper

1. Keep the rabbit whole, or, if it will not fit your pan or casserole, just cut it in two between hind legs and rib cage. Dust it over with seasoned flour.
2. Heat lard in a pan and turn rabbit over in it to brown. Lift out of fat on to a plate.
3. Fry onion gently to soften.
4. Put rabbit in a pan or a casserole. Put vegetables on top and add other ingredients. Cover with a lid or foil. *Either* bring to boil and simmer until tender, about 1½ hours, *or* put casserole into a warm oven, Gas 3, 325°F, 160°C, for about 2 hours or until tender.
5. Lift out rabbit, remove all meat from bones and return it to pan. Be careful to remove the small pieces of bone. Re-heat.

Serve as a stew with potatoes and green vegetables, or with pasta shells. Or try one of the following:
As a pie, enough for 6.

Choose a pastry from pages 104 and 105. Allow meat to cool and put it in a dish which it nearly fills so that it supports pastry.
Bake in a hot oven, Gas 7, 425°F, 220°C, for 30 minutes. Check after 15 minutes, reducing temperature to moderately hot, Gas 5, 375°F, 190°C, if it is browning too quickly.

As a cobbler, enough for 6. Delicious with wholewheat flour.
225 g/8 oz self-raising wholewheat* or white flour
A pinch of salt
25 g/1 oz margarine
A bare 150 ml/¼ pint milk

*Use 1½ teaspoons baking powder if you cannot buy self-raising flour.

1. Put rabbit and gravy into a casserole which allows 5 cm/2 inches headroom. Let it cool.
2. Mix flour, salt and baking powder, if used. Rub in margarine and mix to a soft dough with milk.
3. Using a floured board, roll out 2 cm/¾ inch thick. Cut 5 cm/2 inch rounds and lay these overlapping on top of meat.
4. Bake above middle of a hot oven, Gas 7, 425°F, 220°C, for 30 minutes. If using wholewheat flour, check after 15 minutes and reduce temperature to Gas 5, 375°F, 190°C, if browning too quickly.

With dumplings, for 4 people.
175 g/6 oz self-raising flour
½ teaspoon salt
75 g/3 oz shredded suet
About 6 tablespoons water

1. Mix ingredients, using enough water to make a firm dough. Form into small balls and drop into bubbling pan or casserole.
2. Cover and simmer for 15 minutes.

Try also Sussex Swimmers (*see page 54*).

Mrs Angela Mottram
Axbridge, Somerset

Chapter 4

Beef, Lamb, Pork, Ham and Bacon

STEAK WITH BLACK PEPPER AND CREAM SAUCE

For 4 people for a very special occasion

15 g/½ oz crushed black peppers
4 large steaks, either rump, sirloin or fillet
50 g/2 oz butter
1 tablespoon olive oil
1 small onion, chopped
A 142 ml/¼ pint carton of double cream
Salt to taste

1. Press the crushed black pepper into the steaks
2. Fry steaks in the butter and oil for no more than 5 minutes each side.
3. Remove steaks to a hot dish. Fry chopped onion in steak pan for 2 minutes.
4. Add cream, heat but do not boil. Add salt to taste.
5. Pour over steaks and serve without delay.

Judith Adshead
Mottram St. Andrew, Cheshire

RUMP STEAK WITH RICE

For 2 people

275 g/10 oz rump steak
125 g/4 oz brown or white rice
1 large onion, sliced
2 sticks celery, sliced
1 red pepper (optional) cored and sliced
1 to 2 tablespoons wholewheat or plain four
1 teaspoon Salt and Pepper Mix
(see opposite)
150 ml/¼ pint stock
2 teaspoons Worcestershire sauce
Chopped parsley

1. Cut fat from meat. Cut fat up small, put it in frying pan and fry to extract dripping. You will need 1 tablespoon. Discard the scraps of skin.
If meat is all lean use 25 g/1 oz beef dripping and heat it in frying pan.

2. Follow instructions for Boiled Rice (*see page 86*).
3. Put onion and celery into frying pan to cook for 5 minutes till softening.
4. Meanwhile, cut steak into strips, 1·2 by 6 cm/½ by 2½ inches. Dust lightly with flour seasoned with Salt and Pepper Mix.
5. Add meat to frying pan and turn it over to seal. Add red pepper. Cook for 7 to 8 minutes.
6. Stir in 3 to 4 tablespoons stock and Worcestershire sauce and let it bubble for 2 minutes, adding a little more stock if it is too thick. Taste and season with more salt and pepper if it is needed.
7. Make a border of rice on a warmed serving dish. Pour meat mixture in centre.
8. Sprinkle on chopped parsley and serve at once.

Serve with green vegetables or green salad.

DOROTHY SLEIGHTHOLME'S SALT AND PEPPER MIX

A mixture of 3 parts salt to 1 part pepper, black for flavour.
Keep in a sprinkler-topped jar.
Useful for flavouring savoury dishes, sauces, gravy, etc.

SEASONED FLOUR

Can be made and stored in a labelled jar. Use for coating fish or meat before grilling, frying, etc.

450 g/1 lb wholewheat flour
50 g/2 oz salt
15 g/½ oz black pepper
15 g/½ oz dry mustard
7 g/¼ oz paprika

This mixture can be divided into separate labelled jars, each incorporating a herb of your choice.

Sybil Norcott
Irlam, Manchester

STROGANOFF

Made with either beef or pork.

Enough for 6 to 8 people, but easy to make less

A 1 kg/2 lb single piece of fillet of beef or fillet of pork
3 medium-sized onions
225 g/8 oz button mushrooms
About 25 g/1 oz butter
A little chopped fresh parsley

Sauce

25 g/1 oz butter
25 g/1 oz plain flour
1 level tablespoon tomato purée (*see below*)
¼ level teaspoon nutmeg, freshly-grated if possible
600 ml/1 pint beef stock
150 ml/5 fl oz yoghurt or soured cream
Salt and pepper

1. Start with the sauce. In quite a large saucepan melt butter, remove from heat and stir in flour.
2. Stir in tomato purée and nutmeg, then gradually stir in stock.
3. Bring to the boil, stirring as sauce thickens, and simmer for 2 minutes.
4. Stir in yoghurt or soured cream and season with salt and pepper.
5. Now for the main part of the dish. Cut meat into strips about 5 cm/2 inches long and 1 cm/½ inch wide.
6. Peel and chop onions. Wipe and finely-slice mushrooms.
7. Heat half of the butter in a large frying pan and quickly brown the meat on all sides. Remove from pan into sauce.
8. Add a little more butter to the pan if necessary and fry onions slowly until tender and light brown. Put these in sauce.
9. In the last of the butter fry mushrooms for just 1 or 2 minutes. Put these with meat and onions.
10. Bring the Stroganoff to the boil and simmer it for 15 minutes.

Serve with boiled potatoes or rice (*see page 86*).

TO KEEP TOMATO PURÉE FRESH

To keep tomato purée fresh once a tin has been opened, spoon it into a screw-topped jar. Smooth top and pour in a layer of cooking oil. Keep in a cool place. When it is required, pour off oil, spoon out what you need, then return the oil once again.

BEEF CASSEROLE

For 4 to 5 people
Remember to start the night before.
675 g/1½ lb stewing beef

Marinade (*see page 52 for a note on marinades*)
3 tablespoons oil
1 tablespoon wine or cider vinegar, or lemon juice
1 wineglass of red wine
1 carrot, sliced in fine rings
1 onion, sliced in rings
1 teaspoon chopped fresh thyme, or ½ teaspoon dried
1 bay leaf

To cook
40 g/1½ oz lard
350 g/12 oz carrots, cut in 1 cm/½ inch slices
450 g/1 lb tomatoes, skinned (*see page 72*) and chopped or a
400 g/14 oz tin of tomatoes
Salt and pepper
675 g/1½ lb potatoes, peeled and thinly-sliced
150 ml/¼ pint beef stock

1. Put marinade ingredients in a pan and simmer for 15 minutes. Leave to cool.
2. Trim meat and cut it into 2·5 cm/1 inch cubes. Put in a basin.
3. Pour cold marinade over meat and leave overnight in refrigerator or a cool place.
4. Strain marinade off meat and reserve it.
5. Brown meat in hot lard and place in a very deep casserole.
6. Add carrots, tomatoes and seasoning to casserole.
7. Top with potato slices.
8. Pour over marinade and stock.

9. Cover casserole and cook in a warm oven, Gas 3, 325°F, 160°C, for 2 hours. For the last 15 minutes of cooking time remove lid to let the potatoes brown a little.

BRAISED STEAK WITH VEGETABLES

For 4 or 5 people

A 675 g/1½ lb single piece of lean braising steak cut about 2·5 cm/1 inch thick
675 g/1½ lb mixed vegetables, onions, leeks, carrots, celery, turnip—whatever you prefer
2 teaspoons flour
25 g/1 oz beef dripping
Salt and pepper
150 ml/¼ pint beef stock (*see page 8*)

Marinade (*see page 52*)
2 tablespoons oil
2 tablespoons vinegar
1 small onion, chopped
A clove of garlic chopped (optional)
6 peppercorns

1. Mix the marinade in a flat dish and soak the meat for 3 to 4 hours, turning occasionally.
2. Meanwhile, prepare vegetables and cut into 5 cm/2 inch pieces.
3. Remove meat from marinade, pat dry and dust well with flour.
4. Heat dripping in frying pan, seal meat quickly on both sides. Lift it out on to a plate.
5. Fry vegetables quickly in the frying pan until just golden.
6. Place them in the bottom of a casserole large enough to hold the steak in one piece. Season with salt and pepper. Place steak on top.
7. Remove peppercorns from marinade and pour it with stock into frying pan. Bring to the boil and pour into casserole.
8. Cover tightly to prevent drying up. If casserole has no lid, cover tightly with greaseproof paper and foil.
9. Cook in a warm oven, Gas 3, 325°F, 160°C for 1¼ to 1½ hours.

Can be served with jacket potatoes. Choose small ones, and rub well with butter, bacon dripping or oil. Spear them on skewers and they will cook at the same time as the meat.

SRI LANKAN BEEF CURRY

For 4 people

450 g/1 lb braising beef
2 tablespoons oil
1 medium-sized onion, finely-chopped
3 cloves of garlic, crushed
3 whole cardamoms*
3 whole cloves
A 2·5 cm/1 inch piece of cinnamon stick
50 g/2 oz creamed coconut*
125 ml/4 fl oz hot water
1 teaspoon fresh ginger (*see page 38*) chopped fine
2 teaspoons malt vinegar
1½ teaspoons ground coriander
1½ teaspoons ground cumin
1 teaspoon chilli powder
1 teaspoon salt
¼ teaspoon ground fenugreek
¼ teaspoon turmeric
¼ teaspoon freshly-milled black pepper

*Can be bought at oriental food shops.

1. Cut beef into 2·5 cm/1 inch pieces.
2. Heat oil and fry onions and garlic till just golden.
3. Add the meat and fry over a low heat until quite brown.
4. Grind together in a mortar or electric grinder the cardamom seeds, cloves and cinnamon stick and add to meat.
5. Dissolve the creamed coconut in the hot water and add it with all the other ingredients.
6. Put on the lid and simmer for 1 hour.

Priya Wickramasinghe
Cardiff

46

CASSEROLED SHIN OF BEEF

This casserole may be made with varying quantities of meat and vegetables according to what you have and how many are to eat it. It is just as good reheated as when it is freshly made, so it is worth making enough for two meals.

2 large onions
2 large carrots
1 stick of celery
1 small parsnip or turnip
A clove of garlic
1 kg/2 lb shin of beef or stewing steak
40 g/1½ oz wholemeal or plain flour
½ teaspoon dried marjoram
½ teaspoon salt
Freshly-grated black pepper
40 g/1½ oz dripping
A wineglass of red wine, or cider or 2 tablespoons vinegar
A 400 g/14 oz tin of tomatoes
Water
Fresh parsley

1. Peel onions and cut them into large pieces. Scrub carrots and cut them into large chunks. Cut up very finely the celery and parsnip or turnip. Crush the garlic.
2. Trim off excess fat and hard gristle from the meat and cut it into easy pieces, about 5 cm/2 inches long, 2·2 cm/½ inch thick. Mix together flour, marjoram, salt and pepper on a plate or in a clean paper bag or polythene bag. Toss the meat in this seasoned flour to coat it well. (*See page 44 for a tip about seasoned flour.*)
3. Heat half of the dripping in a heavy saucepan or a flameproof casserole. (Flameproof means one which can stand direct heat on top of the stove and can also go into the oven.) Add onion and fry till it begins to brown. Then lift it out with a draining spoon on to a plate.
4. Now add remaining dripping and heat till it begins to smoke. Then add the meat, turning it over quickly to brown.
5. Turn down heat and add wine or cider but not the vinegar. Let it bubble for a minute.
6. Now, if you are using a saucepan which cannot go into the oven, turn the contents into a large casserole.
7. Add the onions, garlic, carrots, celery, parsnip or turnip.
8. Add vinegar, if used instead of wine or cider.
9. Now empty the tin of tomatoes on top, refill the tin with cold water and pour in enough just to cover the meat and vegetables.
10. Tie a bunch of parsley together with cotton or string and lay it on top.
11. Cover the casserole and put it in a moderate oven, Gas 4, 350°F, 180°C, for 2½ to 3 hours. After half an hour, when pot will be bubbling nicely, reduce heat to very cool Gas ¼, 250°F, 120°C, and let it go on cooking for another 2 hours. If you are using shin of beef a total of 3½ hours is not too long.
12. Remove the bunch of parsley and add freshly-chopped parsley, if you can spare it, just before serving.

STUFFED SKIRT OF BEEF

A very old Gloucestershire recipe, economical and nourishing.

1 kg/2 lb skirt of beef

Stuffing
100 g/4 oz medium oatmeal
50 g/2 oz shredded suet
1 dessertspoon chopped parsley and other herbs to taste
25 g/1 oz finely-chopped onion
Salt and pepper
A little milk

To cook
50 g/2 oz dripping
225 g/8 oz chopped onions
1·2 litres/2 pints brown stock
(*see page 8*)
Salt and pepper
125 g/4 oz carrots
125 g/4 oz turnips
50 g/2 oz cornflour
2 tablespoons water

1. Buy the skirt in one piece. Remove skin and with a sharp knife slice a deep pocket in the meat.

47

2. Combine all stuffing ingredients using enough milk just to bind it.
3. Stuff the pocket in meat and sew up the opening.
4. Melt dripping in a heavy saucepan and brown meat and onions.
5. Add stock and salt and pepper if necessary. Bring to the boil and simmer very gently for 2½ to 3 hours.
6. About 45 minutes before end of cooking time add carrots and turnips, scrubbed and sliced into even-sized pieces.
7. Blend cornflour with water and add to pan at last minute to thicken.
8. Lift out meat and remove sewing thread.
9. Put meat on a hot dish surrounded by carrots and turnips.

Gloucester College of Agriculture, Hartpury

STUFFED BEEFBURGERS

A good way to use up any kind of stuffing.

For 4 people

350 g/12 oz minced beef
Salt and pepper
1 teaspoon Worcestershire sauce
4 heaped teaspoons stuffing
25 g/1 oz flour
1 to 2 tablespoons dripping
1 sliced onion
Half a cup of stock

1. Season mince with salt, pepper and Worcestershire sauce.
2. Divide mince into 8 portions and flatten each one into a thin round.
3. Place stuffing on four of the rounds and cover with remaining four. Pinch edges well together.
4. Dust beefburgers with flour.
5. Meanwhile fry onions in dripping until golden. Make space for the beefburgers and fry them until brown on both sides.
6. Remove browned beefburgers to a plate.
7. Mix in with fried onions any remaining flour. Stir in stock and let it thicken.
8. Replace beefburgers in pan, put on

lid and cook very gently for about 30 minutes.
Serve with creamed potatoes and a green vegetable.

Anne Wallace
Stewarton, Ayrshire

MINCED MEAT CURRY

For 4 people

2 tablespoons oil
1 medium onion, chopped
3 cloves garlic, chopped
2 green chillis, finely chopped
¼ teaspoon chopped fresh ginger
2 teaspoons ground coriander
2 teaspoons ground cumin
1 teaspoon garam masala*
¼ teaspoon turmeric
450 g/1 lb lean mince
1 teaspoon tomato purée
50 g/2 oz creamed coconut
125 ml/4 fl oz hot water
1 cup fresh or frozen peas
*Can be bought at wholefood shops and oriental food shops.

1. Heat oil and fry onions in it until just golden.
2. Add garlic, chillis, fresh ginger and other spices, and fry for a few seconds.
3. Add meat and continue to fry over a low heat.
4. Mix in tomato purée.
5. Dissolve creamed coconut in the water, mix it in, cover pan and allow to simmer for ¾ to 1 hour.
6. Toss in the peas and cook for a further 10 minutes.
Serve with Boiled Rice (*see page 86*), Curried Bhindi (*see page 73*) or Cauliflower Bhaji (*see page 74*) and salad.

Priya Wickramasinghe
Cardiff

SAVOURY BEEF CHARLOTTE

This recipe won first prize in a cooking competition judged by Dorothy Sleightholme and was given to her for this book.

For 3 or 4 people

1 tablespoon oil
1 onion, finely chopped

2 carrots, scrubbed and finely
chopped
225 g/8 oz minced beef
15 g/½ oz plain flour, wholewheat or white
2 level tablespoons tomato
purée*
125 g/4 oz mushrooms, sliced
2 teaspoons chopped fresh
parsley
Salt and Pepper Mix (see page 44)
6 large slices bread, wholewheat
is best
50 g/2 oz margarine
1 small beaten egg

Sauce

2 level tablespoons tomato
purée
2 tablespoons vinegar
1 level tablespoon golden syrup
A pinch of dry mustard

To keep tomato purée fresh, see page 45.

1. Heat oil in a large pan and put in
onions and carrot. Put on lid, turn
heat very low and cook for 10 minutes.
2. Stir in meat, flour and tomato
purée. Cook, stirring to break up meat,
for 5 minutes.
3. Mix in mushrooms, 1 teaspoon of
the parsley and salt and pepper. Cook
for 5 minutes, then remove from heat
to cool a little.
4. Meanwhile, spread margarine on
one side of slices of bread. Cut them to
fit and line sides and bottom of a
greased 1·5 litre/2¼ pint oven dish. A
20 cm/8 inch soufflé dish is suitable.
5. Beat egg into cooled meat mixture
and turn into prepared dish. Cover
with a lid or greaseproof paper and
foil.
6. Put dish on a baking tray and into a
moderately hot oven, Gas 5, 375°F,
190°C, for 20 minutes.
7. Blend sauce ingredients together.
Pour over the charlotte and return
dish to oven uncovered for 10 minutes
more.
8. Sprinkle on the rest of the parsley
just before serving.

Mrs Jean Barnard
Harrogate, Yorkshire

MEAT BALLS IN A TANGY TOMATO SAUCE

Plenty for 6 people

Mixture makes about sixteen 50 g/2 oz
balls. Smaller balls can be made for a
fork-meal.

Meat Balls

2 rashers of smoked bacon
450 g/1 lb stewing beef
1 small onion
1 cup fresh wholewheat
breadcrumbs
1 egg
225 g/8 oz sausage-meat
1 level teaspoon salt
½ teaspoon pepper
2 tablespoons flour, seasoned
with salt and pepper
50 g/2 oz lard

Tomato Sauce

1 large onion
A 400 g/14 oz tin of tomatoes
25 g/1 oz lard
5 tablespoons brown sugar
4 tablespoons malt vinegar and
2 tablespoons water
1 tablespoon Worcestershire
sauce
2 teaspoons lemon juice
1 teaspoon dry mustard
Salt and pepper

1. Remove rinds from bacon. Mince
rashers together with beef and onion.
2. To this add breadcrumbs, egg,
sausage-meat, salt and pepper. Mix
thoroughly.
3. Make small balls of the mixture
about 4 cm/1½ inches in diameter and
roll them in seasoned flour.
4. Using a heavy frying pan, heat the
50 g/2 oz lard and fry meat-balls until
well browned all over. Lift out with a
draining spoon on to kitchen paper or
brown paper.
5. Cover casserole and put it in oven
while you quickly make sauce. Set
oven to moderate, Gas 4, 350°F, 180°C.
6. Peel onion and chop finely.
Liquidise tomatoes.

7. Fry onion in lard until soft but not brown.

8. Add all other ingredients. Simmer for 3 minutes.

9. Pour sauce over meatballs.

10. Cover casserole and return to the pre-heated oven for a further 30 minutes. *Or*, complete cooking on top of stove instead of oven, simmering for 30 minutes.

Don Oldridge
Goole, N. Humberside

POTTED BEEF

8 helpings

1 bacon knuckle
Water
450 g/1 lb shin of beef, cut into large pieces
1 stick of celery, sliced
8 peppercorns
1 bay leaf
A pinch of ground allspice

1. Place bacon knuckle in a large saucepan, cover with cold water. Bring to boil, then discard water.

2. Put beef, celery and rest of ingredients into pan with knuckle and add 1.1 litres/2 pints fresh cold water.

3. Bring to boil, skim off any scum, then lower heat. Cover pan and simmer for 2 to 2½ hours until beef is very tender. *Or*, pressure cook in 600 ml/1 pint of water for 50 minutes.

4. Strain off stock and reserve. Discard bay leaf and peppercorns. Allow meat to cool.

5. Slice beef finely, removing any fat or gristle.

6. Remove skin from bacon knuckle. Cut bacon into fine cubes.

7. Place meat into an 850 ml/1½ pint mould or bowl. Add stock to almost fill mould. Top up with cold water if necessary. Stir well and cover. Chill and leave to set, overnight if possible.

8. To serve, loosen mould around edges with fingers. Place serving plate on top, invert and shake to release meat.

ROAST STUFFED HEART

Enough for 4 or 5 people
Remember to start the night before.

1 calf's heart, about 1 kg/2 lb in weight
Water
Salt
Vinegar
300 ml/½ pint beef stock
1 level dessertspoon cornflour
2 tablespoons cold water

Stuffing

50 g/2 oz prunes, soaked overnight
50 g/2 oz cooked brown rice (*see page 86*)
50 g/2 oz walnuts, chopped
1 large cooking apple, peeled, cored and chopped
Grated rind of a lemon
25 g/1 oz melted butter
Pepper and salt

1. To prepare heart, cut away the membranes, gristle and veins. Wash thoroughly in cold running water to remove congealed blood. Soak for 4 hours in cold, salted water with 1 tablespoon of vinegar to each 600 ml/1 pint of water.

2. Meanwhile, prepare stuffing. Drain prunes, remove stones and chop flesh.

3. In a bowl, combine all stuffing ingredients.

4. Using a sharp knife enlarge the cavity of the heart and spoon in the stuffing.

5. Tie up like a parcel and place the heart with its stuffing downwards in a roasting tin.

6. Pour over the stock. Cover and bake for 1½ to 2 hours in a moderate oven, Gas 4, 350°F, 180°C, basting frequently.

7. Put the stuffed heart on to a warm dish and keep hot.

8. Pour juices from the tin into a small pan.

9. Slake cornflour in water and stir into juices. Heat gently, stirring as sauce thickens. Serve sauce separately.

Serve with green vegetables.

OXTAIL STEW

It is better to do the first part of the cooking the day before the stew is needed. This ensures that a great deal of the fat can be skimmed off.

1 oxtail
Salt and pepper
225 g/8 oz carrots, diced
225 g/8 oz turnips, diced
225 g/8 oz onions, chopped
2 tablespoons flour
Chopped fresh parsley

1. Trim any surplus fat from the oxtail and cut it into its separate joints. Put into a bowl, cover with water and leave for 1 hour.
2. Drain and put the pieces in a stewpan. Add seasoning and cover with fresh water. Bring to the boil, reduce heat and simmer for 1½ hours.
3. At this point leave overnight.
4. Next day, skim off fat which has risen to the top.
5. Add chopped vegetables. Simmer again for 1½ hours or until tender.
6. Thicken just before serving. Mix flour to a smooth paste with a little cold water. Add to the stew, stir well and simmer again for a further 10 minutes.
Sprinkle generously with chopped fresh parsley if you have it.

Mrs A. Greenwood
Boroughbridge, Yorkshire

OXTAIL MOULD

1 oxtail
225 g/8 oz bacon in a piece or bacon pieces
1 small onion
4 cloves
Water
Pepper and salt to taste

1. Wash and joint the oxtail.
2. Put in a pan, with the bacon cut in chunks and the onion stuck with the cloves. Cover with water. Put on lid and simmer gently for three hours. *Or*, pressure cook for one hour.
3. Strain off liquid. Remove the onion.
4. Take all meat from the bones and cut it up discarding fat. Cut up bacon quite small.

5. Return the strained liquid and meat to the pan. Season with pepper and salt. Bring to the boil.
6. Pour into a mould and leave to set.
Serve cold with hot creamed potatoes.

HONEYED WELSH LAMB

Oen Cymreig Melog

Good Welsh lamb needs no dressing up and is amongst the best and least adulterated meat that can be bought in Britain. This recipe gives a spicy gloss to the joint and a delicious gravy. It was served to us with medlar jelly (*see page 171*).

A 1·5 to 2 kg/3 to 4 lb joint of lamb, leg or shoulder
Salt and pepper
1 teaspoon ginger
1 dessertspoon dried or 2 sprigs fresh rosemary
2 tablespoons runny honey
About 300 ml/½ pint cider

1. Use a roasting tin in which joint will be a fairly snug fit.
2. Rub salt, pepper and ginger all over joint and put it in tin.
3. Sprinkle rosemary over it and dribble on the honey. Pour cider around it.
4. Allowing 30 minutes per ½ kg/1 lb, roast near top of a moderately hot oven, Gas 6, 400°F, 200°C for the first half hour. Then baste meat and reduce oven heat to moderate, Gas 4, 350°F, 180°C, for remaining cooking time. Baste every 20 minutes and add a little extra cider if necessary.
5. Lift meat on to a warmed dish and make gravy using residue in roasting tin.

Mrs Joyce Powell
Llanddewi Rhydderch W.I., Gwent

MOSSLANDS SADDLE OF LAMB

Enough for 10 people
For a special occasion.

1 saddle of lamb
1 pork fillet

2 tablespoons chopped fresh
parsley or rosemary jelly
Salt and pepper

1. Bone and skin the saddle, or ask the
butcher to do this for you.
2. In place of the bone, lay the pork
fillet.
3. Sprinkle inside meat with parsley
(or spread on the jelly). Season with
salt and pepper.
4. Roll up, tie in place and weigh joint.
5. Roast in a moderate oven, Gas 4,
350°F, 180°C, for 35 minutes per ½ kg/
1 lb.
6. Remove from oven and allow to rest
for 10 minutes before carving.

Sybil Norcott
Irlam, Nr. Manchester

FAST SWEET AND SOUR LAMB CHOPS
For 4 people

4 lamb chops, best end of neck
3 level tablespoons mango
chutney or good home-made
chutney
2 teaspoons made mustard
½ teaspoon mixed herbs
Salt

1. Put chops in a roasting tin with a
cover.
2. Mix sauce ingredients, chopping
mango pieces if they are large.
3. Pour half of the sauce over chops.
Cover.
4. Roast in a moderate oven, Gas 4,
350°F, 180°C for 15 minutes.
5. Turn chops over and pour rest of
sauce over them.
6. Cover and cook 10 to 15 minutes
more until chops are done. If chops are
very thick allow 5 to 10 minutes
longer. If the sauce becomes sticky,
moisten with a little water.

MARINATED LAMB CHOPS
For 4 people
Remember to start the night before.

4 loin or chump chops
A little melted lard

Marinade*
2 tablespoons oil
2 tablespoons lemon juice or
wine vinegar
A clove of garlic, crushed
1 bay leaf
½ teaspoon thyme and ½
teaspoon basil, or 1 teaspoon
chopped fresh mint
½ teaspoon dry mustard
Salt and pepper to taste
*For a note on marinades, see below.

1. Mix marinade ingredients
2. Put chops in a flat, shallow dish and
pour over the marinade. Leave in
refrigerator or a cool place overnight.
Turn chops in marinade every now and
then.
3. Next day, drain chops and pat dry.
4. Brush with lard and cook under a
hot grill for about 15 minutes, turning
frequently.

A marinade is a highly seasoned liquid
in which meat, fish or game may be soaked
as a preliminary to cooking. The object is
to impregnate the meat with certain
flavours. It also helps to tenderise. This is
particularly helpful with chops and steaks
to be grilled or fried. Lemon juice, oil,
vinegar, wine and aromatic flavourings
such as bay leaf, parsley, thyme, rosemary,
etc., can be used. The marinade itself is
often used up by incorporating it in the
final sauce. It is not always necessary to
cover the meat—sometimes only enough
marinade is used to moisten the meat,
which can be turned over two or three
times during the waiting period. See
marinated Fried Tarragon Chicken (*page
35*), Marinated Lamb Chops (*above*),
Beef Casserole (*page 45*), Marinated
Smoked Mackerel (*page 13*), and others.

SHEPHERD'S PIE
A 19th century Sussex pie said to have
been a traditional favourite of
shepherds tending the Southdown
sheep.
For 4 people

1 large onion, chopped
4 tablespoons lentils
4 lamb chump chops
1 tablespoon wholewheat flour

¼ teaspoon curry powder
Salt and pepper
About 450 g/1 lb small whole
peeled potatoes
1 level tablespoon brown sugar
About 600 ml/1 pint stock

1. Cover the bottom of a 1.1 litre/2
pint casserole with onion and lentils.
2. Season the flour with curry
powder, salt and pepper. Coat chops
and put them on top of lentils.
3. Pack potatoes around and on top of
chops.
4. Sprinkle over remaining seasoned
flour and the sugar and pour in the
stock. Put lid on casserole.
5. Cook in middle of a warm oven, Gas
3, 325°F, 160°C, for 2½ or even 3 hours,
removing lid for last 20 minutes to
brown potatoes.

Mrs Ruth Brooke & Mrs Sheila Powell
Hove & Portslade, Sussex

MOUSSAKA
A delicious Greek dish.
Enough for 6 people
450 g/1 lb aubergines
1 tablespoon salt
Good cooking oil
2 large onions, thinly-sliced
A clove of garlic, crushed
450 g/1 lb lean lamb, from the
shoulder or leg, minced
A 400 g/14 oz tin of tomatoes
2 tablespoons tomato purée
Salt and pepper

Topping
2 eggs
A 142 ml/5 fl oz carton of single
cream
50 g/2 oz grated Cheddar cheese
25 g/1 oz grated Parmesan
cheese

1. It is necessary to salt aubergines.
(This will help them absorb less oil
when fried.) Wipe, top and tail, slice
into 7 mm/¼ inch thick slices and lay
out in a colander, sprinkling with 1
tablespoon salt. Leave for one hour.
Press gently and pat dry on kitchen
paper.

2. Fry aubergines lightly in 1 or 2
tablespoons hot oil, adding more oil if
needed. Lift aubergines out of pan on
to kitchen paper or brown paper.
3. Using 1 tablespoon oil, fry onions
and garlic until golden.
4. Add lamb and cook for 10 minutes,
stirring every now and then.
5. Add tomatoes and purée and mix
well. Bring to the boil and simmer
with lid on pan for 20 to 25 minutes.
Season with salt and pepper.
6. Arrange alternate layers of
aubergine and lamb in a 1·1 litre/2 pint
soufflé dish or shallow casserole.
7. Cook in a moderate oven, Gas 4,
350°F, 180°C, for 35 to 40 minutes.
8. Meanwhile, prepare topping. Beat
eggs and cream together. Stir in
grated cheeses.
9. Pour this on top of the moussaka
and return it to the oven for a further
15 to 20 minutes until topping is well-
risen and golden brown.

LAMB HOT-POT
WITH PARSLEY
DUMPLINGS
For 4 people
1 medium-sized onion
2 carrots
2 sticks of celery
40 g/1½ oz lard or dripping
8 best end or middle neck lamb
chops
1 tablespoon plain flour
A 400 g/14 oz tin of tomatoes
150 ml/¼ pint water
1 level teaspoon rosemary or
mixed dried herbs
1 teaspoon salt
Black pepper

Parsley Dumplings (*or try*
Sussex Swimmers, see over)
100 g/4 oz self-raising flour
¼ level teaspoon salt
40 g/1½ oz shredded suet
1 level tablespoon chopped
parsley
A little water

1. Peel and slice onion. Scrub and slice
carrots. Wash and slice celery.

2. Melt half the lard in a frying pan. Add onion, carrots and celery and fry for 2 to 3 minutes. Lift out into a 1·5 litre/2½ pint shallow casserole.

3. Coat chops in plain flour.

4. Add remaining lard to pan, then brown the chops quickly on both sides.

5. Arrange chops on vegetables in casserole.

6. Pour excess fat out of pan, put in tomatoes, water, rosemary, salt and pepper. Bring to boil, stirring, and pour over lamb.

7. Cover casserole and cook in centre of a moderate oven, Gas 4, 350°F, 180°C, for 1 to 1½ hours until meat is tender.

8. For the dumplings: sift flour and salt into a bowl. Mix in suet and parsley. Mix to a soft but not sticky dough with water. Form into 8 small balls.

9. Place dumplings on top of hot-pot and cook, uncovered, for a further 15 to 20 minutes, until dumplings are risen and cooked.

Serve immediately.

SUSSEX SWIMMERS

These dumplings used to be served with a good gravy and, like Yorkshire Puddings in Yorkshire, before the meat course. The rule was that those who ate most puddings could have most meat, a canny way to save meat.

Can also be served as a sweet course with golden syrup.

100 g/4 oz self-raising whole-wheat flour*
100 g/4 oz self-raising white flour
100 g/4 oz shredded suet
¼ teaspoon salt
7 to 8 tablespoons milk
Boiling stock or water

*If you cannot buy this use plain wholewheat flour and add 1½ level teaspoons baking powder.

1. Mix dry ingredients and suet.

2. Mix to a stiff dough with milk.

3. Take tablespoons of mixture and form into balls.

4. Have ready a saucepan of boiling stock or water in which the dumplings can be submerged.

5. Slip dumplings into pan and boil for 15 to 20 minutes.

6. Drain well and serve with a very good gravy, or, if for a sweet, golden syrup.

Mrs Ruth Brooke and Mrs Sheila Powell
Hove and Portslade, Sussex

LAMB AND MINT JELLY

Economical

450 g/1 lb scrag end of lamb
850 ml/1½ pints stock, preferably bone-stock (see page 8)
1 carrot, scrubbed and cut small
1 onion, chopped
A bunch of mint, about 25 to 50 g/1 to 2 oz
2 tablespoons water
15 g/½ oz powdered gelatine
1 level teaspoon salt

1. Simmer scrag end in stock for about 30 minutes with carrot, onion and bunch of mint (keeping out 2 or 3 mint leaves for later).

2. Strain off liquid and set aside.

3. Scrape all meat from the bones, separating all the fat, and chop up meat into fairly small pieces.

4. Put 2 tablespoons water in a cup and stand it in a saucepan containing about 4 cm/1½ inches hot water. Heat gently. Sprinkle gelatine into cup and stir until dissolved.

5. Strain gelatine mixture into a bare 600 ml/1 pint of strained stock. Stir and leave until on the point of setting.

6. Add the diced lamb, a few small pieces of cooked carrot, the finely-chopped mint leaves and salt to taste.

7. Pour into a wetted mould to set.

Serve cold turned out on to a plate with salad, or with creamy mashed potatoes and a green vegetable.

BRAISED LAMB HEARTS

For 2 or 3 people

2 lamb's hearts
2 teaspoons salt

Stuffing

1 teaspoon lard or margarine
1 small chopped onion
1 rasher of bacon, de-rind and chop small
4 tablespoons brown breadcrumbs
1 tablespoon finely-chopped suet
1 teaspoon chopped fresh parsley
Grated rind of half a lemon or orange
1 beaten egg, to bind
Salt and pepper

1. Wash hearts well in cold water and cut away veins or gristle.
2. Place hearts in a pan, add salt and cover with water.
3. Bring to the boil and remove any scum. Put on lid and simmer for 1¼ hours.
4. Remove hearts and save the liquid.
5. Cut hearts in half or in slices if large. Lay in a casserole or shallow pan.
6. **Meanwhile make the stuffing.** Melt lard or margarine. Fry onion and bacon until cooked. Remove from heat.
7. Add the other ingredients and mix well. Season with salt and pepper to taste.
8. Spread stuffing over the heart slices.
9. Pour 300 ml/½ pint of the reserved liquid around the slices of heart. Cover with lid or foil.
10. Simmer on top of cooker for about 1 hour. *Or* cook for 1 hour in a moderate oven, Gas 4, 350°F, 180°C. Test meat with a skewer.

Serve with creamed potatoes and a green vegetable.

Mrs A. Greenwood
Boroughbridge, N. Yorkshire

PORK SLICES IN A CAPER SAUCE

For 4 people

4 slices of pork fillet cut about 5 cm/2 inch thick
A little plain flour
1 beaten egg
About 40 g/1½ oz fresh whole-wheat or white breadcrumbs
2 tablespoons oil

Sauce

50 g/2 oz butter or margarine
Half a large onion, chopped
1 anchovy fillet, or 1 teaspoon anchovy essence
2 tablespoons capers, or pickled nasturtium seeds*, or use pickled gherkin
1 tablespoon chopped parsley
1 tablespoon flour
2 tablespoons vinegar
300 ml/½ pint water
Salt and pepper

*French capers, the pickled flower heads of a trailing plant from Southern Europe, are now rather forgotten, although they can still be bought. A good substitute is home-pickled nasturtium seeds (*see page 173*).

1. Smack the pork slices with a rolling pin to flatten.
2. Flour each slice, dip in beaten egg and then in breadcrumbs.
3. Heat oil and gently fry the slices until cooked. Put on a serving dish and keep hot.
4. **Meanwhile make sauce.** Melt half of the butter or margarine and slightly brown onions.
5. Chop anchovy and mash it down with a wooden spoon. Chop capers. Add these with parsley and flour. Cook gently for 3 or 4 minutes.
6. Add vinegar and water gradually, stirring as sauce thickens. Simmer 2 or 3 minutes.
7. Remove pan from heat, stir in rest of butter and pour sauce over pork slices.

PORK CHOPS WITH ORANGE SAUCE

For 4 people, but easy to do for just 1 or 2

4 pork chops
175 g/6 oz brown or white rice (*see Boiled Rice, page 86*)

Orange Sauce

1 level dessertspoon cornflour
1 tablespoon demerara sugar
Finely-grated rind and juice of 2
oranges
1 tablespoon chopped fresh
parsley
Salt and Pepper Mix (*see page 44*)

1. Put chops on to grill and rice on to
boil.
2. Meanwhile, mix together cornflour,
sugar, rind and juice of oranges.
3. When chops are done, put 1
tablespoon of their dripping into a
small saucepan. Mix in prepared sauce
ingredients and stir over gentle heat
until thick. Stir in parsley. Season to
taste.
4. Put rice on a hot dish. Put chops on
top and pour over the sauce.

PORK CHOPS IN MUSHROOM AND CREAM SAUCE

For 4 people

4 pork loin chops
25 g/1 oz butter
1 onion, finely-chopped
25 g/1 oz plain flour
300 ml/½ pint single cream
225 g/8 oz mushrooms, chopped
Salt and pepper
Chopped parsley (optional)

1. Grill chops for about 8 minutes each
side.
2. Meanwhile, fry onion in the butter
till golden brown.
3. Mix in mushrooms and fry for 2
minutes.
4. Add flour and stir to a paste.
5. Add cream and cook *very* gently to
thicken.
6. Season to taste.
7. Pour sauce over chops and garnish
with chopped parsley if desired.

Judith Adshead
Mottram St. Andrew, Cheshire

PORK IN CIDER WITH WALNUT-STUFFED PRUNES

*For 4 to 6 people but easy to cut
down for fewer*
This dish freezes well for about 3
months.
Remember to start the night before.

16 prunes
½ to ¾ kg/1 to 1½ lb diced pork,
from the shoulder
1 heaped tablespoon cornflour
1 onion, chopped
1 tablespoon oil
300 ml/½ pint dry cider
300 ml/½ pint chicken stock
A clove of garlic, crushed
4 cloves or ¼ teaspoon ground
cloves
½ teaspoon marjoram
Salt and pepper
16 walnut halves

1. Start by pouring boiling water over
prunes and leaving to soak and plump
up for at least 12 hours. If using ready
softened prunes, soak in cold water.
2. Toss pork in cornflour.
3. Fry onion gently in oil until
softened.
4. Add meat to pan and stir until
surfaces are brown.
5. Add cider, stock, garlic, marjoram,
salt and pepper.
6. Bring to boil, cover pan and let it
just simmer until meat is tender, about
1½ hours. Or transfer into a covered
casserole and cook in a slow oven, Gas
2, 300°F, 150°C, for about 2 hours.
7. Meanwhile, remove stones carefully
from prunes and stuff with walnuts.
8. 20 minutes before end of cooking
time drop stuffed prunes in with meat.
Serve with rice, pasta or boiled
potatoes and freshly-cooked green
vegetables.

Mrs Angela Mottram
Axbridge, Somerset

SWEET AND SOUR PORK

Deep-fried pork in batter with
vegetables in a sweet and sour sauce.

For 4 people
450 g/1 lb lean pork
75 g/3 oz cornflour
50 g/2 oz plain flour
1 teaspoon salt
1 egg, separated
3 tablespoons cold water
Oil for deep frying

Sweet and sour vegetables

1 green pepper
2 carrots
1 small onion
2 cloves of garlic
2 tablespoons sugar
1 tablespoon soya sauce
3 tablespoons wine or cider
vinegar
1 tablespoon rice wine* or dry
sherry
1 tablespoon oil
½ teaspoon grated fresh ginger
(*see page 38*)
1 tablespoon cornflour
1 tablespoon water

*Can be bought at Chinese
supermarkets.

1. Trim any fat from pork, cut it into
fairly thin slices and cut these into
2·5 cm/1 inch pieces.
2. In a bowl mix the 75 g/3 oz cornflour, plain flour and salt.
3. Lightly mix egg-yolk and water.
4. Make a well in centre of flour and
work in the egg-yolk and water to
form a smooth batter.
5. Beat egg-white until stiff. Fold it
into batter.
6. Heat the oil until it is nearly smoking
hot. To test: drop into it a small piece
of dry bread; if it immediately rises
bubbling to the surface and goes
golden in 1 minute, oil is ready.
7. Cooking just a few pieces of pork at
a time, dip them into the batter and
deep fry until golden brown and crisp,
about 3 to 5 minutes.
8. Drain on kitchen paper and keep
warm in a low oven until all the pieces
are fried.
9. Meanwhile, wash and dry green
pepper and cut into bite-sized squares.
10. Scrub carrots, slice lengthwise
into fine strips. Cut these into 2·5 cm/
1 inch pieces.

11. Chop onion quite small.
12. Finely chop the garlic.
13. In a small bowl, mix together the
sugar, soya sauce, vinegar and wine.
14. In a wok or frying pan heat 1
tablespoon of oil until it is just
smoking hot. Add carrots, pepper and
onion and stir-fry over a medium heat
for 2 minutes.
15. Add garlic, ginger and the vinegar
mixture. Allow to boil for 1 minute.
16. Slake the cornflour by mixing it
with 1 tablespoon of water and then
add it to pan and cook for half a
minute, stirring until the sauce has
thickened and becomes clear.
17. Arrange the pork pieces in a
serving dish and pour the sauce over.
Serve at once with Boiled Rice (*see
page 86*) or noodles.

Priya Wickramasinghe
Cardiff

LIVER AND BACON HOT-POT

450 g/1 lb pig's liver
225 g/8 oz streaky bacon
rashers
2 medium-sized onions or 3
sticks of celery
2 medium-sized, sharp, cooking
apples
2 tablespoons chopped parsley
1 teaspoon chopped fresh
marjoram or ½ teaspoon dried
marjoram
75 g/3 oz soft breadcrumbs
Salt and pepper
About 600 ml/1 pint stock or
water

1. Cut liver into thin slices.
2. Cut bacon rashers into small pieces.
3. Peel and chop onions. Peel, core and
chop apples and mix with onion.
4. Place a layer of liver in a greased
casserole, cover it with a layer of
bacon and a layer of onion and apple.
5. Mix parsley and marjoram into
breadcrumbs and sprinkle over onion
and apple. Add a shake of salt and
pepper.
6. Repeat these layers until dish is
full, saving enough breadcrumbs to

cover the final layer of onion and
apple.
7. Pour in enough stock or water
almost to cover.
8. Put lid on casserole and cook in a
warm oven, Gas 3, 325°F, 160°C, for 2
hours.
9. Half an hour before serving, remove
lid to let the top brown.

Mrs Becky Blackmore
Exeter, Devon

FAGGOTS

Ffagod Sir Benfro, which means
faggots as made in Pembrokeshire.

*Enough for 5 or 6 people but easy to
cut recipe down*

700 g/1½ lb pig's liver
2 large onions
125 g/4 oz fresh brown or white
breadcrumbs
75 g/3 oz shredded suet
2 level teaspoons sage
1 teaspoon salt
¼ teaspoon pepper
To serve: green peas and gravy

1. Mince liver and onion into a bowl.
2. Add remaining ingredients and mix
thoroughly.
3. Form into balls to fit palm of hand.
Traditionally, faggots were wrapped
in caul to cook. Nowadays, the best
way is to use or make foil cups to hold
them in shape. Set these in a small
roasting tin and pour boiling water
around them.

Or, make a loaf of the mixture. Press
into a greased 1 kg/2 lb loaf tin. Set
this in a roasting tin and pour boiling
water around it to come halfway up
sides.
4. Bake in middle of a moderate oven,
Gas 4, 350°F, 180°C, for 30 minutes for
individual faggots, 1 hour for loaf.

Serve faggots in a bed of peas with a
good gravy in a separate jug.

Leave loaf in tin for 10 minutes in a
warm place. This gives it time to set
and it can then be turned out and will
slice quite easily.

Mrs Joyce Porvell
Llanddewi Rhydderch W.I., Gwent

SAUSAGE SAUTÉ

2 tablespoons oil
450 g/1 lb pork sausages
1 medium-sized onion
1 green pepper
225 g/8 oz fresh or tinned
tomatoes
1 large cooking apple
Salt and Pepper Mix (*see page 44*)

1. Heat 1 tablespoon of the oil in a
large frying pan. Separate the
sausages and cook gently for 15 to 20
minutes, turning frequently.
2. Peel and slice onion.
3. Wash and dry green pepper. Cut
out core and remove pips. Cut flesh
into thin strips.
4. Warm 1 tablespoon oil in another
pan. Cook onion and green pepper
gently, stirring occasionally, for 5
minutes.
5. Skin the tomatoes (*see page 72*) and
chop roughly.
6. Roughly chop the apple.
7. Add tomatoes and apple to onion
mixture and continue cooking for 5
minutes, stirring occasionally. Season
slightly.
8. Drain sausages and keep hot.
9. Turn out onion mixture into a
warmed dish and arrange sausages on
top.

Serve with plain boiled potatoes.

SAUSAGE AND
KIDNEY HOT-POT

For 4 people
Could be made in electric frying pan.

4 sheep's kidneys
4 large sausages
100 g/4 oz bacon
3 small onions or 3 sticks of
celery
100 g/4 oz mushrooms
225 g/8 oz carrots
25 g/1 oz butter
15 g/½ oz flour
300 ml/½ pint stock
1 teaspoon tomato purée, or
ketchup
1 tablespoon sherry
Salt and pepper
1 small packet frozen peas

1. Remove skins from kidneys, cut them into 4 pieces and cut out core.
2. Skin the sausages and make each into 2 or 3 small balls.
3. De-rind bacon and cut it into strips.
4. Peel and chop onions or celery. Wipe and slice mushrooms. Scrub carrots and cut into short, very thin strips.
5. Melt butter in pan and fry bacon a little. Add kidneys and sausages and fry them quickly till lightly-browned. Lift out of fat on to a plate.
6. Add onions and mushrooms to pan. Reduce heat and cook slowly for 5 minutes, stirring occasionally.
7. Stir flour into pan and let it cook 1 minute.
8. Stir in stock, tomato purée and sherry and bring to simmering point, stirring as it thickens. Season with salt and pepper.
9. Add carrots, bacon, kidney and sausage balls.
10. Cover pan with a well-fitting lid and simmer gently for ¼ hour. 10 minutes before end of cooking time add frozen peas.

Ann E. Craib
King's Park, Glasgow

GAMMON IN CIDER

This Somerset method best suits a large joint such as a half gammon but non-gammon joints such as slipper, forehock and hock can be used. It is boiled then roasted.

If the meat is smoked, soak it first for 12 hours in plenty of cold water. To speed up process, cover pan, bring to boil. Leave until cold. Then discard water, and proceed as follows:

For a large joint
2·4 litres/4 pints water
600 ml/1 pint dry cider
1 chopped onion
6 allspice berries
4 cloves
2 bay leaves

Place joint in a saucepan with the above ingredients, put lid on, bring slowly to the boil and simmer for 10 minutes to the ½ kg/1 lb.

For smaller joints
Reduce liquid in same ratio of 1 part cider to 4 parts water using sufficient to cover meat generously. Reduce onion and spices accordingly. Cook as above.

Then lift out joint, skin it and score fat in a criss-cross pattern.

For basting
Dry cider
2 tablespoons demerara sugar
1 teaspoon dry mustard } mixed together
1 teaspoon mixed spice

1. Put joint in a baking tin, moisten with cider, sprinkle on some of the dry mix, sufficient to cover surface.
2. Bake near top of a hot oven, Gas 6 to 7, 400 to 425°F, 200 to 220°C, for 10 minutes to the ½ kg/1 lb, basting every 10 to 15 minutes with more cider and dry ingredients. When all is used up, baste from liquor around joint.

For decorating
Sliced oranges
Glacé cherries

Arrange these over joint as it comes out of oven, or if joint is being baked to eat cold, decoration can be done before baking, or part way through for a large joint.

Mrs Angela Mottram
Axbridge, Somerset

FOREHOCK OF BACON

A big joint for a special occasion. Remember to start the night before.
1 forehock of bacon, weighs about 3·25 kg/7 lb before serving
3 level tablespoons demerara sugar
2 sprigs of fresh rosemary or 1 teaspoon dried
Whole cloves

The forehock is to be boned and this is what you do:
1. Soak overnight in cold water.
2. Then working on the underside of the joint, take a small sharp knife and cut off rib bones.

3. Slit meat down to the inner bones and work round them to expose completely. Remove them.

To prepare and cook

4. Sprinkle inside of meat with 2 tablespoons demerara sugar.

5. Then tie up joint with strings at 5 cm/2 inch intervals.

6. Weigh joint and calculate boiling time at 25 minutes per ½ kg/1 lb.

7. Put joint in a pan, cover with water, add rosemary. Bring slowly to the boil. Simmer gently for the calculated time. Leave in the cooking water until cool enough to handle.

8. Skin carefully and score fat in a lattice pattern. Press a clove in each 'box' and sprinkle on the last tablespoon of sugar.

9. Set under a pre-heated grill until brown and bubbly.

Serve cold.

Stock will make excellent soup.

Freezes well.

Remember to boil up the bones separately for more stock.

SUSSEX BACON ROLY POLY

This is a lovely, crusty, baked version of the traditional Sussex Roly Poly which used to be wrapped in a cloth and boiled for 3 to 3½ hours.

Enough for 4 or 5 people, but easy to make less

225 g/8 oz self-raising flour
A pinch of salt
100 g/4 oz shredded suet
7 to 8 tablespoons water
350 g/12 oz lean bacon rashers, cut small
1 onion, finely-chopped
Finely-chopped fresh or dried sage
Black pepper
Beaten egg or milk, to glaze

1. Sift flour and salt into a bowl. Add suet and mix with water to a soft but not sticky dough.

2. Using a floured board, roll out very thin.

3. Cover generously with bacon and onion and add sage and pepper to taste. Brush edges of pastry with water.

4. Roll up into a long roll, sealing edge and ends. Place on a greased baking tray with join underneath.

5. Decorate with the trimmings made into little leaves. Brush all over with beaten egg or milk.

6. Bake near top of a moderately hot oven, Gas 6, 400°F, 200°C, for 30 to 40 minutes, when it will be crusty and golden.

Mrs Janice Langley
Shoreham-by-Sea, West Sussex

TRADITIONAL SUSSEX BACON PUDDING

For 2 people

125 g/4 oz wholewheat flour
1½ teaspoons baking powder
50 g/2 oz shredded suet
1 onion, finely-chopped
3 to 4 rashers streaky bacon, chopped
1 teaspoon mixed fresh herbs or ½ teaspoon dried
Pepper and a little salt
1 medium to small egg
Milk, if necessary

1. Mix together flour, baking powder, suet, onion, bacon, herbs and seasoning.

2. Mix with egg, adding milk if necessary to make a soft dropping consistency.

3. Grease a 600 ml/1 pint basin and put in a piece of greaseproof paper just to cover bottom.

4. Put pudding mixture into basin. Cover with greaseproof paper and foil, tucked in neatly under the rim.

5. Steam for 1½ hours. If you haven't a steamer, stand basin on a trivet or upturned saucer in a pan of boiling water. Put on lid and boil for 1½ hours, replenishing with boiling water when necessary. Do not let it go off the boil.

Serve with Parsley Sauce (*see page 95*).

Mrs Sheila Powell
Portsiade, Sussex

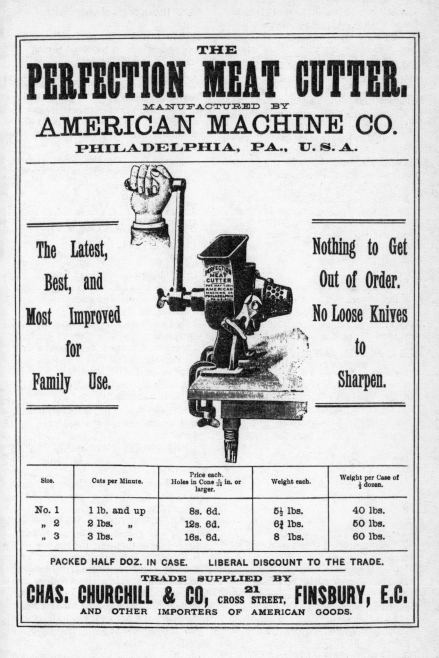

Chapter 5

Salads and Vegetables

SALAD DRESSINGS

Some basic dressings and many variations.

French Dressing

Made in a jar in quite a large quantity, will keep in a cool place for several weeks, to be used a little at a time as required. Saves a lot of time.

1 rounded teaspoon French mustard, try Dijon
1 rounded teaspoon cooking or sea salt
½ level teaspoon freshly-ground black pepper
½ level teaspoon sugar (optional)
Juice of 1 lemon (optional)
300 ml/½ pint olive or good salad oil
4 tablespoons wine or cider vinegar

Put all ingredients in a jar with a well-fitting screw top. Shake vigorously to combine.

Try different flavourings but add these to the small amount of dressing required when salad is made. They go stale if kept in the dressing for long:

Crushed garlic or chopped onion; chopped fresh parsley, chives, tarragon, basil, chervil or fennel. Try combinations of one or two. Dried herbs can also be added but take care because most are twice as strong as the fresh ones.

Simple Dressing Without Oil

A mild dressing especially if young children are to eat the salad.

3 tablespoons tarragon vinegar, plain vinegar can be used
2 tablespoons water
½ teaspoon sugar
Salt and pepper to taste
1 large teaspoon chopped fresh mint, parsley, chives, tarragon, fennel or onion

Mix all ingredients thoroughly in a salad bowl and at last minute toss in the salad ingredients

Basic mayonnaise

Made in liquidiser. Keeps in refrigerator for 3 to 4 weeks. Can be thinned down when required with milk or single cream, or more lemon or orange juice, or vinegar.

2 to 4 egg-yolks, according to how extravagant you feel
300 ml/½ pint of good salad oil, olive or sunflower are best
2 dessertspoons lemon or orange juice or wine or cider vinegar
1 rounded teaspoon French mustard, try Dijon
½ level teaspoon cooking or sea salt
¼ level teaspoon freshly-ground black pepper
¼ level teaspoon sugar (optional)

1. Put egg-yolks in liquidiser and switch on for 2 minutes or until thick and creamy.
2. With machine running, add juice or vinegar. Then add oil gradually until 150 ml/¼ pint has been absorbed.
3. Now add all the seasonings, switch on again and gradually add the last of the oil.

Try different flavours but always add them to mayonnaise after it is made: tomato purée, anchovy purée, crushed garlic, chopped chives, capers or cucumber, etc.

Sour Cream and Chive Dressing

Delicious with crunchy salads—e.g., chopped white cabbage, grated carrots, finely-chopped onion.

A 142 ml/5 fl oz carton of soured cream
2 level tablespoons chopped fresh chives
1 tablespoon wine vinegar
1 level tablespoon made mustard
Salt and freshly-ground black pepper
A little milk (optional)

Combine all the ingredients, adding milk to thin it down if necessary.

Cooked Salad Dressing

A good economical dressing of mayonnaise quality but using no oil, therefore not so rich and fattening.

2 teaspoons sugar
½ level teaspoon dry mustard
1 level teaspoon salt
25 g/1 oz margarine
2 tablespoons vinegar
1 tablespoon lemon juice
1 egg

A double saucepan is ideal for this but it can also be made as follows:

1. Put sugar, mustard and salt in a bowl.
2. Cut the margarine into small pieces and add it to the bowl.
3. Add vinegar and lemon juice.
4. Beat egg and strain it into bowl.
5. Stand bowl over a pan of simmering water. Do not let bowl touch water. Let the dressing cook, stirring occasionally with a wooden spoon, until it is thick enough to coat the back of the spoon.
6. Then take bowl off pan and let it cool.

Keeps for a week in a cool place. Keeps for at least two weeks, covered, in a refrigerator.

Margaret Heywood
Mankinholes, Todmorden, Yorkshire

Yoghurt and Tahini Dip

This is a lovely dressing for salads. It may also be used as a dip served with Greek Pitta Bread (*see page 139*). It is used in the recipe for Chicken Kebabs (*see page 33*).

Tahini is made from sesame seed pulp and can be bought at a delicatessen.

3 tablespoons natural yoghurt
1 tablespoon tahini
A clove of garlic, crushed (optional)
Lemon juice
Salt and pepper

Mix yoghurt, tahini and garlic. Beat in lemon juice, salt and pepper to taste.

Serve cold. Will keep in refrigerator for a few days. Stir before serving.

Elizabeth Mickery
Pudsey, West Yorkshire

COOKING WITH DRIED BEANS, PEAS, LENTILS AND GRAINS

Aduki beans: a small red bean, much prized by the Chinese for its goodness. Very useful substitute for mince when cooked with bouquet garni, onion, carrot, tomato purée.
Barley: moist and chewy. Best in soups or roasted for savoury bakes.
Black-eye beans: earthy flavour. Used often in Mexican cooking. Combines very well with red kidney beans.
Brown rice: nutty flavour. Used for risotto, curry, pilaff and sweet puddings.
Buckwheat: a Russian delicacy. Particularly strong nutty flavour; adds meatiness to dishes.
Bulgar wheat: creamy tasting. Quick to use as it needs no cooking when used for salads. Often confused by people with white rice.
Butter beans: rather bland taste.
Chick peas: very popular in Middle Eastern cookery. Nutty in flavour and appearance. Delicious in salads and for making savoury dips.
Field beans: at last something British! Best in soups and stews with root vegetables.
Haricot beans: the traditional baked bean when cooked with treacle and tomatoes.
Lentils: the whole variety: brown, earthy-flavoured; green, more delicate flavour. Hold their shape and make a quick addition to soups and stews. The split red variety purée easily and are excellent for pâtés, rissoles and go well with curry spices.

65

TO COOK DRIED BEANS, PEAS, LENTILS AND GRAINS

This chart can be followed in conjunction with notes opposite

Bean, Pea, Lentil, Grain	Soak overnight in cold water	Cooking time in fresh cold water	Time needed for hard boil at some stage in cooking	A minimum amount of fresh cold water for 1 cup of beans, etc.
		Minutes	*Minutes*	
Aduki beans	Yes	60–80	10	4 cups
Barley— pot or pearl	No	45–50	Nil	3 cups
Black-eye beans	Yes	40–45	10	3 cups

Brown rice
  long grain
  short grain
	No	20–25
		20
			Nil	2 cups
				(*see Boiled Rice page 86*)

Buckwheat	No	20–25	Nil	4 cups
Bulgar wheat	Just soak in boiling water for 5 to 10 minutes, then it is ready for salads			
Butter beans	Yes	40	10	4 cups
Chick peas	Yes	2 hours	10	5 cups
Field beans	Yes	60	10	4 cups
Haricot beans	Yes	45–50	10	3 cups

Lentils—brown
  green
  red
	No	40–45
		40–45
		15–20
			Nil	4 cups
				4 cups
				3 cups

Lima beans	Yes	40–45	10	3 cups
Millet	No	20–25	Nil	3 cups
Mung beans	No	40–45	Nil	3 cups
Oats	No	25–30	Nil	3 cups
Pinto beans	Yes	60	10	6 cups
Red kidney beans	Yes	45–50	10	4 cups
Soya beans	Yes	2½–3 hours	30	6–7 cups
Split peas— green and yellow	No	40–45	Nil	3 cups
Wheat	No	60	Nil	5 cups

Lima beans: similar to butter beans but tastier. Good for salads and when combined in creamy dishes and soups.

Millet: a delicate flavoured grain. Easily digested and can be used for sweet and savoury dishes.

Mung beans: best for sprouting.

Oats: sweet creamy-tasting. Main ingredient for muesli.

Pinto beans: rather like speckled eggs. Can be used instead of black-eye or red kidney beans.

Red kidney beans: beautiful distinctive colour. Brightens stews and salads. Popular with chilli spices.

Soya beans: good source of protein. Excellent for absorbing the flavour of all that is cooked with it. Best in soups and casseroles.

Split peas: best for soups. Green type best cooked with mint or rosemary; yellow type go well with spices.

Wheat: very chewy berries. Adds texture to bean dishes. Also when cooked, a good addition to bread.

NOTES ON COOKING DRIED BEANS, PEAS, LENTILS AND GRAINS

Grains only need bringing to the boil and simmering. But the flavour of some is improved if they are lightly toasted in a little oil in the pan in which they are to be boiled. Use ¼ teaspoon oil to the 125 g/¼ lb grain. This applies to buckwheat, millet, rice and barley.

1. Pick over beans, lentils, etc., for sticks and stones then wash before soaking and cooking.

2. Soak beans and peas overnight. This swells them and helps loosen grit and dirt. It also removes excess starch and carbohydrates which cause flatulence. Soak by covering with 8 cm/3 inches of water. Beans, etc., should double in size. This water is then thrown away, the beans washed thoroughly and covered with fresh water.

3. Cook beans, etc., in plenty of water as it is useful stock—125 g/4 oz beans in 850 ml/1½ pints water.

4. All beans and some peas must be fast-boiled for at least 10 minutes. This destroys the anti-nutritional factors on the surface of the beans. Then lightly boil for the remaining time, in a covered pan.

5. Salt is not added during boiling because it tends to harden the outer skin and prevent the bean from becoming soft. The same applies if lemon juice, wine or vinegar is put in at the beginning of cooking. However, adding herbs, spices or vegetables to the cooking water improves the flavour. Adding caraway, aniseed or fennel seed helps counteract flatulence. Fennel is the least dominating. Add ½ teaspoon to 125 g/4 oz beans, etc., during last ½ hour.

6. When cooked, drain liquid and save it for stock. It will keep 3 to 4 days in refrigerator.

7. Cooked beans, etc., drained of ALL liquid to stop fermentation will keep 4 to 5 days in covered containers in refrigerator.

8. Red and brown beans turn the water dark during cooking and will colour any white beans or grains cooked with them. It is best to keep dark beans separate from white during cooking to keep the appearance of each bright and natural.

9. Some people find this type of food indigestible. Dried beans, peas, etc., contain water soluble sugars that the body cannot break down. Some people develop the necessary enzymes to cope with this. Those who have found problems must attack them more thoroughly before cooking. Boil for 3 minutes. Leave to soak in that water for 4 to 5 hours. Drain. Reboil in fresh water for 3 minutes. Leave to soak for 4 to 5 hours. Drain and then cook for use adding 30 minutes on to the recommended times to ensure softness.

10. *Pressure cooking* saves time and fuel and soaking time can be reduced or even eliminated. The anti-nutritional problem (see note 4 above) does not apply because of the higher temperature involved. *Be sure* to follow instructions in your pressure cooker handbook.

MARINADE FOR BEANS

Dried beans are delicious in salads when they have been marinated immediately after cooking.

This is enough for ½ kg/1 lb cooked beans. 225 g/8 oz uncooked beans will weigh about ½ kg/1 lb when cooked.

175 ml/6 fl oz best salad oil, ideally use a mixture of olive and safflower or sunflower oils
125 ml/4 fl oz cider vinegar
Juice of 1 lemon
A clove of garlic, crushed
1 teaspoon fresh chives, chopped
1 teaspoon marjoram
1 teaspoon oregano
1 teaspoon pepper
½ teaspoon salt

1. Mix everything together.
2. Pour over hot, freshly-cooked, thoroughly-drained beans.
3. Allow beans to remain in marinade until quite cold.
4. Drain marinade into a jar. Beans are ready for use in salads.

Marinade can be used again but will keep only a few days because fresh herbs will go stale. If there is water in it from the beans it will not keep well.

Marinated Bean Salad

Red kidney beans, lima beans and chick peas make a good mixture of contrasting colours, textures and tastes.

1. Cook beans according to directions on previous page.
2. Marinate hot beans as above.
3. Choose favourite salad vegetables, such as radish, celery, green, red or yellow pepper, tomato. Add fresh herbs. No extra dressing is necessary.

Sarah Brown
Scarborough, Yorkshire

BUTTER BEAN AND WATERCRESS SALAD

Enough for 4 small side salads— easy to make less or more

For a more substantial salad, cubes of Cheddar or Gouda cheese may be added.

Salad

125 g/4 oz cooked lima or baby butter beans
A quarter of a cucumber
1 firm small pear, Comice or Beurre Hardy are best
Half a bunch of watercress (about 50 g/2 oz)
Salt and pepper

Dressing: for this you need a liquidiser

2 tablespoons natural yoghurt
25 g/1 oz blue cheese
1 dessertspoon mayonnaise (*see page 64*)
40 g/1½ oz cottage cheese

1. Remember to start the day before by soaking beans overnight and then cooking (*see page 66*).
2. Put dressing ingredients in liquidiser and blend till smooth. This can be done some time ahead.
3. Cut unpeeled cucumber and pear into small cubes.
4. Save a few nice sprigs of watercress to garnish and cut up rest finely.
5. Mix all salad ingredients with dressing. Taste for seasoning.
6. Chill before serving.
7. Garnish with watercress.

Sarah Brown
Scarborough, Yorkshire

BEANSPROUT AND WALNUT SALAD

Enough for 4 to 6 people but easy to make less

2 large crisp apples, unpeeled
3 sticks of celery
225 g/8 oz beansprouts
50 g/2 oz walnuts
50 g/2 oz raisins

Dressing

1 teaspoon lemon juice
200 ml/7 fl oz natural yoghurt

1 tablespoon chopped fresh mint
Pepper and salt

1. Chop apples and celery and mix
with beansprouts, walnuts and raisins.
2. Mix dressing ingredients and stir
into salad.
3. Chill slightly before serving.

Janet Horsley
Headingley, Yorkshire

BEETROOT AND CELERY SALAD

Equal quantities of cooked beetroot in vinegar and fresh
celery, seasoned with a little
salt

1. Cut the celery into thin slices and
lay it in the dish from which it will be
served.
2. Sprinkle with a little salt.
3. Lift the beetroot out of the vinegar,
cut it into quarters or neat lumps and
lay it on top of the celery.
4. At the last minute pour over a little
of the beetroot vinegar.

CAULIFLOWER SALAD

Make as much as you need, but make
it fresh each time.

Cauliflower
Carrot
Green pepper
Celery

Dressing

Choose one from *pages 64/65*

1. Wash cauliflower and break into
small sprigs.
2. Scrub carrot and grate it coarsely.
3. Wash green pepper, remove core
and seeds and slice flesh finely.
4. Wash and finely slice celery.
5. Combine all with the dressing.

CUCUMBER IN YOGHURT

An oriental version of a well-known
and exceptionally refreshing salad.

For 4 people

300 ml/10 fl oz yoghurt
1 cucumber, finely-sliced
1 green chilli, finely-chopped
(optional)
½ teaspoon salt
¼ teaspoon dried ginger—
freshly-ground if possible

To garnish: fresh coriander
leaves, chopped

Mix all ingredients in a bowl, cover
with a well-fitting lid and refrigerate
before serving.

Eat this fresh. It does not keep.

Delicious with Cashew Nut Curry (*see
page 88*).

Priya Wickramasinghe
Cardiff

LAYER SALAD

For 4 to 6 people

Layer the following ingredients in a
large glass bowl:

100 g/4 oz shredded cabbage
175 g/6 oz grated carrot
75 g/3 oz chopped peanuts
100 g/4 oz chopped celery
2 chopped red apples, unpeeled
75 g/3 oz chopped dates
100 g/4 oz cooked brown rice (*see
page 86*)
25 g/1 oz sesame seeds
1 box mustard and cress,
chopped
Garnish with slices of tomato

Janet Horsley
Headingley, Yorkshire

LETTUCE WITH PEANUT DRESSING

For 4 people

1 crisp lettuce, washed and
dried
Half a cucumber, sliced

Dressing

2 tablespoons oil
¼ teaspoon mustard seed
½ teaspoon salt
¼ teaspoon cumin seed
A pinch of turmeric
1 tablespoon lemon juice
50 g/2 oz peanuts, coarsely-ground

1. Start with dressing. Heat oil and splutter the mustard seeds in it. To do this put seeds in hot oil, put lid on pan, keep pan over medium heat and listen while seeds leap up against lid for a few seconds until the spluttering sound has stopped. Remove pan from heat before lifting lid.
2. Add salt, cumin and turmeric and fry for 5 seconds.
3. Remove from heat and add lemon juice and peanuts. Leave to cool.
4. Just before serving, break up lettuce into small pieces into a salad bowl. Add cucumber and dressing and toss salad thoroughly.

Priya Wickramasinghe
Cardiff

ONION SALAD

For 4 people

225 g/8 oz onions
2 green chillis, finely-chopped
Juice of 1 lemon
½ teaspoon salt
¼ teaspoon freshly-milled black pepper

1. Slice onions into fine rings.
2. Mix all ingredients and leave for at least 1 hour before serving.

Before serving, finely-sliced tomatoes can be added.

Delicious as an accompaniment to rice dishes.

Priya Wickramasinghe
Cardiff

NEW POTATO SALADS

New potatoes, scrubbed
Chopped chives, onion tops or leak tops
4 tablespoons French dressing
(*see page 64*)

1. Steam potatoes or cook them in their jackets over low heat in a very little water. Drain. Skin and slice when they have cooled down a bit.
2. Meanwhile, mix dressing ingredients.
3. Toss potato while still hot in the dressing, adding chives, onion or leek tops.

Ideas for more substantial salads

Add any of the following:

Cubes of garlic sausage
Strips of green pepper
Tuna fish, drained and chopped

POTATO SALAD

With capers and mayonnaise. Old potatoes can be used.

450 g/1 lb potatoes cut into 1 cm/½ inch dice
Water
Salt
1 tablespoon chopped capers
3 tablespoons mayonnaise or salad cream (*see page 64*)

1. Put potatoes in a saucepan with salted water just to cover. Bring to the boil, put on lid and cook for 3 to 5 minutes until almost tender.
2. Drain quickly and thoroughly and toss lightly with capers.
3. When cold coat with mayonnaise, mixing gently.

Anne Wallace
Stewarton, Ayrshire

RICE SALAD WITH APPLE DRESSING

A well-balanced meal in itself.

Enough for 4

350 g/12 oz cooked brown rice
(*see page 66*) or 150 g/5 oz
uncooked
50 g/2 oz cashew nut pieces,
toasted
50 g/2 oz raisins
50 g/2 oz bean sprouts*
Half a red pepper
Lettuce leaves
1 dessert apple

Dressing

2 tablespoons apple juice
1 tablespoon sunflower oil
1 tablespoon lemon juice
1 teaspoon shoyu (*see page 80*)
¼ teaspoon ground ginger
Salt and pepper

1. Cashew nut pieces are cheaper than whole nuts. They can be toasted under a moderately-hot grill until crisp and just turning golden. Toasting makes them crisp and fresh.
2. Mix together salad ingredients, except lettuce and apple.
3. Mix dressing ingredients. Beat well. Mix into salad.
4. Serve on a bed of lettuce, garnished at last minute with apple slices.

Sarah Brown
Scarborough, Yorkshire

A SALAD OF RED CABBAGE AND MUSHROOMS WITH BROWN RICE

For 3 or 4 people

Keeps for a day or two.

Juice of 1 small orange
25 g/1 oz sultanas or raisins
4 tablespoons French dressing
(*see page 64*)
100 g/4 oz red cabbage
1 small onion
50 g/2 oz mushrooms
100 g/4 oz brown rice
1 tablespoon chopped parsley
2 tablespoons Chinese beansprouts (optional)

1. Put sultanas or raisins to soak in the orange juice.
2. Prepare French dressing and divide it between two small bowls.
3. Finely shred red cabbage and toss it in one bowl of dressing.
4. Peel and finely chop onion and toss it with cabbage.
5. Wipe the mushrooms and slice them thinly. Toss them in the other bowl of dressing.
6. Leave both bowls for at least one hour.
7. Meanwhile, cook the rice (*see Boiled Rice, page 86*).
8. When rice is done, drain off any liquid. Then spread it out thinly to cool. If when it is cool it is not nicely dry, put the dish in a very slow oven, less than Gas ¼, 225°F, 110°C, for 20 minutes or so to draw the moisture out.
9. All these preparations may be done some time in advance, even the day before it is to be served.
10. Stir each bowl of ingredients then combine all together in a serving dish with rice, parsley and bean sprouts.

INDONESIAN TOMATO SALAD

For 4 people

4 ripe tomatoes
Salt to taste
2 fresh green chillis
3 tablespoons sugar
Juice of 2 lemons

1. Slice the tomatoes and arrange in a serving platter. Sprinkle with a little salt.

2. Slice the green chillis slantwise into elongated rings and arrange over the tomato slices.
3. Sprinkle with sugar and lemon juice and allow to stand for an hour or two before serving.

Priya Wickramasinghe
Cardiff

TO PEEL TOMATOES

Either: Put tomatoes in a bowl, pour boiling water over them and leave for 1 minute. Plunge them into cold water and skin when required.

Or, if only one is needed, spear it on a fork and turn it in the hot air just above a gas flame. Skin will contract and burst and tomato can be easily peeled.

WATERCRESS AND GRAPEFRUIT SALAD

For 4 people

25 g/1 oz lightly-roasted hazelnuts
1 bunch of watercress
1 small lettuce
1 large grapefruit

1. To roast hazelnuts, put them in a shallow tin in a moderate oven, Gas 4, 350°F, 180°C, for 10 minutes. Or put under grill, turning often. Then rub the skins from them and chop coarsely.
2. Wash watercress and lettuce and dry well.
3. Peel grapefruit and remove membrane and pips, working over a bowl so as to retain the juice. Chop flesh into bowl.
4. Break lettuce and watercress into small pieces. Toss it with grapefruit and put it in a salad bowl.
5. Sprinkle hazelnuts over the top.

Janet Horsley
Headingley, Yorkshire

HOME BAKED BEANS
For 4 people

A delicious home-made version of that ever-popular and nourishing tinned commodity, baked beans in tomato sauce. Remember to start the night before.

225 g/8 oz haricot beans, soaked overnight
50 g/2 oz butter or margarine
1 large onion, chopped
A clove of garlic, crushed
A 400 g/14 oz tin of tomatoes
2 teaspoons brown sugar
1 tablespoon chopped fresh parsley
Salt and pepper

1. Cook beans as directed on *page 66*.
2. Melt butter and fry onion and garlic until soft but not brown.
3. Break up tomatoes in the tin and pour into pan.
4. Simmer uncovered for about 10 minutes to reduce tomato juice.
5. Add sugar, parsley, salt and pepper.
6. Pour sauce over the hot beans and keep warm for at least 30 minutes so that beans absorb the flavour.

Sue Maddison
Chislehurst, Kent

RUNNER BEANS AND ALMONDS
For 4 people

15 g/½ oz flaked almonds
40 g/1½ oz butter
275 g/10 oz frozen runner beans or whole green beans
Salt and pepper

Lightly-cooked, drained, fresh (not frozen) beans can be used.

1. Fry the almonds in butter till both are pale golden brown.
2. Add frozen beans, shake them in amongst butter and almonds. Cover pan and simmer gently for 3 minutes.
3. Uncover pan, turn up heat and stir-fry for 1 minute.
4. Season and serve.

Lightly-cooked non-frozen beans are added to pan when almonds are brown. Stir-fry for 1 minute. Season and serve.

Sybil Norcott
Irlam, Nr. Manchester

CURRIED BHINDI

Also known as okra and ladies' fingers.

For 4 people

450 g/1 lb bhindi
1 tablespoon oil
1 small onion, finely-chopped
½ teaspoon ground cumin
½ teaspoon coriander
½ teaspoon chilli powder (optional)
¼ teaspoon ground turmeric
¾ teaspoon salt
150 g/5 oz tinned tomatoes

1. Wash and dry the bhindi. Trim the tops and tails and cut into 2·5 cm/1 inch pieces.
2. In a pan, heat oil and fry onion until it is lightly browned.
3. Add spices and salt and cook for 2 minutes on a low heat.
4. Add bhindi and stir until it is well mixed and coated with spices.
5. Lastly, add tomatoes and bring to the boil. Cover and simmer for about 7 minutes or until the bhindi is cooked.

Serve with Boiled Rice (*see page 86*), Chicken Curry (*see page 35*) and Onion Salad (*see page 70*); or with Puris (*see page 142*) and Cauliflower Bhaji (*see page 74*) as part of a vegetarian meal.

Priya Wickramasinghe
Cardiff

BAKED CARROTS WITH HONEY AND MUSTARD

450 g/1 lb carrots
2 tablespoons water

2 tablespoons oil
2 tablespoons honey
1 teaspoon made mustard, try a whole grain one
Pepper and salt
A few sesame seeds for decorating (optional)

1. Scrub carrots and chop into small sticks.
2. Mix water, oil, honey and mustard.
3. Put carrots in a shallow oven dish, pour over the honey mixture. Sprinkle with pepper and a very little salt.
4. Cover dish (greaseproof paper and foil will do) and bake in a moderately hot oven, Gas 5, 375°F, 190°C, for 50 to 60 minutes until tender.

Serve with a sprinkling of sesame seeds.

Sarah Brown
Scarborough, Yorkshire

BUTTERED CARROTS AND THYME

225 g/8 oz small carrots
15 g/½ oz butter
1 teaspoon chopped fresh thyme

1. Trim carrots and gently scrub clean, leaving skin on. Cut into match-stick strips (known as julienne).
2. Steam carrots for 10 minutes or simmer in a very little water in a tightly-covered pan until nearly tender.
3. Toss in butter, sprinkle with thyme and serve at once.

Janet Horsley
Headingley, Yorkshire

BROCCOLI WITH BUTTER SAUCE

450 g/1 lb broccoli sprigs

Sauce

65 g/2½ oz butter
25 g/1 oz flour

300 ml/½ pint boiling water
Salt and pepper
1 egg-yolk
2 teaspoons lemon juice

1. Steam the broccoli until it is just tender, or cook in a very little water in a saucepan with a well-fitting lid.
2. Meanwhile, prepare sauce. Melt a third of the butter in a pan.
3. Stir in flour and cook for 1 minute.
4. Pour in boiling water, whisking all the time until sauce thickens, but do not boil it.
5. Remove pan from heat, beat in egg-yolk and remaining butter.
6. Season to taste and add lemon juice.
7. Pour over cooked broccoli or serve in a separate sauce-boat.

If sauce is not served at once it can be reheated in a double saucepan.

Anne Wallace
Stewarton, Ayrshire

SPICY CABBAGE WITH COCONUT

For 4 people

225 g/½ lb spring greens, cabbage or Chinese leaves, finely-shredded as for coleslaw
½ medium-sized onion, chopped
2 cloves of garlic
½ teaspoon ground cumin
½ teaspoon ground coriander
¼ teaspoon turmeric
1 teaspoon salt
2 tablespoons unsweetened desiccated coconut
2 green chillis, finely-chopped
1 tablespoon water

1. In a bowl mix all the ingredients thoroughly.
2. Using a heavy-bottomed frying pan, stir-fry the cabbage on a low flame for about 5 minutes.

Priya Wickramasinghe
Cardiff

CAULIFLOWER WITH ALMOND SAUCE

1 cauliflower
50 g/2 oz butter
50 g/2 oz flour
125 g/4 oz ground almonds
600 ml/1 pint water or 450 ml/¾ pint water mixed with 150 ml/¼ pint milk
½ teaspoon nutmeg
Salt and pepper

1. Steam cauliflower whole or in florets, or simmer it in as little water as possible in a saucepan with well-fitting lid. Do not overcook. The texture should be almost crisp.
2. Meanwhile, melt butter in a pan, stir in flour and cook for 2 minutes.
3. Mix almonds with water (or water and milk mixture).
4. Pour almond milk over roux, bring to the boil, stirring continuously. Simmer for 3 minutes seasoning with nutmeg, salt and pepper.
5. Pour sauce over hot, well-drained cauliflower and serve immediately.

Sarah Brown
Scarborough, Yorkshire

CAULIFLOWER BHAJI

Bhaji is the Indian name for a vegetable dish.

For 4 people

1 medium-sized cauliflower
2 medium-sized potatoes
2 tablespoons oil
¼ teaspoon mustard seed
3 cloves of garlic, chopped
2 green chillis, chopped
½ teaspoon ground cumin
¼ teaspoon ground coriander
¼ teaspoon turmeric
¼ teaspoon garam masala (see page 38)
125 ml/4 fl oz warm water

To garnish: fresh coriander leaves, when available

1. Cut cauliflower into florets and potatoes into matchsticks.

2. Heat oil in a pan and splutter the mustard seeds in it. To do this, put seeds into the hot oil, put lid on pan, keep pan over medium heat and listen while seeds leap up against lid for a few seconds until the spluttering sound has stopped. Remove pan from heat before lifting lid.

3. Add potatoes and fry gently for about 3 minutes.

4. Add the other ingredients, except water, and stir-fry for about 5 minutes.

5. Pour in water and allow to simmer for about 15 minutes until cauliflower and potato are just cooked but not soft.

6. Garnish with freshly-chopped coriander leaves.

To vary the flavour of this dish 1 tablespoon of desiccated coconut may be added during cooking, at paragraph four.

Priya Wickramasinghe
Cardiff

BRAISED CELERY AND BACON

A nice way to serve celery if the oven is on for something else.

For 4 people

1 head of celery
15 g/½ oz butter or margarine
Salt
Black pepper
½ level teaspoon nutmeg
300 ml/½ pint chicken stock
2 or 3 rashers of streaky bacon, without rinds

1. Wash and trim the celery and cut it into 2·5 to 5 cm/1 to 2 inch lengths.

2. Use the butter or margarine to grease an oven dish with a lid.

3. Lay celery in dish and season with a little salt, freshly-grated black pepper and nutmeg.

4. Pour over the stock.

5. Cut bacon into thin strips and fry them a little, then lay the strips over celery.

6. Put lid on dish and cook in a moderate oven, Gas 4, 350°F, 180°C, for 30 minutes.

7. When celery is tender, drain off excess liquor, toss bacon amongst celery and serve.

COURGETTES

A vegetable with a lovely appearance but so delicate a taste that it needs some other flavour with it. Takes only 5 minutes to prepare.

450 g/1 lb courgettes, do not peel
25 g/1 oz butter
Half a clove of garlic, crushed
Salt and black pepper

1. Wash courgettes, trim off the stalks and cut into even-sized very fine rings. This can be done very quickly on the mandolin cutter of a grater.

2. Melt butter and fry garlic for 1 minute.

3. Add courgettes and stir over moderate heat so that garlic butter is well distributed. Season with a little salt and plenty of freshly-ground black pepper.

4. Put on lid, lower heat and let courgettes just heat through for 3 to 4 minutes. Shake pan every now and then.

Serve at once while the green slices are still brilliantly green and not jaded with over-cooking.

ONIONS BAKED IN CIDER

A delicious recipe to serve with meat dishes, especially pork.

450 g/1 lb onions
25 g/1 oz butter
1 level teaspoon sugar
150 ml/¼ pint cider
½ teaspoon salt
Freshly-ground black pepper

1. Slice onions thickly, place in a casserole, dot with the butter. Sprinkle on sugar, salt and pepper.
2. Pour the cider over, and cover casserole tightly. Greaseproof paper and foil will do.
3. Cook in a moderate oven, Gas 4, 350°F, 180°C, for 1¼ hours. Then remove lid and cook a further 15 minutes.

NEW POTATOES

Served in a sweet glaze.

New potatoes
25 g/1 oz butter
25 g/1 oz sugar

1. Boil new potatoes in their jackets until tender.
2. In a clean pan melt butter and sugar and cook gently until golden.
3. Put in potatoes with or without skins. Turn them over in glaze until they are coated and light brown.

Nice with cold ham and a green crisp salad.

SCALLOPED NEW OR OLD POTATOES

Can be made with old potatoes, but choose really waxy ones like Desirée or Dr Mackintosh.

450 g/1 lb new potatoes, scrubbed
125 g/4 oz mushrooms, chopped
15 g/½ oz butter
125 g/4 oz cooked ham, cut in small pieces

Cheese Sauce

50 g/2 oz butter
50 g/2 oz flour
1 teaspoon made mustard
A grating of nutmeg
600 ml/1 pint milk
50 g/2 oz grated cheese

1. Steam potatoes or cook them over low heat in a very little water. Then drain and slice.
2. Meanwhile, chop mushrooms and fry for 1 minute in the 15 g/¼ oz butter.
3. Make sauce. Melt butter, stir in flour and cook 1 minute.
4. Stir in mustard and nutmeg. Then add milk gradually, stirring as sauce thickens, and simmer for 3 minutes.
5. Stir in cheese and reheat but do not boil.
6. Arrange slices of potato over-lapping in a buttered, shallow oven dish.
7. Cover with mushrooms and ham.
8. Pour over the cheese sauce.
9. Cook at top of a moderately hot oven, Gas 6, 400°F, 200°C, for 15 minutes.

GLAZED PARSNIPS WITH WALNUTS AND ROSEMARY

450 g/1 lb parsnips
Salt
50 g/2 oz butter
75 g/3 oz broken walnuts
½ teaspoon dried rosemary
Freshly-ground black pepper
Chopped parsley (optional)

1. Scrub parsnips and slice into rings of even thickness.
2. Steam with a little salt or simmer with a good lid on pan in as little water as possible until just tender. Drain.
3. Melt most of butter in saucepan and toss parsnips and walnuts in it until both are lightly-browned.
4. Mix in rosemary and black pepper.
5. Serve with an extra dot of butter or parsley to garnish.

Sarah Brown
Scarborough, Yorkshire

SPINACH WITH CREAM

1 to 1·5 kg/2 to 3 lb fresh
spinach
25 g/1 oz butter or margarine
3 to 4 tablespoons fresh breadcrumbs
2 to 3 tablespoons single cream
A good grating of whole nutmeg
Pepper and salt

1. Trim, and wash spinach. Put it in a
large saucepan with no extra water.
Boil for 4 or 5 minutes.
2. Meanwhile heat butter or
margarine and fry breadcrumbs till
golden, stirring often.
3. Drain spinach, chop, drain again
and squeeze out moisture.
4. Mix in cream, nutmeg, pepper and a
little salt. Put in a warmed dish and
sprinkle piping hot breadcrumbs on
top.

Serve at once.

Mrs Joyce Langley
Shoreham-by-Sea, West Sussex

TOMATO AND ONION CASSEROLE

450 g/1 lb onions
Salt and pepper
½ level teaspoon marjoram
450 g/1 lb tomatoes, skinned (see
page 72) and sliced
75 g/3 oz breadcrumbs
75 g/3 oz grated cheese
25 g/1 oz melted butter,
margarine or bacon fat

1. Peel and slice onions and boil in
salted water for about 20 minutes.
2. Drain well and season with pepper
and herbs.
3. Put half onion into a greased
casserole.
4. Add a layer of half the sliced
tomatoes.
5. Next, add a layer of crumbs and
grated cheese.
6. Repeat the layers.

7. Pour over the melted butter,
margarine or bacon fat.
8. Bake in a hot oven Gas 7, 425°F,
220°C, for 20 minutes.

Sybil Norcott
Irlam, Nr. Manchester

STIR-FRY VEGETABLES WITH BEANSPROUTS

Served with brown rice (see page 86) or
wholewheat pasta this makes an
appetizing light meal for 4 or 5 people.

2 tablespoons oil, sesame oil is
best
1 onion, cut into rings
A clove of garlic, crushed
½ to 1 teaspoon ground ginger
1 green pepper, thinly-sliced
1 large carrot, scrubbed and
thinly-sliced
1 leek, sliced
125 g/4 oz small button
mushrooms
150 ml/¼ pint water
1 to 2 tablespoons white wine
(optional)
1 to 2 teaspoons soya sauce
225 g/8 oz beansprouts

1. Heat oil in a large frying pan with a
lid.
2. Fry onion, garlic and ginger until
soft but not brown.
3. Add green pepper and fry for 1
minute more.
4. Toss in carrot and fry 3 or 4
minutes more, stirring often.
5. Add leek and mushrooms and stir-
fry 3 or 4 minutes more.
6. Stir in water, wine and soya sauce
and lay beansprouts on top.
7. Cover pan, bring to boil and simmer
very gently for 1 minute before
serving.

Janet Horsley
Headingley, Yorkshire

AUBERGINES AND TOMATOES

6 firm ripe tomatoes
2 aubergines, fairly large
1 onion, finely-sliced and
chopped small
A clove of garlic
½ level teaspoon fresh basil, or a
good pinch of dried
1 tablespoon oil
Salt and pepper

1. Put tomatoes in a bowl, cover with boiling water and leave for 30 seconds. Plunge one at a time into cold water and skin.
2. Slice the tomatoes and arrange half of them in a well-greased, shallow oven dish.
3. Wash the aubergines. Trim off stem ends. Cut in half lengthways.
4. Now, with skin side up make lengthways cuts 1 cm/½ inch apart to within 1 cm/½ inch of stem end.
5. Transfer to dish. Space the aubergine fans out in a single layer. Fill the spaces between the fans with slices of tomato.
6. Arrange the rest of the tomatoes, onion, garlic and basil around the fans. Brush all over with oil. Season with salt and pepper.
7. Cover with lid or foil and bake in a very hot oven, Gas 8, 450°F, 230°C, for 10 minutes. Reduce heat to moderate, Gas 4, 350°F, 180°C for another 25 minutes or until the aubergines are tender.

Serve on its own as a snack or as an accompaniment to grilled lamb.

BUTTER BEANS AND MUSHROOMS

Under a crisp cheese topping, this is a light but nourishing dish to eat on its own, with lightly-cooked green beans or just with some crusty French bread and green salad.

Remember to start the night before.

175 g/6 oz butter beans, soaked overnight
225 g/8 oz mushrooms
A little butter
Salt and pepper

White Sauce

25 g/1 oz butter
1 dessertspoon wholewheat flour
150 ml/¼ pint milk
1 tablespoon lemon juice
Salt and pepper

Topping

40 g/1½ oz grated cheese
40 g/1½ oz fresh wholewheat breadcrumbs

1. Having soaked beans overnight in water to cover, drain off water. Put beans in saucepan and cover with fresh water. Boil hard for 10 minutes then reduce heat and simmer until tender, about 40 minutes more. Drain (saving liquid for soups, etc.).
2. Put beans in a well-buttered 1·1 litre/2 pint pie dish. Season well with salt and pepper.
3. Meanwhile, cut stalks from mushrooms and chop them finely, leaving mushroom caps whole.
4. Simmer mushroom caps in a very little water for 2 or 3 minutes to soften a little. Then drain, saving the liquid.
5. For the sauce, melt butter and fry mushroom stalks for 2 minutes.
6. Add flour and cook 1 minute.
7. Add milk and lemon juice to pan, stir as sauce thickens and add enough mushroom liquid to make a smooth pouring sauce. Add salt and pepper to taste. Simmer for 3 minutes.
8. Pour sauce over beans.
9. Lay mushroom caps on top with undersides up.
10. Mix grated cheese and breadcrumbs and sprinkle over mushrooms.
11. Bake near top of a moderate oven, Gas 4, 350°F, 180°C, for 15 minutes to brown the top and heat through.

CHESTNUT HOT-POT

Can be cooked on top of stove or as a casserole in oven. Freezes well.

Enough for 4 people, but this dish improves with keeping and reheating. So 1 or 2 can enjoy it more than once. Baked potatoes and spiced red cabbage go well with it, also wholewheat bread rolls.

50 g/2 oz whole lentils
125 g/4 oz whole dried chestnuts*
1·1 litres/2 pints water
1 medium-sized onion
225 g/8 oz carrots
2 sticks of celery
1 tablespoon oil
2 tablespoons fresh parsley or 1 tablespoon dried
1 teaspoon sage
½ teaspoon thyme
½ to 1 tablespoon shoyu (*see page 80*)
½ teaspoon mustard powder
Salt and pepper

*Can be bought at good wholefood shops

1. Wash lentils and pick them over for stones.
2. Boil chestnuts and lentils in the water for 40 minutes.
3. Meanwhile, peel onion and scrub carrots and celery and cut into bite-sized pieces.
4. Heat oil and gently fry chopped vegetables for 10 minutes, stirring occasionally so that they do not brown.
5. Combine in one saucepan or casserole the fried vegetables, chestnuts, lentils and their cooking liquid.
6. Add all remaining ingredients and more liquid, either water or stock, if necessary.
7. Cover pan and simmer for 30 minutes. If using casserole, cook in middle of a moderate oven, Gas 4, 350°F, 180°C, for 45 minutes to 1 hour.

Sarah Brown
Scarborough, Yorkshire

CHESTNUT AND MUSHROOM LOAF

A party dish. Delicious cold as a pâté or served hot in the style of a traditional Sunday lunch.

Enough for 8 to 10 people, but easy to reduce quantities

125 g/4 oz dried chestnuts, whole or kibbled*
1·1 litres/2 pints boiling water
50 g/2 oz butter
1 onion, chopped
2 cloves of garlic, crushed
1 tablespoon chopped fresh parsley
2 teaspoons sage
¼ teaspoon winter savory
½ teaspoon paprika
2 tablespoons wholewheat flour
150 ml/¼ pint stock from cooking chestnuts
150 ml/¼ pint red wine
350 g/12 oz walnuts, ground
50 g/2 oz fresh wholewheat breadcrumbs
4 sticks celery, chopped
1 teaspoon salt
1 tablespoon shoyu (*see page 80*) or Worcestershire sauce
225 g/8 oz mushrooms, sliced
1 beaten egg

*Kibbled is the name given to chestnuts which are sold in small broken pieces.

1. Soak chestnuts in the boiling water for 1 hour.
2. Then cook them in the same water in a covered pan until soft. If whole this will take about 40 minutes; if kibbled, about 20 minutes. Save the cooking water as you drain them. Chop coarsely (not necessary with kibbled chestnuts).
3. Melt butter in a large frying pan and fry onion and garlic gently until transparent.
4. Stir in herbs, paprika and flour and cook 2 minutes.
5. Add the 150 ml/¼ pint stock from chestnuts and wine, stir well. When sauce thickens remove pan from heat.

6. Mix together in a bowl chestnuts, ground walnuts, breadcrumbs, celery, salt, shoyu or Worcestershire sauce and mushrooms.

7. Mix in sauce and beaten egg. Check seasoning.

8. Grease a 1 kg/2 lb loaf tin and line it with greased greaseproof paper. Fill with mixture and press down well.

9. Bake in a moderately hot oven, Gas 5, 375°F, 190°C, for 1 hour until firm to the touch. Remove from oven.

When serving hot, leave loaf in tin for 10 minutes before cutting.

Sarah Brown
Scarborough, Yorkshire

SHOYU OR TAMARI

It is a natural fermentation of soya beans and wheat, not dissimilar to commercial soy sauce. Wholefood and vegetarian cooks use it in preference to that and yeast extracts because they find it is a more versatile condiment. It is also highly concentrated food containing valuable vitamins and minerals. It adds depth of flavour, stimulates the appetite and compliments a wide range of foods. It can be used in a number of dishes from seasonings, soups and stews, to dips and dressings.

Although there is no direct substitute, alternatives are yeast extract, soy sauce, tomato purée, mustards and herbs. Also meat extracts or stock cubes if you are not vegetarian.

CIDER WITH ROSEMARY

A well-flavoured casserole of vegetables. The chick peas, wheat grain and cheese provide protein to make this a substantial and nutritionally-balanced main course.

For 4 people

150 g/5 oz cooked chick peas (*see page 66*) or 50 g/2 oz uncooked

150 g/5 oz cooked wheat grain (*see page 66*) or 75 g/3 oz uncooked grain
About 1 kg/2 lb mixed root vegetables, carrot, swede, turnip, parsnip
1 tablespoon oil
175 g/6 oz fennel, cut in chunks
25 g/1 oz butter
50 g/2 oz wholewheat flour
450 ml/¾ pint cider
450 ml/¾ pint water or stock
1 bay leaf
1 dessertspoon chopped fresh parsley
1 teaspoon rosemary
1 teaspoon sage
1 teaspoon thyme
Salt and pepper

1. Don't forget to soak chick peas and wheat grain overnight before cooking, according to instructions on *page 66*. Save cooking liquid.

2. Cut up root vegetables into even-sized chunky pieces.

3. Heat oil and gently fry fennel for about 5 minutes. This draws out flavour.

4. Add chopped root vegetables and stir well so that all is coated in a very little oil to seal in flavour.

5. Add butter, letting it melt. Stir in flour and let it cook 2 to 3 minutes.

6. Stir in cider and water or stock and bring to the boil.

7. Mix in chick peas, grain and herbs. Bring back to boil, lower heat and simmer for 1 hour. Check seasoning before serving.

Delicious served with baked potatoes and a sprinkling of grated cheese.

Sarah Brown
Scarborough, Yorkshire

CREAMY OAT AND ALMOND CASSEROLE

For 4 to 6 people, but easy to make less

50 g/2 oz whole oats, or barley
50 g/2 oz whole green

continental lentils
225 g/8 oz leeks
225 g/8 oz carrots
125 g/4 oz celery
1 parsnip
1 green pepper
25 g/1 oz butter
½ teaspoon thyme
½ teaspoon mustard

Sauce

50 g/2 oz ground almonds, or
grind whole, unblanched
almonds yourself if you can
300 ml/½ pint stock from
cooking grain and lentils
25 g/1 oz butter
25 g/1 oz wholewheat flour
Salt and pepper

Topping

50 g/2 oz porridge oats
50 g/2 oz wholewheat breadcrumbs
1 tablespoon sunflower seeds

1. Pick over lentils for sticks and
stones. Then rinse with the grain. Put
them together in a pan of fresh water,
about 900 ml/1½ pints, and boil for 45
minutes. Then strain off the liquid and
keep it for use later.
2. Meanwhile, scrub and chop
vegetables finely.
3. Melt 25 g/1 oz butter in a large
frying pan and fry vegetables, stirring
so that they are coated in butter.
4. Pour in about half a cupful of
cooking liquid from grain and lentils.
Cook 10 to 15 minutes until vegetables
are just about tender but not soft.
5. Mix in thyme, mustard and well-
drained grain and lentils. Cook
another 5 minutes.
6. Meanwhile, make sauce. Mix
ground almonds with the stock to form
'milk'.
7. Melt butter in pan, stir in flour,
cook for one minute.
8. Pour in almond milk—stirring
continuously. Bring sauce to boil.
Season.
9. Pour sauce over cooked vegetables.
Turn into a greased oven dish.

10. Mix topping ingredients and
sprinkle over.
11. Bake near top of a moderate oven,
Gas 4, 350°F, 180°C for 20 minutes,
when it will be nicely browned.

Sarah Brown
Scarborough, Yorkshire

MASHED SWEET POTATO

With ham, turkey or chicken

450 g/1 lb sweet potatoes
2 tablespoons milk
50 g/2 oz butter or margarine
300 ml/½ pint béchamel sauce
(see page 95)
Slices of cold meat
2 tablespoons sharp apple purée

1. Cook sweet potatoes with skins on
in water just to cover. Then skin and
mash with milk and half of the butter
or margarine to a creamy consistency.
2. Make up béchamel sauce.
3. Arrange cold meat in a buttered
oven dish.
4. Cover with apple purée and
béchamel sauce.
5. Top with sweet potatoes.
6. Smooth the surface and score in a
pattern. Dot with butter and brown
under the grill.
7. Reheat for 30 minutes in a
moderate oven, Gas 4, 350°F, 180°C.

MUSHROOM AND BUCKWHEAT GOULASH

*Enough for 6 to 8 people, but easy to
reduce for small households*

Contains kidney beans, so remember
to start the day before.

125 g/4 oz uncooked red kidney
beans (or a mixture of these
with pinto and black-eye beans)

1 onion
1 green pepper
2 sticks of celery
2 tablespoons oil
2 teaspoons cinnamon
2 teaspoons paprika
50 g/2 oz unroasted buckwheat
2 tablespoons wholewheat flour
1 to 1·25 litres/1½ to 2 pints
stock, from cooking beans
50 g/2 oz walnuts
50 g/2 oz currants
225 g/8 oz mushrooms
Salt and pepper

1. Soak beans overnight in plenty of cold water (see pages 66 and 67).

2. Next day, drain and rinse beans and cook in 1·1 litres/2 pints fresh water. Boil them hard for 10 minutes then simmer for a further 45 minutes.

3. Meanwhile, chop up onion, green pepper and celery into bite-sized pieces.

4. Heat oil and fry onion gently with cinnamon and paprika for 3 minutes.

5. Add green pepper, celery and buckwheat. Stir well so that all the vegetables get a light coating of hot oil, which will seal in the flavour, and the buckwheat has a chance to toast slightly, which will enhance the flavour.

6. Stir in flour. Cook for 2 or 3 minutes.

7. Save the liquid as you drain the cooked beans and pour 1 litre /1½ pints over vegetables.

8. Add beans, walnuts, currants and mushrooms. Bring to the boil, stirring well. Put into a casserole and put on lid.

9. Cook in a warm oven, Gas 3, 325°F, 160°C for 2 or even 3 hours. Check seasoning before serving.

This dish needs slow cooking to bring out the full flavour. The end result is a beautiful dark, rich stew. Goes well with a contrasting vegetable, such as creamed potatoes or leeks.

Sarah Brown
Scarborough, Yorkshire

NEW ENGLAND CASSEROLE

Can be cooked on top of stove or in oven. Very good with Corn Muffins (see page 147).

For 6 people

Remember to start the day before.

50 g/2 oz red kidney beans
50 g/2 oz black-eye beans
1·1 litres/2 pints water
1 medium-sized onion
1 green pepper
225 g/8 oz marrow or courgettes
1 aubergine
50 g/2 oz raisins
1 cooking apple (about 175 g/6 oz)
Salt and pepper

Sauce

A 400 g/14 oz can of tomatoes
2 tablespoons cider vinegar
1 tablespoon treacle
1 tablespoon apple juice concentrate
½ tablespoon shoyu (see page 80)
Juice of ½ lemon

1. Mix beans together and soak in water overnight.

2. Next day, drain beans, rinse and put in saucepan with 1·1 litres/2 pints fresh cold water. Boil hard for 10 minutes then simmer for 45 minutes more.

3. Meanwhile, mix all sauce ingredients together and simmer for about 20 minutes, or until flavours are well-blended.

4. Chop vegetables into bite-sized pieces.

5. Saving the cooking liquid, drain beans and combine them with vegetables, sauce, raisins and apples. Add some of the bean stock or more tomatoes to moisten if necessary, and salt and pepper according to taste.

6. Cover pan, bring to boil and simmer 20 minutes. *Or*, transfer to a casserole and cook in a moderate oven, Gas 4, 350°F, 180°C for 45 minutes.

If making muffins while casserole is in oven put dish in coolest part.

Sarah Brown
Scarborough, Yorkshire

RED BEAN HOT-POT

A well-flavoured substantial main course.

Enough for 5 people, but easy to make less

Remember to start the night before.

225 g/8 oz red kidney beans
1·1 litres/2 pints water
1 tablespoon oil, olive oil is best
1 onion, sliced
1 green pepper, sliced
225 g/8 oz courgettes
225 g/8 oz mushrooms
225 g/8 oz tomatoes, peeled (*see page 72*) and chopped
2 teaspoons soya sauce
2 teaspoons sage
300 ml/½ pint bean stock
Pepper and salt
450 g/1 lb potatoes, peeled and sliced
25 g/1 oz butter

1. Soak beans overnight.
2. Next day, drain beans and put them in a saucepan with 1·1 litres/2 pints of fresh water. Cover pan and boil beans hard for 10 minutes. Then reduce heat and cook until tender, about 1 to 1½ hours. *Or*, pressure cook for 15 minutes.
3. Saving the cooking liquid, drain beans well.
4. Preheat oven to moderately hot, Gas 6, 400°F, 200°C.
5. Heat oil and fry onion, green pepper, courgettes and mushrooms for 5 minutes.
6. Add tomatoes, cooked beans, soya sauce, sage and 300 ml/½ pint of the bean stock. Add pepper and salt to taste.
7. Put mixture into a greased shallow casserole and lay sliced potatoes on top. Cover with a lid or greaseproof paper and foil.
8. Cook for 45 minutes to 1 hour until potatoes are cooked. Then remove cover, dot potatoes with butter, return to top shelf of oven and cook for 10 minutes more until potatoes are brown on top.

Serve with fresh green vegetables.

Janet Horsley
Author of 'The Bean Cuisine'

RED KIDNEY BEAN RISSOLES

Makes 12 to 14 rissoles

Remember to start the night before.

225 g/8 oz red kidney beans
1·1 litres/2 pints water
2 onions, finely-chopped
50 g/2 oz wholewheat flour
1 tablespoon soya sauce
1 teaspoon dried rosemary or sage
Pepper and salt

For frying: a little oil

1. Soak beans overnight. Drain away the water.
2. Next day, put beans in 1·1 litres/2 pints of fresh cold water. Cover pan and boil hard for 10 minutes, then reduce heat and cook for 1 to 1½ hours until beans are tender. *Or*, pressure cook for 15 minutes.
3. Drain, keep aside half of the beans and mash the rest.
4. Combine all the ingredients, seasoning to taste. Leave aside in a cool place to firm up, about 30 minutes.
5. Shape round rissoles using about 2 tablespoons of mixture for each one. Leave aside in a cool place for 15 minutes to firm up.
6. Heat oil and fry rissoles for 3 to 4 minutes each side until cooked through and lightly-browned and crisp on the outside.

Serve with fried potatoes and a green salad.

Janet Horsley
Headingley, Yorkshire

ENGLISH VEGETABLE COBBLER

For 6 people, but easy to make in quite small quantities

Can be made without cobbler. Really economical.

1 tablespoon oil
2 onions, sliced

225 g/8 oz parsnip
225 g/8 oz swede or white turnip
225 g/8 oz carrot
2 sticks of celery, diced
125 g/4 oz cooked field beans or
carlins or 50 to 75 g/2 to 3 oz
uncooked beans (*see page 66*)
600 ml/1 pint stock, save
cooking water from beans
1 tablespoon parsley
2 teaspoons dried sage
Salt and pepper

Cobbler Topping

125 g/4 oz self-raising brown* or
white flour
A pinch of salt
25 g/1 oz butter or vegetable
margarine
25 g/1 oz grated cheese
About 3 tablespoons milk

*81% extraction rather than pure
wholewheat self-raising flour is
preferable and often easier to
obtain.

1. Heat oil and fry onions until
transparent.

2. Chop root vegetables into bite-sized
pieces and toss in the saucepan with
onions. Add celery. Allow these
vegetables to cook gently for 10
minutes.
3. Add cooked field beans and stock,
herbs and seasoning. Bring to the boil,
cover pan and simmer gently for 20
minutes. Check seasoning.
4. Meanwhile, make topping, just like
a scone. Mix flour and salt.
5. Rub in butter or margarine to form
fine breadcrumbs. Mix in cheese.
6. Mix with enough milk to form a
soft dough.
7. Knead lightly on floured board.
Roll out 7 mm/¼ inch thick. Cut into
circles.
8. Put vegetable and bean mix in an
oven dish.
9. Lay scone circles overlapping on
top.
10. Bake near top of a moderately hot
oven, Gas 6, 400°F, 200°C, for 20
minutes. Topping will rise slightly and
brown. Mixture will bubble underneath.

Nice with baked potatoes.

Chapter 6

Rice, Pasta, Pancakes, Cheese & Egg, Savouries, Snacks and Sandwich Spreads

BOILED RICE

For 4 people

This is the best way of making fluffy white rice to serve with curries and other savoury dishes.

1 cup rice (washed in a sieve under running cold water until the water runs clear)
2 cups water
1 teaspoon salt

1. Put rice, water and salt in a saucepan and bring to the boil.
2. Stir, cover pan, put on a well-fitting lid, reduce heat and simmer for 15 minutes. At the end of that time the rice will have absorbed all the water and be perfectly cooked, but *it is vital* that the lid be kept on for the full 15 minutes.
3. Fluff with a fork and serve.

The above method is suitable for all good rice, Basmati, Patna, Chinese, Japanese and Italian. For part-cooked rice follow manufacturers' instructions on packet.

Brown Rice may also be cooked in exactly the same way but 25 minutes is required for it to absorb the water.

Priya Wickramasinghe
Cardiff

SRI LANKAN YELLOW RICE

This delicately flavoured dish goes well with chicken curries (*see pages 35–38*), Cashew Nut Curry (*see page 88*), Onion Salad (*see page 70*) and poppadoms.

For 4 people

1 cup rice
125 g/4 oz creamed coconut*
2 cups hot water
½ medium-sized onion, finely-chopped.
2 tablespoons ghee (*see page 38*), butter or oil
A few curry leaves (*see page 38*)
3 cloves
3 cardamoms
A 2·5 cm/1 inch piece of

cinnamon stick
1 teaspoon salt
¼ teaspoon saffron or turmeric
8 peppercorns

*Can be bought at wholefood and oriental food shops.

1. Wash rice in a sieve under running water and leave to drain.
2. Dissolve creamed coconut in the hot water.
3. Fry onion in the oil.
4. Add all the other dry ingredients and fry over a low heat, stirring until the grains of rice become yellow.
5. Add coconut liquid and bring to a rapid boil.
6. Cover with a well-fitting lid, reduce heat and simmer for 15 minutes. Simmer 25 minutes if brown rice is used.

Priya Wickramasinghe
Cardiff

KIDNEYS IN A SAUCE WITH MUSHROOMS

For 2 people

3 lamb's kidneys
25 g/1 oz plain flour
Salt and pepper
25 g/1 oz lard
1 medium-sized onion, chopped
50 g/2 oz mushrooms, thickly-sliced
300 ml/½ pint beef stock, a stock cube will do

1. Remove skins from kidneys, cut them in half and cut out the core. Then chop up.
2. Season the flour with salt and pepper. Toss chopped kidneys in it.
3. Melt lard in a frying pan and gently fry onion.
4. Add kidneys to pan and fry gently for 2 to 3 minutes, turning them over in the fat.
5. Toss mushrooms in with kidneys for 2 or 3 minutes more.
6. Stir remaining flour into pan and let it sizzle for a minute. Gradually stir in stock and bring to the boil. Taste and season if necessary with more salt and pepper.

7. Cover pan and simmer for 10 minutes.

Serve with plain boiled brown or white rice (see *opposite*) and green vegetables.

EGG CURRY

6 eggs
2 teaspoons salt
¼ teaspoon turmeric
3 tablespoons oil
Half a medium-sized onion, chopped
25 g/1 oz creamed coconut*
300 ml/½ pint hot water
2 cloves of garlic, chopped
¼ teaspoon fresh ginger (see page 38) chopped
A 5 cm/2 inch piece of cinnamon stick
1 dessertspoon ground coriander
1 teaspoon ground cumin
1 teaspoon chilli powder
¼ teaspoon ground fenugreek
A sprig of curry leaves*, if available
Juice of half a lemon

*Can be bought at oriental and some wholefood shops.

1. Boil eggs for 11 minutes and shell them.
2. Mix salt and turmeric and rub it into eggs. Use a pin and prick them in several places so that they do not burst when fried.
3. Heat 3 tablespoons oil and fry eggs until golden brown, about 2 minutes. Lift eggs out of pan.
4. Fry onions until golden brown.
5. Dissolve creamed coconut in the hot water. Add this to pan with all other ingredients, except eggs and lemon juice. Simmer, stirring occasionally, until sauce is thick.
6. Add eggs and lemon juice and allow to simmer for a further 5 minutes.
Serve with Boiled Rice (see *opposite*), or Sri Lankan Yellow Rice (see *opposite*) and vegetables and salads.

Priya Wickramasinghe
Cardiff

SAUSAGES IN A CURRY SAUCE

For 4 people, but easy to make less for 1 or 2

No need for oven.

700 g/1½ lb sausages
25 g/1 oz dripping
225 g/8 oz brown rice
1 onion, chopped
1 apple, chopped
1 level tablespoon curry powder
1 rounded tablespoon plain flour
A 225 g/8 oz tin of apricot halves
1 green pepper, cut in thin strips
1 dessertspoon mango or good chutney
2 teaspoons lemon juice
Salt and Pepper Mix (see page 44)

1. Fry sausages gently in dripping until golden brown. Remove on to a plate, draining all but 1 tablespoon of the fat. (Save this tasty extra fat for something else.)
2. Meanwhile, put rice on to cook, following instructions for Boiled Rice on *page 86*. Keep sausages warm on top of rice pan.
3. Fry onion in sausage pan until softening.
4. Add apple and fry for 2 to 3 minutes.
5. Stir in curry powder, let it sizzle, then stir in flour and cook for 1 minute.
6. Strain juice from apricots into a measure and make up to 300 ml/½ pint with water.
7. Add liquid to pan, stir until boiling.
8. Add green pepper, chutney, lemon juice, salt and pepper. Let sauce simmer for 20 minutes, adding a little more water if it becomes too thick. Add apricots to heat through.
9. Put rice around edge of a serving dish, sausages in the middle, and pour sauce over sausages. Garnish with apricots.

87

LENTIL RICE

For 4 people

½ cup yellow moong dhal*
½ cup long grained rice, white or
brown
2 tablespoons oil
1 medium-sized onion, sliced
½ teaspoon salt
½ teaspoon turmeric
2 cups hot water, use same cup
as for lentils and rice
½ teaspoon ground cumin
¼ teaspoon mustard seed
A few curry leaves (*see page 38*)

*Moong dhal is the lentil most
widely used in Asian countries.
When used whole it can be sprouted
and becomes the familiar Chinese
beansprout (*see page 65*). Yellow
moong dhal is the split version with
the green husk removed.

1. Wash the lentils and soak them in
plenty of water for 2 hours. If using
brown rice, soak it also.
2. Wash and drain lentils and rice in a
sieve.
3. Heat oil and fry onion until lightly-
browned.
4. Add rice and lentils and fry over
low heat for about 5 minutes.
5. Add all the other ingredients and
bring to the boil.
6. Cover with a well-fitting lid, reduce
heat and simmer for 15 minutes.

It is nice to eat this with pickles such
as Date Chutney (*see page 174*), or
Tomato Relish (*see page 176*), and
with Poppadoms (*see page 38*).

Priya Wickramasinghe
Cardiff

CASHEW NUT CURRY

A favourite Sri Lankan dish.

For 4 people

225 g/8 oz cashew nuts
900 ml/1½ pints cold water
½ teaspoon bicarbonate of soda
1 tablespoon oil
1 medium-sized onion, finely-
chopped
2 cloves

2 cardamoms
2 pieces of cinnamon stick, each
about 2·5 cm/1 inch long
1½ teaspoons ground coriander
1 teaspoon ground cumin
¼ teaspoon turmeric
1 teaspoon salt
25 g/1 oz creamed coconut
125 ml/4 fl oz hot water

1. Soak the cashew nuts for 8 hours in
cold water to which bicarbonate of
soda has been added. Drain away
water and wash cashew nuts.
2. In a pan, heat oil and fry onions
until lightly-browned.
3. Pound or grind the cloves,
cardamoms and cinnamon sticks.
4. Add them to pan with rest of spices,
salt and cashew nuts and mix
thoroughly.
5. Add creamed coconut dissolved in
the hot water and bring to the boil.
6. Put lid on pan, lower heat and
simmer for 15 minutes.

Serve with Lentil Rice (*see opposite*),
or Sri Lankan Yellow Rice (*see page
86*) and a meat dish such as Chicken
Curry (*see page 35*), or Egg Curry
(*see page 87*). Also Cucumber in
Yoghurt (*see page 69*) and Onion
Salad (*see page 70*).

Priya Wickramasinghe
Cardiff

SPICY RISOTTO

For 4 people

This is an ideal way of using meat left
over from the Sunday joint. When
served with a green salad it provides a
balanced meal.

1 cup Basmati* or long-grain
brown or white rice
2 tablespoons oil
1 medium-sized onion, finely-
chopped
2 medium-sized carrots, grated
Half a green pepper, chopped
225 g/8 oz cooked meat cut into
small pieces (lamb, pork or
chicken)
1 teaspoon salt
½ cup frozen peas
¼ teaspoon ground cardamom

¼ teaspoon ground cinnamon
¼ teaspoon ground cloves
2 cups hot water, use same cup
as for rice

*Basmati rice is the best of all the
varieties of white rice. It has a
distinctive aroma and flavour.

1. Wash the rice in a sieve and allow
to drain.
2. Heat oil and fry onion until lightly-
browned.
3. Add the rice and fry for about 5
minutes on a low heat, stirring all the
time.
4. Add rest of ingredients and bring
rapidly to the boil.
5. Reduce heat to a minimum, put on
well-fitting lid and cook for 15
minutes. If using brown rice cook 25
minutes.

Priya Wickramasinghe
Cardiff

CANNELLONI

For 4 people

Freezes well, but this should be done
before final cooking in oven.

12 cannelloni tubes, the ready-
to-bake variety are easiest to
use

Filling

1 medium onion, finely-chopped
A clove of garlic, crushed
2 tablespoons oil
175 g/6 oz minced beef
1 tablespoon tomato ketchup
1 tablespoon Worcestershire
sauce
1 teaspoon oregano
Salt and pepper
1 tablespoon grated cheese
A 250 g/9 oz tin of spinach
1 beaten egg

Tomato Sauce

1 dessertspoon cornflour
2 tablespoons milk
About 600 g/1 lb 6 oz tomatoes
1 tablespoon tomato ketchup

1 teaspoon sugar
1 level teaspoon oregano
1 level teaspoon sweet basil
Salt and pepper

To cover: 40 g/1½ oz grated
cheese

1. Fry onion and garlic in oil until
soft but not brown.
2. Stir in the mince and cook about 10
minutes. Turn off heat.
3. Stir in remaining filling
ingredients, except egg. Allow to cool.
4. Mix in beaten egg.
5. Fill cannelloni tubes with mixture
and place them in a buttered, shallow,
oven dish.
6. For the tomato sauce, slake
cornflour by mixing it with milk till
smooth.
7. Put all sauce ingredients with cornflour mixture into a pan. Stir over
medium heat until boiling.
8. Reduce heat and cook the sauce for
3 minutes, stirring all the time.
9. Pour sauce over cannelloni,
sprinkle with grated cheese.
10. Cook at top of a moderate oven,
Gas 4, 350°F, 180°C for 30 minutes.

Elizabeth Mickery
Pudsey, West Yorkshire

CASHEW AND APPLE SAVOURIES

Baked in a tray of 6 Yorkshire
pudding tins, allowing one for each
person. Served with pasta and a cold
creamy piquant sauce.

Enough for 6 generous helpings

225 g/8 oz ground cashew nuts*
1 onion, chopped
A clove of garlic, crushed
50 g/2 oz butter
1 green pepper, chopped
¼ teaspoon each of marjoram,
thyme, ground cumin and
paprika
50 g/2 oz wholewheat flour
2 tablespoons sweet sherry or
madeira

89

150 ml/¼ pint light vegetable
stock (water from cooking
chestnuts is ideal) or use apple
or grape juice
50 to 75 g/2 to 3 oz fresh breadcrumbs, wholewheat if possible
1 large cooking apple, grated
skin and all
Salt and pepper
50 to 75 g/2 to 3 oz fancy pasta,
wholewheat if possible

To garnish: slices of tomato and
lemon

*If you cannot buy ground cashew
nuts you can grind your own in an
electric coffee grinder.

1. Fry onion and garlic gently in
butter until transparent.
2. Add green pepper, herbs and spices
and fry a further 3 minutes.
3. Stir in flour and cook for 1 minute.
4. Stir in sherry or madeira and stock
or fruit juice. Bring to boil and stir
over low heat for 2 minutes.
5. Remove pan from heat. Mix in
cashews, breadcrumbs and apple.
Season with salt and pepper to taste.
6. Spoon mixture into greased tins.
7. Bake in middle of a moderately hot
oven, Gas 5, 375°F, 190°C, for about 20
minutes or until cooked thoroughly
and browned on top.
8. Meanwhile, cook pasta in boiling,
slightly-salted water until tender.
9. Make the sauce.

Creamy Piquant Sauce

225 g/8 oz cottage cheese
2 tablespoons mayonnaise or
cream cheese
2 tablespoons yoghurt
2 tablespoons oil
1 tablespoon cider vinegar
1 tablespoon lemon juice
Herbs to taste—e.g., dillweed,
chives or tarragon

Put all ingredients together in a
liquidiser and blend until smooth.

Or, if you do not have a liquidiser,
press cottage cheese through a sieve,
then beat in remaining ingredients.

Sarah Brown
Scarborough, Yorkshire

LASAGNE

*For 4 people. Served with salad,
enough for 6.*

350 g/12 oz lasagne
1·4 kg/3 lb fresh spinach
175 g/6 oz Mozzarella cheese,
thinly-sliced*
125 g/4 oz grated Parmesan
cheese

*Cheddar cheese can be used

Sauce

40 g/1½ oz butter or margarine
1 finely-chopped onion
A crushed clove of garlic
1 chopped green pepper, core
and seeds removed
225 g/8 oz minced beef
Two 400 g/14 oz tins of tomatoes
4 tablespoons tomato purée
1 teaspoon paprika pepper
Pepper and a little salt

1. Put lasagne on to cook in boiling
salted water, but put it into water 2 or
3 sheets at a time to prevent it
sticking together. Then let it all boil
together for about 15 minutes.
2. Wash spinach and simmer it without extra water until just tender.
Drain and chop.
3. Meanwhile start sauce. Heat butter
or margarine in a pan. Fry onion,
garlic and green pepper for 5 minutes.
4. Stir in beef and fry until it loses its
pinkness.
5. Add remaining sauce ingredients,
bring to the boil and simmer for 30
minutes.
6. Line the bottom of a well-greased
oven dish with about a third of the
lasagne.
7. Cover with half of the cooked
spinach, then half of the Mozzarella,
then half of the sauce.
8. Sprinkle on about a third of the
grated Parmesan cheese.
9. Continue making layers, finishing
with a thick layer of Parmesan cheese.
10. Put into a moderate oven, Gas 4,
350°F, 180°C and cook for about 40
minutes.

Judith Adshead
Mottram St. Andrew, Cheshire

LASAGNE WITH VEGETABLES

Enough for 4 to 6 people

A substantial dish, nutritionally well-balanced.

125 to 175 g/4 to 6 oz aduki
beans, soaked overnight
125 to 175 g/4 to 6 oz Brussels
sprouts
125 g/4 oz cabbage
125 g/4 oz mushrooms
1 leek
1 carrot
½ green pepper
1 onion
A clove of garlic (optional)
1 tablespoon oil
600 ml/1 pint stock saved from
cooking aduki beans
2 tablespoons tomato purée
1 teaspoon oregano
1 teaspoon marjoram
Salt and pepper
175 g/6 oz lasagne, wholewheat
if you can get it
75 g/3 oz grated cheese

Sauce

20 g/¾ oz butter or vegetable
margarine
20 g/¾ oz wholewheat flour
450 ml/¾ pint milk
Salt and pepper

1. Remember to start the night before
by soaking aduki beans in cold water
(*see page 66*).
2. Drain beans, rinse and bring to boil
in at least 1·1 litres/2 pints fresh
water. Boil for 40 minutes.
3. Cut up all vegetables, except onion
and garlic, into even-sized, quite small
pieces.
4. Chop onion finely, crush garlic and
fry in oil in a large pan until
translucent.
5. Mix in prepared vegetables and
cook for 5 minutes, stirring
occasionally.
6. Drain aduki beans, saving the
water, and add them to vegetables.
7. Mix tomato purée into 600 ml/1 pint
of the bean stock and pour this over
vegetables and beans.

8. Mix well, adding herbs and salt and
pepper to taste. Allow to simmer for 30
minutes, stirring occasionally. Adjust
seasoning.
9. Meanwhile, make sauce. Melt
butter or margarine over low heat, stir
in flour and let it sizzle for 1 minute.
Gradually add milk, stirring as it
thickens and comes to boil. Cook for 3
minutes.
10. Soak lasagne in hot water for 3 to
5 minutes.
11. Grease an oven dish. Make layers
of lasagne, vegetables and sauce,
ending with a layer of sauce.
12. Put grated cheese on top.
13. Bake near top of a moderate oven,
Gas 4, 350°F, 180°C, for 30 minutes
until cheese is golden and bubbling
and lasagne is cooked.

Serve with green salad, steamed
courgettes or broccoli (*see page 75*).

Freezes well for a week or so.

Sarah Brown
Scarborough, Yorkshire

CREAMY MACARONI AND VEGETABLES

A nice macaroni cheese which is also
pleasant to eat cold as a salad.

For 4 people

142 ml/5 fl oz natural yoghurt
50 g/2 oz cottage cheese
50 g/2 oz cream cheese
125 g/4 oz leeks, weighed after
preparing
125 g/4 oz macaroni, try wholewheat
2 sticks of celery
Half a green pepper
Half a red pepper
½ teaspoon caraway seeds, or
dill weed*
1 dessertspoon shoyu (*see page
80*) or Worcestershire sauce
Salt and pepper
50 g/2 oz grated Cheddar cheese

*If you are not fond of the flavour of
caraway or dill you can use instead
a mixture of mustard and paprika.

1. Mix together yoghurt, cottage and cream cheeses.
2. Wash leeks well and slice quite finely.
3. Blanch leeks by immersing them in a pan of boiling water. Bring to the boil and then drain.
4. Cook macaroni in boiling salted water until just tender.
5. Chop celery and peppers finely.
6. Combine vegetables, macaroni and yoghurt mixture, add caraway seeds and shoyu and taste for seasoning.
7. Put in an oven dish and cover with grated cheese.
8. Bake near top of a moderate oven, Gas 4, 350°F, 180°C, for 30 minutes.

Sarah Brown
Scarborough, Yorkshire

MIXED FRIED NOODLES, INDONESIAN-STYLE

Made with chicken and prawns.

For 4 people

225 g/8 oz egg noodles
1 to 2 tablespoons vegetable oil
Half a medium-sized onion, finely-chopped
2 cloves of garlic, finely-chopped
125 g/4 oz uncooked chicken flesh, cut into very small pieces
125 g/4 oz prawns, shelled
1 stick celery, finely-chopped
50 g/2 oz Chinese cabbage
¼ teaspoon salt
1 tablespoon soya sauce
3 spring onions, sliced
Half a cucumber, finely-sliced
1 tablespoon onion flakes

1. Cook the noodles according to the directions on the packet, making sure not to overcook them. Then drain in a colander until needed.
2. In a wok or large frying pan heat the oil.
3. Add onion, garlic, chicken and prawns and stir-fry over a medium to high heat until the chicken and prawns are cooked, about 3 to 5 minutes.

4. Add the celery and cabbage and stir-fry for a few seconds.
5. Add noodles and salt and mix thoroughly.
6. Lastly, add soya sauce and cook for a further minute or so until the dish is heated through.
7. Serve in 4 shallow bowls and garnish with spring onion, cucumber and fried onion flakes.

Priya Wickramasinghe
Cardiff

A RICH MEAT SAUCE FOR SPAGHETTI

This sauce freezes well.

2 rashers streaky bacon
1 onion
A clove of garlic
1 small pig's kidney
2 tablespoons oil
225 g/8 oz beef mince
1 carrot
1 tablespoon tomato purée
150 to 300 ml/¼ to ½ pint stock
A pinch of mixed herbs
Black pepper
Salt
2 teaspoons wholewheat flour or cornflour
1 tablespoon water

To serve

Wholewheat spaghetti, if you can get it. A little grated cheese, preferably Parmesan.

1. Remove rinds from bacon and cut it very small.
2. Peel and finely chop onion. Crush garlic.
3. Dice the kidney very finely.
4. Heat oil and fry bacon gently.
5. Add onion, garlic, mince and kidney. Cook gently for 5 minutes. Stir occasionally.
6. Grate the carrot and add it with tomato purée, 150 ml/¼ pint stock, herbs, pepper and salt. Bring to the boil.
7. Lower heat, cover pan and simmer for 20 minutes. Stir occasionally to prevent sticking, and add more stock if necessary.

8. Meanwhile, cook spaghetti in plenty of boiling salted water.
9. Thicken meat sauce at last minute, if necessary, by mixing flour and water, stirring in and bringing back to the boil.

Serve the grated cheese separately in a small bowl.

BUCKWHEAT PANCAKES

Makes about 10 pancakes
Keep for a day or two in refrigerator. Freeze well.

425 ml/¾ pint milk
1 large egg
A pinch of salt
75 g/3 oz buckwheat flour
75 g/3 oz wholewheat flour
Oil to grease pan

1. If you do not have a liquidiser: put flours and salt in a bowl, make a well in centre and drop in egg. Beat in the milk, gradually incorporating flour. Beat thoroughly.
If you have a liquidiser: put in milk, eggs and salt and switch on for 15 seconds. Then add flours and switch on again for 30 seconds.
2. Heat a frying pan and lightly grease it. Pour in a little mixture swirling it around to make thin pancakes. Cook till browning a little underneath and drying on top.
3. Toss or flip them over to cook other side.
4. When done, flip on to a cold plate so that they cool quickly. This will prevent them becoming leathery.
5. When cold, stack the pancakes on a plate, layered with greaseproof paper. Delicious as a sweet with soured cream and maple syrup. In Brittany they are often filled with ham, eggs and onions.

Try also:

Buckwheat Pancakes with Creamy Leek Filling
For 4 people for a special occasion
The filling is delicious to eat on its own.

10 buckwheat pancakes
15 g/½ oz butter

Filling

450 g/1 lb leeks, finely-chopped
25 g/1 oz butter
125 g/4 oz cottage cheese
2 tablespoons mayonnaise
2 tablespoons yoghurt
1 tablespoon single cream
1 tablespoon lemon juice
1 tablespoon oil
¼ teaspoon tarragon
Pepper and salt

1. Prepare leeks.
2. Heat butter and fry leeks for 5 to 8 minutes until just softening but not brown.
3. Put remaining ingredients together in liquidiser and switch on for 30 seconds. If you do not have a liquidiser, push cottage cheese through a sieve, then mix it with remaining ingredients and beat hard till you have a soft cream.
4. Mix this with leeks.
5. Spoon filling on to each pancake, roll up and place in a greased dish, seam side down.
6. Dot with butter.
7. Bake in middle of a moderate oven, Gas 4, 350°F, 180°C, for 15 to 20 minutes until just heated through.

Sarah Brown
Scarborough, Yorkshire

SAVOURY FILLINGS FOR PANCAKES OR VOL-AU-VENTS

Ham

For this you need:

300 ml/½ pint thick basic white sauce (*see over*), made, if possible, with ham stock—otherwise a chicken or ham stock cube will do
125 g/4 oz chopped cooked ham
1 dessertspoon cooked peas
¼ teaspoon chopped fresh parsley

Mushroom

300 ml/½ pint thick basic white sauce (*see below*), using chicken stock.

175 g/6 oz chopped, lightly-cooked mushrooms
1 dessertspoon cooked peas

Prawns

300 ml/½ pint thick basic white sauce (*see below*), using stock made from simmering prawn shells in a little water, then making up to 300 ml/½ pint with milk. Otherwise use all milk.

125 g/4 oz chopped prawns
1 hard-boiled egg, chopped
1 dessertspoon chopped fresh parsley

BASIC WHITE SAUCES

40 g/1½ oz butter or margarine
40 g/1½ oz plain flour
Salt and pepper

Thick sauce
300 ml/½ pint milk or stock

Medium thick
450 ml/¾ pint milk or stock

Thin
600 ml/1 pint milk or stock

Several methods

I. Traditional

1. Melt butter in a heavy pan.
2. Add flour and work it into butter, stirring until it forms a smooth paste which leaves the sides and base of the pan clean.
3. Cook for a minimum of 2 minutes, stirring all the time. This is to start flour cooking.
4. Pour in milk or stock a little at a time until all the liquid is incorporated. Beat vigorously between each addition of liquid in order to avoid lumps. Season to taste with salt and pepper.

II. Shortcut

1. Put three tablespoons of milk or stock into a screw-topped jar or a shaker.
2. Heat rest of milk or stock in a pan until almost at boiling point. Add butter and melt.
3. Add flour to shaker or jar, put on lid, then pour contents into the pan and stir well until the sauce thickens and comes to the boil.

III. All-in

For a thick sauce using 300 ml/½ pint liquid.

1. Put all ingredients together into a pan over gentle heat and stir continuously while sauce thickens and comes to the boil.
2. Boil for 5 minutes.

Savoury Sauces

Anchovy

Anchovies pounded to a purée and added at last minute to medium-thick or thin white sauce, made with milk or stock as above. Quantity of anchovies to your taste.

Cheese

50 to 75 g/2 to 3 oz grated hard, well-flavoured cheese added at last minute to medium thick or thin sauce, made as above with milk. Reheat but do not boil or cheese may go stringy.

Egg

1 or 2 hard-boiled eggs, chopped small, added at last minute to medium thick or thin sauce made with milk, as above.

Parsley

Medium thick white sauce made with milk or stock as above, adding plenty of chopped fresh parsley at the last minute until sauce is nearly green.

Tomato

Using medium thick or thin white sauce made as above with stock. Remove pan from heat and stir in tomato purée, thyme or basil to taste and a pinch of sugar. Reheat.

Sweet sauces

Coffee

Make up thin sauce as above with half milk and half strong coffee. Add sugar to taste—but no salt and pepper.

Vanilla

Make up thin white sauce as above, using milk. Add a vanilla pod while sauce is simmering. Then remove it, wash and dry and store for further use.

BÉCHAMEL SAUCE

A gently-flavoured classic white sauce.

300 ml/½ pint milk
½ bay leaf

2 peppercorns
1 blade of mace
A piece of carrot, 5 cm/2 inches
¼ of a medium onion
25 g/1 oz butter
25 g/1 oz flour
Salt and pepper

1. Put milk, bay leaf, peppercorns, mace, carrot and onion in a pan. Heat for 10 minutes and strain.
2. Use this milk to make a white sauce. Melt butter, stir in flour and let it sizzle for 1 minute.
3. Gradually add milk, stirring as sauce thickens, and let it cook gently for 3 minutes.

POTATO OMELETTE

This is the Spanish Tortilla.
For 2 or 3 people

For this you need a heavy frying pan about 23 cm/9 inches in diameter.

4 small potatoes, 275 g/10 oz total weight
1 small onion
About 200 ml/7 fl oz good quality oil (it would be olive oil in Spain)
A clove of garlic (optional)
3 large lightly-beaten eggs
Sea salt and freshly-ground black pepper

1. Peel and chop potatoes into 1 cm/½ inch cubes. Rinse and dry.
2. Peel and chop onion finely.
3. Heat the oil and fry the peeled garlic clove for a minute, then remove.
4. Put potato cubes into hot oil and cook gently until soft, turning occasionally.
5. Towards the end of the cooking add onion. Do not let oil get too hot.
6. Remove potatoes and onion and mix gently with eggs.
7. Pour off oil, leaving a light film in pan and heat again. Put in the mixture of eggs, potato and onion and cook gently until the underside is cooked but not too brown and the top is still moist. Season well with sea salt and freshly-ground black pepper.

8. Traditionally the tortilla is turned over at this point. It is inverted on to a large plate, then slid back into the pan, cooked-side uppermost. That is the correct way to do it but a satisfactory method is to put the frying pan and its contents under a hot grill for a couple of minutes. The aim is to serve the tortilla with the centre just a little moist.

Grainne Mulligan
Madrid

OVEN-BAKED OMELETTE

Enough for 4 for a light meal with salad

25 g/1 oz butter
6 eggs
Salt and pepper
50 g/2 oz grated cheese
1 teaspoon chopped fresh parsley or chives (optional)
2 tomatoes, skinned (*see page 72*) and sliced

1. Preheat oven to moderately hot, Gas 6, 400°F, 200°C.
2. Put butter in an ovenproof dish into the oven to melt and get hot.
3. Beat eggs lightly, add grated cheese, seasoning and parsley or chives if used.
4. Put tomatoes in oven dish, pour egg mixture over and bake in centre of oven for about 15 minutes until set.
5. Serve immediately.

Margaret Heywood
Todmorden, Yorkshire

CHEESE AND POTATO SOUFFLÉ

For 2 or 3 people

350 g/12 oz mashed potato
3 eggs, separated
25 g/1 oz margarine, softened
100 g/4 oz grated cheese
2 teaspoons grated onion

2 tablespoons milk
A level teaspoon Salt and Pepper Mix (*see page 44*)

1. Preheat the oven to moderately hot, Gas 5, 375°F, 190°C, and have ready the shelf above the middle.
2. Grease a 1 to 1·5 litre/2 to 2½ pint soufflé dish.
3. Have potato well-mashed in a large bowl.
4. Add egg-yolks, margarine, cheese, onion, milk, salt and pepper and mix all well together.
5. Beat up egg-whites till they are stiff and will stand up in peaks.
6. Using a metal spoon, fold egg-whites into the mixture and pour straight into greased dish. Put in the oven without delay.
7. Bake for 50 minutes. Do not be tempted to open oven door while it is cooking.

Serve immediately.

TOMATO AND CHEESE SOUFFLÉ

15 g/½ oz butter
3 large tomatoes skinned (*see page 72*)
Salt and Pepper Mix (*see page 44*)
50 g/2 oz fresh breadcrumbs
150 ml/¼ pint single cream
¼ teaspoon dry mustard
A pinch of cayenne pepper
100 g/4 oz grated cheese
2 large eggs, separated

1. Preheat oven to moderately hot, Gas 5, 375°F, 190°C.
2. Grease a 15 cm/6 inch soufflé dish with the butter.
3. Slice the skinned tomatoes and lay them in dish. Season with a little salt and pepper.
4. Put breadcrumbs in a bowl and pour cream over them. Leave 5 to 6 minutes to soak.
5. Then add mustard and cayenne to bowl. Beat in cheese and egg-yolks.
6. Whisk egg-whites until stiff but not dry. Fold them in.

7. Pour cheese mixture on top of tomatoes and put dish straight into the pre-heated oven. Bake for 40 to 45 minutes.

Serve as soon as it is ready.

POTATO CHEESE CAKES

Like tiny soufflés, these can be cooked in oven or frying pan.

Enough for 3 people

225 g/8 oz potatoes
2 eggs, separated
175 g/6 oz grated cheese
1 medium-sized onion, grated
1 tablespoon chopped parsley
Try also 1 teaspoon kelp powder
1 tablespoon sunflower seed oil, for frying

1. If baking these, pre-heat oven to moderately hot, Gas 5, 375°F, 190°C.
2. Cook the potatoes in their skins in a little water, cutting them into reasonable-sized pieces. Peel them while hot and mash.
3. Whisk egg-yolks until fluffy and mix in mashed potato, cheese, onion, parsley and kelp powder.
4. Whisk egg-whites until stiff and fold in.
5. Heat oil in frying pan. Put mixture into pan in small mounds and fry quickly till crisp and brown on both sides. If baking, put small mounds on a greased baking tray and bake for 15 minutes, till they are crisp and brown outside and puffy inside.

Eaten with a green salad, these can make a meal in themselves. Nice with home-made tomato sauce (*see Cannelloni, page 89*).

To vary the flavour use chives, paprika, chopped tomato, mixed herbs or a dessertspoon of curry powder.

For extremely light cheese cakes replace potato by 50 g/2 oz wholewheat flour and use two more eggs. Otherwise, make as for potato cheese cakes.

Elizabeth Shears
Author of 'Why Do We Eat'

ONION TART

For 4, but easy to make a smaller tart

Case
12 to 13 cream crackers (175 g/ 6 oz)
50 g/2 oz melted butter or margarine

Filling
2 medium-sized onions
25 g/1 oz butter or margarine
2 lightly-beaten eggs
200 ml/7 fl oz milk
1 teaspoon Salt and Pepper Mix (*see page 44*)
50 g/2 oz grated cheese
A sprinkle of paprika

1. Crush crackers to fine crumbs. Mix in melted butter or margarine and press into bottom and sides of a shallow, 20 cm/8 inch pie plate or quiche dish.
2. Peel and quarter onions and cut thin slices.
3. Cook in butter or margarine until soft but not brown. Put in tart case.
4. Combine eggs, milk, salt and pepper. Pour over onions.
5. Sprinkle grated cheese on top.
6. Bake near top of a moderate oven, Gas 4, 350°F, 180°C, for about 35 minutes, or until set.
7. Sprinkle paprika on top.

Nice hot or cold.

CHEESE CRISPIES

Good with grilled sausages, bacon or liver.

225 g/8 oz grated potato
25 g/1 oz self-raising flour
50 g/2 oz grated cheese
Pepper and salt
1 egg
About 50 g/2 oz lard for frying

1. Grate potato coarsely into a basin, add self-raising flour, cheese and seasoning.
2. Beat egg and mix in.
3. Heat lard in a frying pan until a

light blue smoke rises from it. Then
drop in spoonfuls of the mixture.
4. Fry until golden brown on both
sides. Then turn down heat until
cooked through.
5. Drain on kitchen paper or brown
paper.
6. Serve immediately.

Stella Boldy
Sykehouse, N. Humberside

BACON FLODDIES

A way to use up a small amount of cold
cooked meat. Turkey or chicken
floddies can also be made.

1 large potato peeled
1 medium onion peeled
1 beaten egg
25 g/1 oz self-raising flour
75 g/3 oz bacon, finely-chopped
A pinch of mixed herbs
(optional)
Salt and pepper
Oil for frying

1. Grate potato and onion into a
basin.
2. Mix in egg.
3. Add flour, chopped bacon, herbs and
seasoning and mix well.
4. Heat oil in a heavy-based frying
pan.
5. Fry tablespoons of the mixture,
turning until golden brown both sides.

Sybil Norcott
Irlam, Nr. Manchester

QUICK PIZZA

No need for the oven.

*Enough for 3 or 4 but easy to make
less*

Base

125 g/4 oz self-raising flour
¼ teaspoon salt
3 tablespoons oil
A little cold water

Filling

25 g/1 oz butter
1 small onion, finely-chopped

225 g/8 oz tinned or fresh
tomatoes skinned (*see page 72*)
and chopped
1 teaspoon mixed herbs

To finish

125 g/4 oz grated cheese
2 or 3 rashers of streaky bacon
cut in strips, or anchovies
soaked for 10 minutes in a little
milk to remove excess salt, or
olives

1. Mix together flour and salt. Stir in
1 tablespoon of the oil and enough
water to make a fairly stiff but pliable
dough.
2. Using a floured board, roll out to fit
a frying pan about 18 cm/7 inches in
diameter.
3. Heat rest of oil in the pan and cook
dough over moderate heat for about 5
to 6 minutes.
4. Turn it over and cook 4 to 5
minutes on the other side.
5. Meanwhile make filling. Melt
butter and fry onion until beginning
to soften but not to colour.
6. Add tomatoes and herbs and cook
for 1 minute. Drain off excess liquid.
7. Spread tomato mixture on top of
cooked base in pan.
8. Sprinkle with cheese.
9. If using **bacon**, arrange the strips
on top of cheese and put under a
moderate grill for a few minutes. If
using **anchovies**, pat dry, arrange on
top of cheese and grill. If using **olives**,
use them to decorate after cheese has
melted under grill.

HAM AND LEEKS WITH CHEESE SAUCE

No need for the oven. The quantity
can be varied to suit your household,
but there will be *enough sauce for 4
people.*

For each person

1 leek, not too large
1 slice cooked ham

Sauce

40 g/1½ oz butter or margarine

40 g/1½ oz white or wholewheat
flour
Salt and Pepper Mix (see page 44)
150 ml/¼ pint cooking liquid
from leeks
A bare 300 ml/½ pint milk
A grating of nutmeg
50 g/2 oz grated cheese

To finish: 50 g/2 oz grated
cheese and 2 tablespoons fresh
wholewheat breadcrumbs

1. Trim and wash leeks and cook them
in a little boiling water until just
beginning to become tender, about 10
minutes. Save the liquid as you drain
them.
2. Wrap a slice of ham around each
leek and place in a shallow, greased
oven dish.
3. Melt butter or margarine, add flour
and let it sizzle for 1 minute.
4. Add liquid gradually, stirring as it
thickens. Add nutmeg. Bring to the
boil and cook for 2 minutes.
5. Add cheese, stir to dissolve and
heat but do not boil.
6. Pour sauce over leeks and ham.
7. For the top, mix the second 50 g/2 oz
cheese with the breadcrumbs and
sprinkle over the sauce.
8. Place dish under a moderately hot
grill to heat through and brown a
little.

FRIED TRIPE WITH ONIONS

*A light meal for 4—enough for 2 or 3
for a main meal*

450 g/1 lb tripe
Salt
Milk
Water
2 tablespoons wholewheat flour
Pepper
Deep fat or oil for frying
2 onions, sliced
A small clove of garlic, crushed
25 g/1 oz butter
1 tablespoon cooking oil
A few grains cayenne
1 tablespoon chopped parsley
2 lemons

Slices of wholemeal bread,
buttered

1. Although tripe is blanched or
partially cooked when bought it may
need to be cooked again before being
used. If it will cut with a knife it is
cooked enough. If not, put it in a pan,
add a little salt and cover with mixed
milk and water. Put lid on pan and
cook until tender.
2. Drain and dry the tripe and cut it
into strips.
3. Season the flour and toss in it the
strips of tripe. Wholewheat flour gives
a nutty flavour and a nice, crisp
texture.
4. Deep fry until golden and crisp, 5 to
7 minutes. Drain on kitchen paper and
keep hot.
5. Meanwhile, heat butter and oil in a
pan. Fry onions and garlic till golden
but not brown. Then add parsley and
juice of 1 lemon and cook 1 minute
more.
6. Turn out on to a warmed dish and
put tripe on top.

Serve with quarters of lemon and
brown bread and butter. Best just like
this, not with extra vegetables.

CHEESE AND WALNUT PÂTÉ

Enough for 8 to 10

Keeps for several days in refrigerator
and freezes well.

225 g/8 oz cottage cheese
75 g/3 oz ground walnuts
3 tablespoons butter
75 g/3 oz Cheddar cheese, finely
grated
1 teaspoon caraway seeds, nice
but not essential
1 to 2 teaspoons wholegrain
mustard
Salt and black pepper
5 to 6 tablespoons fresh wholewheat breadcrumbs

To garnish: lettuce leaves,
cress, tomato slices, walnut
halves

1. If you like a fine-textured pâté, first
sieve the cottage cheese.

2. Walnuts may be ground in an electric coffee grinder.

3. Cream butter and cottage cheese.

4. Add grated cheese, walnuts, caraway seeds and seasonings. Mix well.

5. Mix in breadcrumbs.

6. Press pâté into a nice dish or into ramekins. Or serve with an ice cream scoop on individual plates garnished with lettuce, cress, tomato slices and extra walnut halves.

Sarah Brown
Scarborough, Yorkshire

SPICED HAM AND EGG SALAD

Enough for 8, but easy to make less

Can be made with a boiled bacon joint or with sliced boiled ham or pork shoulder.

12 hard-boiled eggs
350 g/12 oz long grain brown or white rice
A small piece of saffron
150 ml/¼ pint mayonnaise (*see page 64*)
450 g/lb boiled ham or bacon

Dressing

3 tablespoons olive oil, or good salad oil
2 tablespoons wine or cider vinegar
2 tablespoons tomato ketchup
2 tablespoons mango chutney
A dash of tabasco
Salt and pepper

To garnish: watercress

1. Cook rice with saffron following instructions for Boiled Rice *on page 86.*

2. Mix mayonnaise with rice and spread it on a large serving plate to cool.

3. Cut eggs in half and arrange them on rice.

4. Shred ham finely and place it on top of eggs.

5. Thoroughly mix dressing ingredients, cutting mango chutney pieces very small. *Or*, put all these ingredients into a liquidiser and switch on for 1 minute.

6. Pour dressing over ham and eggs. Garnish with watercress.

Judith Adshead
Mottram St. Andrew, Cheshire

SAVOURY PEANUT LOAF

Nice hot or cold. If hot, serve with a well-flavoured tomato sauce, see Cannelloni (*page 89*) or Meat Balls in Tangy Tomato Sauce (*page 49*). Good for picnics and packed lunches.

175 g/6 oz peanuts, finely-chopped or ground
125 g/4 oz carrot, grated
125 g/4 oz celery, finely-chopped
75 g/3 oz fresh wholewheat breadcrumbs
2 beaten eggs
2 tablespoons milk
2 teaspoons tomato purée
2 teaspoons mixed herbs
Pepper and salt

To finish: 50 g/2 oz butter

1. Pre-heat oven to moderate, Gas 4, 350°F, 180°C.

2. Mix ingredients, adding pepper and salt to taste.

3. Line the bottom of a greased ½ kg/1 lb loaf tin with greaseproof paper.

4. Spoon mixture into tin and press it down lightly. Dot with butter.

5. Bake near top of oven for 30 to 35 minutes.

6. Leave to cool for 5 minutes before turning out of tin.

Janet Horsley
Headingley, Yorkshire

SANDWICH SPREADS

Tuna and Walnut

A 100 g/3½ oz tin of tuna, drained and chopped
25 g/1 oz walnuts, chopped
A 5 cm/2 inch piece of cucumber, chopped small
2 dessertspoons salad cream
2 dessertspoons chutney

1 level teaspoon dry mustard
Pepper and salt

Combine all ingredients and season to taste. If too thick to spread add a little more salad cream or chutney.

Roe Paste

225 g/8 oz cooked cod's roe
50 g/2 oz melted butter
Pepper and salt
A dash of vinegar

1. Skin the roe and mash it.
2. Add melted butter and pepper, salt and vinegar to taste.

3. Beat well or use a liquidiser to blend.

Liver Spread

125 to 175 g/4 to 6 oz lightly-cooked lamb's liver
1 large spring onion, chopped
25 to 50 g/1 to 2 oz melted butter
Pepper and salt

Put all ingredients in a liquidiser and blend for 2 or 3 minutes.

See also Potted Meat from Clear Beef Soup (*page 9*).

Chapter 7

Pies
and
Pastries

PASTRY

A few tips

1. All pastry is less likely to shrink during cooking if it is allowed to rest in a cool place or refrigerator for 10 to 15 minutes before rolling out, and again immediately before baking. Cover it with greaseproof paper, polythene or cling-film.

2. When recipes indicate a certain quantity of home-baked pastry is required it means that you make up pastry using that quantity of flour—e.g., for 225 g /8 oz short-crust you make up pastry based on 225 g/8 oz flour.

3. Quantity of pastry required for different-sized flans. It is usually rolled out to 7 mm/¼ inch thick:

15 cm/6 inch
18 cm/7 inch   } 125 g/4 oz flour

20 cm/8 inch
23 cm/9 inch   } 150 g/6 oz flour

25 cm/10 inch 225 g/8 oz flour

4. To prepare a flan case for baking 'blind' requires:
(a) a circle of pastry 5 cm/2 inches wider than diameter of flan tin, ring or dish.
(b) not to stretch pastry when fitting it into tin.
(c) to prick base all over with a fork.
(d) a circle of foil to fit into bottom and sides of flan.
(e) dried peas or beans to fill and hold pastry in shape during baking (ceramic 'beans' can now be bought).

5. To bake a flan case with hard-to-handle, rich shortcrust pastry. Lay pastry on the *outside* of an upturned flan or cake tin. Prick base and bake as usual.

6. To bake flan cases blind:
(a) White shortcrust: hot oven, Gas 7, 425°F, 220°C, 10 to 12 minutes. Remove beans, foil, reduce temperature to moderate, Gas 4, 350°F, 180°C, and bake for a further 7 to 8 minutes.
(b) Cheese pastry, either white or wholewheat, also wholewheat short-crust and sweet wholewheat: moderately hot, Gas 6, 400°F, 200°C, for 15 minutes. Remove beans and foil

and return to oven for 10 minutes more.
(c) Rich sweet shortcrust: moderately hot, Gas 5, 375°F, 190°C, for 10 minutes. Remove beans and foil and return to oven for a further 10 to 15 minutes. If you have your pastry on the outside of the tin, allow it 20 to 25 minutes complete baking time.

7. To avoid a soggy bottom in a flan which has a moist filling:
(a) If flan case is ready-baked, paint inside with beaten egg and allow to dry before putting in filling.
(b) If flan case is uncooked, pre-heat a baking sheet at the highest possible oven temperature. Put flan into oven on to this, then turn heat down immediately to the baking temperature required.

8. Half-cooked flan cases. These are useful when a flan filling needs lower heat than temperature required to seal pastry. Prepare as if baking blind and bake near top of a moderately hot oven, Gas 6, 400°F, 200°C, for 10 to 12 minutes. Remove from oven, cool, then fill and bake to suit filling.

Shortcrust, white or wholewheat

225 g/8 oz plain white or whole-wheat flour or a mixture
½ level teaspoon salt
50 g/2 oz hard margarine (add 25 g/1 oz for wholewheat pastry)
50 g/2 oz lard or hard vegetable fat
2 tablespoons cold water (3 for wholewheat) use a measure

Sieve or mix flour and salt in a bowl. Cut fats into small pieces, put them into bowl and rub between fingers until mixture is like fine breadcrumbs. Add water and, using a round-ended knife, stir until mixture begins to bind. Then use your hand to knead lightly and quickly until dough is formed.

Rich sweet shortcrust

Ideal for rich dessert flans and tartlet cases. Almost as rich as shortbread and needs careful handling. See tip 5 *opposite*.

225 g/8 oz plain white flour*
A pinch of salt
150 g/5 oz butter or margarine,
softened
25g/1 oz sugar
1 egg-yolk
A squeeze of lemon juice
2 or 3 tablespoons cold water
*There is no benefit in making this
with wholewheat flour. The
previous recipe is rich enough
especially if some of the fat is
replaced with butter and 1 teaspoon
sugar is added.

Sieve flour and salt into a bowl. Rub
in butter or margarine as lightly as
possible. Add sugar. Mix together egg-
yolk, lemon juice and 2 tablespoons
water. Stir it into flour with a round-
ended knife. Then use your hand to
knead lightly to a firm dough, adding 1
or 2 teaspoons more water only if
necessary.

Cheese pastry

Delicious for savoury flans, meat pies,
sausage rolls, etc.

225 g/8 oz plain white or wholewheat flour
½ level teaspoon salt
½ level teaspoon dry mustard
A pinch of cayenne pepper
75 g/3 oz hard margarine or
vegetable fat
75 g/3 oz well-flavoured cheese,
finely-grated
1 egg-yolk
2 tablespoons water (3 for
wholewheat pastry) use a
measure

Sieve or mix flour, salt, mustard and
cayenne pepper. Rub in margarine
with fingertips until mixture is like
breadcrumbs. Mix in cheese. Mix egg-
yolk with water and stir it with a
round-ended knife. Then knead lightly
until smooth and a firm dough is
formed.

RICH PIE PASTRY

For savoury pies. Can be used where a
more difficult hot water crust is
normally used. The following

ingredients make enough pastry to
line and cover a ½ kg/1 lb loaf tin.

275 g/10 oz plain flour, or half
white and half wholewheat
1 teaspoon salt
140 g/4½ oz lard
1 beaten egg
About 65 ml/2½ fluid oz water

1. Sieve or mix flour and salt in a
bowl. Rub in lard.
2. Keep 1 teaspoon of the beaten egg
for glazing. Mix the rest with water
and use it to bind flour and lard into a
soft elastic dough. If using wholewheat flour it may take a bit more
water.
3. Leave dough to rest for at least 1
hour before rolling out.

Anne Wallace
Stewarton, Ayrshire

GROUND ALMOND
FLAKY PASTRY

275 g/10 oz plain flour
125 g/4 oz ground almonds
50 g/2 oz ground rice
Pinch of salt
350 g/12 oz butter
1 tablespoon lemon juice
6 tablespoons iced water

1. Sift flour, ground almonds, ground
rice and salt into a bowl.
2. Rub one quarter of the butter into
flour mixture and mix to a pliable but
not sticky dough with lemon juice and
iced water as required.
3. Cover and put aside in a cool place
to rest for 10 to 15 minutes.
4. Soften remaining butter with a
knife and divide into thirds.
5. Using a floured board, roll out
pastry 3 times as long as wide, about
7 mm/¼ inch thick.
6. Using one third of the butter, place
in dabs over the top two-thirds of
pastry.
7. Fold bottom third up, and top third
down. Seal edges lightly with rolling
pin. Turn, leaving pressed edges at top
and bottom and at right-hand side.
Wrap in greaseproof paper and put to

rest in the refrigerator or in a cold place for 10 minutes.

8. Repeat rollings with second and then third portions of butter. Then wrap and leave in a cold place for 1 hour, or overnight. If leaving it overnight, wrap a damp cloth around greaseproof covering to make quite sure it is still soft and has no crust when you need to use it.

This pastry will keep in refrigerator for 2 or 3 days. Freezes well.

Mrs Angela Mottram
Axbridge, Somerset

PUFF PASTRY

Usually bought ready made, frozen. This is nevertheless satisfying to make but a long, slow job with frequent use of the refrigerator to chill the pastry at various stages. It is used for very special pastries like vol-au-vents. *See page 93* for a variety of fillings.

225 g/8 oz plain white flour
A pinch of salt
225 g/8 oz unsalted butter
A squeeze of lemon juice
Cold water to mix

1. Sift flour and salt into a bowl and rub in 50 g/2 oz of the butter.
2. Add lemon juice and a little water to make a stiffish dough.
3. Place on a wooden board and knead until smooth.
4. Allow the butter to soften until it is pliable enough to form into a neat brick about 2 cm/¾ inch thick.
5. Roll out dough into a rectangle 30 by 15 cm/12 by 6 inches. Place butter on one half and fold the rest over to enclose it completely. Seal edges. Wrap in a polythene bag and chill for 10 minutes.
6. Put pastry on board with the fold to the left. Roll it out lightly to a long strip about 45 by 15 cm/18 by 6 inches. Fold into 3. Seal edges by pressing lightly with rolling pin. Replace in polythene bag and chill for 10 minutes.
7. Repeat rolling, folding, sealing and chilling so that this process has been done about 7 times in all. For the final chill in refrigerator allow 30 minutes.

Pastry is then ready for use. Or it can be frozen.

8. Roll out 7 mm/¼ inch thick for use. When shaped, chill again for 30 minutes before baking.

ROUGH PUFF PASTRY

As the name implies, an economical and a quickly-made puff pastry. Excellent for Christmas mince pies, sausage rolls and used also in Cheese Strudel Slices (*see page 17*).

225 g/8 oz strong plain flour
A pinch of salt
75 g/3 oz firm margarine
75 g/3 oz firm lard
½ teaspoon lemon juice
About 125 ml/¼ pint water

1. Sieve flour and salt into a basin.
2. Cut fats into 1 cm/½ inch cubes. Mix lightly into flour, but do not break up.
3. Mix to a dough with lemon juice and water. It usually takes the full amount. Form dough into a brick-shape and chill for 10 minutes.
4. On a well-floured board, lightly roll out pastry 7 mm/¼ inch thick, 3 times as long as wide. Fold bottom third up and top third down. Press edges lightly with rolling pin to seal. Wrap in greaseproof paper, polythene or cling-film and chill for 10 minutes.
5. Put pastry on board, folded edges to right and left. Repeat rolling, folding, sealing and chilling 3 times more.

Chill for 30 minutes before using. Freezes well at this stage.

CHOUX PASTRY

This pastry is made in an unusual way. It is almost always associated with éclairs and profiteroles, but it also makes an excellent container for savoury fillings (*see page 93 for some fillings for pancakes or vol-au-vents*). They can be served hot or cold.

65 g/2½ oz flour
A pinch of salt
50 g/2 oz butter
100 ml/4 fl oz water
2 well-beaten eggs

1. Sift the flour and salt on to a piece of paper (this is a help when adding the flour to the hot water and butter).
2. Cut up butter into small pieces and put this with the water into a saucepan. Bring this mixture to the boil. When the butter has melted shoot in the flour and remove pan from heat. Beat well with a wooden spoon until there are no lumps left.
3. Now beat in half of the beaten egg with care and when well mixed add the second egg a bit at a time.
4. At this point the mixture should be slack enough to pipe easily, but firm enough to retain its shape. Put lid on pan and let it cool a little.
5. Put mixture into a forcing bag with a 1 cm/½ inch plain nozzle. Pipe either small rounds or sausage shapes on a well-greased tin or on a baking sheet lined with non-stick paper.
6. Bake in a moderately hot oven, Gas 6, 400°F, 200°C, for 20 to 25 minutes or until crisp, golden and puffy.
7. Cool on a wire rack. They are now ready to be filled.

SARAH BROWN'S WHOLEWHEAT PASTRY

An unorthodox approach to pastry-making but one that answers complaints that wholewheat pastry is unmanageable and hard. It is meant to be wet as you make it. This way it will roll out easily and thinly.

225 g/8 oz wholewheat flour
75 g/3 oz mixed hard fats, solid vegetable fat and butter are suitable
15 g/½ oz soft brown sugar
A pinch of salt
A pinch of baking powder
100 ml/4 fl oz water
1 teaspoon oil

1. Rub fats into flour.
2. Mix in sugar, salt and baking powder.
3. Add water and oil and mix to a dough, which should be fairly wet.

If it seems too wet leave it for a few minutes for flour to absorb some of moisture. Otherwise simply squeeze out excess water.
4. Roll out as required on a floured board.

Keeps a week in refrigerator if well-wrapped.

To bake blind

1. Using a floured board, roll out very thinly and line the tin. Prick bottom all over with a fork.
2. Bake near top of a moderately hot oven, Gas 6, 400°F, 200°C, for 12 minutes.

CHEESE AND ONION PIE

A simple-to-make pie which can be made with either wholewheat or white shortcrust pastry (see page 104). The strong flavoured Canadian Cheddar gives the filling a bite.

Enough for 4 or 5 people

350 g/12 oz shortcrust pastry

Filling

2 large onions, minced or finely-chopped
225 g/8 oz Canadian Cheddar cheese, grated
Pepper
2 tablespoons milk
25 g/1 oz butter

1. Line a 25 cm/10 inch pie tin or flan ring on a baking sheet with two thirds of the pastry. Roll out the rest for the lid.
2. Mix onions and cheese, season to taste and add a little milk to keep pie moist.
3. Put filling into pastry base, dot top with small pieces of butter.
4. Brush edges of pie with water, fit on lid, press to seal. Brush top with milk to glaze. Make two or three slits to let out steam.
5. Bake in centre of a hot oven, Gas 7, 425°F, 220°C, for 30 to 35 minutes. If

using wholewheat pastry, bake just above middle of a moderately hot oven, Gas 6, 400°F, 200°C.

Best served just warm or cold.

Can be frozen either before baking, in which case do not glaze, or after cooking when quite cold.

Mrs Iris Dargavel
Llanellen, Gwent

COLD SAVOURY FLAN

For 4 people

For this you need a 20 cm/8 inch flan case baked blind. Cheese or wholewheat pastry is nice for this filling (*see pages 104/105*).

3 eggs
25 g/1 oz butter
2 tablespoons thin cream or top-of-the-milk
75 to 125 g/3 to 4 oz lean cooked ham or bacon, chopped small
2 tablespoons mayonnaise
125 g/4 oz frozen mixed vegetables, cooked and cooled
Black pepper and a little salt

To garnish: tomato or cucumber slices

1. Scramble eggs with butter and cream.
2. Add chopped ham, mayonnaise, vegetables and seasoning.
3. Fill flan case and decorate with slices of tomato and or cucumber.

COURGETTE TART

For this you need a 20 or 23 cm/8 or 9 inch pastry case baked blind. Choose a pastry on page 104 and follow instructions given for baking blind (*see page 104*).

350 g/12 oz courgettes
15 g/½ oz butter
1 small onion, chopped
1 teaspoon chopped fresh tarragon or ½ teaspoon dried
2 large eggs

142 ml/5 fl oz soured cream
3 heaped tablespoons grated Parmesan cheese
Salt and pepper

1. Wash courgettes and trim off stalks, but do not peel. Cube them. Do not slice.
2. Melt butter, add courgettes, onion and tarragon. Put on lid and cook over a low heat, shaking pan occasionally, until courgettes are barely done. Leave to cool.
3. Beat together eggs and cream. Stir in Parmesan.
4. Fold this sauce into courgettes. Add pepper and a little salt to taste.
5. Pour into pastry case.
6. Bake above middle of a moderate oven, Gas 4, 350°F, 180°C, for 30 to 40 minutes.

HAM, EGG AND ONION FLAN

150 g/5 oz wholewheat or white shortcrust pastry (*see page 104*)

Filling

25 g/1 oz ham fat or lard
1 small onion, finely-chopped
125 g/4 oz cooked ham
2 beaten eggs
300 ml/½ pint milk
Pepper and a little salt
50 g/2 oz grated Cheddar cheese

1. Using a floured board, roll out pastry to fit a 20 cm/8 inch flan tin, or a ring set on a baking tray, or a flan dish.
2. **For the filling.** Heat fat and fry onion gently to soften.
3. Put onion and ham in flan.
4. Mix eggs, milk and seasoning and strain into flan.
5. Sprinkle cheese on top.
6. Bake near top of a moderately hot oven, Gas 6, 400°F, 200°C, for 20 minutes. Then reduce heat to moderate, Gas 4, 350°F, 180°C, for another 10 minutes.

LEEK FLAN

Tarten Gennin in Wales.

An excellent, rich and well-flavoured flan. Easy to make half the given quantity.

Pastry

A 25 cm/10 inch ready-baked flan case, of either wholewheat or white shortcrust pastry (*see page 104*)
Or, two 15 cm/6 inches in diameter

Filling

6 large leeks
25 g/1 oz butter
150 g/5 oz bacon, chopped
4 well-beaten eggs
300 ml/½ pint milk or cream
Pepper and salt
75 g/3 oz grated cheese (optional)

1. Wash leeks and cut both white and green into 2·5 cm/1 inch pieces.
2. Heat butter in a saucepan and cook leeks over very low heat with lid on pan until they are soft.
3. Spread leeks in pastry case. Arrange bacon on top.
4. Beat eggs with milk or cream, adding pepper and a little salt. Pour into flan case.
5. Sprinkle cheese over and put at once in the middle or lower part of a moderate oven, Gas 4, 350°F, 180°C, for 35 minutes.

If making 15 cm/6 inch flans bake for 25 to 30 minutes.

Serve hot or cold.

Mrs Eileen Trumper
Llanvair Kilgeddin, Gwent

MINCED BACON AND PORK PIE

Makes about 6 portions
275 g/10 oz rich pie pastry (*see page 105*)

Filling

175 g/6 oz cheapest bacon

175 g/6 oz minced pork luncheon meat
Pepper and salt
2 eggs
75 ml/2½ oz milk

This quantity is enough for a loaf shape or round pie with a lid.

1. Roll out two thirds of the pastry and line a ½ kg/1 lb loaf tin, an 18 cm/7 inch pie plate or flan ring set on a baking sheet.
2. Mince bacon, mix it with pork and season with pepper if necessary.
3. Put it into pastry-lined tin.
4. Beat eggs, adding milk and a little salt, and pour over meat, saving 1 or 2 teaspoons to glaze the pie.
5. Roll out the pastry lid, damp edges, place it over filling and seal all round.
6. Use trimmings to decorate and brush over with remaining egg and milk to glaze. Do not make holes in top yet or filling may boil over and spoil top.
7. Bake near top of a moderately hot oven, Gas 6, 400°F, 200°C for 1 hour, moving pie down to middle when it has begun to brown.
8. Remove pie from oven and pierce lid in one or two places to let out steam.

Serve hot or cold.

Anne Wallace,
Stewarton, Ayrshire

SAVOURY SAUSAGE PIE

Quantities given makes two 15 cm/6 inch pies, so it is easy to make just one.

Freezes well.

Mrs Odell had this recipe given her many years ago by a 90-year-old Worcester woman who remembered the filling being minced up pork pieces left after the pig was killed. It was known as 'Bits and Pieces'.

350 g/12 oz shortcrust pastry, white or wholewheat or a mixture (*see page 104*)

Filling

450 g /1 lb pork sausagemeat

125 g/4 oz bacon bits, fat pork
or streaky bacon
1 medium-sized cooking apple
1 tablespoon chopped fresh
parsley
2 beaten eggs
Pepper and salt

An optional addition: 1 hard-
boiled egg for each pie, but if
you are going to freeze pies it is
best to leave this out.

1. Using a floured board, roll out
225 g/8 oz of the pastry to fit two
15 cm/6 inch flan rings or dishes,
saving the rest for the lids.
2. **Now for the filling.** Mash up
sausagemeat in a large bowl.
3. Mince bacon or pork.
4. Grate the apple.
5. Mix all filling ingredients together,
except hard-boiled egg, seasoning with
pepper and a little salt if necessary.
Save a dessertspoon of beaten egg to
glaze pie tops.
6. Divide filling between the two
flans. Arrange a quartered hard-boiled
egg in each if desired, covering them
carefully with sausage mixture.
7. Roll out lids. Moisten edges, secure
them in place and pinch edges to seal.
Use trimmings to decorate.
8. Prick tops in several places with a
fork. Mix a dessertspoon of milk with
remaining beaten egg and brush tops
of pies to glaze.
9. Bake for 45 minutes in all at top of a
moderately hot oven, Gas 5, 375°F,
190°C, for 30 minutes, then if
browning too quickly reduce heat to
moderate, Gas 4, 350°F, 180°C, for the
last 15 minutes.

Mrs Olive Odell
Hartlebury, Worcestershire

CORNISH PASTY

We sampled this pasty with members
of the Women's Institute in Truro and
it was excellent—but the variations
are as many in Cornwall as elsewhere.

**100 g/4 oz shortcrust pastry
using the flour of your choice**
(*see page 104*)

Filling
125 g/4 oz skirt of beef
1 potato
1 small onion
A small piece of swede
Salt and pepper
A little milk
A small piece of butter

1. Make up pastry and leave it in a
cool place to rest.
2. Cut meat into strips and then slice
finely (but do not mince).
3. Slice vegetables finely and mix
together.
4. Roll out pastry into a round, about
23 cm/9 inches in diameter.
5. Place mixed vegetables on one half
of pastry and season to taste. Put meat
on top of vegetables and season again.
6. Damp edges of pastry with milk and
fold it over into a pasty. Seal edges.
7. Crimp the sealed edges. Brush
pastry with milk. Cut two slits in top
of pasty.
8. Bake in a hot oven, Gas 7, 425°F,
220°C, for 20 minutes or until pastry
starts to brown. Then reduce heat to
moderately hot, Gas 5, 375°F, 190°C,
and bake for a further 30 minutes.

About 10 minutes before cooking time
is completed, remove pasty from the
oven and put butter in the slits in
pastry. Replace in oven to finish
cooking.

Mrs Jean Wootton
Cornwall Women's Institute

DEEP-FRIED PASTIES

**175 g/6 oz white shortcrust
pastry** (*see page 104*)
Fat for deep-frying

Filling
225 g/8 oz cooked meat, beef,
chicken, bacon or ham, minced
2 teaspoons Worcestershire
sauce
1 teaspoon Salt and Pepper Mix
(*see page 44*)

1. Using a floured board, roll out
pastry, 7 mm/¼ inch thick. Cut 10 cm/
4 inch rounds.

2. Mix together minced meat, sauce, salt and pepper.
3. Place a dessertspoonful on each round of pastry. Damp edges, fold into pasties and seal edges.
4. Heat fat, 340°F, 170°C is the correct temperature. Otherwise you can test heat by dropping in a 1 cm/½ inch cube of bread. The bread should turn golden in 30 seconds. If it turns brown the fat is too hot, allow to cool a little. If fat is not hot enough the bread will not colour.
5. Cook for 4 to 5 minutes until golden. Drain on brown paper or kitchen paper. Eat piping hot.

Fillings can be varied: add 50 g/2 oz chopped mushrooms if you don't have sufficient meat. Also try minced pork with a little onion, a small apple and 2 to 3 teaspoons sage and onion stuffing or a pinch of dried sage.

DEVONSHIRE PORK PASTIES

Makes about 6 or 7 pasties

Especially good made with whole-wheat pastry and eaten cold with salad.

350 g/12 oz white or whole-wheat shortcrust pastry (*see page 104*)
350 g/12 oz cooked pork
1 small onion or 1 stick of celery
1 teaspoon Worcestershire sauce
Salt and pepper

1. Make up pastry and leave it to rest in a cool place while preparing filling.
2. Cut up pork into 1 cm/½ inch cubes.
3. Grate onion or chop celery very finely.
4. Mix pork and onion with Worcestershire sauce, adding salt and pepper to taste.
5. Using a floured board, roll out pastry about 7 mm/¼ inch thick and cut rounds about 15 cm/6 inches across, saucer size.
6. Place equal amounts of filling in centre of each pastry round.

7. Damp edges of pastry and bring edges together to make a join across top. Press lightly to seal and flute edges with fingers and thumb. Make 2 slits alongside the join.
8. Bake above middle of a moderately hot oven, Gas 6, 400°F, 200°C, for 30 minutes until firm and just golden.

Mrs Becky Blackmore
Exeter, Devon

SUSSEX CHURDLES

Delicious pasties with a crisp cheese topping.

Makes 6

225 g/8 oz shortcrust pastry

Filling

100 g/4 oz lamb's liver
100 g/4 oz bacon
1 medium-sized onion
25 g/1 oz lard
50 g/2 oz mushrooms*
½ dessertspoon chopped fresh parsley
½ teaspoon dried rosemary (optional)
Salt and pepper

Topping

1 tablespoon grated cheese
1 tablespoon wholewheat bread-crumbs
Beaten egg to glaze
*Mushrooms can be replaced with tomatoes or apple if preferred

1. Skin liver and cut up small. Cut up bacon and chop onion finely.
2. Fry these together in the lard for 5 minutes.
3. Add mushrooms, herbs and seasoning and cook 2 or 3 minutes more.
4. Using a floured board, roll out pastry about 7 mm/¼ inch thick. Cut rounds about 15 cm/6 inches in diameter.
5. Divide filling between rounds of pastry.
6. Damp edges of pastry.
7. Make pasties leaving the centre open.
8. Mix cheese and breadcrumbs and put a little topping in each pasty.

111

9. Brush pastry with beaten egg.
10. Bake on a greased baking sheet in a moderately hot oven, Gas 5, 375°F, 180°C, for 30 minutes.

Serve hot with vegetables. Delicious with redcurrant jelly.

Mrs Janice Langley
Shoreham-by-Sea, West Sussex

VOL-AU-VENTS

Large
225 g/8 oz puff pastry (*see page 106*)
Beaten egg

1. Using a floured board, roll out pastry 2 cm/¾ inch thick into an oval or a round.
2. Put pastry on to a baking sheet. Using a sharp knife or cutter and keeping at least 1 cm/½ inch in from edge of pastry, cut another oval or round, but cut only half-way through the pastry. This inner piece will form the lid of the vol-au-vent.
3. Brush top with beaten egg and leave to rest for 30 minutes.
4. Bake above middle of a hot oven, Gas 7, 425°F, 220°C, for 8 to 10 minutes until well-risen and golden brown. Then reduce heat to moderately hot, Gas 6, 400°F, 200°C, and cook for a further 25 to 30 minutes.
5. Remove from oven on to a wire cooling rack. Lift off the lid and press down the pastry beneath so that there is room for the filling.

Small vol-au-vents are rolled out 1 cm/½ inch thick. Cut and glaze as above. Bake at above temperatures, reducing heat after 8 minutes and continuing at the lower temperature for a further 8 to 10 minutes.

ALMOND TART
Shortcrust pastry made up with 100 g/4 oz flour (*see page 104*)

Filling
75 g/3 oz butter or soft margarine
75 g/3 oz sugar
1 beaten egg
50 g/2 oz cake crumbs
25 g/1 oz ground almonds
A few drops almond essence
Raspberry jam
A few split almonds

1. Roll out pastry on a floured board and fit it into an 18 cm/7 inch flan ring.
2. Now mix the filling. Cream butter and sugar together and then beat in the egg.
3. Fold in cake crumbs and ground almonds and add the almond essence.
4. Spread jam inside flan case then fill it with mixture. Make sure filling spreads nicely to sides of flan case.
5. Scatter split almonds over the top.
6. Bake in a moderately hot oven, Gas 5, 375°F, 190°C, for 30 to 40 minutes. Look in oven after 20 minutes and reduce heat to Gas 4, 350°F, 180°C, if browning too quickly.

DUTCH APPLE PIE
A much travelled recipe. It reached our contributor from Canada.

For this you need 225 g/8 oz unbaked pastry (*see page 104*) rolled out to fit a 25 cm/10 inch flan tin or ring

Filling
225 g/8 oz cooking apples, peeled and cored
2 tablespoons plain flour
½ teaspoon salt
175 g/6 oz sugar
1 beaten egg
A 150 g/5 oz carton natural yoghurt
¼ teaspoon nutmeg
1 or 2 drops vanilla essence

Spicy Topping
65 g/2½ oz flour
40 g/1½ oz butter
50 g/2 oz sugar
1 teaspoon cinnamon

1. Dice apple.
2. Mix other filling ingredients well.
3. Stir in apple and fill flan.

4. Bake near top of a moderately hot oven, Gas 6, 400°F, 200°C, for 15 minutes. Then reduce heat to moderate, Gas 4, 350°F, 180°C, for about 30 minutes more until filling is firm and golden.
5. Meanwhile, prepare topping. Rub butter into flour, and mix in sugar and cinnamon.
6. Sprinkle topping on pie and bake 10 minutes more.

June Lambton
Goole, N. Humberside

FUDGE TART

First published in a book of family recipes 'In a Bisley Kitchen', collected over 100 years.

For this you need a ready-baked shallow 15 cm/6 inch pastry case (*see page 104*)

Filling
50 g/2 oz butter
50 g/2 oz light soft brown sugar
200 ml/⅓ pint sweetened condensed milk
25 g/1 oz roughly-chopped walnuts
25 g/1 oz seedless raisins
25 g/1 oz glacé cherries, chopped

1. Melt butter in pan. Add sugar and condensed milk. Stir over low heat until sugar is dissolved and mixture boils. Boil for 5 minutes stirring all the time.
2. Take pan off heat. Stir in walnuts, raisins and cherries.
3. Pour mixture into pastry case and leave to cool.

Mrs A. Bucknell
Bisley, Gloucestershire

MINCEMEAT AND ALMOND DELIGHT

For 6 people

Pastry
150 g/5 oz self-raising flour—if using plain wholewheat flour add ¼ level teaspoon baking powder

50 g/2 oz butter
25 g/1 oz lard
1 egg yolk
½ teaspoon lemon juice

Filling
50 g/2 oz butter
50 g/2 oz castor or soft brown sugar
2 lightly-beaten eggs
50 g/2 oz ground almonds
A few drops almond essence
4 heaped tablespoons mincemeat
2 bananas, thinly sliced

1. Put flour in a bowl (with baking powder if wholewheat flour is used). Rub in butter and lard.
2. Add egg-yolk and lemon juice and mix to a firm dough.
3. Roll out pastry on a floured board to fit a 20 cm/8 inch flan tin or pie plate.
4. Filling. Cream butter and sugar.
5. Stir in eggs, ground almonds and essence and mix well.
6. Fill pastry case with alternate layers of mincemeat and bananas. Then spread almond mixture on top, taking care that it covers fruit right to pastry edge.
7. Bake in middle of a hot oven, Gas 7, 425°F, 220°C, for half an hour, when it will be firm on top and nicely browned. If using wholewheat pastry, reduce heat after 15 minutes to moderately hot, Gas 5, 375°F, 190°C, and cook for another 15 to 20 minutes.

Mrs Becky Blackmore
Exeter, Devon

PECAN AND RAISIN FLAN

A rich pudding.

Pastry
225 g/8 oz rich sweet shortcrust pastry (*see page 104*)

Filling
125 g/4 oz seedless raisins
120 ml/4 fl oz water
1 tablespoon cornflour

Grated rind and juice of 1
orange
Grated rind and juice of ½ lemon
50 g/2 oz soft brown sugar
50 g/2 oz pecans or walnuts,
chopped to size of raisins

To decorate
A 142 ml/5 fl oz carton of double
cream
1 tablespoon rum

1. Using a floured board, roll out
pastry 7 mm/¼ inch thick and line a
20 cm/8 inch flan dish or a flan ring on
a baking sheet. Prick base with a fork.
Chill it for 10 minutes.
2. Cut a piece of foil big enough to line
base and sides of flan case. Fill with
baking beans.
3. Bake near top of a moderately hot
oven, Gas 5, 375°F, 190°C, for 10 to 15
minutes. Remove beans and foil at 10
minutes and return flan to oven to
crisp up base. If pastry is already very
brown, reduce temperature to warm,
Gas 3, 325°F, 160°C, for final few
minutes. (Save beans and foil for
another occasion.)
4. Take flan out of oven, remove from
dish or ring on to a wire rack to cool.
(Return it to dish or ring for support
while filling.)
5. Put raisins in water and simmer for
10 minutes.
6. Mix cornflour to a paste with 1
tablespoon of the juice and add sugar.
7. Stir cornflour mixture and rind
into raisin mix and cook until thick. If
too thick add more juice, but
consistency should be like jam. Allow
to cool.
8. To this cooled mixture add chopped
pecans. Pour into cold flan case.
9. Whip cream and add rum. Whip
again.
10. Fill a piping bag and, using a star
nozzle, decorate surface of flan.

TOFFEE CREAM
TART

First make an 18 cm/7 inch
shortcrust flan case and bake it
blind (see page 104)

Filling
150 ml/¼ pint milk
65 g/2½ oz margarine or butter
40 g/1½ oz white or soft brown
sugar
25 g/1 oz plain flour
75 g/3 oz golden syrup

For special occasions decorate with
grated chocolate and whipped cream.

1. Heat the milk but do not boil it.
2. Melt margarine and sugar in a
small pan and stir in flour.
3. Whisk in the hot milk. Stir as it
thickens and reaches boiling point.
Cook for 2 or 3 minutes, stirring.
4. Remove from heat, add syrup and
whisk again.
5. Spread filling in flan case.

Mrs A. E. Phillips
Selsey, Sussex

YORKSHIRE CURD
TART

Sometimes called Cheesecake, but not
quite the same. This recipe uses home-
produced curd.

To make curd
1·2 litres/2 pints milk (Channel
Islands milk is best*)
1 teaspoon Epsom salts
*Ordinary pasteurized milk can
be used but skimmed,
homogenised, sterilised and
'long-life' milks are not suitable.

1. Bring milk to boiling point.
Remove from heat and stir in Epsom
salts.
2. Leave for a few hours or overnight
for curds to form. Strain.

To make tart
175 g/6 oz shortcrust pastry (see
page 104)
225 g/8 oz curd
25 g/1 oz butter or margarine
25 g/1 oz washed currants
1 large beaten egg
1 tablespoon castor sugar
1 tablespoon golden syrup
1 tablespoon rum

1. Roll out pastry and line an 18 cm/7
inch flan ring placed on a greased
baking sheet.

2. Combine all other ingredients and fill the pastry case.

3. Bake above middle of a moderately hot oven, Gas 6, 400°F, 200°C, for 30 minutes until pastry is cooked and the filling firm and golden.

DATE PASTY

Crisp, short pastry with a thick filling.

300 g/11 oz dates, chopped
300 ml/½ pint water

Pastry

125 g/4 oz fine wholewheat flour
125 g/4 oz fine wholewheat semolina
150 g/5 oz butter
5 to 6 teaspoons cold water

To glaze: beaten egg or milk

1. Simmer dates in the water for 10 to 15 minutes until soft. Leave to cool.

2. Pre-heat a moderately hot oven, Gas 5, 375°F, 190°C.

3. To make the pastry, mix dry ingredients in a bowl and rub in butter.

4. Add enough water to make a soft dough.

5. Cut dough into 2 pieces and, using a board well dusted with semolina, roll out each piece to a 23 cm/9 inch square.

6. Lift one piece of pastry on to a lightly-oiled baking tray. Spread cooked dates to within 1·2 cm/½ inch of the edges.

7. Moisten edges with a little water, put on top piece of pastry, pressing edges to seal. Trim off any surplus pastry.

8. Brush with beaten egg or milk. Prick through top layer of pastry several times with a fork.

9. Bake near top of oven for 20 to 25 minutes.

10. Leave pastry on baking tray for 15 to 20 minutes to cool. Then cut into squares and lift them on to a cooling wire to go quite cold.

Janet Horsley
Headingley, Yorkshire

DELUXE MINCEMEAT PUFFS

For this you need ground almond flaky pastry—make up quantity given on *page 105*

Filling

225 g/8 oz chopped eating apple, weighed after peeling and coring
225 g/8 oz currants
225 g/8 oz seedless raisins
150 g/5 oz chopped candied orange peel, mixed peel will do but orange is nicer
275 g/10 oz flaked or chopped blanched almonds
Half a nutmeg, grated
4 to 6 tablespoons brandy

Mix all filling ingredients together and leave to soak and infuse for at least 1 hour.

To make the mincemeat puffs

1 beaten egg
Demerara sugar

1. Roll out cold pastry to about 3·5 mm/⅛ inch thick. Cut into 10 cm/4 inch squares.

2. Place 1 tablespoon of filling on each square.

3. Fold over diagonally, sealing join with beaten egg.

4. Brush top with egg, sprinkle with demerara sugar and place on baking trays.

5. Bake above middle of a hot oven, Gas 7, 425°F, 220°C, for 12 to 15 minutes until risen, golden brown and firm. Puffs at centre of tray may need another 2 to 3 minutes if pastry is still pale underneath.

Delicious served with Rich Brandy Butter (*see page 123*) or a simple Brandy Sauce (*see page 123*).

Instead of individual puffs, a large roly-poly can be made. Roll out pastry as above, spread over it all the filling and roll up, sealing edges with beaten egg. Brush with beaten egg and sprinkle with demerara sugar. Bake for 30 minutes as above, then reduce

115

temperature to moderately hot, Gas 5, 375°F, 190°C, for a further 15 minutes until well-risen, brown and set. Centre of roly-poly will remain quite soft inside.

Mrs Angela Mottram
Axbridge, Somerset

HOW D'YOU DO CAKE

For this you need 350 g/12 oz shortcrust pastry (see page 104), made up with self-raising flour

Filling

350 g/12 oz currants
50 g/2 oz mixed peel
1 tablespoon golden syrup
1 tablespoon demerara or soft brown sugar
1 level teaspoon nutmeg or cinnamon
A pinch of ground cloves. Or, instead of these spices, 1 level teaspoon mixed spice

To glaze: 1 dessertspoon golden syrup warmed with 1 dessertspoon sugar

1. Divide pastry into 2 pieces, one to line tin, the other for top. Shape these into rectangular blocks. Put in a cool place or refrigerator to rest for 20 minutes.
2. Using a floured board, roll out pastry about 7 mm/¼ inch thick and line a Swiss roll tin, about 28 by 18 cm/11 by 7 inches.
3. Warm filling ingredients together in a pan so that they mix easily. Spread filling over pastry in tin.
4. Damp edges of pastry and cover filling with second piece, pressing to seal.
5. Brush with the glaze. Prick top all over with a fork.
6. Bake in a hot oven, Gas 7, 425°F, 220°C, for 25 minutes when it will be shining and golden.
7. Allow to cool in tin and then cut into slices.

Mrs Jill Marshall
Hythe, Kent

KIDDERMINSTER PLUM CAKES

Makes 12 cakes

For this you need a 375 g/13 oz packet of puff pastry, just thawed. Or make up your own using recipe *on page 106*. There will be some pastry over if you use home-made.

Filling

4 glacé cherries
225 g/8 oz mixed dried fruit
50 g/2 oz plain flour
50 g/2 oz soft brown sugar
50 g/2 oz soft margarine
1 egg
½ level teaspoon mixed spice

To finish: water, granulated sugar.

1. Start with filling. Roughly chop cherries and put them in a bowl.
2. Add remaining filling ingredients and beat with a wooden spoon for about 3 minutes to mix thoroughly.
3. Roll out pastry on a lightly-floured board to 3·5 mm/⅛ inch thick.
4. Cut twelve rounds 10 cm/4 inches across; a saucer may be useful to cut round.
5. Place 2 teaspoons of filling in centre of each round. Brush edges with water.
6. Gather pastry together over filling and seal well.
7. Turn each plum cake over and roll out lightly to form a round about 7·5 cm/3 inches across.
8. To finish, brush tops of cakes with water and invert on to a saucer of granulated sugar to give a thick sugary coating on top.
9. Put cakes on a baking sheet and, using a sharp knife, make 3 cuts on top of each.
10. Bake on shelf just above centre of a moderately hot oven, Gas 6, 400°F, 200°C, for 20 minutes when cake will be golden brown.
11. Remove from oven and slide cakes on to a wire rack to cool.

Mrs Cynthia Cooksey
Cofton Hackett, Worcestershire

PARADISE BARS

Makes 20 pieces

**175 g/6 oz white or wholewheat
shortcrust pastry** (*see page 104*)

Filling

75 g/3 oz margarine
75 g/3 oz castor sugar
1 beaten egg
75 g/3 oz currants, washed and
dried
50 g/2 oz chopped glacé cherries
65 g/2½ oz ground rice

50 g/2 oz ground almonds
3 drops of vanilla essence

1. Using a floured board, roll out
pastry 7 mm/¼ inch thick and line
bottom and sides of a Swiss roll tin,
27 by 18 cm/11 by 7 inches.
2. Cream margarine and sugar. Mix in
egg and other ingredients gradually.
3. Smooth filling over pastry base.
4. Bake above middle of a moderate
oven, Gas 4, 350°F, 180°C, for about 40
minutes.
5. Leave to cool in tin.

117

6. Then turn out, cut into four and then into bars.

SUSSEX PLUM HEAVIES

Adapted from an old recipe in 'Sussex Cooking'. The original called for 3 lb flour.

225 g/8 oz self-raising flour
A pinch of salt
175 g/6 oz butter or butter and margarine mixed
75 g/3 oz currants
1 tablespoon castor sugar
About 2 tablespoons cold water
A little milk

1. Put flour and salt into a bowl.
2. Divide fat into 3 even amounts. Rub one third into flour.
3. Add currants and sugar and mix to a firm dough with water.
4. Using a floured board, roll out to an oblong three times as long as it is wide.
5. Using second lot of fat, put little pieces on to the top two thirds of pastry. Fold up bottom third and fold down top third. Turn pastry so that folds are at sides.
6. Roll out again, use remaining fat and fold as before. If pastry has got hot and sticky leave in a cool place or refrigerator for 15 minutes to firm up.
7. Roll into a 20 cm/8 inch round cake, score top and brush with milk. Place on a greased baking sheet.

8. Bake in middle of a moderately hot oven, Gas 6, 400°F, 200°C, for 30 minutes.
9. Slide off on to a wire rack to cool.

These freeze well.

Mrs Janice Langley
Shoreham-by-Sea, West Sussex

SUSSEX TARTLETS

100 g/4 oz shortcrust pastry, white or wholewheat (*see page 104*)

Filling

1 large or 2 small cooking apples, peeled and cored
2 lightly-beaten eggs
Grated rind and juice of 1 lemon
50 g/2 oz castor sugar
A pinch of cinnamon

1. Using a floured board, roll out pastry 7 mm/¼ inch thick and line 18 tartlet tins.
2. Grate apple and put it in a bowl.
3. Mix in eggs, lemon, sugar and cinnamon.
4. Spoon filling into pastry cases.
5. Bake near top of a moderately hot oven, Gas 5, 375°F, 190°C, for 15 to 20 minutes.
6. Allow to cool in tins for 10 minutes and then remove on to a wire rack.

Mrs Ruth Brooke and Mrs Sheila Powell
Hove and Portslade, Sussex

Chapter 8

Puddings, Hot and Cold

APPLE AND FIG CRUMBLE

For 3 or 4 people

Crumble

50 g/2 oz wholewheat flour
40 g/1½ oz porridge oats
15 g/½ oz desiccated coconut
50 g/2 oz melted butter, or 2
tablespoons vegetable oil
Several drops of vanilla
essence

Filling

125 g/4 oz figs, chopped
150 ml/¼ pint water
225 g/8 oz cooking apples,
peeled, cored and sliced

1. Pre-heat oven to moderately hot,
Gas 5, 375°F, 190°C.
2. Mix crumble ingredients well
together.
3. Put figs in a pan with water and
simmer for 5 minutes.
4. Mix apple and figs in an oven dish
and pour over remaining fig juice.
5. Sprinkle crumble on top and bake
near top of oven for 25 to 30 minutes.

Janet Horsley
Headingley, Yorkshire

DORSET APPLE CAKE

Enough for 6 people

250 g/8 oz self-raising flour
A pinch of salt
125 g/4 oz margarine, butter,
lard or dripping or a mixture of
these fats
350 g/12 oz sour cooking apples
125 g/4 oz sugar
1½ to 2½ tablespoons milk
Demerara sugar for sprinkling

1. Sift flour and salt into a bowl and
rub in fat.
2. Peel, core and roughly chop up
apples.
3. Mix in apple and sugar, adding
enough milk to form a soft but not
sticky dough.

4. Dust with flour, shape into an oval
about 20 by 15 cm/8 by 6 inches and
place on a greased baking sheet.
5. Bake in centre of a moderate oven
Gas 4, 350°F, 180°C, for about 50
minutes until the cake is lightly
browned and slightly firm when
pressed in centre. Cake will spread
during baking.
6. Eat hot, straight from oven,
sprinkled with demerara sugar.

Very nice buttered or with
Lancashire cheese. Also nice cold.

Miss Betty Butt
Woodsford, Dorset

GOLDEN APPLE BETTY

*For 4 people, easy to make for 1 or
more people*

175 g/6 oz wholewheat or white
bread
125 g/4 oz butter
1 level teaspoon cinnamon
125 g/4 oz plus 1 tablespoon
light soft brown sugar
450 g/1 lb cooking apples

1. Use a little of the butter to grease a
1·2 litre/2 pint shallow oven dish.
2. Slice bread thickly, remove crusts
and cut each piece into 4 triangles.
3. Put remaining butter in a large
frying pan and melt over a low heat.
Stir in cinnamon and 125 g/4 oz of the
sugar. Add bread and turn the pieces
over carefully until melted butter and
sugar are absorbed.
4. Place one-third of bread mixture in
base of dish.
5. Peel and core apples and cut into
thick slices. Arrange these in dish.
Sprinkle over remaining tablespoon of
sugar.
6. Cover with remaining bread
mixture.
7. Place dish on a baking sheet in
centre of a warm oven, Gas 3, 325°F,
160°C, and bake for 1 to 1¼ hours until
bread is crisp on top.

Serve hot with custard or cream.

MALVERN APPLE PUDDING

Malvern is apple-growing country. Although this dish is made with Russet apples, small sweet eating apples can be used.

Enough for 6, but it is easy to make half quantity

Freezes well.

125 g/4 oz butter
125 g/4 oz sugar
2 beaten eggs
125 g/4 oz plain or self-raising flour
A pinch of salt
2 smallish Russet apples (about 225 g/8 oz, peeled and cored)
Grated rind of 1 lemon
50 g/2 oz currants
2 to 3 tablespoons brandy*

*It is nearly as nice with sherry, or ½ teaspoon brandy flavouring with 2 tablespoons milk, or even with apple juice.

1. Cream butter and sugar.
2. Add beaten eggs.
3. Fold in flour and salt.
4. Peel, core and chop apples and mix with lemon rind, currants and brandy.
5. Grease a 1·1 litre/2 pint pudding basin. If making half quantity a 450 ml/¾ pint basin suits. Put a small square of greased, greaseproof paper to cover bottom of basin to help when pudding is turned out.
6. Put mixture in basin and cover with greaseproof paper and foil, or tie a double layer of greaseproof paper firmly in place with string.
7. Steam pudding for 1½ to 2 hours. If making half quantity 1 hour will be enough.

If you haven't a steamer, stand basin on a trivet or upturned saucer in a saucepan with a lid. Pour in boiling water to come halfway up sides of basin. Cover pan and boil, replenishing with more boiling water if necessary.

8. Turn pudding out on to a warmed dish and serve it with custard or brandy or sherry sauce (*see page 123*).

If freezing, do so as soon as pudding is cold, covering with fresh paper and foil. To reheat, thaw first, then steam or boil in basin for ½ hour.

Mrs Cynthia Cooksey
Cofton Hackett, Worcestershire

SPICY APPLE BARS

Makes 6 pieces

175 g/6 oz plain flour
½ level teaspoon salt
75 g/3 oz margarine
75 g/3 oz light soft brown sugar

Topping

1 tablespoon soft brown sugar
1 level teaspoon cinnamon
2 small or 1 large cooking apple
25 g/1 oz butter

1. Sift flour and salt and rub in margarine until it is like breadcrumbs.
2. Stir in soft brown sugar.
3. Spread this mixture loosely in a greased shallow baking tin, about 18 cm/7 inches square.
4. Now start the topping. Mix together sugar and cinnamon.
5. Peel, core and slice the apples into neat pieces. Lightly press them into mixture in tin.
6. Sprinkle the sugar and cinnamon on top. Dot with butter.
7. Bake in a moderately hot oven, Gas 6, 400°F, 200°C, for 35 to 40 minutes.
8. Cut into 6 bars and serve hot or cold with cream, ice-cream or custard.

Freezes and re-heats well.

Mrs M. K. Smith
Dartford, Kent

BANANA FRITTERS

For 6 people

50 g/2 oz plain flour
A pinch of salt
2 teaspoons icing sugar
4 tablespoons lukewarm water
2 teaspoons melted butter
White of 1 egg
3 or 4 bananas
Oil for deep frying

1. Sift flour and salt into a bowl.
2. Add sugar and mix with water and butter to a thick, smooth batter.
3. Whisk egg-white until stiff.
4. Fold into batter.
5. Quarter the bananas, cutting each lengthways and then across.
6. Heat the oil until it is nearly smoking hot. Test by dropping in a small piece of bread. If it rises bubbling to surface and turns golden in 30 seconds oil is ready to cook fritters.
7. Dip each piece of banana in the batter and fry until golden brown.
8. Drain on kitchen paper and serve hot with a jam sauce.

Pineapple Fritters

Same as for Banana Fritters except use pineapple rings in place of banana quarters.

Priya Wickramasinghe
Cardiff

CARROT SWEET

450 g/1 lb carrots, finely-grated
50 g/2 oz whole cashew nuts or blanched almonds, whole or chopped a little
150 g/5 oz sugar
650 ml/1¼ pints milk
75 g/3 oz butter or ghee (*see page 38*)
6 cardamoms

1. Put carrots, nuts, sugar and milk in a pan. Stir over low heat to dissolve sugar. Then cook very gently, stirring occasionally, until carrot has absorbed all the liquid.
2. In another pan melt butter. Stir in the carrot mixture and cook for a few minutes.
3. Crush seeds from cardamom pods and mix in.
4. Pile mixture into a nice dish and serve at room temperature.

Priya Wickramasinghe
Cardiff

CHICHESTER PUDDING

For 4 people

A very light bread pudding, almost like a soufflé.

4 slices of white bread, preferably real bread
15 g/½ oz butter
2 eggs, separated
2 tablespoons castor sugar
250 ml/9 fl oz milk
Grated rind and juice of 1 large lemon

1. Preheat oven to moderate, Gas 4, 350°F, 180°C.
2. Cut crusts off bread and make it into coarse crumbs. Use the grater.
3. Use butter to grease a 600 ml/1 pint soufflé or oven dish.
4. Beat egg-yolks with sugar and milk.
5. Add crumbs, lemon juice and rind.
6. Whisk egg-whites quite stiff and fold them in.
7. Turn mixture into prepared dish and put straight into pre-heated oven, near top. Bake 35 to 40 minutes until pudding is set, well-risen and golden.

Serve at once or, like a soufflé, it will fall.

Mrs Sheila Powell
Portslade, Sussex

CHRISTMAS PUDDING

An excellent pudding, full of fruit. Can be made just a few weeks before Christmas but keeps for 6 months.

A pudding made in a 1·1 litre/2 pint basin will provide 10 to 12 helpings

There is enough mixture for a 1·1 litre/2 pint basin plus a 300 ml/½ pint basin, *or* an 850 ml/1½ pint basin and a 600 ml/1 pint basin. Smaller puddings can be cooked with larger ones and removed from steamer slightly sooner.

225 g/8 oz raisins ⎱ washed
225 g/8 oz sultanas ⎰ and
225 g/8 oz currants ⎰ dried

225 g/8 oz fresh breadcrumbs,
wholewheat or white
50 g/2 oz almonds, blanched and
finely-chopped
1 apple
Grated rind and juice of 1 lemon
4 small beaten eggs
250 g/9 oz moist brown sugar,
try muscovado
225 g/8 oz shredded suet
50 g/2 oz cut mixed peel
50 g/2 oz plain flour, wholewheat or white
1 rounded teaspoon mixed spice
3 tablespoons sherry or brandy

1. Grease basins and place in the
bottom of each a circle of greaseproof
paper or foil. This will make sure
puddings are turned out easily.
2. In a very large bowl, mix all
ingredients thoroughly. Make sure
you get some help with the stirring.
3. Fill basins to 1 cm/¼ inch below the
rim. Do not ram the mixture down too
hard.
4. Cover basins with a piece of greaseproof paper, pleated along middle, and
then with a piece of pleated foil. Tuck
foil securely under rim of basin.
5. Steam the puddings 4 hours for 1·1
litre/2 pint basins and 2 hours for
600 ml/1 pint basins. The longer the
steaming, the darker the pudding.
If you do not have a steamer, stand
basins on a trivet in a large pan of
boiling water, put on the lid and boil.
Do not let water go off the boil and
remember to replenish with more
boiling water from time to time.
A pressure cooker will reduce cooking
time considerably. Follow instructions
in the handbook.
6. Remove puddings from steamer,
take off paper and foil covers and leave
to cool under a clean towel. When
quite cold re-cover with fresh greaseproof paper and foil and store in a cool
cupboard until required.
7. On Christmas Day, steam puddings
2 hours for a 1·1 litre/2 pint basin and
1 hour for a 600 ml/1 pint basin. Or
pressure cook to save time and fuel.
Serve with Rum Sauce or Rich
Brandy Butter (see opposite).

RUM SAUCE

For Christmas Pudding.

600 ml/1 pint milk
40 g/1½ oz cornflour
40 g/1¼ oz sugar
2 tablespoons rum, or more if
desired

1. Blend cornflour with 2 or 3
tablespoons of the cold milk.
2. Heat rest of milk and, when near
boiling point, pour a little over
cornflour mixture. Stir and return it
all again to the pan.
3. Bring to the boil and simmer for a
few minutes, stirring all the time.
4. Add rum and keep sauce hot in a
jug.

Brandy or sherry sauce can be
made in exactly the same way.

RICH BRANDY BUTTER

50 g/2 oz butter
100 g/4 oz icing sugar
1 egg
50 g/2 oz ground almonds
1 dessertspoon brandy
150 ml/¼ pint double cream

1. Use soft but not melted butter.
2. Cream butter with icing sugar.
3. Beat in the egg and ground
almonds.
4. Whip cream until it holds soft
peaks, then beat in brandy. Fold into
the creamed mixture.
5. Refrigerate for at least an hour
before use, but preferably overnight.
Serve to accompany the Christmas
pudding.

The mixture can be frozen well in
advance or refrigerated for up to four
days beforehand.

JAMAICAN OMELETTE

Enough for 3

3 eggs, separated
50 g/2 oz demerara sugar

Grated rind and juice of 1
lemon
A pinch of salt
1 dessertspoon apricot jam
1 banana
3 tablespoons rum
40 g/1½ oz butter

1. Put egg-yolks, 15 g/½ oz of the sugar
and 1 teaspoon lemon rind in a basin.
Whisk lightly.
2. In another bowl whisk egg-whites
and salt.
3. **For the filling.** Warm jam. Mash
banana and mix with jam. Add rest of
lemon rind and 1 tablespoon of the
rum. Heat gently.
4. **For the sauce.** Melt 25 g/1 oz of
the butter and the remaining sugar in
a small pan and let it cook for a few
seconds.
5. Stir in 1 teaspoon lemon juice and
the last 2 tablespoons of rum.
6. **Now to complete the
omelette.** Melt remaining 15 g/½ oz
butter in omelette pan.
7. Fold egg mixtures together and
pour into hot butter in pan. Cook until
golden underneath.
8. Place under a low grill for a minute
to firm top and toast it until slightly
golden.
9. Lift omelette out on to a warmed
dish. Place on it the banana mixture
and fold it over.
10. Pour the hot sauce over and serve
at once.

PINEAPPLE
PUDDING

An oven is not required for this
pudding. It is cooked on top of stove
and under grill. Can be made with
stewed rhubarb or plums.

50 g/2 oz margarine
100 g/4 oz plain white flour
425 ml/¾ pint milk
25 g/1 oz sugar
A 450 g/16 oz tin of pineapple
pieces
2 egg-yolks

Meringue
2 egg-whites
75 g/3 oz castor sugar

1. Heat grill just to warm and put a
deep 1·1 litre/2 pint dish under to
warm.
2. Melt margarine in a large pan.
Remove from heat and stir in flour.
Cook for 2 minutes, stirring all the
time.
3. Remove pan from heat and stir in
milk gradually. Now heat gently until
it thickens, stirring all the time.
Simmer for 3 minutes.
4. Mix in sugar and 150 ml/¼ pint of
juice drained from pineapple.
5. Mix in egg-yolks and cook, stirring
for 2 or 3 minutes more. It should
bubble but not boil.
6. Lastly, mix in pineapple pieces and
pour into the warmed dish. Put it back
under grill to keep warm.
7. Whisk egg-whites until they stand
up in peaks. Add sugar and whisk
again.
8. Spread this meringue over pudding
and put dish back under grill. Keep
heat low. Grill for 15 minutes until top
is a lovely golden brown.

This meringue is not crisp, but soft
like marshmallow.

Mrs Patricia Chantry
Hook, Nr. Goole, N. Humberside

PLUM CARAMEL
PUDDING

A delicious bread pudding which can
be made in any quantity to suit your
household.

Plums
Butter or margarine
Brown sugar
**Slices of stale bread, whole-
wheat, brown or white**

1. Wash plums and cut in halves,
removing stones.
2. Thickly grease sides and bottom of a
pie dish and sprinkle all over with
sugar.
3. Line dish with pieces of stale bread.

4. Place a layer of plums over bread cut side uppermost. Sprinkle with sugar. Cover with another layer of bread, and a second layer of plums and sugar.
5. Finish top with slices of buttered bread, butter-side uppermost.
6. Cover with greaseproof paper and bake in middle of a moderate oven, Gas 3 to 4, 325° to 350°F, 160° to 180°C. Remove paper after 30 minutes.
7. Turn pudding out on to a warmed dish.

Serve with cream or custard.

Mrs Cynthia Cooksey
Cofton Hackett, Worcestershire

WHITE LADIES PUDDING

This recipe is named after a village near Worcester called White Ladies Aston where a convent of Cistercian nuns lived in the 12th century. They wore white habits.

Enough for 6 people, but easy to reduce to one third or two thirds for 2 or 4 people

Can be baked in oven or steamed on top of stove.

6 medium-thick slices of white bread
75 g/3 oz butter
125 g/4 oz desiccated coconut
600 ml/1 pint milk
A pinch of salt
Vanilla essence
3 eggs
75 g/3 oz sugar

1. Remove crusts from bread. Butter it thickly and cut into squares or triangles.
2. Use remaining butter to grease a 1·5 litre/2¼ pint pie dish. Sprinkle it with the coconut. Then arrange bread in dish.
3. Heat milk till it feels comfortably hot when tested with little finger. Add salt and a few drops of vanilla essence.
4. Beat eggs with sugar. Pour in milk, stirring to dissolve sugar, and strain into pie dish. Leave to soak for 30 minutes.

5. Stand dish in a roasting tin, pour hot water around it to come halfway up.
6. Bake in middle of a warm oven, Gas 3, 325°F, 160°C, for about 1½ hours until pudding is set.
Or the pudding can be steamed if you prefer not to use oven.
7. Turn pudding out on to a warmed dish. Delicious hot or cold.

To cook on top of stove
Using ingredients scaled down to 2 eggs, pudding will fit a 1·1 litre/2 pint pudding basin. Cover top with greaseproof paper and foil. Steam for 1½ hours. If you do not have a steamer, stand basin on a trivet in a large saucepan. Pour in boiling water to come halfway up sides of basin. Cover pan and boil for 1½ hours, replenishing with more boiling water if necessary.

Mrs Jeanne Round
Cookley, Worcestershire

ALMOND JELLIES

A Chinese confection to eat on their own or with fruit salad, tinned fruits, coffee, etc.

10 g/¼ oz agar agar*
1·5 litres/2½ pints cold water
450 ml/15 fl oz milk
350 g/12 oz sugar
2½ teaspoons concentrated almond essence

*Agar agar is a type of seaweed and unlike gelatine has setting properties that do not need refrigeration. It is colourless and flavourless and sets to a superb solid texture which can be easily cut into cubes. It is available from Chinese supermarkets and some wholefood and health food shops.

1. Using a pair of scissors, snip the strips of agar agar into 2·5 cm/1 inch pieces.
2. In a large bowl, soak agar agar in the water for about 8 hours.
3. In a pan, bring agar agar and water to the boil. Simmer until dissolved.
4. Add rest of ingredients, stirring to dissolve sugar, then boil for a further 10 minutes.

125

5. Remove from heat and pour into shallow oiled dishes or baking tins to a depth of about 2·5 cm/1 inch.

6. When set, cut into cubes and pile on to individual serving dishes.

Eat while fresh.

Priya Wickramasinghe
Cardiff

COLD FRUIT SOUFFLÉ

Can be made with blackberries, blackcurrants, cranberries, plums, raspberries or strawberries.

Enough for 10 people but it is easy to make a smaller quantity scaling ingredients down to 1 or 2 eggs

**900 g/2 lb fruit, fresh or frozen
Water
About 50 g/2 oz sugar
40 g/1½ oz gelatine (3 sachets)
3 large egg-whites**

To decorate: chopped nuts, whipped cream for piping (optional)

This can be served in a 1·75 litre/3 pint glass dish or in a specially prepared 1·1 litre/2 pint straight-sided dish. This measures 15 cm/6 inches across and 7·5 cm/3 inches deep.

To prepare a traditional soufflé dish with a paper collar:

1. Cut from a roll of greaseproof paper a single piece measuring 56 cm/22 inches long and 39 cm/15 inches wide.

2. Now fold this lengthways so that you have three thicknesses, 56 cm/22 inches long and 13 cm/5 inches wide.

3. Wind this strip around the outside of the dish and fix it as tightly as you can. Elastic bands are best to hold it in place. It needs to fit very well especially at rim edge.

Now for the soufflé

1. Wash fruit and put it in a saucepan with water barely to cover. Simmer until soft. If using frozen fruit take care to defrost it and add very little water.

2. Push cooked fruit through a nylon sieve, scraping purée from underneath as you do it.

3. Measure purée and, if necessary, top up with water to 1·25 litre/2¼ pints. Return purée to pan.

4. Add sugar according to taste. Stir until it is dissolved. Pour into a large bowl.

5. Put 3 tablespoons water into a cup and sprinkle on the gelatine. Place cup in a small pan of warm water. Heat gently. Stir until gelatine has dissolved, about 2 or 3 minutes.

6. Now strain gelatine mixture into fruit purée, stir well and leave to set in a cool place, or refrigerator.

7. When fruit is set but still wobbly, take a fork and mix it all up again.

8. In a clean, grease-free bowl, whisk egg-whites until stiff. Fold them into fruit.

9. Pour into prepared dish. If you have used a soufflé dish with paper collar, the soufflé will be about 3 cm/1¼ inches above top of dish. Put it carefully in refrigerator to set, allowing 2 or 3 hours.

10. To serve, peel paper gently away using the blunt edge of a knife. Decorate risen edge by gently pressing on chopped nuts. Top can be decorated with a border of chopped nuts or piped rosettes of whipped cream. Otherwise, a jug of pouring cream is nice.

CHRISTMAS JELLY

Made in a pudding basin so that the jelly looks like a Christmas pudding.

**450 g/1 lb black grapes
1½ packets of dark jelly (black-currant or blackberry)
150 ml/¼ pint port or sherry
Water
50 g/2 oz raisins
50 g/2 oz chopped blanched almonds***

*To blanch almonds: put them in a basin, pour over boiling water to cover. Leave until cool enough to handle when almonds will squeeze easily out of their skins.

1. Cut each grape in half and remove seeds.

2. Make up the jelly according to packet instructions but using the 150 ml/¼ pint of port or sherry so that in all you have 850 ml/1½ pints of liquid jelly.

3. Wet a 1·75 litre/3 pint pudding basin with cold water. Pour the liquid jelly into wet basin.

4. Add to this the grapes, raisins and nuts. Stir occasionally until set.

5. Turn out and decorate with a sprig of holly.

Serve with single cream.

CHOCOLATE CREAM PIE

For at least 6 people

Base

75 g/3 oz butter
75 g/3 oz crushed cornflakes
50 g/2 oz soft brown sugar
25 g/1 oz crushed All Bran

Filling

90 g/3½ oz plain cooking chocolate
1 tablespoon water
5 ml/1 teaspoon gelatine
1 egg
25 g/1 oz sugar
150 ml/¼ pint double or whipping cream

1. Start with base. Melt butter, mix it with cornflakes, sugar and All Bran.

2. Press mixture into a 20 cm/8 inch pie plate.

3. Bake above middle of a moderately hot oven, Gas 5, 375°F, 190°C, for 10 minutes. Remove from oven and leave to cool.

4. Now the filling. Grate 15 g/½ oz of the chocolate and keep it for decorating. Break up the rest of it into a small bowl and stand it over a pan of simmering water to melt.

5. Put water in a cup, sprinkle in gelatine and stand cup in a pan of hot water until dissolved.

6. Beat egg and sugar. Add melted chocolate and then gelatine.

7. Whip cream till it will stand in soft peaks. Put 2 tablespoonfuls in a piping bag with fluted nozzle and keep in refrigerator till required. If you haven't a piping bag you can still save 2 tablespoons cream for decorating in a different way.

8. Fold rest of cream into chocolate mixture and pour into cooled case. Put pie in a cool place or refrigerator to set.

9. When set, sprinkle with grated chocolate and decorate with rosettes of piped cream. If you haven't a piping bag, carefully spread cream over surface of pie, fork it and sprinkle with grated chocolate.

Anne Wallace
Stewarton, Ayrshire

ORANGE CREAM CHEESE CAKE

For this you need a loose-bottomed 20 cm/8 inch flan tin or a ring set on a baking sheet.

Flan case

100 g/4 oz digestive biscuits
50 g/2 oz butter

Filling

70 g/2½ oz sugar
75 ml/3 fl oz concentrated orange juice, the frozen variety gives a good strong flavour
275 g/10 oz cream cheese

To decorate: finely-grated orange rind

1. Start with the flan case. Crush the biscuits. To do this lay biscuits flat in a single layer inside a large polythene bag and press with a rolling pin.

2. Melt butter gently. Add crushed biscuits and turn them over and over until well integrated with butter.

3. Now the filling. Stir sugar and orange juice together until dissolved.

4. Mix in cream cheese very gradually until it is all incorporated.

5. Pour this mixture over the biscuit base and press down gently. Level and smooth the top.

127

6. Return to refrigerator to set.

7. When needed, sit the flan case on an upturned basin. The ring will drop away leaving you to slide the cheese-cake on to a flat plate. Or, if using a flan ring, carefully slide cheesecake and ring on to a flat plate, then lift off ring.

Serve with single cream in a jug.

CHOCOLATE SUPRÊME

Enough for 6 people but you can make half quantity

Freezes well up to 3 months.

Very rich. Best made the day before it is needed so that flavour matures.

125 g/4 oz best quality plain eating chocolate
4 eggs, separated
90 g/3½ oz butter, cut in small pieces
1 tablespoon brandy or very dry sherry
2 level dessertspoons icing sugar, sieved
3 tablespoons double cream

To decorate: toasted flaked almonds, or piped double cream

1. Break up chocolate into a bowl. Stand bowl over a pan of simmering water. Do not let water boil and do not let bowl touch water. Chocolate must melt without getting too hot.

2. Add egg-yolks to melted chocolate and mix gently. Do not beat at any stage in this recipe.

3. Remove bowl from pan. Add the small pieces of butter and stir gently until dissolved.

4. Now add brandy or sherry and sieved icing sugar. Stir until dissolved.

5. Lastly, add cream and stir again.

6. In another bowl, whisk egg-whites until thick and fluffy and fold into chocolate mixture.

7. Pour into tiny glasses, cover with foil or cling film and keep in refrigerator until needed.

8. Just before serving, decorate with a sprinkling of toasted almonds or a whirl of double cream.

CHOCOLATE ORANGE MOUSSE

Makes 6 individual helpings

175 g/6 oz plain cooking chocolate
1 orange
15 g/½ oz butter
3 eggs, separated
150 ml/¼ pint whipped cream (optional)
1 teaspoon castor sugar
Chopped walnuts to decorate

1. Break up chocolate into quite a large basin. Set it to melt over a pan of simmering water. Do not let water touch bowl.

2. Grate zest from orange. Squeeze out juice.

3. Remove bowl of chocolate from pan, stir in butter, orange zest and juice. Mix well.

4. Beat in egg-yolks one at a time.

5. Mix in whipped cream.

6. Whisk egg-whites firmly and then whisk in sugar.

7. Fold egg-whites into chocolate mixture.

8. Serve in small sundae glasses. Decorate with a sprinkling of chopped walnuts when cool.

COCOA COFFEE MOUSSE

For 4 to 6 people

2 eggs
75 g/3 oz castor sugar
1 teaspoon vanilla essence
4 level teaspoons cocoa
1 level teaspoon instant coffee
300 ml/½ pint milk
3 tablespoons hot water
15 g/½ oz gelatine, 1 sachet
150 ml/5 fl oz double cream
Flaked almonds

1. Separate eggs. Put whites in a clean grease-free basin.

2. In another bowl, put yolks, castor sugar and vanilla essence. Beat until light and creamy.

3. In a saucepan, blend cocoa and coffee with a little of the measured milk. Add remaining milk and bring to boil. Remove from heat and let it cool for a minute.

4. Stir into egg-yolk mixture and pour back into pan.

5. Return to heat, bring to the boil and boil for 1 minute, stirring. Remove from heat and pour back into the bowl.

6. Measure 3 tablespoons of hot water into a small bowl, sprinkle on gelatine. Stir a little just to mix. Leave for 5 minutes to soften.

7. Stir gelatine into chocolate mixture. Leave in a cool place until just on setting point.

8. Whip cream until just thick. Keep 2 tablespoons aside until later for decoration.

9. Whisk egg-whites until stiff but not dry.

10. Using a metal spoon, carefully fold cream and egg-whites into chocolate mixture. Pour into a fluted mould or a nice serving dish. Put in refrigerator to set, allow at least 30 minutes.

11. If using a mould, dip it into a bowl of hand-hot water and turn mousse out on to a serving plate.

12. Put remaining whipped cream in a piping bag with a star nozzle. Pipe on stars to decorate and arrange flaked almonds to look pretty.

Chill until ready to serve.

RASPBERRY MOUSSE

This can be frozen and is delicious to eat frozen or just chilled.

A 170 g/6 oz can of evaporated milk
A 369 g/13 oz can of raspberries, or equal quantity of frozen raspberries
1 raspberry jelly

To decorate (optional): 150 ml/¼ pint whipped cream

1. Put evaporated milk into the refrigerator for about 1 hour so that it is thoroughly chilled when needed.

2. Drain liquid from can of raspberries into a measuring jug and make up with water to 300 ml/½ pint. Bring to the boil.

3. Make jelly with this hot liquid. If using frozen raspberries just use water for the jelly. Leave till cool and just beginning to set.

4. Whisk evaporated milk until thick.

5. Whisk jelly, add the milk and continue to whisk. It should double its bulk.

6. Fold in raspberries.

7. Leave to set. It will set almost immediately with frozen raspberries.

8. Decorate by piping with whipped cream.

Sybil Norcott
Irlam, Nr. Manchester

DEVONSHIRE JUNKET

This can be made from pasteurized or farm-bottled milk, but homogenised, sterilised and UHT milk are not suitable. Delicious made with Channel Island milk.

600 ml/1 pint milk
1 tablespoon sugar
2 teaspoons brandy or rum
1 teaspoon essence of rennet
Cinnamon
Grated nutmeg

1. Put milk in a pan with sugar and warm gently till only blood heat, 98°F, 30°C. Stir to dissolve sugar.

2. Remove pan from heat, stir in brandy or rum and pour into a nice dish. Without delay, stir in rennet and put dish aside to set at room temperature. It takes about 1½ to 2 hours.

3. When junket is set, sprinkle cinnamon and nutmeg on top. It can then be chilled.

Serve with sugar to taste and Devonshire cream if you can (*see over*).

Mrs Elizabeth Selby
Exeter, Devon

DEVONSHIRE CREAM

It takes 1 gallon of rich, creamy milk to produce 350 to 450 g/¾ to 1 lb of clotted cream, but the result is delicious. Channel Island milk gives the best result.

1. Put fresh milk in a shallow bowl and leave it at room temperature (55°F, 13°C) for 12 to 24 hours until cream rises to the top.
2. Stand bowl over a pan of boiling water till a crust forms on top of milk. Do not let water touch bowl. This will take about 1 hour.
3. Leave bowl in a cool place till next day.
4. Carefully skim off thick creamy top. Underneath is scalded milk suitable for sauces, soups and puddings.

Mrs Elizabeth Selby
Westleigh, Tiverton, Devon

FLOATING ISLANDS

For 4 people
600 ml/1 pint milk
2 eggs, separated
50 g/2 oz castor sugar plus 2 level teaspoons
1 level tablespoon cornflour
Vanilla essence
A very little water

To decorate: grated chocolate or chocolate vermicelli

1. Pour milk into a saucepan, heat to simmering point.
2. Whisk 1 egg-white until stiff, add 25 g/1 oz of the sugar. Whisk again until stiff. Fold in another 25 g/1 oz sugar.
3. Divide egg-white into 4 and spoon each portion on to milk. Poach until set, about 4 to 5 minutes. Lift on to greaseproof paper with a draining spoon.
4. Blend cornflour, egg-yolks, 2 teaspoons sugar and a few drops of vanilla essence with just enough water to slake cornflour.
5. Sowly stir in the milk in which meringue was poached. Return to pan, stir as it thickens but do not let it quite boil.

6. Cool a little. Pour into 4 glass dishes and place 1 egg island on top of each.
7. Sprinkle on a little grated chocolate or vermicelli.

FRESH PEACHES (OR PEARS) IN A FUDGE SAUCE

For 4 people but easy to make less

Tinned fruit can be used but the contrast of fresh fruit and fudge sauce is particularly delicious.

4 ripe peaches or pears
A little butter

Sauce
225 g/8 oz light soft brown sugar
15 g/½ oz butter
2 tablespoons milk

1. Start with sauce. Put sugar, butter and milk in a heavy pan. Stir over low heat to dissolve sugar.
2. Bring to boil and boil to soft ball stage, 235°F, 114°C. This stage is reached when dribbles of sauce dropped in some cold water set to a soft ball, not crisp. Stir frequently.
3. Peel, stone and halve the peaches. For pears, use soft ripe fruit, peel, quarter and core.
4. Place fruit cut side down in a buttered heat-proof dish.
5. Pour hot sauce over the fruit. Cool and serve really chilled.

FRESH FRUIT WITH ORANGE CREAM

For 4 people

1 small punnet raspberries or strawberries, or 2 large bananas*
A 150 g/5 fl oz carton of double cream
1 dessertspoon castor sugar
1 large orange
½ lemon

1. Divide raspberries or strawberries between 4 small bowls or sundae glasses. If using bananas, follow instructions below to keep them from going brown, then slice and divide between 4 bowls.
2. Beat cream and sugar until thick.
3. Grate zest only from orange and half lemon. Squeeze juice from half lemon.
4. Peel orange and roughly chop flesh, catching the juice.
5. Fold orange, juices and zest into the cream.
6. Spoon cream mixture on top of the fruit in the bowls.
7. Chill before serving.

Elizabeth Mickery
Pudsey, West Yorkshire

*To keep sliced bananas from going brown

Put unpeeled bananas in cold water for 5 to 10 minutes. They may then be peeled, sliced and kept for at least 4 hours without going brown.

Miss M. Owen
Elworth, Cheshire

LEMON DELIGHT

Another recipe from the West Sussex Federation of Women's Institutes' book 'Come Cooking Again'. A truly delightful sweet, set off by the egg-custard which accompanies it.

450 ml/¾ pint water
25 g/1 oz cornflour
150 g/5 oz sugar
Grated rind and strained juice of 2 lemons
2 egg-whites

Custard

2 egg-yolks
1 tablespoon sugar
300 ml/½ pint milk

1. Bring to the boil all but 2 tablespoons of the water. Remove from heat.
2. Mix cornflour with remaining water, stir it into boiled water, return to heat. Stir as it thickens and boil for 1 minute.

3. Stir in sugar until dissolved. Allow to cool a little and add lemon rind and juice.
4. Whisk egg-whites until really firm. Fold into mixture. Pour into a dish, leave to set in a cool place or refrigerator.
5. Make custard by mixing egg-yolks, sugar and milk. Pour into a saucepan and heat gently, stirring as it thickens. Do not let it boil.

Mrs Janice Langley
Shoreham-by-Sea, West Sussex

LEMON SOLID

An old family recipe.

Rind and juice of 2 lemons
175 g/6 oz castor sugar
600 ml/1 pint milk
15 g/½ oz gelatine

1. Finely grate rind from the lemons and squeeze the juice.
2. Put lemon rind into a basin with sugar and half of the milk.
3. Heat remaining milk with the gelatine, stirring continuously until gelatine is dissolved. Be very careful not to boil it.
4. Mix heated milk with cold milk mixture, stirring to dissolve sugar.
5. Add lemon juice. Don't be alarmed if milk appears to curdle.
6. Pour into a wet jelly mould and leave to set in a cold larder for about 12 hours or 5 hours in refrigerator.
7. Turn pudding out of mould. It should have separated with a clear jelly at top and 'curds' at bottom.

Mrs Marion Wightman
Piddletrenthide, Dorset

MANGO MOUSSE

For 6 people

2 tablespoons water
2 heaped teaspoons gelatine
340 ml/12 fl oz tinned evaporated milk, chilled in refrigerator
2 tablespoons sugar

A 454 g/16 oz tin of 'Kissan'
mango pulp*

*Can be bought from oriental food
shops.

1. Measure water into a cup. Sprinkle
in gelatine. Stand cup in hot water to
dissolve gelatine, stirring once to
combine.
2. Whisk the chilled evaporated milk.
Gradually add sugar. Whisk in the
gelatine.
3. Fold in the mango pulp and set in a
covered mould in refrigerator for 3
hours.

This dish may be decorated with
whipped cream and mango slices.

Priya Wickramasinghe
Cardiff

PORT AND PRUNES

*A party dessert for 15 people but
easy to make less*

Can be made with less expensive wine
than port.

Remember to start the day before, or
even sooner, as it improves with
keeping. A liquidiser is useful.

450 g/1 lb dried prunes
175 to 225 ml/6 to 8 fl oz ruby
port, sweet sherry or mature
home-made dessert wine
284 ml/½ pint double cream
50 g/2 oz castor sugar

1. The day before, soak prunes in
water to cover.
2. Next day simmer prunes gently
until very soft. Leave to cool. Drain.
3. Remove stones and liquidise prunes
with 175 ml/6 fl oz port to produce a
very thick purée. Add more port if
necessary.
4. Whisk cream with sugar until it is
as thick as purée.
5. Fold purée into cream and spoon
into tiny glasses.

Serve with crisp biscuits such as
Shortcake Biscuits (*see page 158*) or
Shortbread Biscuits (*see page 157*).

A SYLLABUB FROM KENT

For 4 people

2 egg-whites
50 to 75 g/2 to 3 oz castor sugar
Juice of ½ large lemon
150 ml/¼ pint white wine
150 ml/¼ pint double cream,
whipped till thick

1. Beat egg-whites until stiff and
frothy.
2. Beat in sugar
3. Add lemon juice and wine.
4. Beat in the thickly-whipped cream.
5. Pour the thick curdy mixture into
little glass dishes and put in a cool
place or refrigerator for 4 to 5 hours so
that flavours blend.

Mrs Jill Marshall
Hythe, Kent

ICE-CREAM

A delicious variation on Anne
Wallace's recipe printed in
Farmhouse Kitchen II, giving a
subtle caramel flavour and a creamy
appearance.

2 eggs, separated
50 g/2 oz light soft brown sugar
142 ml/5 fl oz double cream

1. Whisk egg-whites until stiff, add
sugar and whisk again.
2. Whip cream till stiff.
3. Whisk egg-yolks.
4. Combine all three and whisk
together.
5. Pour straight into a plastic food box
or margarine carton, put on lid and
freeze.

Two ideas for bought ice-cream

Ice-cream Snowball
2 tablespoons sultanas
1 tablespoon currants
1 tablespoon rum, sherry or
orange juice
1 litre/1¾ pint firm vanilla ice-
cream, not the whipped or 'soft'
variety
125 g/4 oz glacé cherries, cut
small

1 tablespoon chopped walnuts

To decorate: 1 teaspoon of the chopped cherries, angelica, marzipan, *or*, whipped double cream for piping

1. Soak sultanas and currants in rum, sherry or orange-juice for 2 hours. Then drain.
2. Allow ice-cream to soften slightly.
3. Reserve 1 teaspoon of the chopped cherries for decorating. Then mix all ingredients together.
4. Pack this mixture into two round pudding basins. (Heat-proof pyrex basins are ideal.) Make sure mixture comes to the very brim of the basins. Any that is left can be frozen separately.
5. Press the two bowls together to form a ball, and freeze until solid.
6. Prepare decorations, cherries and angelica. Or marzipan to look like holly. Or whipped cream in a piping bag.
7. Just before serving, carefully remove basins with the aid of hot damp cloths or a bowl of warm water. Set the snowball on a chilled dish and decorate with the 'holly', or pipe rosettes of cream all over.

Once decorated, the snowball could be returned to freezer, but remember to take it out about 10 minutes before serving so that cream is not too icy.

Ice-cream Surprises

For this you need 10 small washed yoghurt cartons.

1 litre/1¾ pint firm vanilla or strawberry ice-cream, not whipped or 'soft' variety
About 1 dozen small meringues
1 dozen grapes
225 g/8 oz toasted* desiccated coconut

*To toast coconut: spread it in grill pan and toast under moderate heat, stirring often until it is evenly-golden. Take care, it burns easily.

1. Allow ice-cream to soften a little. Then fill each carton about ¾ full. Return to freezer.
2. Meanwhile, crumble the meringues and remove pips from grapes.

3. When cartons of ice-cream have frozen hard, take them out one at a time. Scoop out a cavity in the middle of each and fill with one grape and crumbled meringue. Seal up again with a dollop of ice-cream and return to freezer.
4. When frozen again, remove ice-cream from cartons and roll each one in toasted coconut, shaping a rough ball at same time. Either wrap each ball in foil and return to freezer, or open-freeze on a tray and pack in a polythene bag until required.

FUDGE SAUCE

For plain ice-cream.

50 g/2 oz butter
50 g/2 oz granulated sugar
75 g/3 oz soft brown sugar
150 g/5 oz golden syrup

Combine ingredients in a pan and stir over low heat until all the sugar grains have dissolved.

MELBA SAUCE

For puddings or ice-cream.

This sauce freezes well.

Raspberries, fresh or frozen
Icing sugar

1. Sieve uncooked raspberries to make a purée.
2. Sift icing sugar and beat it into purée, one teaspoon at a time, until sauce is sufficiently sweet.

Anne Wallace
Stewarton, Ayrshire

QUICK CHOCOLATE SAUCE

50 g/2 oz sugar
65 ml/2½ fl oz water
50 g/2 oz dark cooking chocolate
A small nut of butter

1. Dissolve sugar in water over low heat. Then boil for 3 minutes.
2. Add chocolate broken in pieces, stir until it is melted and simmer sauce for 1 minute.
3. Stir in butter.

Serve hot or cold.

Anne Wallace
Stewarton, Ayrshire

MINT PARFAIT

150 g/5 oz castor sugar
150 ml/¼ pint water
2 egg-whites
A pinch of salt
45 ml/3 tablespoons Crème de Menthe
275 ml/½ pint double cream, whipped to soft-peaks

Toppings

Grated chocolate or sugared mint leaves* or Quick Chocolate Sauce (see above)

1. Dissolve sugar in water over a low heat. Do not let it boil until sugar is dissolved. Then, using a sugar thermometer if you have one, boil to 238°F, 110°C. If you have not got a thermometer, the syrup is boiled when a little forms a very soft ball when tested in a cup of cold water.
2. Whisk egg-whites with salt until stiff but not dry. While still whisking, pour on boiling syrup in a steady stream and keep on whisking until it has cooled.
3. Mix in Crème de Menthe, then fold in cream.
4. Put into a covered plastic box and freeze.

Serve scoops of the parfait sprinkled with grated plain chocolate, or a topping of your choice.

*Sugared mint leaves

Paint fresh mint leaves with lightly-beaten egg-white. Coat well with castor sugar. Allow to dry in a warm room.

Anne Wallace
Stewarton, Ayrshire

ORANGE AND LEMON ICE

A generous 150 ml/5 fl oz water
200 g/7 oz granulated sugar
Grated rind of 1 lemon
Strained juice of 2 oranges and 2 lemons

1. Put water in a pan and bring to the boil. Reduce heat. Add sugar and stir to dissolve.
2. Bring to boil. Add lemon rind and leave to cool and infuse for 2 hours.
3. Add fruit juice. Stir well.
4. Pour into a shallow container and put into freezer.
5. When almost frozen—i.e., soft in middle and hard around edges, turn it out into a bowl and whisk very well. It will whisk up into almost a froth of snow.
6. Rinse and dry the container and pour in the mixture. Cover lightly with a lid or foil and freeze until required.
7. To serve, scoop into glass dishes or fill hollowed out orange or lemon shells.

PEANUT BRITTLE GÂTEAU

For this you need 1 fatless sponge, about 20 cm/8 inches across and 6 to 7 cm/2½ to 3 inches deep (see page 150)
125 g/4 oz peanut brittle
A 142 ml/5 fl oz carton double cream
120 ml/4 fl oz rum
120 ml/4 fl oz water

1. Crush peanut brittle. The best way to do this is to put it inside 2 polythene bags and knock it with a hammer. Do not crush it too fine because the beauty of this gâteau is the crunchy texture of the brittle with the soft rum and cream centre.
2. Whip cream until thick.
3. Mix rum and water.
4. Cut sponge into 2 layers. Lay bottom half on a serving plate, pour about half of the rum and water mix

over the sponge. Then spread about half of the whipped cream over this.

5. Lay top half of sponge over the cream and drench this with the rest of the rum and water.

6. Cover top and sides with cream.

7. Sprinkle and pat the crushed peanut brittle over the top and sides of the gâteau. Chill and serve.

GRACE'S CHOCOLATE FANCY

For this you need 1 chocolate fatless sponge, about 20 cm/8 inches across and about 7·5 cm/3 inches deep (*see page 150*)

A 110 g/4 oz jar of maraschino cherries in syrup
120 ml/4 fl oz sherry
120 ml/4 fl oz water
300 ml/½ pint double cream, whipped
2 tablespoons of chocolate mousse, or a 105 ml/3·7 fl oz carton of bought mousse

Chocolate curls decoration

50 g/2 oz top-quality plain eating chocolate
2 teaspoons salad oil

1. First start preparing chocolate for decorating. Heat a small empty bowl in a moderate oven, Gas 4, 350°F, 180°C. Take it out and put into it the chocolate broken into small pieces.

2. Add oil and stir gently until dissolved.

3. Spread this mixture very thinly over a hard surface and leave to set in a cool place. Ideally a marble slab should be used but you can use a formica surface, such as a large formica chopping board.

4. Now drain syrup from cherries and mix it with sherry and water.

5. Cut each cherry in two.

6. Slice sponge into 3 layers. Place bottom layer on a large serving plate.

7. Use one third of sherry mixture to pour over bottom layer of sponge. Spread with 2 tablespoons of the whipped cream and 1 tablespoon chocolate mousse. Top this with half of the cherries.

8. Put middle slice of sponge in position and repeat the above process with sherry mixture, cream, mousse and cherries.

9. Put on top layer of sponge. Pour over remaining sherry mixture. Press sponge down gently.

10. Now cover sides and top with rest of cream. Set gâteau aside to firm up in a cool place or refrigerator.

11. Make chocolate curls. Draw a sharp knife, held at an angle, across the board making curls of chocolate. Drop curls and broken bits of chocolate all over the gâteau. Chill and serve.

Can be frozen.

Chapter 9

Yeast Cookery, Teabreads and Scones

SHORT TIME BREAD

White

15 g/½ oz fresh yeast, 7 g/¼ oz dried
A 25 mg Vitamin C tablet (buy from chemist, also called ascorbic acid)
½ teaspoon sugar
About 150 ml/¼ pint warm water
225 g/8 oz strong plain flour
½ teaspoon salt
15 g/½ oz margarine

Wholewheat or Brown

Use 225 g/8 oz wholewheat flour, or half wholewheat and half white

1. Blend together the yeast, crushed Vitamin C tablet and half of the water. If using dried yeast, add sugar also and wait until it froths up before using.
2. Sieve flour and salt, rub in margarine.
3. Pour yeast liquid into dry ingredients and mix well.
4. Add sufficient warm water to make a soft, beatable dough.
5. Beat dough until the bowl is clean.
6. Turn out on to a lightly-floured board and knead until smooth, 10 minutes.
7. Rest dough for five minutes, covered lightly.
8. Shape into bread buns or cottage loaf, twist or plait and put on a greased baking tray. Cover with a damp cloth or greased polythene, and leave in a warm place to rise until doubled in size.
9. Bake near top of a hot oven, Gas 7, 425°F, 220°C.

Bread buns take 10 to 12 minutes. Loaves take 25 to 30 minutes.

Pizza

The above quantity of dough will make 4 pizza bases 18 to 20 cm/7 to 8 inches in diameter.

Filling

For 1 pizza, 2 people

¼ to 1 tin anchovy fillets
50 g/2 oz chopped bacon
1 teaspoon oil or melted butter
25 g/1 oz grated cheese
25 g/1 oz sliced mushrooms
2 sliced tomatoes
A large pinch of basil
Black olives (optional) or pickled prunes (*see page 173*)

To garnish: chopped parsley

1. If you find the flavour of anchovies rather too strong, drain them and soak in milk for about half an hour.
2. Fry bacon lightly.
3. Roll out a piece of dough to 7 mm/¼ inch thick and 18 to 20 cm/7 to 8 inches in diameter.
4. Place it on a well-greased tin. Brush it over with oil or butter.
5. Sprinkle top of dough with cheese, mushrooms and bacon. Finish with tomatoes and basil.
6. Arrange drained anchovies in a lattice design on top. Place olives in the spaces.
7. Cover lightly and leave aside to rise, or until the pizza dough has doubled in size or puffed up well.
8. Bake near top of a hot oven, Gas 7, 425°F, 220°C, for 20 to 30 minutes, reducing heat to moderately hot, Gas 5, 375°F, 190°C, after 15 minutes if browning too quickly.
9. Garnish with chopped parsley.

Wholewheat Tomato Pizza

For 4 people

25 g/1 oz margarine or 1 tablespoon oil
450 g/1 lb onions, chopped
2 cloves of garlic, crushed
Two 400 g/14 oz tins of tomatoes
½ teaspoon oregano
Salt and freshly-ground black pepper
A pinch of sugar
75 g/3 oz finely-grated cheese

To garnish: 2 or 3 mushrooms, or fine slices of green and red pepper

1. Heat margarine or oil and fry onion and garlic until softening.
2. Add tomatoes, oregano, salt, pepper and sugar and cook gently for about 20 minutes until thick.

3. Meanwhile, roll out enough dough to fit a greased Swiss roll tin. Prick all over with a fork. Cover with a cloth and let it rise until puffy.

4. Bake the pizza base near top of a hot oven, Gas 7, 425°F, 220°C, for 5 minutes. Then remove from oven and reduce heat to moderate, Gas 4, 350°F, 180°C.

5. Spread tomato mixture over the hot pizza base. Sprinkle cheese on top and decorate with mushroom slices or rings of pepper.

6. Return to oven near top and bake for 20 minutes until cheese is melted and browning.

Sweet Pears and Cheese Pizza

Eaten hot or cold.

For 3 or 4 people

3 dessert pears
Rind and juice of ½ lemon
50 g/2 oz Lancashire, Cheshire or Mozzarella cheese, grated
25 g/1 oz plain cooking chocolate, grated
50 g/2 oz chopped walnuts
25 g/1 oz butter

1. Peel and core pears and cut into slices, about 3 slices to each quarter. Dip into lemon juice to prevent browning.

2. Roll out dough about 7 mm/¼ inch thick and 18 to 20 cm/7 to 8 inches in diameter.

3. Arrange slices of pear on the dough leaving a 1 cm/½ inch border all round.

4. Scatter on the lemon rind. Cover pears with cheese, sprinkle on chocolate and chopped walnuts. Dot with butter.

5. Cover lightly and leave aside in a warm place to rise.

6. Bake near top of a very hot oven for 5 minutes, Gas 8, 450°F, 230°C, then lower temperature to Gas 7, 425°F, 220°C and bake for about 15 minutes more, or until pizza dough is brown.

PITTA BREAD

2 teaspoons dried yeast
A pinch of sugar

300 ml/½ pint warm water
1 teaspoon salt
1½ tablespoons oil
400 g/14 oz strong plain flour, sifted

1. In a large mixing bowl, dissolve yeast and sugar in 3 tablespoons of the warm water. Let it stand for 10 minutes in a warm place until frothy on top.

2. Add rest of water, salt and oil.

3. Stir 100 g/4 oz flour at a time into yeast mixture, forming a sticky dough. If it is too sticky to work when all flour is used, add a little more flour.

4. Transfer dough to lightly-floured board and knead until smooth, about 10 minutes.

5. Shape dough into a ball and coat lightly with oil. Return it to bowl. Cover and let it rise in a warm place until doubled in bulk, about 1½ hours.

6. Punch dough down and form 6 or 7 balls. On a lightly-floured board, roll or press out the dough with the hands into 15 cm/6 inch circles that are 7 mm/¼ inch thick. Dust lightly with flour.

7. Put on to lightly-oiled baking sheets, cover and allow to rise again for 15 minutes.

8. Preheat oven to very hot, Gas 8, 450°F, 230°C.

9. Bake for 8 to 10 minutes. Wrap the bread in foil immediately after removing from oven to preserve moistness.

Serve hot or reheated under grill.

Freeze well. Reheat from frozen under grill.

Elizabeth Mickery
Pudsey, Yorkshire

KENTISH HUFFKINS

These are plain, white, flat yeast cakes, traditionally baked with a dimple in the middle.

Makes 10

15 g/½ oz fresh yeast or 1½ teaspoons dried yeast
1 teaspoon castor sugar

300 ml/½ pint warm milk and
water mixed
450 g/1 lb strong plain white
flour
¼ teaspoon salt
25 g/1 oz lard

1. Mix yeast and sugar into warmed
milk and water. If using dried yeast,
whisk it in with a fork so that
granules dissolve without clogging
together. Leave in a warm place for 5
minutes until yeast is active and
frothy.
2. Mix flour and salt in a bowl. Rub in
lard.
3. Add yeast mixture. Mix to a pliable
dough and turn out on to a floured
board.
4. Knead well until dough is no longer
sticky, and is smooth and shiny, about
10 minutes.
5. Lightly grease bowl and put in the
dough. Cover with a cloth or greased
polythene. Keep in a warm place, away
from draughts, so that dough will rise
(or 'prove') until doubled in size.
6. Turn on to a floured board. Knead
lightly to let out air and to make
dough pliable again.
7. Divide this dough into 10 equal
pieces.
8. Shape into flat oval cakes about 1·2
cm/½ inch thick. It is best to do this by
forming a roll first and then flattening
to an oval with rolling pin.
9. Place well apart on greased baking
trays and press a floured finger into
the centre of each cake. Cover trays
and leave to 'prove' until doubled in
size.
10. Bake near top of a very hot oven,
Gas 8, 450°F, 230°C, for 15 to 20
minutes.
11. Transfer to a wire rack.

Eat hot or cold, split and buttered.

Mrs Jill Marshall
Hythe, Kent

CURRANT LOAF

15 g/½ oz fresh yeast or 7 g/¼ oz
dried
300 ml/½ pint warm milk

25 g/1 oz castor sugar
450 g/1 lb strong plain white
flour
1 teaspoon salt
1 level teaspoon cinnamon
25 g/1 oz margarine
125 g/4 oz washed and dried
currants
Beaten egg

1. Blend the yeast into the warm milk.
If using dried yeast, add 1 teaspoon of
the sugar and wait until it froths up
before using.
2. Sift together flour, salt and
cinnamon.
3. Add sugar and rub in fat.
4. Stir in yeast and milk and mix to a
soft dough.
5. Turn on to a floured board and
knead until smooth.
6. Cover and leave to rise until
doubled in size, about 1 hour.
7. Work the currants into the risen
dough until evenly distributed.
8. Form into loaf shape and place in a
greased 1 kg/2 lb loaf tin.
9. Brush the loaf with beaten egg.
Cover and leave to 'prove' again,
about 1 hour, until well-risen and
puffy.
10. Bake near top of a moderately hot
oven, Gas 6, 400°F, 200°C, until golden
brown, about 50 minutes.
11. Cool on a wire rack.

Freezes well.

SWEDISH TEA RING

225 g/8 oz strong plain flour
¼ teaspoon salt
50 g/2 oz margarine
40 g/1½ oz sugar
15 g/½ oz fresh yeast or 7 g/¼ oz
dried
150 ml/¼ pint warm milk and
water mixed
1 beaten egg

Marzipan filling

40 g/1½ oz ground almonds
40 g/1½ oz castor sugar
Beaten egg

Decoration

A little glacé icing
4 glacé cherries, chopped
Angelica, chopped
25 g/1 oz chopped walnuts

1. Sieve flour and salt, rub in margarine, add sugar, except for one level teaspoonful.
2. In a small jug work together the yeast and the level teaspoon of sugar until it is liquid. Add a little of the warm milk and water mixture to the jug. If using dried yeast, combine yeast, sugar and enough liquid to dissolve and leave jug in a warm place to froth up.
3. Make a well in the centre of the flour and pour in the yeast liquid. If using fresh yeast, leave it to become frothy, about 10 to 15 minutes. If using dried yeast, it is better to wait until you are certain it is active before adding to flour.
4. Add beaten egg and enough of the liquid to make a soft dough.
5. Turn out and knead well until the dough is smooth and elastic, about 10 minutes. Leave aside in a warm place to rise for about 1 hour until doubled in size.
6. Roll out dough to a rectangle 30 by 10 cm/12 by 4 inches.
7. Make up almond paste by mixing ground almonds and castor sugar with just enough egg to bind. Form it into a roll about 30 cm/12 inches long.
8. Lay the roll of paste on the dough and roll up.
9. Form it into a ring on a greased baking tray and leave aside, covered lightly, to rise again until doubled in size.
10. Bake above middle of a hot oven, Gas 7, 425°F, 220°C, for 20 to 25 minutes.
11. Remove it on to a wire rack to cool.
12. When cold, spread with a little glacé icing and scatter chopped cherries, angelica and nuts on top while icing is wet.

LOAF CAKE
Teisen Dorth

A Glamorgan recipe for a rich fruit loaf. Can be made with white or wholewheat flour or a mixture of wholewheat and white. With wholewheat the loaf will not be as light as with white.

15 g/½ oz fresh yeast, or 2 teaspoons dried yeast
300 ml/½ pint lukewarm milk
450 g/1 lb plain flour
A pinch of salt
¼ teaspoon mixed spice
65 g/2½ oz butter or lard
65 g/2½ oz soft brown sugar
150 g/5 oz sultanas
150 g/5 oz currants
65 g/2½ oz raisins
25 g/1 oz candied peel
1 beaten egg

1. Mix yeast with a little of the warm milk and leave in a warm place for 5 minutes. If using dried yeast, add a teaspoon of the sugar also, wait until it is active and frothy before using.
2. Put flour, salt and spice into a bowl and rub in fat.
3. Mix in rest of dry ingredients.
4. Make a well in centre, add yeast mixture, well-beaten egg and enough warm milk to make a soft dough. Mix and then knead in basin for 5 minutes.
5. Grease the mixing bowl. Put dough in it, cover with greased polythene or a damp cloth and leave it in a really warm place to rise for about 1½ hours, until it has doubled in size.
6. Knead dough again to knock out the bubbles.
7. Shape and place in a well-greased 1 kg/2 lb loaf tin. Cover again and leave 20 minutes in a really warm place to rise again. Dough should rise well above top of tin.
8. Bake just above middle of a hot oven, Gas 7, 425°F, 220°C, for 20 minutes. Then reduce heat to warm, Gas 3, 325°F, 160°C, for 45 minutes more.
9. Turn loaf out on to a wire rack immediately to cool.
Freezes well.

Mrs Doreen Owen
Llanwenarth Citra W.I., Gwent

FRIED INDIAN WHOLEWHEAT FLOUR BREAD

These are known as puris. They are usually eaten with vegetables, or at the start of a meal, and are a great favourite among children and adults alike.

This quantity makes 12 or 13

They go well with Cauliflower Bhaji (*see page 74*), Curried Bhindi (*see page 73*) and Onion Salad (*see page 70*).

175 g/6 oz wholewheat flour
175 g/6 oz plain white flour
1½ teaspoons salt
2 teaspoons oil
150 to 175 ml/5 to 6 fl oz tepid water
Oil for deep frying

1. In a bowl mix flours, salt, 2 teaspoons oil and sufficient water to form a soft pliable dough.
2. Knead the dough thoroughly and leave covered at room temperature for about 1 hour.
3. Roll out one third of the dough at a time into a large pancake, less than 7 mm/¼ inch thick. Cut circles about 6 to 8 cm/2½ to 3 inches in diameter, using a pastry cutter or wine glass.
4. The success of a puri is in its cooking. The oil should be heated until it begins to smoke, and the puris should be carefully immersed one at a time.
5. After about 6 seconds in the hot oil the puri will begin to surface. Using a frying spoon, gently pat it down to keep it submerged in the hot oil until it puffs up.
6. Turn it over and allow it to cook for a couple of seconds more. This whole frying process should take about 15 to 20 seconds per puri.

Priya Wickramasinghe
Cardiff

IRISH SODA BREADS

The mixing of soda bread is done lightly and quickly, like scones. This ensures light fluffy results.
Freezes well, up to 6 months.

Brown
275 g/10 oz wholewheat flour
175 g/6 oz strong plain white flour
2 teaspoons sugar (optional but not traditional)
1 teaspoon bicarbonate of soda
1 teaspoon salt
1 teaspoon cream of tartar*
About 300 ml/½ pint milk*
*It is usually made with sour milk which makes its own contribution to the rising. If fresh milk is used then add cream of tartar, but not otherwise.

1. Put wholewheat flour in a large bowl and sieve in all the other dry ingredients.
2. Mix to a soft dough with the milk, adding extra if required. The dough should be slack but not wet.
3. With floured hands knead until smooth, then flatten the dough into a circle about 3·5 cm/1½ inches thick. Put on a greased baking tin, score a large cross over the top.
4. Bake in a moderatley hot oven, Gas 5, 375°F, 190°C, for about 40 minutes. The bread should feel light when fully cooked.
Eat fresh.

Mrs June Hodgson
Loch Corrib, Ireland

Using Granary Flour
450 g/1 lb granary flour
225 g/8 oz strong plain white flour, or 175 g/6 oz of this plus 50 g/2 oz bran
1 teaspoon bicarbonate of soda
1 teaspoon cream of tartar
1 teaspoon salt
2 teaspoons sugar
Just under 600 ml/1 pint milk or milk and water mixed

1. Put granary flour in a large bowl. Sieve in white flour, bicarbonate of soda, cream of tartar and salt. Add bran, if used.

2. Now gradually mix with milk until dough is soft but not wet.
3. Turn out on to a floured board and knead fairly quickly until smooth.
4. Flatten the dough into a large circle about 3·5 cm/1½ inches thick. Place it on a greased baking tin. Score over the top a large cross (this ensures even distribution of heat).
5. Bake in a moderately hot oven, Gas 5, 375°F, 190°C, for about 50 to 60 minutes. Test with a skewer to check that it is fully cooked. The skewer will come out clean if the bread is ready.

BANANA LOAF

Sliced and thinly-buttered, this is delicious. A good use for over-ripe bananas.

Freezes well packed in a polythene bag with all air excluded.

2 ripe bananas
50 g/2 oz margarine
150 g/5 oz castor sugar
2 eggs
225 g/8 oz self-raising flour*
A pinch of salt

*If you prefer wholewheat flour this works with half wholewheat and half white. If you cannot buy self-raising wholewheat, add ½ teaspoon baking powder.

1. Mash bananas.
2. Cream margarine and sugar.
3. Beat in eggs.
4. Add flour, salt and banana and mix well.
5. Put in a greased and floured 675 g/ 1½ lb loaf tin, or slightly larger.
6. Bake in middle of a moderately hot oven, Gas 5, 375°F, 190°C, for about 1 hour, until loaf is golden brown, springy to touch and shrinking slightly from sides of tin.
7. Turn loaf out on to a wire rack to cool.

Anne Wallace
Stewarton, Ayrshire

GRANDMA BASTON'S FRUIT BREAD

This quantity makes 3 large loaves but easy to make one third or two thirds of this quantity.

They keep well and freeze well.

350 g/12 oz currants
350 g/12 oz raisins
225 g/8 oz sultanas
900 g/2 lb plain white flour
1 dessertspoon baking powder
A pinch of salt
350 g/12 oz butter or margarine
450 g/1 lb moist brown sugar
3 beaten eggs
About 150 ml/¼ pint milk
½ teaspoon bicarbonate of soda
50 g/2 oz mixed peel, grated or fine-chopped
50 g/2 oz glacé cherries, chopped

1. The day before baking put currants, raisins and sultanas in a basin of hot water to cover. Leave to steep for 2 or 3 hours.
2. Then squeeze out excess moisture and spread fruit in a large baking tin. Put it to dry in a warm place, stirring about a bit from time to time.
3. Sieve flour, baking powder and salt into a large bowl.
4. Rub in fat and add sugar.
5. Mix in eggs and enough milk to achieve a fairly stiff mixture. Continue mixing until consistency is smooth.
6. Mix bicarbonate of soda with 1 tablespoon milk and add.
7. Lastly, add fruit, peel and cherries. Stir well.
8. Grease three 1 kg/2 lb loaf tins and line the bottoms with greaseproof paper. Divide the mixture between them.
9. Bake below middle of a moderate oven, Gas 4, 350°F, 180°C, for 2¼ to 3 hours until well-risen and firm to the touch.

Mrs Patricia Chantry
Hook, Goole, N. Humberside

143

MALTED WHOLEWHEAT TEABREAD

350 g/12 oz wholewheat flour
2 level teaspoons baking powder
½ level teaspoon salt
50 g/2 oz muscovado sugar
50 g/2 oz sultanas
50 g/2 oz dates
2 rounded tablespoons malt extract
50 g/2 oz butter or margarine
150 ml/¼ pint plus 1 tablespoon milk
2 beaten eggs

1. Mix flour, baking powder and salt in a large bowl.
2. Add sugar and sultanas.
3. Chop the dates and mix in.
4. Gently heat malt and butter or margarine together until fat has just melted.
5. Add milk to beaten eggs.
6. Combine malt mixture with egg and milk mixture and stir into dry ingredients.
7. Mix together to form a soft dough.
8. Turn mixture into a greased 1 kg/ 2 lb loaf tin, or into two greased 450 g/ 1 lb tins. Level the surface of the mixture.
9. Bake in a warm oven, Gas 3, 325°F, 160°C, for 1 hour. Then turn out to cool on a wire rack.

Wrap in foil and keep one day before eating and the bread will be nice and moist. Freezes well.

Serve sliced and buttered.

MUFFINS

Made on a girdle or griddle or in a heavy frying pan.

125 g/4 oz plain white flour or half wholewheat and half white
½ teaspoon cream of tartar
¼ teaspoon bicarbonate of soda
15 g/½ oz sugar
20 g/¾ oz melted butter or margarine
2 teaspoons of beaten egg

About 4 tablespoons milk
A knob of suet to grease girdle, or a *very* little lard

1. Mix dry ingredients, sifting in cream of tartar and bicarbonate of soda.
2. Mix in butter, egg and enough milk to make a soft dough.
3. Using a floured board, roll out to 1 cm/½ inch thick. Cut rounds.
4. Heat girdle, grease lightly and cook muffins for 3 to 4 minutes each side until nicely golden brown.

Good to eat hot or cold.

Freeze well.

OATMEAL SCONES

50 g/2 oz medium oatmeal
50 g/2 oz plain wholewheat or white flour
A pinch of salt
1 teaspoon soft brown sugar (or more, to taste)
½ teaspoon cream of tartar
¼ teaspoon bicarbonate of soda
15 g/½ oz dripping or bacon fat
About 3 tablespoons milk, to mix

1. Put oatmeal, wholewheat flour, salt and sugar in a bowl.
2. Sift in cream of tartar and bicarbonate of soda to be sure there are no lumps.
3. Rub in fat.
4. Mix to a soft dough with milk.
5. Using a floured board, roll out about 7 mm/¼ inch thick and cut rounds.
6. Cook on a hot, lightly-greased girdle or heavy frying pan for about 4 minutes each side. Cool in a towel.

SAVOURY DROP SCONES OR PANCAKES

Can be made on a girdle, griddle, bakestone or hot-plate—whatever name you give it—or in a heavy frying pan.

225 g/8 oz plain white or whole-wheat flour
1 teaspoon cream of tartar
½ teaspoon bicarbonate of soda
A pinch of salt
1 dessertspoon finely-chopped onion
1 egg
About 150 ml/5 fl oz milk

To grease girdle: a knob of beef suet or a very little lard or margarine

1. Put flour in a bowl. Sieve in cream of tartar, bicarbonate of soda and salt. Mix in chopped onion.
2. Mix to a thick pouring batter with egg and milk.
3. Heat girdle and grease it if necessary.
4. Drop spoonfuls of batter on girdle. When bubbles appear, turn over and cook other side.
5. Cool scones in a towel. This stops them drying out.

Freeze well.

WELSH CAKES

Makes 40 to 50, but they freeze well

Or you can make half quantity, using 1 small egg and very little milk.

These are cooked on a bakestone, as it is known in Wales, or a girdle, as used in Scotland. A heavy-based frying pan gives best results if you have neither of these.

450 g/1 lb self-raising flour
A pinch of salt
125 g/4 oz lard
125 g/4 oz margarine
175 g/6 oz granulated sugar
50 g/2 oz currants
1 beaten egg
About 3 tablespoons milk
A little extra lard to grease pan

1. Sift flour and salt into a basin.
2. Rub in lard and margarine.
3. Add sugar and currants.
4. Mix to the consistency of pastry dough with beaten egg and milk.

145

5. Roll out on a floured board to approximately 7 mm/¼ inch thick. Cut with a 6·5 cm/2½ inch plain scone cutter.

6. Heat bakestone, girdle or heavy frying pan and grease it lightly with lard. It is wise to test heat by cooking one cake on its own. If it is too hot, cakes burn before inside is cooked. Cook cakes on both sides until just golden. Grease pan very lightly between batches.

7. Put on wire rack to cool. Store in a tin or plastic box.

Traditionally eaten cold, but they are hard to resist straight from the pan, especially when children are about. They are never buttered.

Mrs Beryl Hawkins
Little Mill W.I., Gwent

POTATO SCONES

Enough for 4 people

Freeze well.

Cooked on a girdle or griddle or heavy frying pan.

15 g/½ oz melted butter or margarine
A pinch of salt
225 g/8 oz cold mashed potato (no lumps)
About 50 g/2 oz plain flour, white or wholewheat

1. Add melted butter or margarine and salt to mashed potatoes.

2. Mix in flour gradually until a working dough is produced.

3. Roll out very thinly. Cut rounds, prick well with a fork.

4. Use a knob of beef suet to grease the girdle lightly.

5. Cook scones on hot girdle for about 3 minutes each side.

6. Cool in a towel.

Eat fresh with butter. Excellent with bacon. Fry in bacon fat with the bacon.

SCONE DROPS

Makes 12 to 15

200 g/7 oz self-raising flour
25 g/1 oz porridge oats
125 g/4 oz margarine
75 g/3 oz sugar
50 g/3 oz mixed dried fruit
6 glacé cherries, chopped
1 large beaten egg
A little milk

1. Mix flour and oats in a bowl.

2. Rub in margarine.

3. Add sugar, dried fruit and cherries.

4. Mix in the beaten egg, using a fork. Add a dessertspoon of milk if too stiff to mix.

5. Put rough heaps on a greased baking sheet.

6. Bake near top of a moderately hot oven, Gas 5, 375°F, 190°C, for 10 to 15 minutes.

Nice hot or cold. Freeze and reheat well.

Margaret Heywood
Todmorden, Yorkshire

WHOLEWHEAT SCONES

175 g/6 oz wholewheat flour
50 g/2 oz plain flour
1 teaspoon cream of tartar
½ teaspoon bicarbonate of soda
¼ teaspoon salt
50 g/2 oz dark brown sugar, try muscovado
1½ tablespoons safflower or sun-flower oil
1 egg
75 to 100 ml/3 to 4 fl oz milk

1. Mix dry ingredients, sifting cream of tartar and bicarbonate of soda with plain flour and salt.

2. Beat oil, egg and milk together.

3. Mix this into the dry ingredients adding a little more milk if necessary, sufficient to make a soft elastic dough.

4. Turn dough on to a floured board and knead it lightly.

5. Roll out just over 2 cm/1 inch thick. Cut into rounds. Place the scones on lightly-greased baking sheets.

6. Bake in a very hot oven, Gas 8, 450°F, 230°C, for 10 to 12 minutes, when scones will be browned and nicely risen.

Note: wholemeal scones tend not to rise as much as plain white ones.

7. Slide scones on to a wire rack to cool.

Anne Wallace
Stewarton, Ayrshire

CORN MUFFINS

Makes 12

175 g/6 oz wholewheat flour
125 g/4 oz cornflour
3 teaspoons baking powder
½ teaspoon salt
1 egg
2 tablespoons honey
300 ml/½ pint milk
2 tablespoons oil
Half a 200 g/7 oz tin of sweetcorn
75 g/3 oz grated cheese

1. Mix flours, baking powder and salt.
2. In another bowl mix egg, honey and milk. Then mix this thoroughly into flours.
3. Stir in oil, sweetcorn and cheese.
4. Grease a tray of 12 deep bun tins. Spoon in mixture.
5. Bake near top of a hot oven, Gas 7, 425°F, 210°C, for 10 to 12 minutes.

Delicious piping hot with cheese or soups, or with New England Casserole (*see page 82*).

Sarah Brown
Scarborough, Yorkshire

SUSSEX HEAVIES

Not a bit heavy, just simple nicely-flavoured fruit scones.

225 g/8 oz self-raising white flour, or half white and half wholewheat*
A pinch of salt
25 g/1 oz castor sugar
50 g/2 oz lard
50 g/2 oz mixed currants and raisins

175 ml/6 fl oz sour milk, or fresh milk 'soured' with juice of half a lemon

*Use ½ teaspoon baking powder if you cannot buy self-raising wholewheat flour.

1. Mix flour, salt and sugar (plus baking powder if needed).
2. Rub in lard and add dried fruit.
3. Mix to a soft dough with most of the liquid.
4. Using a floured board, roll out and cut into 5 cm/2 inch rounds. Brush with remaining sour milk. Place on greased baking sheets.
5. Bake near top of a hot oven, Gas 7, 425°F, 220°C, until golden brown, about 10 minutes.

Mrs Gaye Goodall
Steyning, West Sussex

HONEY BISCUITS

These are like exceptionally good digestive biscuits and are particularly nice with cheese.

Makes about 24 biscuits

225 g/8 oz wholewheat flour
½ level teaspoon salt
100 g/4 oz margarine or butter
2 tablespoons clear honey

1. Mix flour and salt in a bowl.
2. Rub in margarine or butter.
3. Mix with honey.
4. Using a floured board, roll out thinly and cut into rounds with a 5 cm/2 inch cutter.
5. Bake in a cool oven, Gas 2, 300°F, 150°C, for 20 minutes.

OATCAKES

Makes 20 oatcakes 6·5 cm/2½ inches in diameter

100 g/4 oz vegetable margarine
50 g/2 oz soft brown sugar
100 g/4 oz wholewheat flour
100 g/4 oz porridge oats
A little milk

1. Cream margarine and sugar.

2. Mix in flour and oats and work into a paste. Moisten if necessary with a teaspoon of milk.

3. Using a floured board, roll out about 7 mm/¼ inch thick and cut into rounds. Put on a greased baking tray.

4. Bake just above middle of a moderately hot oven, Gas 5, 375°F, 190°C, for 20 minutes, until pale brown.

5. Take straight off baking tin on to a wire rack to cool.

Sarah Brown
Scarborough, Yorkshire

Chapter 10

Cakes, Biscuits and Cookies

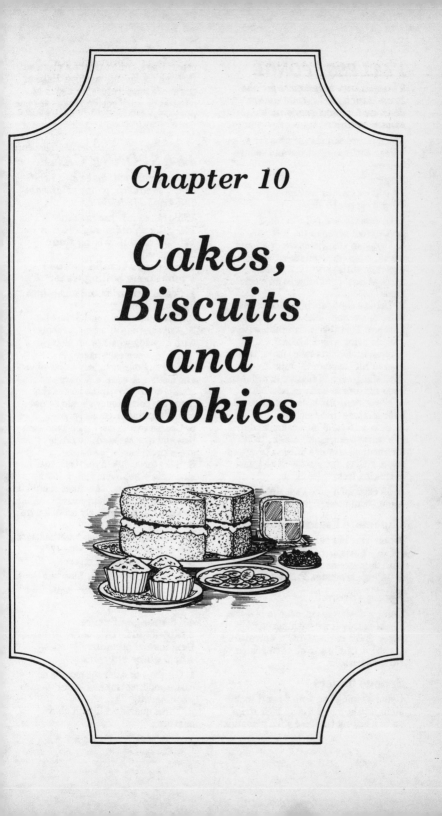

FATLESS SPONGE

This quantity is sufficient for one 20 cm/8 inch tin 7·5 cm/3 inches deep. Or for two 15 cm/6 inch sandwich tins.

The mixture can also be used for a sponge flan, sponge drops and sponge fingers.

3 eggs
75 g/3 oz castor sugar
75 g/3 oz plain flour

1. Grease tin and put a circle of greaseproof paper in the bottom.
2. Using an electric mixer or a hand whisk, whip eggs and castor sugar together until very, very thick. It takes at least 5 minutes in an electric mixer.
3. Using a sieve, sprinkle about one third of the flour over surface of egg mixture. Fold this in carefully with a spatula using a figure of eight movement. Do this twice more, taking care to cut through the mixture only with sharp edge of spatula in order to keep mixture as fluffy as possible.
4. When flour has been incorporated, pour mixture into tin(s).
5. Bake a 20 cm/8 inch cake in centre of a warm oven, Gas 3, 325°F, 160°C, for about 40 minutes until cake is well-risen, golden, firm to touch and just shrinking from sides of tin.

In 15 cm/6 inch sandwich tins bake about 30 minutes.

Chocolate Fatless Sponge

When flour has been weighed out, remove 2 teaspoons and replace this with 2 teaspoons sifted cocoa (not drinking chocolate). Proceed as before.

Sponge drops

Using a dessertspoon, drop in blobs on a baking tray lined with non-stick paper. Bake at the above temperature for about 12 minutes or until golden. Do not overbake.

Sponge fingers

Using a piping bag with 7 mm/¼ inch plain nozzle, pipe 7·5 cm/3 inch strips on to a baking tin lined with non-stick paper. Use a knife to make a clean cut through the sponge mixture. Bake at the above temperature for about 12 minutes or until golden. Take care not to overbake.

4-5-6 SPONGE CAKE

This mixture will make an 18 cm/ 7 inch sandwich, or one small cake and 4 or 5 Madeleines

125 g/4 oz soft margarine
150 g/5 oz castor sugar
175 g/6 oz self-raising flour
2 large eggs
1 or 2 drops vanilla essence
1 tablespoon boiling water

1. Cream margarine and sugar until light and fluffy.
2. Sieve flour into another bowl.
3. Add eggs one at a time, beating with a spring whisk or an electric whisk between each egg.
4. Fold in flour as lightly as possible and lastly the vanilla essence and boiling water. With the last of the flour, the consistency should be not quite dropping from the spoon.
5. Grease two 18 cm/7 inch sandwich tins and line bases with a circle of greaseproof paper.
6. Bake for about 15 to 20 mintues in a moderately hot oven, Gas 6, 400°F, 200°C. When done, the cakes should be golden, firm on top and springy.
7. Turn out immediately on to a wire rack.
8. When cool, sandwich together with jam or lemon curd (*see page 177*). Sprinkle castor sugar on top.

Mrs Joan Gould
Hook, Goole, N. Humberside

Madeleines

4-5-6 sponge mixture
2 tablespoons raspberry jam
Desiccated coconut
4 or 5 glacé cherries

1. Grease 4 or 5 dariole moulds or castle pudding tins and stand them on a baking tray.
2. Three quarters fill with above mixture.

3. Bake for 15 minutes as above or until risen and golden brown.
4. Turn out of tins to cool on a wire rack.
5. Coat with melted raspberry jam all over and cover with coconut. Set a cherry on top.

Mrs Joan Gould
Hook, Goole, N. Humberside

CHOCOLATE SPONGE SANDWICH

Made all in one bowl.

175 g/6 oz self-raising white flour
175 g/6 oz castor sugar
175 g/6 oz margarine, softened
1 level tablespoon cocoa
1½ level teaspoons baking powder
3 eggs
2 tablespoons warm water

1. Grease two round 20 cm/8 inch sandwich tins and line the base of each with a circle of greaseproof paper.
2. Put all the ingredients together in a warm bowl, sifting in the cocoa and baking powder. Mix well until smooth. Beating is not required.
3. Divide mixture between tins, and level tops.
4. Bake above middle of a warm oven, Gas 3, 325°F, 160°C, for 30 minutes until cakes are risen and firm to the touch.
5. Turn cakes straight out of tins on to a wire rack to cool.

Sandwich filling

50 g/2 oz soft margarine
100 to 175 g/4 to 6 oz icing sugar
1 large teaspoon cocoa
1 teaspoon hot water
1 teaspoon sherry or liqueur (optional)

1. Beat margarine in a bowl.
2. Sieve in 100 g/4 oz of the icing sugar and the cocoa.
3. Add other ingredients, including 1 extra teaspoon hot water if sherry is not used.

4. Beat until smooth, sieving in extra icing sugar if necessary.
5. Fill sponge with about half of this quantity.
6. Use the rest to spread on top, saving a little to pipe decorations around edge. Nuts or flaked chocolate can also be used to decorate.

CHOCOLATE BUTTER CREAM

100 g/4 oz plain cooking chocolate
100 g/4 oz butter or table margarine
150 g/6 oz icing sugar

1. Break up chocolate in a bowl and put it to melt over a small pan of simmering water. Do not let water touch bowl.
2. Cream butter or margarine and icing sugar.
3. When light, add melted chocolate and beat again.

This filling is worth making in this quantity as it keeps in a cool place or refrigerator for quite some time and can be used as required to fill or top cakes or biscuits. If too firm to spread beat up with a very little boiling water when using.

Anne Wallace
Stewarton, Ayrshire

SIMPLE LEMON CRUNCH TOPPING FOR A PLAIN SPONGE

Juice of 1 whole lemon (about 2 tablespoons)
125 g/4 oz granulated sugar

Allow the sponge to cool slightly on a wire tray.

Then mix the lemon juice very swiftly with the sugar and before it dissolves the sugar spread evenly over the sponge. The lemon sugar should stay on top of the sponge and the juice

151

should sink into the cake. This gives a lovely crunchy lemon topping with little effort, but it must be done swiftly.

RASPBERRY AND COCONUT TOPPING FOR A PLAIN SPONGE

For a 20 cm/8 inch sponge use:

2 level tablespoons raspberry jam
25 g/1 oz desiccated coconut

Spread jam over top of cooled sponge and sprinkle coconut evenly over the surface.

APPLE CAKE

Looks and tastes superb.

200 g/7 oz self-raising flour
A pinch of salt
150 g/5 oz butter, or half margarine half butter
75 g/3 oz castor sugar
1 egg
350 g/12 oz cooking apples
A squeeze of lemon juice
2 tablespoons apricot jam
2 tablespoons granulated or demerara sugar
A little icing sugar

1. Grease and line a 20 cm/8 inch cake tin, which should be at least 4 cm/1½ inches deep.
2. Sieve flour and salt.
3. Cream butter and castor sugar until light and fluffy.
4. Beat in the egg.
5. Fold in flour and salt.
6. Using a lightly-floured board, gently pat or roll out three-quarters of the mixture and fit it into prepared tin.
7. Peel, core and slice apples and squeeze lemon juice over to keep their colour. Arrange overlapping slices on the cake mixture.

8. Heat jam and brush it over apples. Sprinkle with the 2 tablespoons of sugar.
9. Take small pieces of the remaining mixture, roll into strips with floured hands and arrange a lattice pattern over the apples.
10. Bake above middle of a warm oven, Gas 3, 325°F, 160°C, for 1 hour.
11. Take cake out of tin on to a wire rack to cool.
12. Dust with icing sugar and serve cool or cold.

Mrs Aileen Houghton,
Kemsing, Nr. Sevenoaks, Kent

CHESHIRE PARKIN

Keeps well—freezes well.

225 g/8 oz coarse oatmeal
75 g/3 oz wholewheat or white flour
50 g/2 oz demerara sugar
1 teaspoon ground ginger
A bare ½ teaspoon bicarbonate of soda
A pinch of salt
225 g/8 oz syrup or treacle
125 g/4 oz margarine
70 ml/2¼ fl oz milk

1. Mix the dry ingredients together.
2. Melt the syrup and fat in a pan and add to dry ingredients.
3. Stir in milk to make a soft consistency.
4. Grease a 20 cm/8 inch round sandwich tin, or an 18 cm/7 inch square tin and line it with greased, greaseproof paper. Put in the mixture.
5. Bake in the middle of a moderate oven, Gas 4, 350°F, 180°C, for 1¼ hours when parkin will be firm to the touch.
6. Leave in tin to cool.

Best kept 2 days before eating.

Judith Adshead
Mottram St. Andrew, Cheshire

DEVONSHIRE BLOCK CAKE

This recipe is easily reduced to make a smaller cake. It also freezes well so that the whole quantity can be made

152

and the cake cut in 3 or 4 pieces to freeze. Very good flavour; improves with keeping.

175 g/6 oz butter or margarine
175 g/6 oz sugar
125 g/4 oz black treacle
3 large eggs
1 tablespoon milk
450 g/1 lb currants or sultanas or a mixture of both
125 g/4 oz mixed peel
350 g/12 oz plain flour

1. Work butter or margarine to a cream.
2. Beat in sugar and treacle.
3. Add eggs one at a time, beating well.
4. Add milk.
5. Mix in currants, sultanas, peel and lastly the flour.
6. Use a greased tin 18 cm/7 inch square or two 1 kg/2 lb loaf tins and line with greased, greaseproof paper.
7. Put mixture into tin and bake in middle of a cool oven, Gas 2, 300°F, 150°C, for 2¼ hours, when cake will be a rich brown and firm to the touch. Look in oven after 1½ hours and, if cake is already very brown, reduce heat to Gas 1, 275°F, 140°C, and lay a doubled sheet of greaseproof paper over top.

Mrs Becky Blackmore
Exeter, Devon

DUNDEE CAKE

Keeps very well.

175 g/6 oz soft margarine
175 g/6 oz light soft brown sugar
¼ teaspoon almond essence
200 g/7 oz plain flour
1 level teaspoon baking powder
175 g/6 oz sultanas
175 g/6 oz currants
50 g/2 oz chopped cherries
25 g/1 oz ground almonds
3 large eggs
Whole blanched almonds

1. Grease an 18 cm/7 inch square tin or a 20 cm/8 inch round tin and line it with greased, greaseproof paper.

2. Cream together margarine, sugar and almond essence.
3. Into another bowl sift flour and baking powder. Into this mix prepared fruit and ground almonds.
4. In a third bowl beat the eggs.
5. Fold egg a little at a time, and fruit likewise, into the creamed mixture. Do not beat.
6. Turn into tin. Level the top.
7. Bake in a warm oven, Gas 3, 325°F, 160°C, for about 1¼ hours, when cake will be brown and firm to the touch. During baking whole almonds are carefully placed on cake. Do this while top of cake is still just moist but not too soon or they will either sink into the mixture or burn before cake is cooked.
8. Leave in tin to cool.

HEAVY CAKE

In Cornwall this was made in the fishing villages south of Truro. When the seine net was being hauled in and the men shouting 'heave' with every pull, the wives would know the men would soon be in for tea and would make this quick flat cake to be eaten warm or cold.

225 g/8 oz flour*
¼ teaspoon salt
50 g/2 oz lard
75 g/3 oz sugar
175 g/6 oz currants
About 75 ml/2 to 3 tablespoons milk
50 g/2 oz butter

*If you prefer wholewheat flour it is best made with two thirds wholewheat and one third white flour, otherwise *too* heavy!

1. Mix flour and salt in a bowl and rub in lard.
2. Add sugar and currants. Mix to a soft dough with milk.
3. Using a floured board, roll out to a long strip about 15 cm/6 inches wide and 3 times as long, about 45 cm/18 inches.
4. Dot half of the butter over the top two-thirds of the pastry. Fold the bottom third, without fat, upwards. Then fold the top third down over it.

153

5. Give the pastry a half-turn so that folds are at sides.
6. Roll out again into a thin strip and spread the rest of the butter as before, repeating the folding in the same way.
7. Roll out finally into a square about 1 cm/½ inch thick. Criss-cross the top with a knife, like a net. Brush with a little milk.
8. Bake above middle of a moderately hot oven, Gas 6, 400°F, 200°C, for 25 to 30 minutes. Remove on to a wire rack to cool.
Eat fresh.

Mrs Jean Daybell
Cornwall Women's Institute

KENTISH HOP-PICKERS CAKE

Makes 2 cakes in ½ kg/1 lb loaf tins

Moist and spicy. Inclined to sink in middle. Keeps well.

275 g/10 oz self-raising flour
1 teaspoon ground ginger
1 teaspoon mixed spice
175 g/6 oz margarine
100 g/4 oz soft brown sugar
100 g/4 oz sultanas
100 g/4 oz currants
50 g/2 oz mixed peel
425 ml/¾ pint milk
1 tablespoon black treacle
1 level teaspoon cream of tartar
½ level teaspoon bicarbonate of soda

1. Sift flour and spices into a bowl.
2. Rub in margarine.
3. Add sugar and fruit.
4. Warm milk with treacle and dissolve in it the cream of tartar and bicarbonate of soda.
5. Mix liquid into dry ingredients with a wooden spoon. The mixture should drop from the spoon.
6. Grease and line two ½ kg/1 lb loaf tins and put in the mixture.
7. Bake in middle of a warm oven, Gas 3, 325°F, 160°C, for about 1½ hours until cakes are firm to the touch.
8. Leave cakes to cool in tins.

Mrs Zina Barnard
Whitstable, Kent

PORTLAND RICE CAKE

A recipe from 'What's Cooking in Dorset' published by the Dorset Federation of Women's Institutes.

225 g/8 oz self-raising flour
½ teaspoon bicarbonate of soda
½ teaspoon cinnamon
½ teaspoon nutmeg
125 g/4 oz ground rice
75 g/3 oz butter or margarine
175 g/6 oz lard
75 g/3 oz soft brown sugar
450 g/1 lb currants
50 g/2 oz mixed peel
2 beaten eggs
300 ml/½ pint milk
1 teaspoon vinegar

1. Sift together flour, bicarbonate of soda, cinnamon and nutmeg.
2. Stir in ground rice.
3. Rub in butter and lard.
4. Add sugar, currants and peel and mix well.
5. Add eggs, milk and vinegar and beat into mixture.
6. Grease a 23 cm/9 inch square tin and line it with greased, greaseproof paper. Put in the mixture and smooth the surface.
7. Bake in the lower part of a cool oven, Gas 2, 300°F, 150°C, for 1 hour. Then reduce heat to Gas 1, 275°F, 140°C for a further 30 minutes, when cake will be firm to the touch and golden brown in colour.
8. Leave it to cool in the tin.

Mrs S. Patterson
Buckland Newton, Dorset

SHEARING CAKE

Cacen Gneifo—a seed cake traditionally baked in Wales at sheep-shearing time. Keeps quite well in a tin for over a week.

Easy to make half this quantity.

450 g/1 lb plain white flour, or half wholewheat half white
1 teaspoon grated nutmeg
1 rounded teaspoon baking powder

A pinch of salt
225 g/8 oz butter or margarine
350 g/12 oz soft brown sugar
1 tablespoon caraway seeds
Grated rind and juice of 1 lemon
300 ml/½ pint milk
2 beaten eggs

1. Sift together white flour, nutmeg, baking powder and salt. Mix in whole-wheat flour if used.
2. Rub in butter or margarine.
3. Add sugar, caraway seeds, lemon rind and juice.
4. Pour in milk slowly, mixing well all the time. Finally, mix in well-beaten eggs.
5. Grease a 23 cm/9 inch round cake tin and line base and sides with greased greaseproof paper.
If making half quantity an 18 cm/7 inch round tin is suitable or a ½ kg/1 lb loaf tin.
6. Pour in cake mixture.
7. Bake in middle of a moderate oven, Gas 4, 350°F, 180°C, for 30 minutes, then reduce temperature to cool, Gas 2, 300°F, 150°C, for another 1½ hours when it will be golden brown and firm to the touch.
If making half quantity, bake as above but it will need only 1 hour when temperature has been reduced.
8. Leave cake in tin till slightly cooled. Then turn it out on to a wire rack.

Mrs Eileen Trumper
Llanvair Kilgeddin, Gwent

SOMERSET CIDER CAKE

A moist cake. Keeps well in an airtight tin.

125 g/4 oz butter
125 g/4 oz soft brown sugar
2 beaten eggs (must be at room temperature)
225 g/8 oz plain flour
1 teaspoon bicarbonate of soda, use a measure
Half a nutmeg, grated
About 225 ml/8 fl oz dry cider

1. Cream butter and sugar until really light and fluffy.
2. Beat in eggs a little at a time.
3. Sift together flour, bicarbonate of soda and nutmeg. Fold it in.
4. Add cider slowly to form a soft dropping consistency.
5. Grease an 18 cm/7 inch round tin and line bottom with greased greaseproof paper.
6. Put mixture into tin and bake near top of a moderately hot oven, Gas 5, 375°F, 190°C, for 1 to 1½ hours or until brown on top, shrinking from sides of tin and springy to the touch.

Mrs Angela Mottram
Axbridge, Somerset

ABERNETHY BISCUITS

50 g/2 oz sugar
3 tablespoons milk
225 g/8 oz self-raising flour
A pinch of salt
75 g/3 oz margarine
50 g/2 oz cooking fat such as Cookeen

1. Put sugar and milk in a small pan over low heat and stir until dissolved. Allow to cool.
2. Sift flour and salt into a bowl, rub in fats and bind to a dough with the cooled liquid.
3. Using a floured board, roll out dough to 7 mm/¼ inch thick. Cut round biscuits and place them a little apart on baking trays. Or, make small balls of the dough, place on baking tray and flatten them with fingertips. Prick each biscuit with a fork.
4. Bake near top of a moderatley hot oven, Gas 5, 375°F, 190°C, for 15 minutes when biscuits will be pale golden brown.
5. Slide off baking trays on to a wire rack to cool.

Anne Wallace
Stewarton, Ayrshire

ORANGE CRISPS

Makes about 20 biscuits

125 g/4 oz butter
50 g/2 oz castor sugar
Grated rind of 1 orange
150 g/5 oz self-raising flour

To finish: extra castor sugar

1. Rub butter into other ingredients until mixture resembles fine crumbs. Work together into a dough.
2. Roll small balls about 2.5 cm/1 inch in diameter. Put them 5 cm/2 inches apart on greased baking trays. Flatten with a fork dipped in cold water.
3. Bake above middle of a moderate oven, Gas 4, 350°F, 180°C, for 10 to 12 minutes until pale gold in colour.
4. Remove from baking trays on to a wire rack. Sprinkle with castor sugar while still hot.

From Cheshire W.I. 'Cook Book'

GRASMERE GINGERBREAD

175 g/6 oz wholewheat flour
50 g/2 oz porridge oats
½ level teaspoon bicarbonate of soda
1 level teaspoon cream of tartar
2 level teaspoons ginger
175 g/6 oz margarine
175 g/6 oz brown sugar, nice with muscovado
50 g/2 oz mixed peel, finely-chopped (optional)

1. Put flour and oats in a bowl and sift in bicarbonate of soda, cream of tartar and ginger. Mix well.
2. Rub in margarine, stir in sugar and mixed peel.
3. Press mixture into a greased Swiss roll tin, 28 by 18 cm/11 by 7 inches. They will be thin biscuits.
4. Bake in a warm oven, Gas 3, 325°F, 160°C, for about 30 minutes until firm and brown.
5. Allow to cool in tin for 5 minutes then cut into fingers.

GRANDMA'S GINGER BISCUITS

100 g/4 oz golden syrup
75 g/3 oz lard
50 g/2 oz sugar
1 teaspoon ginger
½ teaspoon bicarbonate of soda
225 g/8 oz self-raising flour

1. Put all ingredients except flour into a fairly large saucepan and heat gently until lard is melted.
2. Remove from heat and stir in flour, 2 tablespoons at a time.
3. Roll mixture into walnut-sized balls. Put them on a greased baking tray 5 cm/2 inches apart.
4. Bake above middle of a warm oven, Gas 3, 325°F, 160°C, for 10 minutes.
5. Leave on tray for a few minutes to firm up. Then lift on to a wire rack to cool.

Mrs Kathleen Smith
Armley, W. Yorkshire

MRS OADES' GINGER CRISPS

Makes about 300 g/¾ lb biscuits

225 g/8 oz plain flour
25 g/1 oz castor sugar
1 teaspoon ground ginger
1 level teaspoon bicarbonate of soda
100 g/4 oz golden syrup
50 g/2 oz butter or margarine

1. Sift dry ingredients into a bowl.
2. To be precise with golden syrup, put a small pan on to scales, weigh it and then weigh syrup into it.
3. Melt fat and syrup together over low heat.
4. Mix this very thoroughly into dry ingredients.
5. Line a ½ kg/1 lb loaf tin with greaseproof paper.
6. Press the soft mixture into tin. Make top level and smooth. Leave for several hours, or overnight, in a cool place or refrigerator.

7. Turn biscuit loaf out of tin and use a sharp knife to cut very thin biscuits, about 7 mm/¼ inch thick or less.

8. Put biscuits on greased baking trays or use non-stick baking paper to line tin.

9. Bake in middle of a warm oven, Gas 3, 325°F, 160°C, until golden. 3·5 mm/⅛ inch thick biscuits take about 12 minutes.

10. Leave on baking tin for 5 minutes to firm up, then put biscuits on to a wire rack to cool.

KRISPIE BISCUITS

Makes about 40 biscuits

150 g/5 oz margarine
150 g/5 oz castor sugar
50 g/2 oz sultanas
1 beaten egg
175 g/6 oz self-raising flour
50 g/2 oz Rice Krispies

1. Put margarine and sugar in a large pan over low heat.

2. When margarine has melted, remove pan from heat and add sultanas, beaten egg and flour. Mix well. Allow to cool and firm up.

3. Put the Rice Krispies in a flat dish and, using a teaspoon, drop in the biscuit mixture. Toss each teaspoonful about so that it is well-covered.

4. Grease baking trays or line with non-stick baking paper. Space biscuits 5 cm/2 inches apart. Press each biscuit down with a fork.

5. Bake in middle of a warm oven, Gas 3, 325°F, 160°C, for 15 to 20 minutes until golden.

6. Leave on baking trays for 10 minutes to firm up. Then slide off on to a wire rack to cool.

SHORTBREAD BISCUITS

Try the variations in flavours and finishing given below.

Can be done by hand or with an electric mixer. Freeze well.

225 g/8 oz unsalted or slightly salted butter
100 g/4 oz castor sugar
350 g/12 oz plain white flour, sifted

To finish: extra castor sugar

1. Use softened butter, do not let it melt and become oily. Put it in a warm bowl.

2. Beat in sugar and flour and work mixture together thoroughly.

If using an electric mixer, warm the bowl, put all ingredients in together and beat until mixture looks like damp breadcrumbs.

3. Form into a fat sausage about 4 cm/1½ inches thick. Roll this on a board sprinkled with castor sugar. Then put into refrigerator for one hour to firm up.

4. Then, using a sharp knife, cut thin slices from the roll, 7 mm/¼ inch thick or less.

5. Place on greased baking trays, or trays lined with non-stick baking paper.

6. Bake above middle of a cool oven, Gas 2, 300°F, 150°C, for about 30 minutes until golden. Take care not to overbake or they will develop a bitter taste.

7. Remove from oven and dredge with castor sugar while still hot. Leave on trays to stiffen up. Then slide off on to a wire rack to cool.

8. When cold, store in airtight tins and remove from tins just before serving.

Variations

1. Delicious made with wholewheat flour, but it is not so easy to make perfectly-shaped biscuits.

2. Unusual fragrance by incorporating ¼ teaspoon dried or ½ teaspoon fresh rosemary, finely chopped. Work it in at paragraph 3.

3. Another unusual flavour using ¼ teaspoon caraway seeds.

4. Dorset Shortbread. The 'sausage' is rolled in demerara sugar at paragraph 3 above. Do not dredge with castor sugar at paragraph 7. Although this recipe is different this method of finishing is typical of traditional

157

Dorset shortbread. This method was contributed by members of Dorset Women's Institute.

SHORTBREAD TOFFEE PIECES

Shortbread

100 g/4 oz margarine
50 g/2 oz castor sugar
150 g/5 oz self-raising white or brown flour

Toffee

100 g/4 oz margarine
100 g/4 oz castor sugar
2 tablespoons golden syrup
Half a 383 g/13·5 oz tin of condensed milk

Topping

100 g/4 oz plain cooking chocolate

1. Shortbread base. Cream margarine and sugar. Mix in flour. Spread in a greased 28 by 18 cm/11 by 7 inch Swiss roll tin.
2. Bake above centre of a moderate oven, Gas 4, 350°F, 180°C, for 20 minutes. Allow to cool in tin.
3. Toffee. Melt margarine, sugar, syrup and condensed milk in a pan and cook gently, stirring, until the mixture leaves the sides of the pan.
4. Pour over the cooled shortbread and leave to cool again.
5. Topping. Heat an ovenproof bowl. Break chocolate into it in small pieces and let it melt in the hot bowl. Spread melted chocolate over toffee. Allow to cool.
6. Turn out on to a board and cut into small pieces.

SHORTCAKE BISCUIT STARS

Swiftly made with an electric mixer but can also be done by hand.

225 g/8 oz softened margarine
50 g/2 oz icing sugar

225 g/8 oz plain white flour or half white and half wholewheat

To decorate: glacé cherries (optional)

1. Cream margarine until soft and fluffy.
2. Sift in icing sugar. Beat again.
3. Add flour and beat until smooth.
4. Using a forcing bag with a large star nozzle, pipe star shapes on to a greased baking tray. Put a tiny piece of cherry on top of each star.
5. Bake in the middle of a cool oven, Gas 2, 300°F, 150°C, for 30 minutes until golden. Do not overbake or biscuits will develop a bitter flavour.

BLAKENEY FRITTERS

Makes 10

75 g/3 oz plain flour
40 g/1½ oz margarine
25 g/1 oz sugar
1 large egg-yolk
Jam

1. Put flour in a bowl and rub in margarine.
2. Add sugar and egg-yolk and work mixture into a paste.
3. Roll little balls of mixture and put them on a lightly-greased baking sheet.
4. Make a hole in each with the end of a wooden spoon. Brush over with a little white of egg.
5. Bake above middle of a moderate oven, Gas 4, 350°F, 180°C, for 30 minutes until just turning golden.
6. Slide off on to a wire rack to cool. Fill the hole in each biscuit with jam.

Mrs Phyl Drinkwater
for Blakeney W.I., Glos.

BRIGHTON ROCKS

Certainly not rock-like.

Made small the yield is 35, easy to make half this quantity.

They freeze well.

100 g/4 oz butter or margarine
100 g/4 oz castor sugar
2 beaten eggs
50 g/2 oz currants
50 g/2 oz ground almonds
225 g/8 oz plain flour
1 teaspoon rose-water or lemon juice

1. Cream butter and sugar.
2. Save 1 tablespoon of egg for glazing and beat in the rest with rose-water or lemon juice.
3. Work in currants, ground almonds and flour.
4. Form into walnut-sized balls and place on greased baking trays. Brush with a little beaten egg.
5. Bake in middle of a hot oven, Gas 7, 425°F, 210°C, for about 10 minutes until just golden.
6. Cool on a wire rack.

Mrs Ruth Brooke and Mrs Gaye Goodall
Hove and Steyning, West Sussex

CHOCOLATE AND CHERRY COOKIES

100 g/4 oz margarine
50 g/2 oz soft brown sugar
1 level tablespoon honey
25 g/1 oz glacé cherries, chopped small
25 g/1 oz chocolate chips
100 g/4 oz plain white flour or half wholewheat half white

1. Beat together margarine, sugar and honey until fluffy.
2. Mix in cherries, chocolate chips and flour and work together.
3. Place teaspoons of the mixture well apart on a greased baking tray.
4. Bake in middle of a moderate oven, Gas 4, 350°F, 180°C, for 15 to 18 minutes until golden.
5. Leave on baking tray for 1 minute to firm up. Then lift on to a wire rack to cool.

CHOCOLATE CLUSTERS

No cooking.

Makes 20

A 150 g/5·3 oz block of plain cooking chocolate
1 level tablespoon golden syrup
2 teaspoons water
75 g/3 oz raisins
75 g/3 oz salted peanuts*
25 g/1 oz mixed peel, finely-chopped

*Can be made with unsalted nuts but rub off brown skins.

1. Place a bowl over a saucepan of boiling water. Do not allow bowl to touch the water. Allow bowl to warm up. Then turn off heat.
2. Break up chocolate and put it in the bowl with the golden syrup and the water. Allow to melt and blend together, stirring occasionally.
3. Stir in raisins, peanuts and mixed peel.
4. Put small teaspoons of the mixture on to a sheet of waxed paper (from a cornflakes packet).
5. Leave to set in a cool place before removing from paper.

CHOCOLATE PEPPERMINT SQUARES

Another recipe from 'What's Cooking In Dorset', published by the Dorset Federation Of Women's Institutes.

100 g/4 oz margarine
50 g/2 oz castor sugar
3 level teaspoons baking powder
100 g/4 oz plain flour
50 g/2 oz desiccated coconut

Butter Cream

50 g/2 oz margarine
75 g/3 oz icing sugar
1 small teaspoon peppermint essence
Drop of green colouring

Topping
175 g/6 oz plain cooking chocolate

1. Beat margarine until soft and cream with the castor sugar.
2. Sift in baking powder and flour.
3. Add coconut and mix well.
4. Press mixture into a greased tin approximately 20 cm/8 inches square.
5. Bake in lower part of a warm oven, Gas 3, 325°F, 160°C, for about 30 minutes when cake will be soft but springy to the touch, slightly risen and golden.
6. Allow to cool in tin until firm, crisp and biscuit-like. Then cover with butter cream.

Butter Cream

1. Beat margarine till soft.
2. Sift in icing sugar adding essence and colouring carefully.
3. Spread over cold cake base.
4. Melt chocolate in a small bowl over a pan of simmering water. Do not let water touch bowl.
5. Spread warm chocolate over butter cream.
6. Cut into squares with a sharp knife when chocolate has almost set. Leave in tin until set.

Mrs Joane Robinson
Cranborne, Dorset

COCONUT BROWNIES

A rich chewy cake.

50 g/2 oz plain cooking chocolate
100 g/4 oz butter or margarine
2 large eggs, lightly-beaten
¼ teaspoon vanilla essence
225 g/8 oz sugar
50 g/2 oz self-raising flour
¼ level teaspoon salt
50 g/2 oz desiccated coconut

1. Break chocolate in pieces. Put it with butter in a pan and heat *very* gently until both are melted.
2. Remove from heat and, using a wooden spoon, gradually beat in the eggs. The mixture will thicken.

3. Add vanilla and sugar, then flour, salt and coconut. Mix thoroughly.
4. Grease an 18 cm/7 inch square shallow tin and line base with greased foil. Pour in mixture.
5. Bake above middle of a moderate oven, Gas 4, 350°F, 180°C, for 50 to 60 minutes when the cake will be crisp at the edges and feel firm in the middle.
6. Leave to cool a little, trim the edges and loosen cake from sides of tin with a knife. Leave to go firm then turn out and remove foil.
7. When quite cold cut into 9 or 12 pieces.

Margaret Heywood
Todmorden, Yorkshire

COCONUT DROPS

225 g/8 oz self-raising flour*
100 g/4 oz margarine
175 g/6 oz castor sugar
50 g/2 oz desiccated coconut
2 medium-sized beaten eggs

***Can be made with half white and half wholewheat flour. If you cannot buy self-raising wholewheat flour, add ½ level teaspoon baking powder. Delicious also with light soft brown sugar.**

1. Put flour in a bowl and rub in margarine.
2. Mix in the rest of the ingredients. Mixture will be firm but not stiff.
3. Roll mixture into balls and place, well apart, on a greased baking tray. Press each biscuit lightly with a fork.
4. Bake near top of a moderately hot oven, Gas 5, 375°F, 190°C, for 10 to 12 minutes or until pale brown. For a crisper result leave in oven till a shade darker.

Mrs Elsie Kaye
Saltmarshe, N. Humberside

COCONUT KISSES

Makes about 30 double kisses!— easy to make half quantity

2 egg-whites
150 g/5 oz castor sugar
100 g/4 oz desiccated coconut

160

Butter Icing

25 g/1 oz butter or margarine
50 g/2 oz icing sugar
Almond essence and pink
colouring
Or, pistachio essence and green
colouring

1. Line baking sheets with oiled
greaseproof paper.
2. Whisk egg-whites till firm. Then
add half of the sugar and whisk again.
3. Fold in coconut and remaining
sugar.
4. Put small teaspoons of the mixture
on to prepared baking sheets.
5. Bake in the 2 middle shelves of a
cool oven, Gas 2, 300°F, 150°C, for 35 to
40 minutes until golden brown.
6. Meanwhile, prepare butter icing.
Beat butter and sifted icing sugar
together, flavouring and colouring as
suggested.
7. Take coconut kisses off baking
sheets to cool on a wire rack. When
they are cold, sandwich in pairs with
butter icing.

These keep well after filling, stored in
airtight containers.

Anne Wallace
Stewarton, Ayrshire

DATE BARS

No baking in oven.

100 g/4 oz margarine
100 g/4 oz sugar
225 g/8 oz chopped dates
225 g/8 oz sweet biscuits, broken
into pieces

1. Melt margarine and sugar in pan.
2. Add chopped dates, mix well and
cook 2 or 3 minutes.
3. Remove from heat and add broken
biscuits. Mix well.
4. Press into a shallow, greased, Swiss
roll tin. Leave to cool.
5. Cut into bars when cold.

May be iced with melted chocolate
before cutting into bars. Or dip the
ends into melted chocolate.

Sybil Norcott
Irlam, Nr. Manchester

DEMERARA BRANDY SNAPS

Makes about 24

50 g/2 oz plain white flour
50 g/2 oz golden syrup
50 g/2 oz demerara sugar
50 g/2 oz butter
1 teaspoon ground ginger
2 teaspoons lemon juice

To finish

Whipped cream
A pinch of sugar
Brandy

1. Put flour to warm in a warm oven,
Gas 3, 325°F, 160°C, for 10 minutes.
2. Weigh a saucepan and weigh into it
the golden syrup. This is the easiest
way to measure syrup without getting
sticky.
3. Melt syrup, sugar and butter.
Remove from heat.
4. Mix in warmed flour, sift in ginger
and add lemon juice. Stir well.
5. Put teaspoons of the mixture on to
well-greased baking trays, or trays
lined with non-stick baking paper.
Keep them 15 cm/6 inches apart
because they spread out very thinly
while baking.
6. Bake in a warm oven, Gas 3, 325°F,
160°C, for 10 minutes or until nicely
golden.
7. Leave for 1 or 2 minutes to firm up
a little. Then quickly roll each brandy
snap into a tube around the handle of
a wooden spoon. Leave to cool.
8. Mix sugar and brandy to taste into
whipped cream. Using an icing bag
with a 1 cm/½ inch star pipe, fill each
brandy snap.

Mrs Amy Cannon
Goole, N. Humberside

JAPS

3 egg-whites
A pinch of cream of tartar
160 g/5½ oz castor sugar
125 g/4 oz ground almonds
20 g/¾ oz custard powder
4 drops almond essence

161

Butter Cream Mousse (*see next recipe*) flavoured with coffee or rum

To Finish

40 g/1½ oz desiccated coconut, toasted*

25 to 50 g/1 to 2 oz plain cooking chocolate

*To toast coconut, spread it in a baking tin and put under a moderately hot grill until golden. Stir often. It burns easily.

1. Whisk egg-whites with cream of tartar until stiff. Add 125 g/4 oz of the castor sugar and whisk again.
2. Add all at once the ground almonds, remaining sugar, custard powder and essence. Fold in carefully.
3. Put this mixture in a piping bag with a 1 cm/½ inch plain pipe.
4. Pipe in small heaps on a well-greased baking tray or a baking tray lined with non-stick paper.
5. Bake in middle of a moderate oven, Gas 4, 350°F, 180°C, for about 20 minutes until just coloured.
6. Cool on a wire tray.
7. Sandwich with the butter cream mousse.
8. Coat sides with more butter cream and roll cakes in toasted coconut.
9. Melt chocolate in a small jug standing in a pan of simmering water and dribble it over the finished cakes.

Mrs Joan Hudson
Finsthwaite, Ulverston, Cumbria

BUTTER CREAM MOUSSE

This is much less sweet than ordinary butter cream and is excellent for filling cakes. The quantity given here would fill two cakes.

50 g/2 oz castor sugar
65 ml/2½ fl oz water
2 egg-yolks
100 g/4 oz unsalted or slightly salted butter
Coffee essence or rum to flavour

1. Dissolve sugar in water and boil till the syrup is sticky and will pull a thread between finger and thumb. Cool slightly.
2. Beat egg-yolks, pour syrup over them and whisk until thick.
3. Cream butter and beat mousse mixture into it by degrees.
4. Flavour with coffee essence or rum.

Keeps for a week in a covered container in refrigerator.

Mrs Joan Hudson
Finsthwaite, Ulverston, Cumbria

MERINGUES

Using an electric whisk.

Notes: Do not use fresh eggs. Be careful to use a grease-free bowl. Store meringues in a tight-lidded tin. Remove from tin at last minute. Sugar attracts moisture and the meringues will go soft if uncovered.

2 large egg-whites
A pinch of salt
A pinch of cream of tartar
125 g/4 oz castor sugar*

*Try also grinding demerara sugar to castor sugar consistency in electric grinder.

1. Whisk the egg-whites. When frothy, add salt and cream of tartar. Continue to whip at high speed until stiff.
2. Now lower the speed and add castor sugar, 2 tablespoons at a time, and continue beating well between each addition until all the sugar is used up and the mixture is thick and peaks easily.
3. Line a baking tray with foil or non-stick baking parchment.
4. Put the meringue mixture into a large icing bag with a 1 cm/½ inch star nozzle. Many different shapes can be made:

Meringue Baskets. Swirl round in a circle about 5 cm/2 inches across. Then pipe round edge to make a small wall. This amount will make about 10 baskets.

Meringue Rounds. For a Pavlova-type cake. Draw three 20 cm/8 inch rounds on the paper or foil. Starting at the centre, pipe round and round until you meet the pencilled edge. This amount will make three rounds.

Bake below middle of a very cool oven,
Gas ¼, 225°F, 110°C, for 1½ hours or
until dry and firm.

SEMOLINA HALVA
For 4 people

300 g/11 oz coarse semolina
100 g/4 oz butter or ghee (*see
page 38*)
600 ml/1 pint milk
275 g/10 oz sugar
50 g/2 oz blanched almonds,
coarsely-chopped
A few drops of almond essence
¼ teaspoon saffron powder,
dissolved in ¼ teaspoon water

1. Using a heavy-based pan, dry roast
semolina over low heat until pale
brown, stirring frequently or it will
burn.
2. Add the butter, milk and sugar and
stir continuously over low heat to
prevent semolina sticking to pan.
3. When quite stiff, add almonds,
essence and saffron.
4. Mix thoroughly and pat on to a
buttered tray to about 7 mm/¼ inch
thick.
5. Cut into 2·5 cm/1 inch squares.

Keep in a cool place and eat within a
day or two of making.

Priya Wickramasinghe
Cardiff

SHERRY SLICES
No cooking.

225 g/8 oz marzipan

Filling
¾ cup digestive biscuit crumbs
½ cup desiccated coconut
½ cup mixed dried fruit, chopped
¼ cup chopped nuts
½ cup raspberry jam
1 tablespoon icing sugar
1 dessertspoon cocoa
1 to 2 tablespoons sherry

To finish: about 175 g/6 oz plain
cooking chocolate

1. You need a tin about 23 cm/9 inches
square.
2. Divide marzipan in half. Using a
board dusted with icing sugar or cornflour, roll each piece out to 23 cm/9
inches square. Put one piece in tin.
3. Mix all the filling ingredients,
spread over marzipan and put on the
marzipan top.
4. Break chocolate into a small basin
and stand it over a pan of simmering
water to melt. Do not let basin touch
water.
5. Spread melted chocolate over and
leave till cold.
6. Slice into small fingers.

Judith Adshead
Mottram St. Andrew, Cheshire

Chapter 11

Preserves and Home-made Sweets

JAMS AND JELLIES

There are two stages in the making of jams and jellies. *First*, there is the gentle simmer in water which breaks down the fruit and extracts the natural setting agent, pectin. With jellies the fruit needs to be crushed well with a potato masher while it is simmering. The initial simmering also softens the fruit. If the sugar is added too soon it makes tough-skinned fruit chewy. *Second*, after the sugar has been added, comes the fast rolling boil to obtain a set quickly which will give the preserve the best flavour and the brightest colour.

Always use dry, fresh fruit, slightly under-ripe, and try to make the preserve on the same day as the fruit is picked. The pectin content does decrease even if the fruit is left overnight. Frozen fruit, if it has been frozen in perfect condition, is excellent but will also have lost a little pectin, and to counteract this add a little extra fruit—e.g., in marmalade making add an extra orange to the recipe weight.

Good Pectin Content

Blackcurrants
Cranberries
Damsons
Gooseberries
Some Plums
Quince
Freshly picked Raspberries
Redcurrants
Seville Oranges

Medium Pectin Content

Fresh Apricots
Early Blackberries/Brambles
Greengages
Lemons
Limes
Loganberries
Sweet Oranges

Poor Pectin Content

Late Blackberries
Cherries
Elderberries
Grapefruit
Marrows
Medlars
Pears
Rhubarb
Strawberries
Tangerines
Tomatoes

The Pectin Test

Half-way through the jam making, before the sugar has been added, it is possible to test the pulp for pectin:

1. Take a teaspoon of juice from the pan of simmered fruit, put it in a glass and cool it.
2. Add three teaspoons of methylated spirit. Shake gently.

If plenty of pectin is present, a clear jelly clot will form. If a medium amount of pectin is present several small clots will form. If a poor amount of pectin is present, no real clot will be formed.

GOOD   FAIR   POOR

If after further cooking no clot is formed, additional pectin should be added:

50 to 100 ml/2 to 4 fl oz per ½ kg/1 lb of fruit—e.g., to 1·8 kg/4 lb fruit, add 2 tablespoons lemon juice, or ¼ level teaspoon citric or tartaric acid, or 150 ml/¼ pint redcurrant or gooseberry juice.

Testing for a Set

Do this when the sugar has been added and boiling has started:

After 10 minutes if fruit is in the high pectin list
After 15 minutes if it is in medium pectin list
After 20 minutes if in poor pectin list

There are several ways.

1) **Volume test.** If you know the expected yield of your fruit—e.g., the recipe says you will get, say, 2·5 kg/5 lb of jam, then measure out in water that amount. Take a 1 lb jam jar (not a 12 oz jar), fill it five times and pour this into your pan. Use a wooden spoon handle, stand it upright in the water and mark this level with a pencil. Keep the spoon handy. Then, when you are testing for a set, draw pan off heat. Wait until bubbling subsides and stand spoon in the jam. When the volume has returned to the level of the pencil mark, the jam is ready to pot.

2) **Cold plate test.** Have some plates cooling in the refrigerator, and take a tea-spoon of jam and drop it on the cold plate. Wait a minute and, if it wrinkles when

pushed, the jam is ready. If not, go on boiling a little longer.

3) **Flake test.** Dip a clean wooden spoon in boiling jam. Allow the cooling jam to drop from the spoon. If the drops run together and form a flake or curtain it is ready to pot.

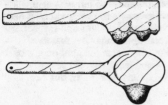

4) **Temperature test.** Use a sugar thermometer. It is important to dip the thermometer in hot water immediately before using it in the jam. Submerge the bulb fully in the boiling jam but do not let it touch bottom of pan. When the thermometer registers 220°F or 150°C the jam is ready to pot.

To Pot the Jam

1. Have your jam pots washed, dried and warming on a low heat in the oven. You should be able to hold them by the rim.
2. Draw the pan off heat, stir in a knob of butter. This helps disperse the foam. If it still persists, scoop it off into a bowl and use it in the kitchen—it is just jam with a lot of air in it.
3. Now, with a heatproof glass or metal jug, fill jam pots to the brim and cover either with a metal twist top lid or seal with a waxed tissue. Make sure that no bubbles of air are trapped underneath.
4. Wipe jars when hot.
5. When cold, cover with dampened cellophane jam pot covers, placing them dry side down. Stretch the cellophane and fix with an elastic band.
6. Label with name of preserve, and the date, and store in a cool, dark, airy place.

Strawberry jam and marmalade may be left to stand for a few minutes before potting to prevent fruit rising in the jars.

Jelly is best potted in small jars so that it is eaten up quite quickly. In large jars it tends to 'weep'.

Aluminium or stainless steel pans are best, then they can be used for pickles and chutneys as well.

Always use a roomy pan for jam and jelly making. The preserve rises very high during the final boiling and spits fiercely. Aim to have your pan not more than half full before you start.

Granulated sugar is excellent but proper preserving sugar crystals are said to give a brighter result when making jelly. Castor and brown sugar produce a lot of extra froth. It is best to warm sugar before adding to pan of fruit. It will then dissolve quickly.

Jelly bags can be bought, but a piece of sheeting or even old blanket can be used. In each case scald it before using by pouring boiling water through it and wringing it out. If jelly is to be clear the bag of pulp must not be squeezed. Allow at least 2 hours for juice to drip through.

BLACKBERRY AND APPLE JAM

No seeds.
Yields about 2·25 kg/5 lb jam for every 1·4 kg/3 lb sugar used

1·8 kg/4 lb blackberries
300 ml/½ pint water
675 g/1½ lb cooking apples, weigh after peeling and coring
Sugar (*see paragraphs 3 and 4 below*)

1. Simmer blackberries very gently in half of the water until tender. Then sieve to remove the seeds.
2. Meanwhile, prepare apples and slice finely. Simmer them in remaining water till soft and pulpy.
3. Combine blackberry purée and apple pulp and weigh it.
4. Weigh out an equal quantity of sugar and put it in a bowl to warm in a very cool oven, Gas ¼, 225°F, 110°C.
5. Boil the pulp until it is thick. Then add the warmed sugar and stir without boiling till it is dissolved.
6. When it is completely dissolved bring to boil and boil rapidly till setting point is reached. It may be only a few minutes (*see notes, page 166*).
7. Fill warmed jars to the brim. Put on at once a well-fitting waxed tissue waxed side down. This is to seal the jam and protect it from the atmosphere.
8. Wipe the jars and put on outer covers, either while hot or when cold, *never* in between.
9. Label with name and date and store in a cool, dark, dry well-ventilated place.

GREEN EGG PLUM JAM

Look out for these plums in mid-August and buy green ones if you can. This is important as it produces a nice tangy jam with a good green colour.

Yields about 2¼ kg/5 lb

1·4 kg/3 lb plums
300 ml/½ pint water
1·4 kg/3 lb sugar

1. Wash plums and remove stalks.
2. Simmer them in the water in a large pan until skins are really tender. Skim off stones as they rise to the surface.
If liked a few plum kernels may be cracked out of the stones and added to the jam at this stage.
3. Meanwhile, put sugar in a dish in a very cool oven, Gas ¼, 225°F, 110°C, for about 20 minutes to warm. Put clean jars in oven to warm at same time.
4. Add warmed sugar to pan of fruit, stir until dissolved without letting it boil.
5. Then boil rapidly, stirring occasionally, until setting point is reached (*see page 166*). Begin testing after 6 minutes.
6. Pot, seal, cover and store as directed on *page 167*.

Mrs Olive Odell
Hartlebury, Worcestershire

POTTED RASPBERRY JAM

Yields 3·6 kg/8 lb—easy to make less

Keeps for only 5 to 6 months. This preserve does not set like ordinary jam. The fruit rises and there is a layer of jelly at the bottom. However, its flavour is superb and it is good for sponges, tarts, etc. Give it a stir in jar before using.

1·8 kg/4 lb raspberries, in perfect condition
1·8 kg/4 lb castor sugar, dissolves more easily than granulated

1. Do not wash raspberries. They must be perfectly dry. Put sugar in another bowl. Put both bowls in the oven. Put clean jars to warm in oven at same time.
2. Heat oven to cool, Gas 2, 300°F, 150°C, for about 25 minutes or until the juice starts to run. Switch off heat.
3. Now mix the sugar and raspberries and stir until sugar has dissolved.
4. Pot into warm jars, put on a waxed tissue and leave till cold before covering jars (*see notes, page 167*).

RHUBARB AND ORANGE JAM

Yields about 3·4 kg/7½ lbs

Good as a filling for a plate-pie.

1·8 kg/4 lb rhubarb
2·3 kg/5 lb sugar
2 oranges
1 lemon
450 g/1 lb seedless raisins*

*****As an economy raisins may be replaced by 450 g/1 lb bananas. Slice them just before they are added at paragraph 4 below.**

1. Wash and trim rhubarb. Cut it into 2·5 cm/1 inch lengths. Put into preserving pan or large saucepan and sprinkle over the sugar.
2. Grate rind from oranges and lemon. Squeeze juice.
3. Add raisins, juice and rind. If using bananas, do not put them in at this stage. Mix with a wooden spoon and allow to stand for 1 hour.
4. Bring to the boil, stirring to ensure there is no undissolved sugar. If using bananas add them now, thinly-sliced. Cook slowly for about 45 minutes, stirring occasionally until liquid evaporates from the fruit and jam is thick. Do not boil this jam hard or rhubarb goes to a mush.
5. Meanwhile, prepare clean jam jars. Put them to dry and warm in a very cool oven, Gas ¼, 225°F, 110°C. Although this jam is not boiled hard to reach setting point it still keeps well as long as it is potted in the usual way, as follows.

6. Fill warmed jars to the brim with the hot jam. Immediately put on well-fitting waxed tissues, waxed side down. This seals the jam and protects it from the atmosphere.

7. Wipe jars and put on outer covers, either while jam is hot or cold, but *never* in between.

8. Label with name and date and store in a cool, dark, dry, well-ventilated place.

Mrs Doreen Allars
Welbourn, Nr. Lincoln

STRAWBERRY JAM

An old recipe. As alum is sold nowadays with a 'not for food use' label, it can be left out. Use sugar-with-pectin in place of 2.25 kg/5 lb sugar.

1·8 kg/4 lb strawberries
2·25 kg/5 lb sugar
10 ml/2 teaspoons alum, can be bought at chemists

1. Allow fruit to thaw a little. Then put it in a large saucepan with the sugar and bring to the boil, stirring all the time until sugar has dissolved.

2. Boil briskly for 10 minutes.

3. Meanwhile, put clean jars to warm in a very cool oven, Gas ¼, 225°F, 110°C.

4. Take pan off heat and allow bubbling to stop.

5. Stir in alum, then return pan to heat and bring to the boil again. Remove from the heat.

6. Allow jam to cool for 10 minutes so that fruit will remain evenly suspended when potted.

7. Pot jam following notes *on page 167*.

Anne Wallace
Stewarton, Ayrshire

MINCED SEVILLE MARMALADE

Yields about 3·2 kg/7 lb

1 kg/2 lb Seville bitter oranges*
1 large lemon
2·3 litres/4 pints water
1·8 kg/4 lb granulated sugar
15 g/½ oz butter

***If using oranges taken from the freezer add one extra orange.**

1. Scrub fruit and remove green stalk ends.

2. Cut each orange in two. Squeeze out all pips and put them in a piece of muslin tied with a long string.

3. Cut lemon in two and squeeze out juice.

4. Put water in a large deep pan. Add lemon juice and bag of pips tied to handle of pan.

5. Put orange shells through mincer or a food processor, then into pan. Leave overnight.

6. Next day, simmer this mixture in pan with the lid on for 15 minutes. Then remove lid and simmer uncovered for about 1 hour, to reduce mixture by about half.

7. Meanwhile put sugar to warm in a very cool oven, Gas ¼, 225°F, 110°C, prepare clean jars and put them to warm in oven too.

8. Test marmalade for pectin strength (*see page 166*).

9. Add warmed sugar. Stir well. Do not let it boil before sugar has dissolved. Then turn up heat and bring to a fast rolling boil, lid off pan. Stir occasionally.

10. After 15 to 20 minutes test for a set (*see page 166*).

11. When setting point has been reached, remove pip bag. Remove pan from heat. Add butter to disperse scum. Stir again.

12. Let marmalade stand for about 5 minutes to cool a little. Otherwise peel may rise in jars, leaving a gap at bottom. Then stir again to distribute peel and pour into warmed jars. Fill to brim.

13. Put on a well-fitting waxed tissue to seal surface and complete according to notes *on page 167*.

Very economical marmalade.

In place of 1 kg/2 lb Seville oranges use:

450 g/1 lb Sevilles
450 g/1 lb peel from sweet oranges and grapefruit

This peel can be frozen at any time of year until enough is collected to make marmalade or until Sevilles season returns.

Proceed with recipe as before.

JELLY MARMALADE

Yields 2·25 kg/5 lb

Grapefruit

2 grapefruit ⎫ combined weight
3 lemons ⎭ 900 g/2 lb
2·6 litres/4½ pints water
1·4 kg/3 lb sugar

Orange

900 g/2 lb Seville oranges
2·6 litres/4½ pints water
Juice of 2 lemons or 1 teaspoon citric or tartaric acid
1·4 kg/3 lb sugar

1. Score the fruit in quarters then scald. To do this, pour boiling water over and leave for 5 minutes. Then drain.
2. Remove peel and cut white pith away from rind. Shred the rind finely.
3. Cut pith and fruit coarsely, put in a saucepan with 1·4 litres/2½ pints of the water (plus lemon juice or acid for Orange Jelly). Put on lid, bring to boil and simmer for 2 hours.
4. Meanwhile, put shredded rind in another pan with 600 ml/1 pint water, put on lid and simmer 1½ hours or until tender.
5. Drain liquid from shreds into pan of pulp.
6. Set up jelly bag (*see notes on page 167*).
7. Empty pan of pulp into jelly bag and allow to drip for 10 to 15 minutes.
8. Return pulp to pan with remaining 600 ml/1 pint of water. Cover pan and simmer for 20 minutes more.
9. Pour this into jelly bag and let it drip without squeezing bag for at least 2 hours.
10. Meanwhile, put sugar to warm in a very cool oven, Gas ¼, 225°F, 110°C, and put small clean jars to warm at same time.

11. Put juice into a roomy pan, bring to the boil, turn down heat and add sugar. Stir until it is dissolved.
12. Then add shredded rind and boil rapidly until setting point is reached (*see notes on page 166*).
13. Quickly skim off froth, then allow jelly to cool until a skin forms, 5 to 10 minutes.
14. Stir gently and pot following notes *on page 167*.

GRAPEFRUIT AND GINGER CHEESE

An interesting way to use the peel remaining after making Grapefruit Jelly (*see previous recipe*). It may be sliced and eaten as a dessert with whipped cream or a few chopped nuts, or with plain biscuits or wholemeal scones and butter.
It is best potted in straight-sided jars, moulds or even old mugs, so that when served it can be turned out on to a plate.

Peel from 2 grapefruit and 3 lemons used for Grapefruit Jelly
Sugar
About 1 level teaspoon ground ginger

For potting

A little glycerine

1. Sieve the pulp.
2. Weigh the purée. It will probably be 350 g/12 oz.
3. Put the same weight of sugar in a dish into a very cool oven, Gas ¼, 225°F, 110°C, for 20 minutes to warm. Put clean, straight-sided jars or moulds into oven to warm at same time.
4. Heat purée in a pan. Remove from heat and add sugar, stirring until it is completely dissolved.
5. Add up to 1 level teaspoon ginger, according to taste. Bring to the boil then simmer, stirring occasionally, for about 10 minutes until mixture coats back of spoon thickly.

6. Smear glycerine inside warmed jars. This helps release cheese from jars when it is turned out.
7. Pour hot cheese into jars, press waxed tissues, waxed-side down, on to the hot surface to seal it. Cover and store as directed for jams (*see page 167*).

Can be eaten a week after making. Best used within 6 months.

Mrs R. Punt
Wychbury W.I., Worcestershire

PLUM BUTTER

Any plums, including greengages and damsons, may be used.

Plums
A little water
Honey
Ground allspice
Ground nutmeg

1. Put plums in a pan with a very little water, barely 1 cm/½ inch deep.
2. Cover pan with a well-fitting lid and allow plums to simmer until they are tender.
3. Put plums through a sieve to make a purée.
4. Measure purée in a measuring jug and put it back in pan.
5. Now measure out honey to exactly half the quantity of purée. Add this to the pan with just enough of the spices to flavour it gently.
6. Cook slowly, stirring often, until it is thick and creamy with no loose liquid.
7. Meanwhile, prepare clean jars with air-tight lids and put jars to dry and warm in a very cool oven, Gas ¼, 225°F, 110°C.
8. Pour hot, plum butter into warmed jars. Put on air-tight lids at once.
9. Label with name and date.

This will not keep for more than a few weeks.

CRANBERRY AND ORANGE PRESERVE

Delicious with roast turkey. Sets like jelly.

450 g/1 lb granulated sugar
450 g/1 lb fresh or frozen cranberries
Finely-grated rind and juice of 1 orange
Water

1. Put sugar to warm in oven on lowest heat, Gas ¼, 225°F, 110°C. Put clean 225 g/½ lb jars into oven at same time.
2. Pick over fruit and discard any that is bruised. Put cranberries into a roomy saucepan.
3. Mix orange juice with water to make 300 ml/½ pint. Add to pan with rind.
4. Bring to the boil over gentle heat and simmer for 10 minutes, stirring occasionally. Cranberries will cook down to a thick pulp. Draw pan off heat.
5. Push pulp through a nylon sieve to make a purée, scraping as much as possible from under the sieve.
6. Put purée in a clean pan, add sugar and stir over low heat until sugar is dissolved.
7. Now turn up heat and boil for 4 to 5 minutes.
8. Pour hot preserve into prepared jars. Finish as indicated *on page 167*.

MEDLAR JELLY

Yields about 1·1 kg/2½ lbs

1·8 kg/4 lbs medlars
1 large lemon or 2 teaspoons citric acid
About 1·7 litres/3 pints water
Sugar

It is a good idea to use small jars for jelly because when it has been opened for a little time it begins to go runny.

1. Wash and cut up medlars and put into a preserving pan or large saucepan with enough water to cover. Simmer slowly, till it is reduced to a pulp.

171

2. Strain through a scalded jelly bag. To be sure of getting a clear jelly it is best not to squeeze the bag.

3. Measure the juice and return it to the pan. To every 600 ml/1 pint juice weigh out 350 g/12 oz sugar.

4. Put sugar in a bowl to warm in a very cool oven, Gas ¼, 225°F, 110°C. Prepare clean, small jars and put them to dry and warm in coolest part of oven.

5. Add citric acid (if lemon has not been used) and bring pan of juice to the boil. Add warmed sugar. Stir without letting it boil until sugar is dissolved.

6. Boil rapidly until setting point is reached (*see page 166*). It usually takes about 25 minutes.

7. Skim off the scum with a metal spoon. Then fill the jars without delay before jelly starts to set.

8. Put on at once well-fitting, waxed tissues, waxed-side down. This is to seal the jelly and protect it from the atmosphere.

9. With jelly it is easier to put outer cover on jars when it is set, but wait until it is quite cold.

10. Label with name and date and store in cool, dark, dry well-ventilated place.

Mrs Doreen Allars
Welbourn, Nr. Lincoln

MINT JELLY

Made from gooseberries.

Yields about 450 g/1 lb

Often made with apples. However the combination of mint and gooseberries is lovely, especially with lamb.

Not a clear jelly.

450 g/1 lb small green gooseberries
Water
Sugar
A bunch of fresh mint, about 10 to 12 fresh stalks, tied together
1 or 2 drops of green food colouring (optional)

1. There is no need to top and tail gooseberries. Just wash and put them into a pan.

2. Just cover with water and cook gently until very mushy.

3. Strain through a nylon sieve, pressing gently but not pushing the pulp through.

4. Measure this juice and for every 600 ml/1 pint add 450 g/1 lb sugar.

5. Put sugar to warm in a very cool oven, Gas ¼, 225°F, 110°C. Put small clean jars to warm also.

6. Put juice, sugar and mint in a pan. Heat gently, stirring until sugar is dissolved.

7. Bring to the boil and boil rapidly, stirring occasionally until setting point is reached (*see notes on page 166*).

8. Remove mint and add green food colouring, if used.

9. Pour carefully in warm jars and finish according to notes *on page 167.*

PICKLES, CHUTNEYS AND SAUCES

Fruits for pickling need to be firm and sound but not of the finest quality. Vegetables should be young, fresh and crisp. Cheaper fruit, provided it is firm, usually forms the basis for chutney.

Aluminium and stainless steel pans are best. Use only wooden spoons, a nylon sieve and stainless steel knives.

Fruit and vegetables for chutney are chopped or minced and cooked to soften in a covered pan with very little water. A pressure cooker is ideal. Vinegar is not usually added at first as it can have a hardening effect and so prolong cooking, thus making the product less economical.

Once all ingredients are combined, chutney is cooked gently until thick, stirring often so that it does not catch. When a spoon drawn through the mixture leaves its trail, and does not at once fill with excess liquid, the chutney is ready to pot.

Pot into clean, dry, warm jars, filling to the brim.

Covers for jars need to be vinegar-resistant—e.g., metal twist top with plastic inner coating, soft plastic snap-on type, or hard plastic screw-on type. Cellophane jam pot covers are not suitable because vinegar will evaporate. Plain metal tops will corrode and rust and impart a metallic taste.

Allow chutneys to mature for 1 or 2 months before using.

Spiced vinegar for pickles can now be bought, but there are 2 methods for home-made:

Best Spiced Vinegar

7 g/¼ oz each of cinnamon bark, whole allspice, whole cloves and whole mace
6 peppercorns
1·1 litre/2 pints white vinegar

Tie spices loosely in a piece of muslin and leave in the vinegar for 2 months, stirring often. Allow to settle for 3 days before straining ready for use.

Quickly Spiced Vinegar

1. Put vinegar and spices in a bowl and cover with a plate.
2. Stand basin in a pan of water. Bring water slowly to boiling point.
3. Remove bowl from heat and leave to stand for 3 hours.
4. Strain and cool.

TO PICKLE NASTURTIUM SEEDS

These are a substitute for capers. Useful for sauces including Sauce Tartare.

1. Pick the green seeds when tiny, about the size of dried peas.
2. Soak for three days in salted water, changing the water daily.
3. Drain and pat dry.
4. Use jars with vinegar-proof lids. Coffee jars with plastic lids can be used.
5. Pack seeds into jars with a little finely-chopped onion if wanted.
6. Cover with cold spiced vinegar (see above) and leave for one week to mature.

SWEET PICKLED PRUNES

These can be eaten immediately, do not need to mature. Keep for a year. Good with cold meat and a good alternative to black olives on pizza.

225 g/8 oz dried prunes
225 g/8 oz soft brown sugar
300 ml/½ pint malt vinegar
150 ml/¼ pint water
A 5 cm/2 inch piece of cinnamon

1. Put prunes in a basin, add sugar, vinegar, water and cinnamon. Cover and leave overnight.
2. Next day, turn everything into a saucepan. Simmer until the prunes are tender, about 10 minutes. Leave to cool.
3. Lift out the prunes, split and remove the stones.
4. Pack prunes into jars.
5. Return the pan of syrup to the heat. Simmer for one minute and pour over the prunes to cover.
6. Put on vinegar-proof lids, label and store.

UNCOOKED CHUTNEY

Yields nearly 1·4 kg/3 lb

This chutney is ready to eat as soon as it is made. Good fill-in between seasons. Best eaten within 6 weeks.

250 g/8 oz each of dates, sultanas, apple, onion
250 g/8 oz soft brown sugar, try muscovado
300 ml/½ pint spiced vinegar (see opposite)
5 g/1 teaspoon salt
A pinch each of pepper, mustard and cayenne pepper

1. Using coarse plates of mincer, mince the dates, sultanas, apple and onion.
2. Mix well with all other ingredients.
3. Use clean dry jars with vinegar-proof lids. Fill jars, cover and store in a cool dry place.

Anne Wallace
Stewarton, Ayrshire

KENTISH APPLE CHUTNEY

Yields about 1·8 kg/4 lbs

Traditionally made late in winter with stored apples. A mild, sweet, firm chutney, quick to make.

1 kg/2 lb apples
600 ml/1 pint spiced pickling vinegar (*see page 173*)
450 g/1 lb sugar
1½ teaspoons salt
1 teaspoon ground allspice
125 g/4 oz preserved ginger
350 g/12 oz sultanas

1. Peel, core and chop apples into small pieces.
2. Put vinegar, sugar, salt and allspice into a large saucepan and bring to the boil, stirring to dissolve sugar. Add apples. Simmer for 10 minutes.
3. Meanwhile, wash syrup from ginger, dry and chop into very small pieces. Add to pan with sultanas.
4. Simmer until chutney thickens, stirring occasionally so that it does not burn. It is thick enough when a spoon drawn through the mixture leaves its trail and does not at once fill with liquid.
5. Meanwhile, choose jars with vinegar-proof lids. Coffee jars with plastic lids are ideal. Put clean jars to warm in a very cool oven, Gas ¼, 225°F, 110°C.
6. Allow chutney to cool slightly before putting into jars. Put on waxed paper discs and, when chutney is quite cold, put on vinegar-proof lids.
7. Label with name and date and store in a cool, dry, well-ventilated cupboard.

Allow to mature 6 weeks before eating.

Mrs Jill Marshall
Hythe, Kent

DATE CHUTNEY

This chutney is made in small quantities to be eaten as soon as it is made. Keeps well.

225 g/8 oz dates
350 ml/12 fl oz malt vinegar
6 tablespoons demerara or muscovado sugar
4 cloves of garlic, finely-chopped
1 teaspoon fresh ginger, finely-chopped
50 g/2 oz sultanas
2 teaspoons paprika
1 teaspoon salt

1. Chop dates quite small.
2. Put vinegar and sugar in a pan, stir over low heat to dissolve sugar, then bring rapidly to the boil.
3. Reduce heat and add dates, garlic and ginger.
4. Cook on a low heat for 5 minutes, stirring all the time.
5. Add the sultanas, paprika and salt and cook for a further 5 minutes.

Do not overcook or it will turn to caramel.

Priya Wickramasinghe
Cardiff

ELDERBERRY CHUTNEY

450 g/1 lb elderberries
450 g/1 lb onions
450 g/1 lb cooking apples or windfalls—weigh them after peeling and coring
125 g/4 oz dried fruit—raisins, sultanas or both
1 teaspoon mixed spice
1 teaspoon ginger
1 teaspoon salt
¼ teaspoon cayenne pepper
300 ml/½ pint malt vinegar
350 g/12 oz sugar

1. Remove elderberries from stalks. To do this, hold them over a large basin and strip off berries with a table fork. (A large basin is necessary because berries tend to fly everywhere.)
2. Peel and finely chop onions. Chop apples finely. Put in a large pan.
3. Add dried fruit, spices, salt, pepper and half the vinegar.
4. Bring to the boil and simmer until ingredients are soft.

5. Add sugar and remaining vinegar. Stir over low heat until sugar is dissolved.

6. Then simmer until chutney is thick. It is thick enough when you can draw a wooden spoon through the mixture and the trail of the spoon remains without filling with excess liquid. Stir frequently to prevent sticking.

7. Meanwhile, prepare clean jars with vinegar-proof lids. Coffee jars with plastic lids are ideal. Warm the jars in a very cool oven—Gas ¼, 225°F, 110°C.

8. Fill jars to the brim with hot chutney and put on waxed paper discs, waxed-side down. Leave to cool.

9. When quite cold, put on the vinegar-proof lids. Label jars with the name and date.

10. Store in a cool, dark, dry, well-ventilated cupboard.

Mrs Lynda M. White
Wroot, Nr. Doncaster

ORANGE CHUTNEY

Yields 2·25 to 2·7 kg/5 to 6 lbs

Delicious with cold pork or hot sausages.

450 g/1 lb onions, peeled and sliced
Water
1 kg/2 lb apples, peeled, cored and sliced
2·3 litres/4 pints good malt vinegar
1·8 kg/4 lb sweet oranges
450 g/1 lb sultanas or raisins
15 to 20 fresh green or red chillis, de-seeded, or 8 dried red chillis*, deseeded and tied in a muslin bag
2 dessertspoons cooking salt
2 teaspoons ground ginger
1 kg/2 lb white sugar

*Fresh chillis are quite mild. It is the dried chillis which are peppery and 4 would be enough if you don't like chutney too hot.

1. Cook onions until tender, in water just to cover. Strain (saving liquid for soup).

2. Add apple and about a cupful of the vinegar and continue cooking gently until mushy. Remove from heat.

3. Meanwhile, scrub oranges and peel them. Remove white pith from outer skin and discard. Reserve the peel.

4. Put peel and orange flesh through mincer, removing as many pips as possible.

5. Mince sultanas or raisins and the chillis, if fresh ones are used.

6. Put dried chillis and other ingredients, except sugar, into the pan with about half the remaining vinegar. Simmer until thick, stirring occasionally.

7. Add sugar and rest of vinegar. Stir to dissolve sugar and simmer again until thick. Stir occasionally or it will stick and burn.

8. Remove muslin bag if dried chillis are used. Finish, pot and store as indicated *on page 172.*

9. Allow to mature for 6 weeks before using.

PLUM CHUTNEY

Yields 1·8 kg/4 lb

Can be made with all types of plums but dark-skinned varieties give it the best colour. Cider vinegar gives chutney a lovely flavour.

1·1 kg/2½ lb plums
450 g/1 lb onions, finely-chopped
Water
900 g/2 lb cooking apples
600 ml/1 pint cider vinegar
A piece of root ginger
1 dessertspoon each of whole cloves, whole allspice and peppercorns
450 g/1 lb soft brown sugar
3 level teaspoons salt

1. Wipe, halve and stone the plums.

2. Put onions in a saucepan, cover with water and boil for 5 minutes to soften them. Drain (saving liquid for soup, etc.).

3. Peel, core and chop apples. Put these and the plums in a large pan with half of the vinegar. Bring to the boil and cook for 20 minutes to a soft pulp.

4. Meanwhile, bruise the ginger by hitting it with a hammer. Then tie it with the other spices in a piece of muslin.

5. Put spice bag with vinegar and sugar into another pan. Bring to the boil and simmer for 5 minutes, stirring all the time. Draw pan off heat and let the vinegar infuse for 30 minutes. Then remove spice bag.

6. Add with onions and salt to apples. Bring to the boil and simmer for about 2 hours until chutney is thick and pulpy. Stir frequently in case it sticks and burns.

7. Finish, pot and store as indicated *on page 172.*

8. Allow to mature for 4 weeks before using.

TOMATO RELISH

1·6 kg/3½ lbs firm ripe tomatoes, skinned (*see page 72*) or use two 675 g/1½ lb tins of tomatoes
1 kg/2 lbs onions, finely-chopped
1 teaspoon salt
1 kg/2 lb sugar
90 g/3½ oz demerara sugar
25 g/1 oz fresh ginger, finely-chopped
7 g/¼ oz chilli powder
600 ml/1 pint malt vinegar

1. Chop tomatoes and place all ingredients, except vinegar, in a pan. Stir over low heat until sugar is dissolved. Cook gently for about 1 hour to a thick consistency, stirring occasionally.

2. Add vinegar and cook for another 10 minutes.

3. Pour the chutney while hot into warmed, clean, dry jars with vinegar-proof lids.

4. Put on the lids when chutney is cold. Label and store in a cool, dry place.

Priya Wickramasinghe
Cardiff

BROWN PLUM SAUCE

Yields about 1·75 litres/3 pints

Keeps very well.
A simple recipe.

1·1 kg/2½ lb red plums
3 medium-sized onions, sliced
125 g/4 oz sultanas
15g/½ oz root ginger
25 g/1 oz pickling spice
1·2 litres/2 pints malt or white vinegar
225 g/8 oz granulated sugar
50 g/2 oz salt
25 g/1 oz dry mustard
1 teaspoon ground nutmeg
1 level teaspoon turmeric

1. Wipe and stone plums and put them in a large pan. Don't worry if stones are firmly anchored—pick them out later.

2. Add onions and sultanas.

3. Bruise the ginger by hitting it with a hammer. Tie it with pickling spice in a piece of muslin. Put it in pan.

4. Add half of the vinegar and boil for 30 minutes.

5. Meanwhile put sugar to warm in a very cool oven, Gas ¼, 225°F, 110°C. Put clean bottles into oven to warm at same time. (Choose bottles with vinegar-proof lids.)

6. Remove spice bag and stir in all the other ingredients. Stir to dissolve sugar and bring to boiling point.

7. Simmer for 40 to 60 minutes, stirring occasionally, then leave to cool.

8. When cool, push contents of pan through a nylon sieve. Remember to scrape all the purée off underside of sieve.

9. If the sauce is too thin, simmer and reduce the volume by evaporation until it is thicker but still of pouring consistency.

10. Pour into warmed bottles, right to the brim and put on clean lids immediately. Label and store.

11. Leave for 4 weeks to mature.

LEMON OR ORANGE CURD

Yields about ½ kg/1 lb

2 lemons or oranges
75 to 100 g/3 to 4 oz butter
225 g/8 oz granulated sugar
2 eggs and one extra yolk

1. Scrub fruit and grate it, removing only the zest. *Or*, peel fruit very finely with potato peeler. Squeeze juice.
2. Put rind and juice with butter and sugar into an earthenware jar or basin. Stand this in a pan of simmering water. A double saucepan is ideal. Take care that water in outside pan never splashes into mixture. Keep water simmering and stir until sugar dissolves.
3. Meanwhile, put clean jars to warm in a very cool oven, Gas ¼, 225°F, 110°C.
4. In another basin fork up the eggs, removing the germ. Do not whisk.
5. Pour fruit mixture over eggs, through a strainer if whole pieces of rind were used, and return to the double cooker.
6. Cook until curd thickens, stirring in one direction. It may take 30 to 45 minutes before it is really thick. Stir every 4 or 5 minutes. Curd thickens a little more in jars as it cools.
7. Pour into warmed jars. Put a waxed tissue on top.
8. When quite cold put on jam pot covers.

Keeps for 6 weeks. Best kept in a refrigerator.

GOOSEBERRY CURD

Yields 900 g/2 lb

700 g/1½ lb young green gooseberries*
300 ml/½ pint water
100 g/4 oz butter
325 g/12 oz sugar
3 eggs

*If you cannot get young gooseberries, 1 or 2 drops of green food colouring can be used.

1. There is no need to top and tail gooseberries. Put them in with the water in a pan, bring to boil and simmer until pulpy.
2. Meanwhile, put clean jars to warm in a very cool oven, Gas ¼, 225°F, 110°C.
3. Push gooseberries through a nylon sieve, taking care to scrape purée from underside of sieve.
4. Put butter and sugar into a double saucepan or into a basin standing in a pan of simmering water. Stir to dissolve sugar. Add gooseberry purée.
5. In another bowl, beat eggs but do not whisk. Stir in hot gooseberry mixture, then return to double cooker.
6. Cook, stirring all the time until mixture thickens.
7. Pour into warmed jars. Put a waxed tissue on top.
8. When quite cold, put on jam pot covers.

Can be eaten straight away. Keeps for 6 weeks. Best kept in a refrigerator.

Delicious as a filling for tartlets and sponges. Also in meringue baskets, but fill them, of course, at the very last minute.

MINCEMEAT

As mincemeat is liable to ferment, it is best if potted in a large jar and kept in refrigerator.

225 g/8 oz seedless raisins
125 g/4 oz sultanas
125 g/4 oz eating apples, peeled
125 g/4 oz mixed peel
50 g/2 oz grated suet
225 g/8 oz currants
Grated rind and juice of 1 lemon
125 g/4 oz soft brown sugar
1 tablespoon golden syrup
1 teaspoon mixed spice
1 teaspoon cinnamon
¼ teaspoon grated nutmeg
4 tablespoons brandy or whisky

1. Mince the raisins, sultanas, apple, peel and suet using the coarse mincing plates. Leave the currants whole.
2. Put all ingredients together and mix well.

3. Pot as suggested in previous recipe with a good lid, and keep in refrigerator.

COCONUT ICE

350 g/¾ lb sugar
150 ml/¼ pint milk
125 g/4 oz desiccated coconut
1 or 2 drops of vanilla essence

The same ingredients are used again for a second batch, which is coloured pink.

1. Put sugar and milk in a saucepan and stir over low heat until sugar is dissolved. Then boil for 5 minutes.
2. Pour into a basin and add coconut and vanilla. Beat until mixture becomes thick.
3. Spread in a buttered dish or tin.
4. Make the second batch, using a few drops of red food colouring. Spread it on top of white.

Nathalie Jowett
Yea, Victoria, Australia

CREAM TOFFEE

A toffee with a soft texture.

175 g/6 oz butter
300 g/12 oz demerara sugar
2 tablespoons golden syrup
A 400 g/14 oz tin of condensed milk

1. Melt butter, sugar and golden syrup. Stir over low heat to dissolve sugar.
2. Add condensed milk.
3. Stirring often, boil for about 10 minutes until the soft ball stage—that is, when a few drops are put into a jug of iced water and the mixture forms a soft ball between the fingers. If it dissolves immediately continue to boil for a further 3 or 4 minutes.
4. Pour into a greased Swiss roll tin 28 by 18 cm/11 by 7 inches.
5. When cold, cut into squares and wrap each one in waxed paper. Because of the soft texture of this toffee it must be wrapped or all the pieces will stick together.

CREAMY CHOCOLATE
Makes about 30

150 g/5 oz plain cooking chocolate
50 g/2 oz butter
A few drops of vanilla essence
175 g/6 oz sweetened condensed milk
100 g/4 oz icing sugar
1 level tablespoon cocoa

1. Break the chocolate into pieces and put in a basin with the butter. Place the basin over a pan containing a little hot water. Heat the water gently to melt chocolate and butter.
2. Remove basin from heat, add vanilla essence and beat in the condensed milk.
3. Add icing sugar sieved with cocoa and beat until creamy.
4. Place a teaspoonful of mixture in paper sweet cases (waxed or foil ones are best) and leave to set.

Margaret Heywood
Todmorden, Yorkshire

FRUIT JELLIES

Blackcurrant, gooseberry and raspberry jellies can be made from the fresh fruit.

Fruit of your choice
Sugar
Lemon juice

1. Make a purée of the fruit by simmering it in the minimum of water to soften. Then rub through a sieve to remove skins and pips.
2. Measure the purée. To every 300 ml/½ pint allow 175 g/6 oz sugar and the juice of half a lemon.
3. Put purée, sugar and lemon juice in a pan. Heat gently, stirring to dissolve sugar before it boils.
4. Boil carefully, stirring most of the time to prevent burning. Test every minute or two after it gets thick by putting a little into a cup of cold water. When this forms a firm ball in the water it is ready.
5. Pour mixture into a wetted baking tin.

6. When the jelly is set, turn it out on to greaseproof paper covered in sugar and leave till completely cold.
7. Cut into suitable shapes. Toss in sugar.

Anne Wallace
Stewarton, Ayrshire

GLACÉ FRUITS

Fresh fruits such as strawberries, orange or mandarin segments, clusters of two grapes, etc., are dipped in caramel, giving them a shiny crisp coating. Canned fruit can also be used, including maraschino cherries, provided the syrup is dried off carefully before they are dipped in the caramel.

Lovely for a party, but cannot be made too far ahead as they go sticky in a day or so, particularly if weather is humid.

The quantity of syrup given is enough to coat about 20 pieces of fruit. You will need tiny crinkled paper sweet cases which can be bought at good stationers. Also, several wooden cocktail sticks for dipping. It is useful but not essential to have a sugar thermometer.

Syrup for caramel
100 g/4 oz sugar
60 ml/2½ fl oz hot water
5 ml/1 teaspoon glucose

1. Brush baking trays lightly with oil.
2. Prepare fruit, making sure it is clean and thoroughly dried.
3. Put sugar in the hot water in a pan, stirring over a low heat until dissolved.
4. Bring to boil and add glucose.
5. Boil to 290–300°F, 145–150°C, or until just before syrup turns brown.
6. Set pan on a wet cloth to stop it boiling.
7. As soon as syrup has stopped bubbling start dipping fruits, holding them by the stems or spearing them with a pair of wooden cocktail sticks.
8. Put each dipped fruit on oiled tray to set. Then place in small paper cases.

Anne Wallace
Stewarton, Ayrshire

PEANUT BUTTER BON-BONS
Makes about 24

100 g/4 oz seedless raisins, chopped
100 g/4 oz icing sugar, sieved
100 g/4 oz peanut butter
25 g/1 oz melted butter or margarine
50 to 75 g/2 to 3 oz plain cooking chocolate

1. Put raisins in a bowl with sugar and peanut butter. Mix to a paste with melted butter or margarine.
2. Shape into balls about the size of a grape and leave on foil or waxed paper to harden overnight.
3. Put chocolate to melt in a small bowl set over a pan of simmering water.
4. Dip the top of each bon-bon in melted chocolate and, when set, put in paper sweet cases.

Margaret Heywood
Todmorden, Yorkshire

RUSSIAN TOFFEE
Makes about 600 g/1¼ lbs

For this it is helpful, but not essential, to have a sugar thermometer.

50 g/2 oz butter
100 g/4 oz sugar
100 g/4 oz golden syrup
400 g/1 large tin condensed milk
25 g/1 oz redcurrant jelly
A few drops of vanilla essence

1. Put butter, sugar and syrup in a large saucepan over a low heat, and stir until sugar is completely dissolved.
2. Bring to boiling point and add condensed milk and redcurrant jelly.
3. Continue to boil to 265°F, 130°C, hard ball stage, stirring all the time.

If using a thermometer, be sure to have it by the pan in a container of very hot water, so that it is hot before it enters the toffee. Hard ball stage can be tested without a thermometer by

dropping a teaspoon of the mixture
into a cup of cold water. When you
feel it between thumb and fingers it is
a hard ball but still chewy.

4. Add vanilla and pour into a greased
18 cm/7 inch square tin.

5. When set, mark into squares. When
cold, cut and wrap in waxed paper.

6. Store in an airtight container.

Anne Wallace
Stewarton, Ayrshire

TOFFEE APPLES

For this you need a large heavy-based
pan, wooden lolly sticks and a large
greased baking tin.

12 small eating apples
450 g/1 lb white or brown sugar
50 g/2 oz butter
1 tablespoon golden syrup
2 teaspoons vinegar
150 ml/¼ pint water

1. Wash and dry the apples. Push a
stick into each stalk end.

2. Put all remaining ingredients into
a large pan. Stir over gentle heat until
sugar is dissolved, then boil rapidly for
5 minutes. Stir just a little.

3. The syrup in the pan has to boil
until it comes to the hard ball stage.
This means that when a little of the
syrup is dropped into a jug of ice-cold
water it forms a hard ball and this tells
you when your toffee is ready. Go on
boiling until this point is reached.

4. Remove pan from heat and, as
quickly as possible, dip the apples.
Twirl them around in toffee for a few
seconds, shake off the surplus and put
on to the greased baking tin to set.

If the toffee starts to set in the pan,
heat it gently again.

SPANISH QUINCE PASTE

1·8 kg/4 lb quinces
300 ml/½ pint water
Sugar

To finish: castor sugar

1. Wash the quinces. Cut them in
quarters and put them in a saucepan
with the water.

2. Simmer until soft, then put them
through a sieve.

3. Weigh the pulp and put it in a
large, clean pan.

4. Weigh an equal quantity of sugar
and mix it in.

5. Stir over low heat until sugar
dissolves. Continue cooking until
mixture becomes very thick. Stir
continuously.

6. Pour into shallow tins lined with
sheets of greaseproof paper.

7. Leave it in a warm place, such as an
airing cupboard, for 3 or 4 days. It will
dry out a little and be easy to handle.

8. Peel off the paper and cut the paste
into pieces. Roll them in castor sugar
and store between layers of greaseproof paper in an airtight tin or plastic
box.

Can be eaten as a dessert with cream
cheese.

Miss Elisabeth Gruber
Winchester

Chapter 12

Beer, Wine and Other Drinks

YEAST STARTER

175 ml/6 fluid oz water
1 dessertspoon malt extract
1 dessertspoon sugar
A pinch of citric acid
A pinch of yeast nutrient
The yeast, as indicated in recipe

1. Put water in a small pan, stir in
malt extract, sugar and citric acid.
Bring to the boil, then turn off heat.
2. Cool this solution a little, then pour
it into a small pop bottle, 300 ml/½ pint.
Plug neck of bottle with cotton-wool
and cool to 21°C, 70°F.
3. Add yeast. If it is a liquid yeast
culture, shake the phial before
emptying it into the bottle. Replace
cotton-wool plug and leave in a warm
place.
4. The yeast will ferment vigorously
and will be ready to use in 3 to 4 days.

PALE ALE

Makes 25 litres/5 gallons

1·4 kg/3 lb dried light malt
extract
450 g/1 lb crushed crystal malt
50 g/2 oz Golding hops
40 g/1½ oz Northern Brewer
hops
450g/1 lb soft light brown sugar

Yeast: British Ale

**For priming bottles: granulated
sugar**

1. Make up a yeast starter 3 to 4 days
before starting to make the pale ale.
Follow instructions *above*.
2. Warm up about 10 litres/2 gallons of
water. When hot, stir in the malts and
hops and boil for 45 minutes.
3. Strain into fermenting bin.
4. Rinse the hops and malt with 1 or 2
kettles full of hot water.
5. Add the sugar and stir to dissolve.
6. Make up volume to 25 litres/5
gallons with cold water.
7. When cool, 18 to 20°C, 65 to 70°F,
pitch the yeast starter.
8. Cover bin loosely. Leave in a warm
place to ferment for about 4 to 5 days.

9. If the bin has an air-tight lid with
an air lock, use this. Otherwise,
syphon pale ale into containers, such
as 4·5 litre/1 gallon jars, or larger
vessels if you have them, to which an
air-lock can be fitted.
10. Leave containers in a warm place
and let pale ale ferment to a gravity of
1·005 or less.
11. Syphon into proper beer bottles.
Be sure to use real beer bottles. Other
bottles are not strong enough to take
the build up of gas during the
secondary fermentation.
12. Prime bottles with ½ teaspoon
sugar per pint (575 ml) and screw in
stoppers tightly or fit new crown
corks.
13. Keep in a warm place for 3 to 4
days to allow priming sugar to ferment
and so give the pale ale condition.
14. Ready to drink 3 to 4 weeks after
bottling but improves if kept 2 to 4
months.

MILD ALE

An ale which is halfway between a
bitter and a stout, dark in colour, a
favourite tipple with many folk.

To make 25 litres/5 gallons

1·8 kg/4 lb malt extract
125 g/4 oz crushed black malt
50 g/2 oz Fuggles hops
350 g/12 oz soft dark brown
sugar

**Yeast: Top-fermenting, British
Ale**

Soft water is necessary for this. If you
do not live in a soft water area 1
teaspoon bicarbonate soda and 1
teaspoon salt can be added to a 25
litre/5 gallon brew. However, it is best
to consult a local home-brew shop
about the most suitable quantity in
your area.

Follow the method given for Pale Ale.
This ale, however, does not require
further maturing after the 3 to 4
weeks in the bottle.

SWEET STOUT

To make 25 litres/5 gallons

**1·5 kg/3 lb dried dark malt
extract
225 g/8 oz crushed black malt
225 g/8 oz crushed crystal malt
450 g/1 lb soft dark brown sugar
50 g/2 oz Fuggles hops
10 to 15 sweetening tablets**

Yeast: Top-fermenting

Soft water is necessary (*see Mild
Ale*).

Follow method given for Pale Ale,
adding sweetening tablets when wort
is still hot.

Dennis Rouston
Kippax, W. Yorkshire

WHITE DRY TABLE WINE

A handy recipe as the *main
ingredients come from the supermarket.* Ready to drink in 3 to 4
months but improves with keeping.

Makes 4·5 litres/1 gallon

**Two 675 ml/24 fl oz bottles pure
apple juice
One 675 ml/24 fl oz bottle pure
grape juice
3 level teaspoons (15 g) tartaric
acid
1 teaspoon Pectolase, or similar
½ teaspoon yeast nutrient
600 g/21 oz granulated sugar**

Sauternes yeast

1. Make up a yeast starter 4 to 5 days
before you want to make the wine.
Follow instructions *on page 182*.
2. Then put all ingredients, including
yeast starter, into a fermentation bin
or bucket with water to make volume
up to 4·5 litres/1 gallon. Stir to
dissolve sugar, etc. Cover loosely.
3. Stir daily for 3 to 4 days.
4. Syphon into a 4·5 litre/1 gallon jar
and top up to within 2·5 cm/1 inch of

top with water. Fit airlock or cover
with a piece of polythene held in place
with a rubber band.
5. Leave in a reasonably warm place,
about 20°C, 70°F, until wine is all but
clear.
6. Syphon wine off sediment into a
clean jar, topping up with cold water,
refitting airlock or polythene cover.
7. After about 3 months the wine will
be clear. If there is any sediment on
the bottom of the jar, syphon into a
clean jar and it should be ready to
drink. But it will improve with
keeping.
8. Once a jar is opened for drinking,
the wine should be bottled, otherwise
it will oxidise and the flavour and
appearance will be spoilt.

Ted Adcock
Northolt, Middlesex

WHITE DRY TABLE WINE—QUICK

Makes 13·5 litres/3 gallons

Gives you plenty of drinkable table
wine in 6 to 8 weeks, but it does
improve with keeping.

**Three 1 litre/35 fl oz cartons of
apple juice
½ litre/1 pint Riesling grape
concentrate (use Southern
Vineyards 'Grandier')
2·5 kg/5½ lb granulated sugar
2 teaspoons each tartaric acid,
yeast nutrient, Pectolase and
Bentonite**

Chablis or Sauternes yeast

1. Make up a yeast starter, at least 3
to 4 days before you want to make the
wine, following instructions *on page
182*.
2. Put all the other ingredients into
fermentation bin with water to make
volume up to 13·5 litres/3 gallons. Stir
well to dissolve.
3. Add the yeast starter. Ferment in
the bin for 14 days, stirring
occasionally. Keep bin covered loosely.

4. Syphon into 4·5 litre/1 gallon jars. Top up with cold water to within 2·5 cm/1 inch of top, fit airlock or a piece of polythene held in place with a rubber band.

5. After 3 to 4 weeks the wine should be clearing. Rack off (i.e., syphon wine off sediment) into clean jars.

6. Rack off the sediment again when clear and it should be ready to drink.

7. Once a jar is opened for drinking the wine should be bottled otherwise it will oxidise and the flavour and appearance will be spoilt.

Keith Simpson
Hartburn, Darlington

FARMHOUSE KITCHEN 'NOUVEAU'

A nice, light, rosé type of wine, with a fresh, clean taste and a pleasant bouquet, that just asks to be drunk young.

Because the various fruits ripen at different times, pick when ripe and freeze, then make the wine at your leisure.

Makes 4·5 litres/1 gallon

700 g/1½ lb blackberries
250 g/8 oz elderberries
125 g/4 oz blackcurrants
12 raspberries
Boiling water
1 kg/2·2 lb sugar
115 ml/4 fl oz white or rosé grape concentrate
1 teaspoon tartaric acid
1 teaspoon yeast nutrient
1 Campden tablet

Bordeaux or Port yeast

1. Make up yeast starter 3 to 4 days before beginning to make the wine. Follow instructions *on page 182*.

2. Put fruit into a large basin and pour over about 1 litre/2 pints of boiling water.

3. Put on rubber gloves and squeeze fruit.

4. Strain juice through muslin into a polythene fermenting bin or bucket.

5. Repeat this process twice—i.e., pour boiling water on to pulp, squeeze and strain. Then throw the pulp away on to the compost heap.

6. Add the sugar and stir to dissolve.

7. Make up the volume of juice to 4·5 litres/1 gallon with cold water. Let it cool to 18 to 20°C, 65 to 70°F.

8. Add the grape concentrate, tartaric acid, yeast nutrient, Campden tablet and the yeast starter.

9. Cover bin loosely with a cloth or lid.

10. Stir daily for 3 to 4 days, then pour into a 4·5 litre/1 gallon jar, top up to 2·5 cm/1 inch from top with cold water.

11. Fit airlock or cover top with a piece of polythene secured with a rubber band.

12. Leave in a warm place, not the airing cupboard, to ferment.

13. After about 3 months, rack off (i.e., syphon wine off sediment) into a clean jar, topping up to 2·5 cm/1 inch from top with water.

14. Rack again once or twice more at 3-month intervals. The wine should be ready to drink in less than a year.

15. Once a jar is opened for drinking, the rest of the wine should be bottled. Otherwise it may oxidise, and flavour and appearance could be spoilt.

Dennis Rouston
Kippax, Yorkshire

THREE WINES SAME METHOD

Each recipe makes 4·5 litres/1 gallon

White table wine

Dry or Sweet

This recipe gives a dry wine in the Muscadet style. If sweetened with white grape concentrate as suggested in the method, it gives it a Vouvray style.

1 kg/2 lb gooseberries, fresh,
frozen or tinned
250 g/8 oz very ripe bananas,
peeled
625 g/1 lb 6 oz sugar
225 ml/8 fl oz white grape
concentrate
3 level teaspoons tartaric acid
½ teaspoon yeast nutrient

Sauternes yeast

Red table wine

This recipe gives a dry red wine in the
Valpolicella style, but can be blended
with the white wine for a Rosé. It can
then be sweetened with white grape
concentrate for an Anjou-style Rosé.

570 g/1 lb 4 oz blackberries
150 g/5 oz elderberries
225 g/8 oz very ripe bananas,
peeled
650 g/1 lb 7 oz sugar
225 ml/8 fl oz red grape
concentrate
2 level teaspoons (10 g) tartaric
acid
½ teaspoon yeast nutrient

Bordeaux or Port yeast

Dessert wine

This wine will become medium-sweet
in the Madeira-style. The sweetness
can be adjusted with white grape
concentrate to give a Malmsey-style.

200 g/7 oz dried rosehip shells
(soak for 1 hour in warm water)
125 g/4 oz dried figs (soak for 1
hour in warm water)
225 g/8 oz very ripe bananas,
peeled
1 kg/2·2 lb sugar
10 g/2 level teaspoons tartaric
acid
½ teaspoon yeast nutrient

Madeira yeast

Sugar syrup made up with 900 g/2 lb
sugar stirred over low heat to dissolve
in 600 ml/1 pint water is added during
fermentation. At paragraph 7 in the
method begin to take gravity readings.
When gravity reaches 1·005 start
feeding in 50 ml/2 fl oz syrup once a
week until fermentation stops. This
could take a month or more.

Method

For this you need a liquidiser.

For each of the above wines you need:

2 Campden tablets
1 teaspoon Pectolase, or similar

1. Prepare a yeast starter and activate
with the suggested yeast 3 to 4 days
before it is required for the wine.
2. Liquidise the fruit with the
minimum of water.
3. Add 1 crushed Campden tablet and
1 teaspoon Pectolase. Cover with a
cloth and leave overnight.
4. Next day dissolve sugar by heating
gently in about 1 litre/1½ pints water,
stirring. Pour over fruit pulp, add the
grape concentrate, tartaric acid and
yeast nutrient.
5. Make up volume to about 4·5
litres/1 gallon then add yeast starter.
6. Ferment on the pulp for 3 to 5 days.
Stir daily.
7. Strain and put into a 4·5 litre/1
gallon jar. Top up with water to
within 2·5 cm/1 inch of top. Fit airlock
or a piece of polythene held with a
rubber band. If possible keep jar at a
controlled temperature of 20°C, 70°F,
while fermenting proceeds.
8. When wine has finished
fermenting, remove to a cool place, add
1 crushed Campden tablet and leave
for 2 to 3 days.
9. Then rack (i.e., syphon it off
sediment). If it throws another
sediment rack again.
10. Once a jar is opened for drinking,
the wine should be bottled. Otherwise
it will oxidise and the flavour and
appearance will be spoilt.
11. If you require the sweeter version,
add white grape concentrate as the
bottle is needed.

Ted Adcock
Northolt, Middlesex

DAMSON WINE

Makes a very nice steady sipping wine for a cold winter's evening. Sugar content can be varied to give a dry or sweet wine.

Makes 4·5 litres/1 gallon

1·8 kg/4 lb damsons
4·5 litres/1 gallon boiling water
125 ml/4 fl oz red grape concentrate
1 teaspoon yeast nutrient
1 teaspoon tartaric acid
1 teaspoon Pectolase or similar
1 kg/2 lb sugar, for a dry wine
Or, 1·5 kg/3¼ lb sugar, for a sweet wine

Port yeast

1. Make up a yeast starter 3 to 4 days before beginning to make wine. Follow instructions *on page 182*.
2. Then chop up damsons, removing stones and put chopped fruit into a fermentation bin or bucket.
3. Pour over boiling water, stir in ¼ kg/1 lb of the sugar and allow to cool.
4. Add other ingredients, including yeast starter.
5. Cover loosely with a cloth or lid and let it ferment on the pulp for 4 to 5 days. Stir at least twice daily.
6. Strain, taking care not to squeeze fruit or it may produce a hazy wine. Return liquor to bin.
7. Over the next 4 to 5 days add sugar, about ¼ kg/1 lb at a time, until the required amount has been used. Stir to dissolve.
8. Syphon into a 4·5 litre/1 gallon jar. Fit an airlock or a piece of polythene secured with a rubber band. Leave in a reasonably warm place.
9. Rack (i.e., syphon wine off sediment) at 3 to 4 month intervals until wine is clear and ready to drink.

It may take a year or more to mature before it will be drinkable, but it is well worth waiting for. Once a jar is opened for drinking the rest of the wine should be bottled. Otherwise flavour may be spoilt.

Dennis Rouston
Kippax, W. Yorkshire

RHUBARB WINE

A medium-sweet wine, which is not only good to drink, but also very useful for blending with other wines. With a freezer, it can be made at your leisure.

2·75 kg/6 lb rhubarb
125 ml/4 fl oz white grape concentrate
1 teaspoon Bentonite
1 Campden tablet
1 teaspoon yeast nutrient
1·35 kg/3 lb sugar

Sauternes yeast

1. Pick the rhubarb as early as possible until the end of June—while it is still pink or red.
2. Trim and wipe clean, cut long sticks in half, put into polythene bags to weigh ½ kg/1 lb. Then put into freezer.
3. Make up a yeast starter 3 to 4 days before beginning to make wine. Follow instructions *on page 182*.
4. Put a strainer over your fermentation bin, put a frozen packet of rhubarb into the strainer. Let it thaw.
5. When the rhubarb has thawed squeeze the last few drops out—throw away the pulp (or use it for a pie).
6. Repeat until 2·75 kg/6 lb rhubarb is used.
7. Add to the rhubarb juice the white grape concentrate, Bentonite, Campden tablet and yeast nutrient and 450 g/1 lb of the sugar. Stir to dissolve. Then stir in yeast starter.
8. Add water to make up volume to 4·5 litres/1 gallon. Cover the bin loosely with a cloth or lid.
9. Stir daily. On third day add 450 g/1 lb sugar. Stir to dissolve.
10. On the fifth day add the last 450 g/1 lb sugar. Stir to dissolve.
11. Next day syphon into a 4·5 litre/1 gallon jar, top up to within 2·5 cm/1 inch of top. Fit airlock or a piece of polythene secured with a rubber band. Leave to ferment in a reasonably warm place.
12. Syphon wine off sediment at 3 month intervals.

Should be ready to drink in 9 months. After opening a jar to drink, bottle the rest of the wine. Otherwise it may oxidise and flavour as well as appearance could be spoilt.

Dennis Rouston
Kippax, West Yorkshire

CIDER

A nice drink. Also very useful in the kitchen for cooking. A press is required which can be bought or made, or it is possible to hire one. Ready to drink in a month or so.

To make 4·5 litres/1 gallon

10 kg/20 lb windfall apples, a mixture of eaters and cookers is ideal
Granulated sugar
1 teaspoon tartaric acid

Sauternes yeast

1. Make up a yeast starter 3 to 4 days before starting to make the cider. Follow instructions *on page 182.*

2. Wipe the apples clean. Do not bother to cut out the bruises.
3. Mince them using coarsest mincer blades.
4. Put the minced apples into a coarse-woven bag, hessian is ideal. Then press, collecting the juice in your fermenting bin. Make up volume to 4·5 litres/1 gallon with water.
5. Measure the gravity with an hydrometer and add sugar until the gravity is 1·055. (15 g/½ oz sugar raises the gravity of 4·5 litres/1 gallon by one degree.)
6. Add tartaric acid and the Sauternes yeast starter. Stir to dissolve acid and sugar.
7. After 3 to 4 days syphon into a 4·5 litre/1 gallon jar, fit airlock or a piece of polythene held in place with a rubber band. Ferment to 1·005.
8. Then syphon off sediment into another jar and if the cider is nice and clear syphon into clean, strong, screw-topped cider or beer bottles. Returnable cider or beer bottles are suitable but the non-returnable are not strong enough. Add 1 level teaspoon sugar per pint. Screw down the top. If it is not clear leave it to settle before bottling.

The cider should be ready to use after a month or so.

CYSER

An old fashioned drink with more of a punch than cider, but a still drink, not sparkling. Matured for a year. As for cider you need a press (*see introduction to previous recipe*).

10 kg/20 lb windfall apples, a mixture of eaters and cookers is ideal
1 kg/2 lb honey
1 teaspoon tartaric acid
1 teaspoon yeast nutrient

Sauternes yeast

1. Make up a yeast starter 3 to 4 days before starting to make the cyser. Follow instructions *on page 182.*
2. Wipe the apples clean. Do not bother to cut out the bruises.

3. Mince them using coarsest mincer blades.
4. Put the minced apples into a coarse-woven bag, hessian is ideal. Then press as for cider, collecting juice in a fermenting bin.
5. Heat up 2 litres/3 pints of the apple juice to 60 to 65°C, 140 to 150°F.
6. Stir honey into hot juice. When dissolved, add to remaining juice. Leave to cool.
7. Add tartaric acid, yeast nutrient and Sauternes yeast starter. Put bin in a warm place.
8. Allow to ferment in the bin for 3 to 4 days.
9. Syphon into a 4·5 litre/1 gallon jar, fit airlock or a piece of polythene held in place with a rubber band. Any liquid over, put into a small bottle and plug neck with cotton wool.
10. Rack at 3 to 4 month intervals (i.e., syphon off the sediment). Top up jar to within 2·5 cm/1 inch of top with liquid from the little bottle. The cyser should be ready to drink in about a year.

Once the jar is opened for drinking the rest should be bottled or it may oxidise and deteriorate in flavour and appearance.

Dennis Rouston
Kippax, Yorkshire

BLACKCURRANT SYRUP

The same method can be used for blackberries, loganberries, raspberries and strawberries.

Blackcurrants
Sugar
Campden tablets
Use really ripe, clean, dry fruit.

1. Put fruit in an earthenware jar or a tall straight-sided jug. Crush it with a wooden spoon or pulper.

2. Cover the container with a thin cloth and leave in a warm room to ferment just a little. It will take 3 to 5 days. Other fruits mentioned above may only take 1 day to ferment, so keep an eye on it.
3. When bubbles of gas are forming on the surface, tip fruit into a scalded jelly bag. Allow it to drain overnight.
4. Next day press the bag thoroughly to remove any remaining juice.
5. Measure juice and to every 600 ml/1 pint add ½ kg/1 lb sugar. Stir until sugar is dissolved.
6. Strain syrup through jelly bag to make sure it is clear but this step is not essential.
7. For every 600 ml/1 pint of syrup add 1 Campden tablet dissolved in 1 tablespoon warm water.
8. Use really clean bottles. To be sure of this put them in a large pan of water. Bring to the boil, take bottles out and drain. Boil the caps for 15 minutes just before use.
9. Fill bottles to 1 cm/¼ inch of the top.
10. Once opened, keep bottles in a cool place or refrigerator.

WILLAWONG LEMON CORDIAL

3 to 4 lemons
450 g/1 lb white sugar
1 dessertspoon tartaric acid
600 ml/1 pint boiling water

1. Peel lemons finely to produce rind with no pith.
2. Squeeze lemons.
3. Put rinds, juice, sugar and tartaric acid into a bowl. Pour over boiling water. Stir till dissolved. Leave to cool, preferably overnight.
4. Strain and bottle.
5. Keep in a cool place or refrigerator.
6. Dilute with water to taste.

Nathalie Jowett
Yea, Victoria, Australia

INDEX

189

193

197

S

FARMHOUSE KITCHEN
COOKING FOR ONE & TWO

CONTENTS

ACKNOWLEDGMENTS.

The compilation of recipes for *Farmhouse Kitchen* books is a rewarding task. There are many viewers who take the trouble to write out and send in recipes and stories about dishes they have made for their family and friends, sometimes over generations. In fact, nearly a third of the recipes in this book have come from viewers, some of whom claim to have been watching *Farmhouse Kitchen* since the series began in 1970. Although I hope we've written to each of them about the recipes chosen for this book, now is my chance to make public my indebtedness and gratitude to all who have contributed or participated in its preparation.

Grace Mulligan is well aware of our viewers' requests and has a wide-ranging selection of recipes in every chapter. Her guest cooks – some who are already familiar faces in the programmes, some who will be introduced in the next year or so – have given recipes to suit their particular interests. They are Yvonne Coull, Head Home Economist of the Sea Fish Industry Authority; Dilwen Phillips from South Wales, well known throughout the Women's Institute, whose current interest is in fresh fast food, with the emphasis on fresh; Jill Myers from the British Diabetic Association; Jennie Siew Lee Cook whose dishes first appeared in her charity publication *My Favourite Chinese Recipes*; Nirmal Singh from Nuneaton whose Indian dishes will be a new feature in the programmes and David Shepperdson, manager of Winn's Fish in Huddersfield market, who brings some everyday fish and some less-so to our attention, and who has forgotten more than some of us ever knew about the handling of fish.

My thanks are due to Joan Tyers, who has been our microwave expert for the last few years, and to Yvonne Hamlett – also an expert in the field – who has done the microwave conversions in this book and who will be seen in forthcoming programmes. Angela Henderson has contributed at least three special-occasion meals and also hopes to be a guest. Angela shared much of the early work with me by writing up recipes for testing. Three more special meals, *A Three-Course Dinner for Two*, have come from the from the winner and two runners-up in the *1987 Junior Cook of the Year* competition conducted by the Young Cooks Club of Great Britain, whose organisers Anna Best and Peta Brown readily agreed to our sharing their recipes. Janet Horsley has given a couple of recipes again; since her last contribution to *Farmhouse Kitchen*, she has produced several more books of her own including *The New Fish Cook Book*, (Piatkus and Futura) and *The Weekend Cook Book* (Collins).

When the idea for this book was announced, we were also invited to choose recipes from *The June Hulbert Cook Book*. June Hulbert, who made and published this collection in aid of Finchale Training College for the Disabled in Durham, is Women's Page Editor of Newcastle Upon Tyne's *Evening Chronicle*. Due recognition must also be given to *Saga Magazine*, whose editor kindly agreed to let us use material from Grace's cookery column.

5

Margaret Heywood has not only given at least twelve recipes to this book, but has been Grace's much-valued helper in the background of *Farmhouse Kitchen* for five years. She and Debbie Woolhead – a recent recruit to that arduous task and who has also dropped in two or three recipes to fill gaps – have with Judith Adshead, Yvonne Hamlett, Angela Henderson and Bunty Johnson, shared nearly all the testing of the recipes in this book. Their valued comments have been the 'Yea' or 'Nay' to many offerings, and their skill at getting worthwhile but incomplete ideas to work is hereby acknowledged with all my admiration and respect.

Almost the last but *never* the least to be admired and thanked are those who type, retype and type again. Julie Cookson has organised this tirelessly; her helpers at YTV have been Joyce Town, Amanda Finney, Hilary Robinson and Kashmir Kaur. And finally, thanks are due to design editor Joy Langridge, whose diplomatic and energetic attention helped the book through its final stages at production.

Thanks and thanks again – to you all.

Mary Watts
Spring 1988

FOREWORD

by Grace Mulligan

Cooking in smaller quantities after a lifetime of feeding a growing, hungry family, is awkward. It took me ages to get used to preparing just enough potatoes and vegetables for my husband and me: three potatoes looked lost in my big pan when I had been used to doing enough for six. Now a large loaf of bread lasts – and lasts! I know you can bake and buy smaller loaves but we do like big slices for our morning toast, so now I divide my wholemeal loaf and repackage it in small plastic bags for the freezer.

The planning and preparation of meals for just one or two is so different. One has to think it all out in a new way. Why cook if you don't have to? What can you make that will last for a day or two? Can one chicken last a week without becoming boring? Can the whole meal be cooked on top of the stove? Is there reason enough to heat the oven when the amounts are so small? Can you *ever* enjoy cooking a whole roast dinner again? If you live alone, I can see why the incentive to cook at all is sometimes missing – but I *do* think it is important to sit comfortably at a properly laid table so that your main meal is something to look forward to and enjoy. A wobbly tray on your knees is no substitute.

This is the first book in which Mary Watts and I have tried to think out quite specifically for the needs of ones and twos. In the programmes it is easy enough to say, 'Just make half-quantities of this family-sized recipe', but quite a few requests – enough in fact to get us moving – have now come in saying, 'Couldn't you do some recipes just for me, just for us two?' Some want it plain, simple and cheap; others are happy to be a bit extravagant, and both young and old have requested dinners for two for special occasions. I am not the only one who knows that for the cost of eating at a restaurant you can dine far more lavishly at home. (See page 179 for Special Occasion Menus.)

I hope our new recipes will remind you that fresh food and home cooking are best in the long run, and often the cheapest. I also hope our recipes will show you different ways of shopping, planning and cooking, to get the best possible value. In some cases we suggest you make up enough for two or three meals and divide it

7

into portions to freeze away for future use. Try filling small containers with just enough for one serving, or making individual pies rather than one large one. Nothing is more depressing than eating your way through a pie which you *know* will last two or three days!

A pot of good home-made soup is easily divided into single portions to come out fresh and tasty just when you need it, and if you haven't much room in your freezer for plastic boxes you can always freeze liquid or semi-liquid food in plastic bags. Just stand the empty bag in a small bowl or – better still – a small, square plastic box. Pour whatever you wish into the plastic and put both the bag and box in the freezer. When the soup or casserole is frozen solid, take the box away and seal up, label and store the bag. The square frozen parcel is easier to stack than a round-bottomed one.

Our viewers often tell me that one of the things they most enjoy about our series is all the tips and suggestions I give as I go along. The tips all come from the experience of doing the recipe many times. All our recipe testers make suggestions about the recipes too as they try them out and we have included their comments to help you as well.

I do hope our new book gives you real pleasure. I love the expression '*Bon Appétit*' but since we *always* go in for plain speaking I will wish you '*Good cooking*!'

Grace Mulligan

INTRODUCTION

If you are looking for recipes that make just one helping for one person then, at a glance, you may think we have not provided enough. However, if you look again I hope you will see that in nearly all recipes where two or more helpings are derived, we have explained whether the dish is good served hot then cold, whether it will keep for a day or two, whether it will freeze well, and if so, how best this is done.

Though it may seem extravagant, I believe a freezer is one of the most important pieces of equipment for a small household. Likewise, a microwave cooker – though a luxury gadget – is ideal if only because you do not have to decide before you go out in the morning what you are going to eat in the evening. The two together, plus your conventional cooker and hob, give maximum flexibility for just one or two to eat what you like – when you like.

I regard this as sufficient reason for quite substantial pastry and baking chapters. There are times, however, when one feels guilty using the amount of fuel it takes to bake one small dish, so to ease your conscience and ours we have included in the book what we call 'All In The Oven' lists. You can see how to fill the oven with a variety of dishes that will cook happily together at the same temperature.

Whatever kitchen equipment you have, I hope you will find plenty of dishes to make. Some recipes require no cooking at all; many can be done entirely on top of the stove, and there are simple snacks on toast to elaborate party pieces.

For microwave cooks
If you decide to compare the results of a recipe cooked first the conventional way and then by microwave, don't be surprised if they look and taste different – sometimes like completely different recipes! Microwave cooking just *is* different for many foods and we have not pretended otherwise. What we have done in the conversions and testing is to satisfy ourselves that the finished dish is pleasant to look at and good to eat.

The timing given relate to microwave cookers of **650 to 700 wattage**. Even if yours is a 600-watt model you may well find that the timings given are suitable. If yours is a 500-watt model, then you should *add 15 seconds in every minute given in the recipe*.

I hope you will approve of the use of **different power levels** in this book compared with our original *Microwave Cook Book* in which we confined ourselves to **Full Power** and **Defrost**, because at that time there were more 2-power-level microwave cookers than variable power models on the market. I have found results infinitely better since I learned how to use the various **Medium** settings on my microwave as well as **High** and **Defrost**.

However, if you have a 2-power microwave cooker you will find we have given details where necessary on dealing with the different power settings recommended by Yvonne Hamlett.

Are you worried about the use of 'clingfilm'?
In my opinion this is the most useful name for the stuff whichever brand you favour, but Grace and I have both gone over to the brand which fits the current scientific notions about toxic substances. So 'clear film' seems to be the handiest name to give to it in this book and, short of advertising, I can only say that one or two manufacturers do offer the purer product as well as the one about which the fuss arose.

Some expert advice about microwaving follows.

Mary Watts

Yvonne Hamlett's Microwave Hints

1　A microwave cooker is just another source of heat, so don't feel you have to cook *everything* in it. There are some foods that cook well in a microwave; with others the results are just not acceptable. The grill is used in many of the recipes in this book to brown and crisp the surface of foods, expecially those with cheese toppings, which might otherwise stay pale and look unappetising.
Meats should roast to an acceptable colour, and it is not always necessary to brush with melted butter before cooking, nor to sprinkle the surface with microwave seasonings or browning mixtures.
Do not salt food to be cooked in the microwave as salt draws the moisture out of the food and cause it to toughen. It causes specks of brown on cauliflower, tough skins on vegetables and a dry surface on meat. Always season at the end of cooking. You can, however, lightly salt sauces and stocks for casseroles and stews as the salt is dissolved in the cooking liquids and not concentrated on the surface of the food.

2　**Timing:** always start checking the results after the minimum cooking time given. Remember that the texture, initial temperature of the food and even the cooking container – its shape, size and the materials of which it is made – will all affect the cooking time. It is all too easy to add extra time but do resist: once overcooked, most foods are irretrievably ruined! Overcooking simply dehydrates and hardens food beyond 'repair'.
Always allow food to stand at the end of cooking. This stand time allows the heat to carry on cooking through the food. If you test it *before* the stand time, it may seem undercooked and you may be tempted to put it back in the cooker for a little longer, thus resulting in overcooking. Meat and poultry need to stand for 5 minutes per 450 g/lb. During this time, the temperature at the centre actually increases; wrapped in foil, shiny side in, the meat stays hot for a good 15 to 20 minutes. In that time, you can be cooking the vegetables to go with the main dish.
Foods with a high fat or sugar content cook very quickly, so check regularly during cooking. Shorten cooking times when using *polyunsaturated fats* as they heat up more quickly than other fats.
Foods with a light airy texture heat more quickly than those with a dense texture.

3　**Dishes:** soup and cereal bowls are ideal for cooking 1 to 2 portions. Make sure they do not have a gold or silver pattern on them.

Generally speaking, Pyrex, ceramic, china and dishwasher-proof plastics are ideal. In fact, any dish that is dishwasher-proof should be fine in the microwave. There are many special microwave dishes available in various shapes and sizes, but check what dishes you already have before buying lots of extras. If you want to buy special dishes, here are the ones to look out for:

'Cook 'n' Roast' sets made from a plastic which can be used in the conventional oven, up to 410 °F, 210 °C. (*NB: Do not put plastic dishes under the grill.*) The plastic rack is ideal for roasting joints, cooking bacon or for reheating pastry items. This is one of the most popular and versatile sets available.

Microwave Tender Cooker This is one of the very latest 'active' cookware accessories: it is a special microwave pressure cooker which will cook and tenderise a stew or casserole in 20 to 25 minutes. It is excellent for chicken, chops and small joints and will even cook a steak and kidney pudding from raw ingredients in just 25 minutes.

4 When cooking: remember that foods arranged in a large flat dish will cook more quickly than those in a smaller deeper dish. Foods in a large flat dish will need stirring quite often to prevent the edge from overcooking.

Arrange items such as chicken portions with the *meatiest parts* to the outside of the dish. This will save turning or shielding the thinner parts. Do not stack foods on top of each other as this will give uneven cooking results.

Cover dishes as recommended in the recipe. It is not always necessary to pierce clear film as it is porous at 212 °F, 100 °C, and will allow the steam to pass through it. In some auto-sensor microwave cookers you must not pierce the clear film. Check with your manufacturer's instructions.

Always release the clear film with a fork on the side of the dish farthest away from you. Lids should always be lifted using oven gloves, and then always lifted *away* from you to avoid steam burns.

5 Cooking complete meals: the secret of cooking complete meals is to have everything ready prepared before beginning to cook so that it is then just a succession of dishes in and out of the microwave.

Always cook jacket potatoes before the main course as these can be wrapped in foil and they will stay very hot for about 25 minutes.

Choose vegetables with similar cooking times so that they can be cooked together. Good combinations are:

Sprouts, carrots, leeks, cauliflower, baby corn.

Or, potatoes, swede, parsnip.

Or, peas and sweetcorn kernels.

Do not mix fresh and frozen vegetables; however, two frozen vegetables can be cooked together.

Vegetables cook better in a flat-bottomed dish rather than a bowl or basin, but if you only have a basin – that will be fine. Boiled potatoes, though may need to be stirred during cooking or those on top will go waxy.

Add two to three 15 ml tablespoons cold water to fresh vegetables. Always cover the dish with a lid or with clear film.

When cooking fish dinners it is better to cook all the vegetables before the fish, as the fish cooks quickly and needs little or no stand time. Vegetables reheat quickly and with better results than fish.

6 Reheating meals on plates: complete servings can be covered with clear film and chilled until required. For successful reheating, make sure to place the foods around the outside of the plate. Do not pile everything in the centre. Flatten piles of mashed potato and dot with a little butter. Pour a little gravy over the meat to keep it moist. If you do not like gravy, then sprinkle a few drops of water on the meat to keep it moist. Small, delicate items such as peas which reheat quickly can be put at the centre of the plate.

Reheat meals on plates one at a time on full power for 2 to 3 minutes. Feel the bottom of the plate and, if this is warm, the meal should be hot enough to eat.

7 Casseroles and stews: a small plate placed on top of the meat and vegetables in a casserole will keep them under the gravy and prevent overcooking of the pieces that would normally rise above the surface of the gravy. It will also eliminate the need to stir food during cooking.

For slow cooking, always use 600 ml/1 pint stock to 450 g/1 lb meat and vegetables. Allow an extra 300 ml/½ pint of stock for each extra 450 g/1 lb meat or vegetables.

Use hot stock rather than cold. This saves more time. Cook the casserole on full power for 10 minutes, then on Simmer (or Defrost in a 2-power microwave cooker) for 60 to 90 minutes. This timing may sound quite long for a microwave but remember the only way to tenderise a tough cut is by long, slow cooking. This is equivalent to 3 hours in the conventional cooker. The microwave also uses less fuel.

Stews and casseroles are always best thickened at the end of cooking.

Vegetables used in a stew should be cut into small dice or slices.

8 Individual steamed sponge puddings can be cooked in teacups, as you will see in the recipes. Allow 1 to 1½ minutes for 1 pudding. For two cups, allow 2 to 2½ minutes on full power.

9 Decreasing recipe servings: if you wish to reduce a recipe from 4 to 2 helpings, halve all the ingredients listed. To reduce 4 to 1 helping, quarter all the ingredients listed. Choose a dish that is proportionately smaller than the one recommended in the recipe. Do take care to see that it is deep enough for the food not to boil over.

Use the power setting recommended in the original recipe. For one serving, allow a quarter to one-third of the time recommended for four. For two servings, allow one-third to two-thirds of the recommended time.

If the original recipe states *stir frequently*, one stir for the reduced amounts is all that is required. For most recipes, providing you use the correct dish and your microwave cooker has a turntable, you will not need to stir. For cookers without a turntable, stir the food or turn the dish through 90° halfway through the cooking time.

10 Lastly, do not try to cook the following in your microwave as they won't be successful:

Yorkshire puddings and batter mixes. They require hot air to crisp and brown them which can only be provided in a conventional cooker.

Choux pastry. This can be made but not baked in the microwave because it needs hot air to crisp and brown it.

Deep fat frying. There is no temperature control.

Reheating in narrow-necked bottles, e.g. tomato sauce bottles, as they easily shatter when the contents expand unevenly – as they can do in a microwave.

Chapter 1

Breakfast

PROPER PORRIDGE

Enough for 1 large or 2 small portions, this is the way it is made and eaten by all Scots!

40 g/1½ oz medium oatmeal
300 ml/½ pint water
2 generous pinches of salt

1 To shorten the cooking time, soak the oatmeal overnight in the cold water.
2 Next morning, bring the porridge up to boiling point, turn the heat down and cook gently until it is thick. Stir often to make sure there are no lumps.
3 Add the salt and serve with cold milk or cream – never with sugar, nor treacle, God forbid!

Grace Mulligan

Microwave ◆◆◆◆◆◆◆◆◆◆◆◆

1 In a 1-litre/1¾-pint basin, soak the oatmeal overnight in the cold water.
2 Next morning, heat the porridge on full power for 2½ minutes, stirring halfway through and then again at the end of cooking.
3 Let it stand for 5 minutes, then add salt and stir well. Serve with cold milk or cream.

PORRIDGE WITH ROLLED OATS

For 2.

50 g/2 oz rolled oats or porridge
**   oats**
300 ml/½ pint cold water
Salt to taste

Traditional method
1 Stir the rolled oats into the cold water in a saucepan. Add salt to taste.
2 Bring up to a boil, stir well, then lower the heat and simmer for 5

minutes, stirring occasionally. Serve with cold milk.

'Fast' method
1 Stir the rolled oats into 240 ml/ 8 fl oz boiling water. Add salt.
2 Boil for 1 minute, then remove from the heat and leave, covered, for 5 minutes. Stir well before serving.

Grace Mulligan

Microwave ◆◆◆◆◆◆◆◆◆◆◆◆

PORRIDGE FOR ONE

25 g/1 oz porridge oats
240 ml/7 fl oz water
A pinch of salt

1 Combine all the ingredients in a deep cereal bowl or small basin. Cook on full power for 4 to 5 minutes, stirring once during cooking and once at the end.
2 Let it stand for 2 minutes before eating – or it will burn your tongue!

HOME-MADE BREAKFAST CEREAL

Delicious served with stewed or fresh fruits, yoghurt and milk or fruit juice to moisten. If you find this muesli 'chewy', try soaking each helping in a little apple juice overnight. Makes 700g/1½ lb.

50 g/2 oz dried apricots
25 g/1 oz nuts
75 g/3 oz raisins
300 g/12 oz porridge oats
50 g/2 oz wheatmeal, or flaked
**   wheat, barley or rye**
25 g/1 oz bran (optional*)
50 g/2 oz soft brown sugar
**   (optional*)**

* If you are not fond of bran, which is simply the husk of ground grains like wheat, oats, barley and rye, it can be left out. When the cereal already

contains whole rolled or flaked grains,
as this one does, there is no dietary need
for extra bran. As for sugar – it would
be better to manage without it or add a
very little to taste when serving.

1 Cut apricots in small pieces. Chop
nuts.
2 Mix all ingredients together and
store in a covered jar or tin. It keeps
for several weeks.

Mrs Margaret Walkinshaw
Ballymena, Co. Antrim, N. Ireland

FARMHOUSE KITCHEN SCRAMBLED EGG

For 1.

1 large egg
1 large tablespoon of milk
Salt and pepper
15 g/½ oz butter or margarine
1 round of hot buttered
    wholemeal toast

1 Beat the egg and milk together with
a fork and add salt and pepper.
2 Melt the butter or margarine in a
small, heavy pan, pour in the beaten
egg and stir gently over a moderate
heat until the egg is creamy.
3 Pile the creamy egg on to the toast.

Variation: for a more substantial
dish for later in the day, add any of
the following as the egg is cooking:

50 g/2 oz chopped and grilled
    bacon
50 g/2 oz cooked prawns
40 g/1½ oz chopped boiled ham
1 tablespoons chopped chives or
    parsley
1 anchovy fillet, finely chopped

Grace Mulligan

Microwave

*As eggs differ in size, and the
temperature varies depending on
whether they are stored in the
refrigerator or at room temperature, and
taking personal preferences into account,
it's hard to give precise cooking times
for microwaving scrambled egg.
However, you will soon learn how long
to allow to suit your taste.*

1 In a small basin, beat together the
egg and milk. Season with a little salt
and pepper. Put in the butter.
2 Heat on full power for 30 seconds
and then stir well. Heat on full power
for a further 15 to 30 seconds, then
stir. The scrambled egg should be
quite creamy as it will continue to
cook slightly and firm up after it is
taken out of the cooker.
3 Pile the egg on to the toast.

For a more substantial dish, add
bacon, prawns etc as above. Add them
to the egg when it is stirred after the
first 30 seconds. You may need to
give an extra 15 seconds to the
cooking time. Sprinkle with chopped
parsley.

POACHED EGG

*For a really tender, softly cooked egg,
use this old foolproof method.*

Water
A generous pinch of salt
A few drops of vinegar
1 egg, as fresh as possible
1 slice of thick hot buttered toast

1 Put the water, salt and vinegar into
a pan and heat to boiling point.
2 Break the egg into a wetted
saucer, then slide the egg into the
water.
3 Bring back to boiling point, remove
the pan from the heat, cover with a
lid and leave for 2 minutes until the
egg is set.

17

4 Drain on a fish slice, shaking off as much water as possible. Serve on hot buttered toast.

Variation: for a change, when it's not for breakfast, spread the toast with a little butter and one of the following before adding the egg:

Yeast extract (e.g. Marmite)
Mango chutney
Good-flavoured pickle
Cheese spread

Grace Mulligan

Microwave

Like scrambled eggs by microwave, you gradually get used to knowing how long it will take. The size of the egg and the temperature at which you store them both affect the timing.

1 Lightly butter a ramekin dish and half-fill it with boiling water. Add a shake of salt and 1 teaspoon vinegar. Heat on full power for 30 seconds until the water is just boiling.
2 Crack an egg into the boiling water and, with a wooden cocktail stick, pierce the yolk once and the white several times. This is to prevent it exploding. Cover the dish with clear film and heat on full power for 30 to 60 seconds, but check it every 30 seconds. If the egg is very large or very cold it will take longer. The white should just be set when you stop the cooking.
3 Leave it covered for 2 minutes then drain away the water and have it on toast as Grace suggests.

SPICED APPLE AND YOGHURT DRINK
A pleasant, creamy drink for 1.

A 150-g/5-oz carton of natural yoghurt
About 100 ml/3 fl oz unsweetened apple juice
A tiny pinch of ground cloves or nutmeg

1 Use chilled yoghurt and apple juice, whisk together with spice and drink while it is still frothy.

Mrs Powell
Enfield, Middlesex

Chapter 2

Soups, Starters and Snacks

SMOKY BACON AND SWEETCORN SOUP

This quickly made soup is a nourishing snack when served with fresh crusty bread rolls. Freezes well, before yoghurt and bacon are added. For 2.

2 rashers rindless smoked
   streaky bacon
15 g/½ oz butter or margarine
1 onion, finely chopped
450 ml/¾ pint milk and water,
   mixed
1 chicken stock cube
1 bay leaf
A 325-g/12-oz can of creamed
   sweetcorn *
Salt and pepper
2 tablespoons cornflour mixed
   with 2 tablespoons cold water
2 tablespoons natural yoghurt

* If you cannot buy this, make your own by putting drained canned sweetcorn kernels through the liquidiser.

1 Grill the bacon until crisp. Allow to cool, then crush into little pieces.
2 Melt butter or margarine in a saucepan, adding a little of the melted bacon fat, if you like. Add onion, then cover and cook very slowly so the onion just sweats for 5 minutes – until soft but not brown.
3 Pour milk and water into the pan, crumble in the stock cube, add the bay leaf, sweetcorn, salt and pepper.
4 Stir in the cornflour mixture and bring the soup to the boil, stirring all the time. Boil for 1 minute.
5 Remove the bay leaf and ladle the soup into hot bowls.
6 Spoon yoghurt over each bowl and scatter with crumbled bacon.

Grace Mulligan

CHICKEN AND SWEETCORN SOUP

A delicately flavoured and nourishing soup. It takes a bit of practice to master the addition of the egg! For 2.

1 small chicken breast,
   uncooked, on the bone
450 ml/¾ pint chicken stock
1 dessertspoon cornflour mixed
   with 1 tablespoon cold water
100 g/4 oz creamed sweetcorn (see
   previous recipe)
Salt and pepper to taste
1 large egg
1 spring onion, trimmed and
   chopped

1 Remove skin and bone from chicken and use to make the stock (or use a stock cube).
2 Chop chicken flesh, then mince or process it.
3 Put the stock in a saucepan with the cornflour mixture, sweetcorn, salt and pepper and stir continuously until it boils. Cook for 2 minutes.
4 Add the minced chicken and reheat until the soup boils. Cook for 1 minute.
5 Lightly beat the egg and pour it into the boiling soup in a fine stream, pulling the strands of egg over the surface of the soup with chopsticks or the prongs of a fork in a slow, circular movement. Do not stir vigorously!
6 When the egg has set, ladle soup into hot bowls and scatter with chopped spring onion.

Jennie Siew Lee Cook
York

FISHERMAN'S CHOWDER

This substantial fish soup makes a filling main meal served with hot, crusty French bread. Makes enough for 2 or 3.

15 g/½ oz butter or margarine
1 small onion, thinly sliced
25 g/1 oz rindless bacon, chopped
2 sticks celery, trimmed and
   chopped
Half a small red pepper, cored
   and diced

125 g/4 oz potatoes, peeled and cut
   into 7-mm/¼-inch dice
300 ml/½ pint fish or chicken
   stock
350 g/12 oz smoked and white
   haddock (or whiting), skinned
   and cubed
150 ml/¼ pint semi-skimmed
   milk
A 15 ml tablespoon cornflour
Salt
Freshly ground black pepper
Chopped parsley for serving

1 Melt the butter or margarine in a
large saucepan and fry the onion,
bacon, celery, red pepper and potato
for 5 minutes.
2 Pour in the stock, lower the heat
and simmer until potatoes are just
tender, then add the fish.
3 Mix together the milk and
cornflour and stir it into the soup.
Bring to the boil, stirring
continuously, then simmer for 5
minutes. Season to taste and serve.

Yvonne Coull
Sea Fish Industry Authority,
Edinburgh

Microwave

1 Put the butter, onion, bacon,
celery, pepper and potato into a 1.4-
litre/3-pint casserole dish. Cook on
full power for 5 minutes, stirring
once.
2 Add the fish and stock, stir well.
Cover with a lid or clear film and
cook on full power for 4 to 5
minutes. The potatoes should then be
tender and the fish cooked.
3 Mix the cornflour to a paste with a
little of the milk. Uncover the fish,
stir in the cornflour paste and the
remaining milk. Cook, uncovered, on
full power for 3 to 5 minutes, stirring
once. The soup should have
thickened.
4 Season lightly, sprinkle with
chopped parsley and serve.

TIP
Instead of using stock and milk with
cornflour to thicken, use a 300 g/10
oz can of condensed asparagus soup.
Stir the soup into the fish, cover and
cook on full power for 5 to 6
minutes. Stir, then serve.

Yvonne Hamlett
Haddenham, Buckinghamshire

CARROT AND
ORANGE SOUP

*Enough for 4: 2 hot servings on the first
day, 2 cold the next. Especially good
liquidised, it freezes well for 2 or 3
weeks. Serve with croûtons or
wholemeal bread.*

15 g/1½ oz butter or
   margarine
1 small onion, chopped
A clove of garlic, crushed
325 g/12 oz carrots, peeled or
   scrubbed and chopped
1 teaspoon dried chopped
   tarragon *or* 2 teaspoons fresh
   chopped tarragon
600 ml/1 pint chicken stock
Finely grated rind and juice of 1
   orange
Salt and pepper
2 tablespoons natural yoghurt

1 In a fairly large saucepan, melt the
butter or margarine and cook the
onion over a low heat until soft but
not browned.
2 Add the garlic and carrot and cook
slowly for a few minutes.
3 Sprinkle in the tarragon, then
pour in the chicken stock, add orange
rind and juice and seasoning.
4 Bring the soup to the boil, then
cover and simmer for 30 minutes or
until the carrots are soft.
5 Serve the soup as it is, or purée in
a liquidiser or food processor.
6 Pour the soup into warmed bowls
and spoon over the yoghurt.

Grace Mulligan

1 Put the butter and onion in a 1.4–litre/3-pint dish. Heat on full power for 3 minutes.
2 Add the garlic and carrot. Pour over orange juice. Cover with a lid or clear film and cook on full power for 6 minutes.
3 Tip the cooked carrots into a liquidiser or processor and blend with 150 ml/¼ pint chicken stock until smooth.
4 Tip back into the dish. Stir in the tarragon, orange rind and remaining stock. Heat on full power for 6 minutes. Stir, then lightly season and serve in warm bowls, with yoghurt.

CREAM OF LENTIL SOUP

This makes 6 helpings, but it freezes well for 2 to 3 weeks. You'll find a liquidiser useful.

225 g/8 oz red lentils
2 sticks of celery
2 large carrots, scrubbed but not peeled
2 medium onions
A clove of garlic, peeled
2 tablespoons safflower or other good-quality oil
2 tablespoons soy sauce
Salt and pepper
1.25 litres/2 pints water

1 Wash lentils and pick them over for stones.
2 Chop vegetables and fry in the oil in a large saucepan for 5 minutes.
3 Add all the remaining ingredients, bring to the boil, then lower the heat and simmer for 45 minutes. Or pressure–cook for 8 minutes.
4 Liquidise the soup – it should be thick and creamy. Adjust seasoning to taste and serve.

Janet Horsley
Leeds, Yorkshire

MUSHROOM SOUP

For this you need a liquidiser or processor. Serve with hot crusty rolls, or croûtons. Enough for 2.

350 g/12 oz dark flat mushrooms, washed and finely chopped
1 onion, finely chopped
25 g/1 oz butter
25 g/1 oz flour
450 ml/¾ pint chicken stock
Salt
Freshly ground black pepper
2 tablespoons cream

1 Put the mushrooms into a saucepan with the onion and butter. Cover and cook very gently over low heat for 10 minutes, shaking the pan from time to time.
2 Stir in the flour, then add the stock. Bring to the boil and simmer for 10 minutes.
3 Allow the soup to cook a little longer, then liquidise.
4 Reheat the soup, season to taste and serve in warm bowls with a swirl of cream in each.

Julie Cookson
Leeds, Yorkshire

Use hot stock for this.

1 Put the mushrooms, onion and butter into a 1.5–litre/3-pint casserole; heat on full power for 5 minutes.
2 Stir in the flour and gradually blend in the hot stock. Heat on full power for 2 minutes, stir, then continue to heat on full power for a further 3 minutes. Allow to cool slightly.
3 Put the soup in a processor or liquidiser and blend until smooth.
4 Tip the soup back into the casserole. Season and heat for 1 to 2 minutes on full power.
5 Serve as above.

PARSNIP SOUP

Very sustaining; keeps a day or two in the fridge. It freezes well. Makes 2 to 3 helpings.

25 g/1 oz butter or margarine
1 large onion, finely chopped
½ level teaspoon curry powder
225 g/8 oz parsnips, scrubbed and diced
125 g/4 oz potato, peeled and diced
600 ml/1 pint hot light stock – a chicken or vegetable stock cube will do
Pepper and salt
Single cream (optional)

1 Melt the butter or margarine in a saucepan and fry onion gently until just softening.
2 Stir in the curry powder and cook gently for 2 or 3 minutes.
3 Toss the parsnip and potato with the onion over gentle heat for 2 or 3 minutes more.
4 Add stock, bring to the boil and simmer soup for about 20 minutes or until vegetables are tender.

The soup is nice to have in its chunky state. For a soft, creamy soup, liquidise and reheat, adding pepper and a little salt if necessary. Add a swirl of cream to each bowlful. Alternatively, strain off liquid into a jug, mash vegetables with a potato masher, then stir stock back in, adjusting seasoning to taste.

Mrs Thelma E Boyne
Aberdeen

Microwave

1 Put the butter and onion into a 1.5-litre/3-pint casserole dish. Heat on full power for 2 minutes.
2 Stir in the parsnip and potato. Add 150 ml/¼ pint hot stock and cover the dish with a lid. Cook on full power for 10 minutes, stirring once.

2 Put the vegetables and stock into a liquidiser or processor and blend until smooth. Return to the casserole.
3 Stir in the curry powder and the remaining hot stock. Season and heat on full power for 4 to 5 minutes, stirring once.
4 Serve in warm bowls with a swirl of cream.

ONION SOUP WITH CHEESE TOAST

This nourishing soup freezes well: a use for stock derived from boiling a Ham Shank (page 67). Makes 4 to 5 helpings.

40 g/1½ oz butter or margarine
1 tablespoon oil
450 g/1 lb onions, peeled and thinly sliced
900 ml/1½ pints ham stock
1 teaspoon yeast extract (e.g. Marmite)
Freshly ground black pepper
1 tablespoon pasta shells or alphabet letters
2 slices wholemeal bread
50 g/2 oz grated Cheddar cheese

1 In a large pan, melt the butter, add the oil and fry the onion very slowly until soft and light brown, stirring often. This will take about 15 minutes.
2 Add the stock, yeast extract and a little black pepper.
3 Bring to the boil, cover with a lid, then simmer for 20 minutes.
4 Add the pasta 5 or 10 minutes before the end of cooking time.
5 To serve – toast the bread under the grill on one side only. Cover the untoasted sides with the cheese and cook under the grill until the cheese has melted and browned. Cut in fingers and serve with the soup.

Grace Mulligan

PEA AND MINT SOUP

For 2: this soup makes a refreshing start to a meal; it needs quite a lot of mint, but at least this is easy to grow. Dried mint could be used. The soup may be served chilled, and it also freezes well.

15 g/½ oz butter
1 small onion, finely chopped
225 g/8 oz frozen peas
2 potatoes, peeled and diced
600 ml/1 pint chicken stock
12 stems of fresh mint, or try 2
    teaspoons dried mint
Salt and pepper
A pinch of sugar
Whipped cream and sprigs of
    mint to garnish

1 Melt the butter in a saucepan, add the onion and cook until soft.
2 Add the peas, potatoes, stock, mint and seasonings and bring up to the boil. Cover with a lid and simmer for 25 minutes.
3 Purée the soup in a blender or food processor, then sieve it to remove the mint stems and to ensure it is completely smooth.
4 Reheat the soup and decorate each bowl with a spoonful of whipped cream and a sprig of fresh mint.

Angela Henderson
Fleet, Hampshire

SPICED VEGETABLE SOUP

The flavour of ginger in this soup is delicious. Serve it hot with croûtons or garlic toast and a dash of Tabasco sauce. Freezes well, and makes plenty for 2 or 3.

100 g/4 oz chopped mixed
    vegetables, fresh or frozen
1 small onion, chopped
A 7-mm/¼-inch piece of fresh
    ginger, peeled and chopped

A clove of garlic, crushed
A 200 g/8 oz can of tomatoes
600 ml/1 pint water
1 vegetable stock cube
2 teaspoons ghee or butter
½ teaspoon cumin seeds
Salt and pepper
Lemon juice to taste

1 Put the mixed vegetables in a saucepan with the onion, ginger, garlic, tomatoes and water. Crumble in the stock cube and bring to the boil. Cover with a lid and simmer for 30 minutes.
2 Purée the soup in a liquidiser or processor and return it to a clean saucepan.
3 Heat the ghee or butter in a frying pan and when very hot, quickly fry the cumin seeds.
4 Add the cumin to the soup, season and add lemon juice to taste before serving.

Nirmal Singh
Nuneaton, Warwickshire

WATERCRESS SOUP

This is a beautiful green, with a delicate flavour –good enough for a special occasion. It freezes well. For 2.

1 small onion, finely chopped
15 g/½ oz butter
1 to 2 bunches of watercress, well
    washed
15 g/½ oz flour
450 ml/¾ pint chicken stock,
    made from a cube if necessary
Salt
Freshly ground black pepper
A grating of nutmeg
A little cream for serving

1 Fry the onion gently in the butter until soft.
2 Add the watercress, put a lid on the pan, lower the heat and let it cook just to sweat it for 5 minutes. Shake the pan from time to time.
3 Stir in the flour and stock, bring to

the boil and cook for 5 minutes more.

4 Liquidise the soup until it is quite smooth, then return it to the pan to reheat.

5 Season to taste with salt, pepper and nutmeg.

6 Serve the soup in hot bowls, pouring in a swirl of cream at the last moment.

Mary Watts

CHILLED TOMATO AND APPLE SOUP

Always serve a chilled soup in smaller bowls than your usual everyday ones. Make this when fresh tomatoes are plentiful and taste the flavour of real tomato soup. It makes 4 helpings and freezes well.

450 g/1 lb fresh ripe tomatoes, chopped
225 g/8 oz onion, chopped
450 g/1 lb cooking apples, peeled, cored and chopped
600 ml/1 pint chicken stock
Salt
Freshly ground black pepper
Finely chopped basil or chives to garnish

1 Put all the ingredients, except the basil or chives, into a saucepan. Bring to the boil, then lower the heat and simmer together for 20 minutes, or until the onions are soft.

2 Purée the soup in a liquidiser or processor, then sieve it to remove the tomato skins and pips and to ensure the soup is completely smooth. (Alternatively, you can skin the tomatoes and remove the pips before cooking them. See Tip, page 26.)

3 Leave to cool, then garnish the soup with the basil or chives.

TIP

If you don't have a liquidiser or food processor, mash up the soup in the pan with a potato masher, then sieve it.

Grace Mulligan

Microwave ━━━━━━━━━━━━━━━━

1 Put the onion in a large mixing bowl with four 15 ml tablespoons of the stock. Heat on full power for 3 minutes, stirring once. The onions should be soft.

2 Add the tomatoes and apples. Cover the dish with clear film and cook on full power for 8 to 10 minutes.

3 Purée the soup in a liquidiser or processor and then sieve it into the cleaned bowl. This will ensure it is completely smooth.

4 Stir in the chicken stock. Chill, then serve the soup garnished with basil or chives.

QUICK CHILLED TOMATO SOUP

For 2. Easy as well as quick to make – but you do need a liquidiser or processor for this one. Serve it with wholemeal bread.

25 g/1 oz canned sweetcorn kernels, drained
25 g/1 oz green pepper or courgette
100 g/4 oz tomatoes, peeled (see next page)
1 teaspoon wine vinegar or lemon juice
1 tablespoon oil
1 shallot or half a small onion, chopped
210 ml/7 fl oz tomato juice
Salt and pepper
Chopped fresh parsley or mint to garnish

1 Put all the ingredients, except the parsley or mint, into a liquidiser or processor and work until well blended. If you want a completely

smooth soup, sieve it.
2 Chill, then serve the soup garnished
with parsley or mint.

Dilwen Phillips
Gileston, South Glamorgan

CHILLED SOUP WITH AVOCADO

*This variation on the classic Spanish
Gazpacho has a very pleasant avocado
flavour. It keeps in the refrigerator for
a day or two; you'll need a liquidiser
or processor for the right consistency.
Makes 2 or 3 generous helpings.*

450 ml/¾ pint chicken stock,
  either home-made or from a
  stock cube
Half a small onion, chopped
Half a small green pepper, flesh
  only, chopped
2 small tomatoes, skinned (see
  below), and quartered
A 2.5-cm/1 to 2-inch piece of
  cucumber, peeled and sliced
Half a ripe avocado, peeled and
  sliced
1 teaspoon white wine vinegar
2 large tablespoons natural
  yoghurt
Salt and pepper

1 Prepare the stock and let it cool.
2 Put onion, green pepper, tomato,
cucumber, avocado, vinegar, yoghurt
and half the stock in the liquidiser or
processor and run it until smooth.
3 Empty the soup into a large serving
bowl or a jug and stir in the
remaining stock. Season to taste and
serve chilled with hot rolls and
butter.

Grace Mulligan

TIP
To skin tomatoes, put them in a
basin, cover with boiling water
and wait 30 seconds. Then drain
and cover with cold water. After a
minute, the skin should easily
peel off.

26

MINTED CUCUMBER MOUSSE

*Simon Dunn, 14, came third in the
1987 Junior Cook of the Year
competition organised by the Young
Cooks' Club of Great Britain with this
delicious starter. (See page 179 for his
complete, three-course menu.) This keeps
for a day in the fridge; serve it with
brown bread and butter or rolls. For 2.*

7.5 cm/3 inches of cucumber,
  peeled and finely diced
Salt
1½ level teaspoons gelatine
60 ml/2 fl oz chicken stock
100 g/4 oz cream cheese
A small pinch of ground mace
1 tablespoon chopped fresh mint
2 teaspoons wine or cider vinegar
1 teaspoon caster sugar
60 ml/2 fl oz double cream
1 egg white
A little oil
Cucumber curls and sprigs of
  mint to decorate

1 Put the cucumber in a sieve over a
bowl and sprinkle with salt. This will
draw out some of the liquid. Leave it
for 30 minutes, then rinse the
cucumber pieces very thoroughly in
cold water and drain well on kitchen
paper.
2 In a small saucepan, sprinkle the
gelatine over the chicken stock, leave
it for a few minutes, then gently
warm it until all the gelatine has
dissolved. Let it cool a little.
3 Beat the cream cheese with the
mace, mint, vinegar, sugar and the
gelatine mixture. Stir in the cucumber
and put aside until it begins to set
slightly.
4 Whip the cream until just thick,
then fold it into the cucumber
mixture.
5 Whisk egg white stiffly and fold
into the mousse.
6 Lightly oil a small ring mould or 2
ramekins, pour in the mousse and
chill until set.

7 Turn it out and decorate with cucumber curls and sprigs of mint.

Simon Dunn
Bickley, Kent

EGGS IN A FOREST

This luxurious starter, with the other two dishes listed on page 179, won Sally Wilson, 14, the title of Junior Cook of the Year, 1987. It makes a good light meal with crusty rolls or toast. For 2.

3 tablespoons good olive oil
2 garlic cloves, crushed
1 large green pepper, chopped
225 g/8 oz chopped courgettes
½ teaspoon grated nutmeg
Freshly ground pepper
Salt
Half a small cauliflower
Juice of half a lemon
A pinch of chilli powder
1 rounded teaspoon caraway seeds
2 eggs
Parsley to garnish

1 Heat half the oil over a medium heat. Add garlic and green pepper, cook over low heat until the pepper has softened, stirring often.
2 Add courgettes and cook for 3 to 5 minutes, stirring carefully, until soft but still bright green.
3 Pour into a liquidiser or processor and process until smooth. Add nutmeg, pepper and salt. Spoon purée into a large, shallow serving dish.
4 Divide cauliflower into small florets; boil until just tender.
5 Put the lemon juice, chilli powder, caraway seed, salt and 4 teaspoons olive oil into a bowl. Add hot cauliflower and coat with the dressing. Leave to cool.
6 Soft-poach the eggs (page 17).
7 When everything is cold, place the eggs on the green purée surrounded by cauliflower florets. Garnish with parsley.

Sally Wilson
Pinner, Middlesex

Microwave ~~~~~~~~~~~~~~~~~~~~~~~~~~~~~~~

1 Put half the oil in a basin with the garlic and green pepper; heat on full power for 3 to 5 minutes, until soft.
2 Add the courgettes and heat on full power for 2 minutes.
3 Pour into a liquidiser or processor and blend until smooth. Season with the nutmeg, pepper and salt. Pour the purée into a large shallow dish.
4 Divide the cauliflower into florets. Put it into a small bowl and sprinkle with three 15 ml tablespoons cold water. Cover with clear film and cook on full power for 4 minutes.
5 Put the lemon juice, chilli powder, caraway seed, salt and 4 teaspoons olive oil into a bowl. Drain cauliflower and add to the dressing, stirring well so that it is coated. Leave to cool.
6 Meanwhile poach the eggs, following instructions on page 17, but heating the dishes for 30 to 60 seconds, and cooking the eggs for 1 to 1½ minutes, checking every 30 seconds. The whites should just be set. Remove film and cool. Drain off the water.
7 When everything is cold, slide the eggs on to the green purée. Surround with cauliflower florets and garnish with parsley.

PEAR WITH STILTON SAUCE

A sophisticated starter for 2. The sauce can be made in advance, but prepare the pear and assemble the dish at the last minute.

50 g/2 oz blue Stilton cheese
1 to 2 tablespoons cream or top-of-the-milk
1 large ripe pear
Toasted flaked almonds*
Lettuce leaves and brown bread and butter or Melba Toast (page 29) to serve

27

* *Flaked almonds can be toasted under the grill but watch them as they easily burn.*

1 Grate the cheese and mix in enough cream or milk to make a thick sauce.
2 Peel the pear, cut it in half and remove the core with a teaspoon.
3 Place each pear flat-side down and cut it into thin slices.
4 Arrange the slices like a fan on 2 small plates and spoon over the Stilton sauce. Scatter the almonds on top.
5 Garnish the plates with lettuce leaves and serve with brown bread and butter or toast.

Grace Mulligan

SMOKED MACKEREL AND LEMON DIP

For 2 or more.

225 g/8 oz 'hot' smoked
   mackerel fillets*
15 g/½ oz butter or
   polyunsaturated margarine
Half an onion, finely chopped
1 teaspoon horseradish relish
1 teaspoon lemon juice
3 to 4 tablespoons soured cream
   (natural yoghurt is a suitable
   substitute)
Freshly ground black pepper
Lemon slices to garnish

* *Hot smoked mackerel means that the fillets have actually been cooked during the smoking process.*

1 Remove skin and bones from the fish.
2 In a small saucepan, melt the butter or margarine. Add the onion and cook until soft.
3 Stir in the mackerel, horseradish and lemon juice, and heat gently for 1 to 2 minutes.
4 Allow to cool, then blend with the soured cream and ground black pepper in a liquidiser or processor until smooth and creamy. Spoon into a serving dish and chill before serving with chunks of colourful fresh vegetables and fingers of toast.

Yvonne Coull
Sea Fish Industry Authority,
Edinburgh

1 Remove the skin and bones from the fish.
2 Put the butter or margarine in a bowl with the onion and cook on full power for 3 minutes until the onion is soft.
3 Stir in the mackerel, horseradish and lemon juice, and heat on full power for a further 1½ minutes.
4 Cool, then blend with the soured cream and ground black pepper in a food processor until smooth and creamy. Spoon into a serving dish and chill before serving with chunks of colourful fresh vegetables and fingers of toast.

QUICK LIVER PATE

For 1 or 2, but easy to make more. Particularly nice made with chicken livers.

15 g/½ oz butter
50 g/2 oz liver
25 g/1 oz cooked ham
Salt and pepper
A few drops of soy sauce

1 Melt the butter in a small pan and fry the liver until cooked, but not dry.
2 Put the liver and butter into a food processor or liquidiser and add the remaining ingredients. Process until smooth.
3 Put the pâté into a small dish, cover with clear film and chill slightly in the refrigerator.
4 Serve with toast, Melba toast (see right) or rolls.

Dilwen Phillips
Gileston, South Glamorgan

1 Cut the liver into small pieces. Put it with the butter into a small 600-

ml/1-pint basin. Cover with clear film and cook on full power for 1 minute; allow to cool slightly.
2 Tip the liver and butter into a food processor or liquidiser with the remaining ingredients. Blend until smooth.
3 Put the pâté in a small dish, cover with film and chill.

The pâté can also be topped with a little melted butter – this will stop the surface from drying.

TUNA FISH PATE

The pâté freezes well. It tastes best served at room temperature, with toast, rolls or oat cakes. For a change it may be served in lemon shells. For 2.

85 g/3½ oz can of tuna fish in oil
50 g/2 oz butter, softened
2 teaspoons lemon juice
½ teaspoon anchovy essence
2 tablespoons cream or top-of-the-milk
A pinch of cayenne pepper
Salt and pepper
Cucumber slices for decoration

1 Drain the tuna and mash it in a bowl, gradually working in the softened butter.
2 When thoroughly mixed, stir in the lemon juice, anchovy essence, cream and seasonings. Alternatively, place all the ingredients in a liquidiser or processor and blend until thoroughly mixed and smooth.
3 Put the pâté in a small bowl or individual ramekins and decorate with twists of cucumber.

Angela Henderson
Fleet, Hampshire

MELBA TOAST

Lovely with pâté or soups.

2 large slices white or wholemeal bread

1 Toast both sides of the bread until nicely golden, then carefully trim off the crusts.
2 Hold the toasted bread flat down on a wooden board with the palm of your hand and, using a sharp knife, cut through horizontally to make two slices.
3 Return to the grill and toast the uncooked sides until crisp and golden.
4 Cool and store in an airtight tin until needed.

Grace Mulligan

STUFFED MUSHROOMS
For 2.

10 medium mushrooms
75 g/3 oz smooth pâté (try Quick Liver Pâté, page 29)
Seasoned flour
1 egg, lightly beaten
Dried breadcrumbs
Oil for frying
Tartare sauce, lemon wedges and slices of tomato and cucumber to serve

1 Wipe the mushrooms and remove the stalks. Using a knife, spread the pâté into the hollows, making it level with the caps.
2 Dip the mushrooms in seasoned flour, then coat with the beaten egg and finally the breadcrumbs.
3 Heat the oil and deep-fry the mushrooms for a few minutes until golden brown. Drain on kitchen paper, sprinkle lightly with salt and serve immediately.
4 Garnish with lemon wedges and slices of tomato and cucumber and serve the tartare sauce separately.

TIP
These mushrooms may be fried earlier in the day and reheated in the oven or microwave just prior to serving. The stalks from the mushrooms may be used in soups, stocks or casseroles.

Angela Henderson
Fleet, Hampshire

HOT SAVOURY TOASTED SNACKS FOR ONE

HAM

1 slice of bread, preferably wholemeal
Butter
1 small slice of cooked ham, finely chopped
1 pickled onion, chopped
25 g/1 oz grated cheese

1 Toast the bread on one side under the grill.
2 Turn the bread over and butter lightly, then cover first with the chopped ham, then the pickled onion, lastly the cheese.
3 Replace under the hot grill to reheat and melt the cheese. Eat at once.

FRANKFURTER

1 slice of bread, preferably wholemeal
Butter
1 Frankfurter sausage, cut in 1-cm/½-inch slices
1 mushroom, finely sliced
25 g/1 oz grated Edam cheese

1 Toast the bread on one side under the grill.
2 Turn the bread over and butter it lightly. Cover with sliced Frankfurter sausage, then the finely sliced mushroom and lastly the grated cheese.
3 Replace under the hot grill to reheat and melt the cheese. Eat at once.

CORNED BEEF

1 slice of bread, preferably
   wholemeal
Butter
1 finely sliced spring onion or 1
   teaspoon finely grated raw
   onion
1 tablespoon finely chopped sweet
   apple
1 slice corned beef
25 g/1 oz Edam cheese, grated

1 Toast the bread on one side under
the grill.
2 Turn it over and butter lightly,
then cover with the onion, the apple,
the corned beef and lastly the grated
cheese. Replace under the hot grill to
reheat and melt the cheese. Eat at
once.

FAST GARLIC TOAST
Rub a cut clove of garlic vigorously
over a slice of toast and butter. Eat
hot.

CREAM CHEESE AND CELERY
Beat finely chopped raw celery and
celery leaves into a well-seasoned
cream cheese and spread on cold
squares of toast. This makes a nice
savoury end to a meal.

Grace Mulligan

EGG-IN-A-NEST
*For 1: hot, quick, nourishing and
filling. Only the grill used.*

A thick slice of white or
   wholemeal bread
Grated Cheddar cheese
1 size 3 egg

1 Toast the bread on one side only.
2 On the untoasted side, make a
'wall' of grated cheese, leaving a well
in centre. Press cheese a little so that
the wall is firm enough to hold the
egg in.

3 Break the egg into the nest, then
return to a moderately hot grill until
the egg is lightly cooked and cheese
has melted. If grill is too hot, the top
of the egg goes hard before the rest
of it is cooked.

Mrs Mary Potts
Bedlington, Northumberland

HAM TITBITS
For 1 or 2 or more . . .

Slices of wholemeal or white
   bread
Thick slices of ham
Rings of well-drained canned
   pineapple
Grated Cheddar cheese

1 Toast the bread lightly on both
sides, then cut rings about 9 cm/3½
inches across with a biscuit cutter.
2 Now cut rings of ham.
3 Lay slices of ham on the toast.
(The offcuts can be tucked in, too.)
4 Place a pineapple ring on each
piece of ham and cover with grated
cheese.
5 Grill until cheese bubbles and
browns. Serve at once on warm
plates.

Save the toast offcuts to make
croûtons or breadcrumbs. For another
recipe using canned pineapple rings,
see page 55.

Mrs Riseborough,
Widdrington Station,
Northumberland.

CHEESE AND SARDINE FINGERS
*For 2 but easy to make for 1. Nice
served with grilled tomatoes.*

A 120 g/4½ oz can of sardines
   in oil
25 g/1 oz fresh breadcrumbs,
   wholemeal or white
½ teaspoon made mustard

1 teaspoon Worcestershire sauce
50 g/2 oz grated cheese
Salt and pepper
4 slices of buttered toast

1 Drain oil from sardine can and mix
some of it with breadcrumbs,
mustard, sauce and cheese to form a
crumbly mixture.
2 Mash sardines and season well with
salt and pepper.
3 Spread sardines on toast, top with
crumbly mixture and grill.

Mrs Margaret Heywood
Todmorden, Yorkshire

WELSH RAREBIT
For 2, but easy to make for 1.

2 slices of wholemeal bread,
  toasted and warm
25 g/1 oz butter
100 g/4 oz strong Cheddar cheese,
  grated
1 teaspoon dry mustard
2 tablespoons beer
Salt and pepper

1 Put the slices of toast on to
heatproof plates.
2 In a small pan, melt the butter,
then add all the other ingredients,
stirring all the time with a wooden
spoon.
3 When the cheese mixture is hot,
but not boiling, pour it over the slices
of toast.
4 Put the toast under a very hot grill
to give a brown bubbly finish. Serve
at once.

Variation: top the cheese with a
poached egg or crispy bacon.

Grace Mulligan

SWEET TOASTED SNACKS

HOT CINNAMON TOAST

1 teaspoon ground cinnamon
2 teaspoons caster sugar
40 g/1½ oz soft butter
Toast

Mix together the cinnamon, sugar and
butter, then spread it on slices of hot
toast. This spiced butter can be kept
in the refrigerator for several days if
it is not all used up at once.

HOT DEMERARA TOAST

Toast
40 g/1½ oz soft butter
Demerara sugar

1 Butter warm slices of toast and
sprinkle over some Demerara sugar.
2 Cut into fingers and serve while
the sugar is still crunchy. Children
love this if coloured sugar crystals are
used instead of Demerara.

BANANA TOAST

Mash a banana with a dusting of
sugar and a dash of rum. Spread on
hot buttered toast. Eat instead of
pudding.

Grace Mulligan

CHICKEN PASTE
*Eat this like a pâté with fingers of
toast, or make a softer spread for
sandwiches. Excellent in sandwiches
with sliced cucumber. Keep refrigerated.*

75 g/3 oz very finely chopped or
  minced cooked chicken
1 tablespoon soft butter
Salt and pepper
Pinch of sage
Extra butter, melted, to seal pots

33

1 Mix all the ingredients, except melted butter, together until smooth.
2 Spoon into two small pots, smooth the surface and cover with a film of melted butter.
3 To make a softer paste, add a very little chicken stock.

Grace Mulligan

SMOKED FISH SPREAD

Can be spread on toast as a light meal or used as a sandwich filling. Keeps in refrigerator for several days. Makes enough for 2 or 3.

200 g/8 oz smoked fish fillet
2 tablespoons milk
50 g/2 oz margarine or butter
75 g/3 oz cream cheese
35 g/1½ oz fresh breadcrumbs
Grated rind and juice of half a lemon
Pepper

1 Cut fish into small pieces and put it in a small pan with the milk and margarine or butter. Cook gently for about 5 to 7 minutes, then mash with a fork and leave to cool.
2 Beat in the cream cheese, breadcrumbs, finely grated lemon rind and juice. Add pepper to taste but no salt.

If you think the fish may be too salty for you, put it in a pan, cover with water and bring to the boil. Then drain off the water and start at step 1.

Mrs Margaret Heywood
Todmorden, Yorkshire

Microwave

1 Put the fish on a plate. Cover with clear film and cook on full power for 2 minutes. Cool slightly, flake with a fork, removing any skin or bones, then mash well.
2 Beat in the cream cheese, breadcrumbs, lemon rind and juice. Add pepper to taste but it is unlikely to need salt.

HAM SANDWICH SPREAD

This works well with meat from a Ham Shank (page 67). The proportions for this recipe don't really matter, but as a guide you need about twice as much ham as butter.

Cooked ham, very finely cut or minced
Soft butter
Freshly ground pepper
A little ham stock

Mix all the ingredients together until you have a moist, spreading consistency.

TIP
If you have a food processor you can make this ham spread in only a few seconds. It is delicious in sandwiches or rolls with a few slices of cucumber and it will keep for several days in a refrigerator.

Grace Mulligan

34

Chapter 3

Fish and Shellfish

SHRIMP-STUFFED TOMATOES

For 1 or 2, delicious!

2 large tomatoes
225 g/8 oz shrimps which, when
　peeled, give 50 g/2 oz for this
　recipe
25 g/1 oz white or wholemeal
　breadcrumbs
A little beaten egg, to bind
Salt and pepper
A little chopped parsley

1 Preheat over to moderate, Gas 4,
350°F, 180°C.
2 Cut tomatoes in half, scoop out a
little of the flesh and place them in
an ovenproof dish.
3 Mix the scooped-out tomato with
shrimps and breadcrumbs and use
just enough beaten egg to bind the
mixture. Season with salt, pepper and
parsley and fill the tomato halves.
4 Cook for 15 to 20 minutes until the
tomatoes are tender.

Mrs A. M. Taylor
Boyton, Suffolk

SEAFOOD WITH TAGLIATELLE

For 2. Make this for a special occasion.
Frozen cooked mussels may be used.

25 g/1 oz butter or margarine
Half an onion, finely chopped
Half a red pepper, deseeded and
　chopped
1 teaspoon chopped fresh basil
Freshly ground black pepper
A 400 g/14 oz can of tomatoes,
　chopped
1 wineglass of red wine
1 dessertspoon of tomato purée
A clove of garlic, crushed
125 g/4 oz tagliatelle verde
50 g/2 oz peeled prawns
125 g/4 oz white fish fillet, skinned
　and cut in 1.5-cm/¾-inch cubes

125 g/4 oz cooked shelled mussels
Chopped fresh basil to garnish

1 In a large saucepan, melt the butter
or margarine and fry the onion until
soft.
2 Add all the other ingredients except
the tagliatelle, fish and shellfish.
Simmer for 30 minutes with the lid
off.
3 Add the tagliatelle to the sauce and
simmer for a further 10 minutes, or
until the pasta is cooked.
4 Add the prawns, cubed white fish
and mussels, and continue to simmer
with the lid on for a further 3 to 4
minutes, until the white fish is
cooked.
5 Serve sprinkled with chopped fresh
basil.

Yvonne Coull
Sea Fish Industry Authority,
Edinburgh

Microwave

1 Put the butter or margarine and
onion in a medium-sized bowl and
cook on full power for 2 minutes,
stirring halfway through.
2 Add all ingredients, except the fish,
cover and cook on full power for 5 to
6 minutes until the pasta is cooked.
3 Add the prawns, cubed white fish
and cooked shelled mussels; cover and
cook on full power for 2 minutes
more.
4 Serve sprinkled with fresh basil.

SPAGHETTI WITH MUSSELS

Delicious for 2.

900 g/2 lb fresh mussels,*
　scrubbed
175 g/6 oz spaghetti
2 to 3 tablespoons oil
1 medium onion, chopped
A clove of garlic, crushed

A 200 g/8 oz can of tomatoes,
  drained and chopped
½ teaspoon dried oregano
2 tablespoons chopped fresh
  parsley
Pepper and a little salt

* 225 g/8 oz frozen or canned mussels
can be substituted.

1 If using fresh mussels, make sure
that they are all tightly closed before
cooking and discard any that do not
shut when the shell is tapped. Put the
cleaned mussels into a pan with 1
cm/½ inch of water, put on the lid
and steam them for 6 to 7 minutes
until they are open. If any do not
open, discard them. Remove the meat
from the shells.
2 Cook the spaghetti in plenty of
boiling salted water with 1 tablespoon
oil until tender. When cooked, drain
and keep warm.
3 Heat 2 tablespoons oil and fry the
onion and garlic until lightly
browned. Pour in the tomatoes and
cook for about 5 minutes, mashing
them down so the mixture resembles
a sauce.
4 Add the oregano and mussels and
allow to warm through. Season to
taste.
5 Pile the spaghetti on to a warmed
dish and pour the mussels and sauce
over the top. Sprinkle with chopped
parsley.

David Shepperdson
Huddersfield, Yorkshire

SQUID WITH GREEN PEPPERS IN A BLACK BEAN SAUCE

*The black bean sauce in this unusual
recipe goes particularly well with squid.
It is sold in Chinese and Oriental food
shops. Serve this with boiled rice.
For 2.*

325 g/12 oz cleaned squid tubes
A clove of garlic, crushed

3 tablespoons water
2 tablespoons light soy sauce
1½ tablespoons black bean sauce
2 tablespoons oil
1 green pepper, deseeded, and cut
  into 2.5 cm/1 inch squares
6 spring onions, cut into 5 cm/2
  inch pieces
1 teaspoon cornflour mixed with 2
  teaspoons water
Pepper and a little salt

1 Cut the squid into pieces 2.5 cm/1
inch square and put them into a bowl
with the garlic. Cover the bowl and
leave it in a cool place for at least half
an hour.
2 Mix together the water, soy sauce
and black bean sauce and set aside.
3 Put the oil into a frying pan or wok
and heat until very hot. Add the
squid and fry for about 4 minutes.
4 Remove the squid from the pan,
drain well, and set aside.
5 Wipe out the pan and then heat 1
tablespoon fresh oil. Stir in the
pepper and cook for 2 minutes. Add
the onions and cook for about 1
minute, then return the squid to the
pan.
6 Pour the black bean sauce mixture
and cornflour into the pan and stir
until the sauce thickens. Season if
necessary with pepper and a little
salt.

David Shepperdson
Huddersfield, Yorkshire

COD WITH NOODLES IN A LEEK AND CHEESE SAUCE

*For 2, but can be made in separate
dishes for two different meals for 1
person.*

225 g/8 oz cod, skinned
25 g/1 oz butter
75 g/3 oz noodles, pasta shells or
  macaroni

The white part of 1 leek, well
    washed and cut in fine rings
15g/½ oz flour
150 ml/¼ pint milk
Pepper and a little salt
50 g/2 oz (or 1½ tablespoons)
    grated cheese

1 Lay cod in a shallow flameproof
dish and dot with half of the butter,
cut in tiny pieces.
2 Cook it under a medium-hot grill.
3 Meanwhile cook the noodles or
pasta shells in boiling water until just
done. Drain and spread over cooked
fish. Keep warm.
4 Melt remaining butter, add leek,
cover pan and cook gently for 5
minutes.
5 Stir flour into leeks and then
gradually add milk, stirring over
gentle heat as sauce thickens. Let it
simmer for 1 minute. Season with
pepper and a little salt.
6 Pour sauce over noodles, cover with
grated cheese and return to grill to
brown the top.

If making two individual dishes, the
second can be kept covered in the
refrigerator overnight. Reheat in a
moderately hot oven, Gas 5, 375°F,
190°C for 20 minutes.

Mrs Ivy Hopes
Oxford

Microwave

1 If using macaroni or pasta shells,
put them in an 18-cm/7-inch soufflé-
type dish. Cover with boiling water
and add a 15 ml tablespoon oil. Heat
on full power for 5 to 6 minutes.
Drain.
2 Put the leeks and butter in a 600
ml/1 pint jug. Heat on full power for
3 minutes.
3 Stir in the flour, then gradually
blend in the milk. Cook on full power
for 1 minute then stir in the salt and
pepper and cook for a further 30
seconds on full power.

4 Arrange the fish in a single layer
in a shallow 18-cm/7-inch flan dish.
Cover with clear film and cook on
full power for 2 minutes. Drain off
any juices.
5 Tip the pasta over the fish, then
pour the sauce over the pasta.
Sprinkle over the grated cheese. Heat
on full power for 2 minutes then
brown the cheese under a hot grill if
desired.

COD BAKED WITH SWEETCORN

*For 1, wrapped in foil like a parcel and
baked in the oven. However, to make
larger quantities, layer the ingredients in
a casserole, cover and bake for 30
minutes.*

50 g/2 oz canned or frozen
    sweetcorn
1 tomato, skinned (page 26) and
    sliced
Salt and pepper
100 g/4 oz fillet of cod or haddock,
    or a cod steak
1 teaspoon lemon juice
A few sprigs of parsley or
    watercress
25 g/1 oz Cheddar cheese, grated

1 Preheat oven to moderately hot,
Gas 6, 400°F, 200°C.
2 Spread out a piece of cooking foil
and on it make a layer of sweetcorn,
then tomato and season it.
3 Place fish on top, sprinkle with
lemon juice and a little more salt and
pepper.
4 Coarsely chop parsley or watercress
and lay it over fish.
5 Finally, cover with cheese.
6 Close the foil tightly and put the
parcel on a baking tray. Cook near top
of oven for 20 minutes.

Mrs J. Macdonald
Aberfeldy, Perthshire

1 Put the fish in a small dish – a cereal bowl is ideal. Sprinkle the sweetcorn over and arrange two tomato slices on top.
2 Sprinkle with lemon juice. Coarsely chop the parsley or watercress and scatter over the tomato slices.
3 Sprinkle with the cheese. Cover the dish with clear film and cook on full power for 1½ minutes. If the fish is thick it may take another minute or two.

TASTY FISH PIE

For 2. A good recipe and very tasty, especially if you use new potatoes. Cod, haddock, coley and whiting are all suitable.

3 medium potatoes
2 teaspoons flour
Salt and pepper
225 g/8 oz cod fillet, skinned and cut into 2 portions
A little butter or margarine
150 ml/¼ pint milk
100 g/4 oz grated Cheddar cheese
50 g/2 oz prawns (optional)
4 medium mushrooms, chopped
25 g/1 oz diced red pepper

1 Slice potatoes thickly and parboil them for 6 minutes, then drain.
2 Meanwhile, preheat oven to moderately hot, Gas 6, 400°F, 200°C.
3 Season flour with salt and pepper and toss the fish in it to coat.
4 Grease an ovenproof dish quite liberally with butter or margarine and put in the fish.
5 Pour in the milk and sprinkle fish with half the grated cheese.
6 Add prawns, mushrooms and red pepper and season with a little salt and pepper.
7 Arrange the potatoes on top and cover with the remaining cheese.

8 Cook near top of preheated oven for 30 minutes. Serve with whole green beans.

Mrs Kay Fussey
Denby Dale, Yorkshire

FISH TIKKA

For 2. Nice served with a green salad and the marinade.

2 cod steaks, each about 225 g/8 oz

MARINADE
3 tablespoons natural yoghurt
A clove of garlic, crushed
A pinch of ground chilli
½ teaspoon garam masala
A pinch of ground ginger
1 dessertspoon lemon juice
Salt and freshly ground black pepper
1 to 2 drops of red food colouring (optional)

1 Place the fish in a shallow dish.
2 In a small bowl, mix together the remaining ingredients and pour over the cod steaks.
3 Cover and refrigerate for 2 to 4 hours.
4 Lift the fish out of the marinade and grill it under a low heat on both sides, for 15 to 20 minutes in all. Serve with the marinade as a cold sauce.

1 Place the fish in a shallow dish.
2 In a small bowl, mix together the remaining ingredients and pour over the cod steaks.
3 Cover and refrigerate for 2 to 4 hours.
4 Cook on full power for 3 to 4 minutes. Serve with the marinade.

Yvonne Coull
Sea Fish Industry Authority, Edinburgh

SMOKED HADDOCK AND CHEESE SAVOURY

For 2. Serve this with fresh toast and halved tomatoes, sprinkled with a little sugar and grilled.

225 g/8 oz smoked haddock
Pepper and a little salt

SAUCE
25 g/1 oz margarine or butter
25 g/1 oz flour
300 ml/½ pint milk
2 teaspoons capers
50 g/2 oz cheese, cut in slices

1 Sprinkle fish with pepper but not too much salt. Place between two plates to steam over a pan of simmering water. It will cook in about 15 minutes.
2 Make a sauce by melting margarine and stirring in flour with a wooden spoon. Allow to cook for 1 minute.
3 Remove pan from heat and gradually stir in half the milk until blended and smooth.
4 Return pan to heat and stir continuously as sauce thickens, gradually adding remaining milk. Bring to the boil and stir as it cooks for 2 to 3 minutes more.
5 Add capers and season with a little salt and pepper.
6 Now flake the cooked fish and mix it into sauce. Pour into a warmed ovenproof serving dish and cover with the thin slices of cheese.
7 Place dish under a hot grill until cheese bubbles and browns nicely.

H. R. Kelman
Aberdeen

Microwave

1 Put the fish on a plate and cover with clear film. Cook on full power for 2 minutes.
2 Put the margarine in a 600-ml/ 1-pint jug, heat on full power for 1 minute.
3 Stir in the flour and gradually blend in the milk. Cook on full power for 1 minute, then stir. Cook for a further 1 minute.
4 Then stir in the capers and season with a little salt and pepper.
5 Flake the fish into the sauce and tip into a shallow 600-ml/1-pint pie dish, cover with thin slices of cheese and grill until the cheese browns.

SMOKED HADDOCK IN A CREAM SAUCE

For 2, but easy to make just for one.

2 fillets smoked haddock, about
    175 g/6 oz each
60 ml/2 fl oz single cream
120 ml/4 fl oz milk
2 eggs
2 tomatoes, skinned (page 26)
    and chopped
A knob of butter or margarine
Salt and pepper
Finely chopped fresh parsley

1 Poach the haddock fillets in a pan in the cream and milk until cooked, 10 to 15 minutes.
2 Poach the eggs (page 17).
3 Warm the tomatoes through in a little butter, then spread them on a warmed serving dish. Put the drained haddock on top and finally top with the poached eggs.
4 Boil the milk and cream mixture to reduce it slightly, add salt and pepper to taste, then strain it over the fish. Garnish with parsley and serve.

David Shepperdson
Huddersfield, Yorkshire

SMOKED FISH SOUFFLÉ

For 2.

225 g/8 oz smoked haddock, cod
    or halibut

Water
Pepper
2 large eggs, separated
1 teaspoon chopped parsley

1 Preheat the oven to moderate, Gas 4, 350°F, 180°C.
2 Poach the fish on top of the cooker in a covered pan in just enough water to come halfway up the thickest part of the fish. The fish is cooked when it looks opaque (about 5 to 8 minutes).
3 Drain the fish and break into small pieces, removing any bones.
4 Season the fish with pepper and beat in the two egg yolks and the parsley.
5 In another bowl, whip the egg whites until stiff and fold them into the fish mixture.
6 Tip this mixture into a buttered ovenproof dish. Ensure that the dish or tin is big enough to allow the soufflé to rise. A 20–cm/8-inch casserole is nicely filled.
7 Bake for 20 minutes. Serve immediately with a good salad or just crusty bread.

Grace Mulligan

Soufflés cannot be made in the microwave but you can use it to cook the fish. At step 2 above: put the fish on a plate, cover with clear film and cook on full power for 2 to 2½ minutes. It is cooked when it is opaque and flakes easily.

SALMON PARCEL
For 2. Serve with Herb Sauce (page 51), Casseroled Potatoes (page 114), and peas, courgettes or a salad.

450 g/1 lb tail piece of salmon
25 g/1 oz butter, softened but not melted
Juice of half a lemon

½ teaspoon chopped chives
½ teaspoon chopped parsley
Salt and pepper
175 g/6 oz flaky or puff pastry
Milk or beaten egg to glaze

1 Skin the salmon and bone it. This will give you two fillets.
2 Mix together the butter, lemon juice, chives, parsley and seasoning.
3 Spread half of the butter mixture on one salmon fillet, cover with the other fillet and spread the remaining butter mixture all over the fish.
4 Roll out the pastry and wrap the fish in it, damp and seal the edges well, keeping the join on top. Cut the pastry trimmings into small leaf shapes. Put the parcel on a baking tray.
5 Glaze the pastry with milk or beaten egg. Arrange the pastry leaves on top and glaze them. Make a small hole in top of the pastry to allow the steam to escape. Leave the salmon parcel to rest for 10 minutes in a cool place.
6 Preheat the oven to hot, Gas 7, 425°F, 220°C.
7 Bake the parcel towards the top of the oven for 30 minutes.

Dilwen Phillips
Gileston, South Glamorgan

SEA FISH CAKES
Enough for 2.

225 g/8 oz white fish fillet, skinned
225 g/8 oz potatoes, peeled
1 egg yolk
Salt and freshly ground black pepper
Milk
2 tablespoons wholemeal flour
1 egg, beaten
4 tablespoons fresh wholemeal breadcrumbs

1 Finely dice the fish, or put it through a liquidiser or processor.

41

2 Put the potatoes in a saucepan with a little lightly salted water and cook until tender.
3 Drain and mash with the egg yolk and seasoning. Allow to cool, then mix into the fish.
4 Form into 2 large or 4 small fish cakes. If the mixture is too stiff add a few drops of milk. Coat the fish cakes in flour, then beaten egg and breadcrumbs. Chill for 30 minutes.
5 Grill the fish cakes for 5 minutes on each side.

Yvonne Coull
Sea Fish Industry Authority,
Edinburgh

CRISP-FRIED FISH PIECES WITH A PIQUANT SAUCE

Enough for 2 generous helpings. If quantities are increased, this makes a good party dish with the sauce as a dip. Use an assortment of filleted fish, e.g. cod, haddock, plaice, sole, whiting, even a few prawns.

250 g/8 oz fish, boned, skinned
15 g/½ oz seasoned flour
A little beaten egg
50 g/2 oz fine dried breadcrumbs
Oil for deep frying

DRESSING
2 large tablespoons mayonnaise
¼ teaspoon each of English and French mustard
½ level teaspoon each of chopped capers, gherkins and fresh parsley
A pinch of chervil

1 Make dressing well in advance to allow flavours to blend. Thoroughly mix all ingredients.
2 Cut fish into bite-sized strips and dust with seasoned flour.
3 Dip strips in egg, then pat on breadcrumbs.

4 Drop into deep hot fat, moving them around with a draining spoon to keep pieces separate.
5 When evenly browned and cooked through – 3 minutes will be enough – lift out on to kitchen paper to drain. Do not overcook.
6 Serve piping hot with the cold dressing in a separate bowl.

TIP
If serving this for a party, fish strips can be 'egged and crumbed', then fried at last minute.

Anne Wallace
Stewarton, Ayrshire

CRISP AND BUTTERY HERRINGS

For 2. The wholemeal coating is delicious and the brown butter sauce is very rich.

2 herrings, heads and gut removed
Wholemeal flour
1 small egg, beaten
50 g/2 oz fresh wholemeal breadcrumbs
25 g/1 oz butter

SAUCE
25 to 50 g/1 to 2 oz butter
1 tablespoon vinegar
½ teaspoon mustard
Lemon slices and wholemeal toast for serving

1 Using the back of a knife, scrape off the scales, then rinse the herrings and dry well.
2 Toss each fish first in flour, then beaten egg, and finally coat with the breadcrumbs.
3 Melt the butter and gently fry the herrings for about 5 to 6 minutes on each side. When cooked, remove from the pan, drain well and set aside to keep warm while preparing the sauce.
4 Melt the butter in a small pan and allow it to brown a little. Mix the

vinegar and mustard together and add to pan. Stir as it heats, season with a little salt and pour the sauce over the herrings.
5 Serve with lemon slices and toast.

Grace Mulligan

HERRING KEBABS WITH REDCURRANT JELLY

For 2.

2 herring fillets, 175 g/6 oz each
8 bay leaves
1 small onion, halved and quartered
Salt and freshly ground black pepper
3 tablespoons redcurrant jelly, melted

1 Cut each herring into 4 and thread on to skewers, alternating with the bay leaves and onion pieces.
2 Season with salt and black pepper and cook under a moderate grill for 8 to 10 minutes, turning the kebabs once and brushing over with some of the redcurrant jelly.
3 Heat the remaining redcurrant jelly but do not let it boil.
4 Serve the kebabs on a bed of brown rice and pour the sauce over the top.

Microwave

1 Cut each herring into 4 chunks and thread on to wooden skewers along with the bay leaves and onion pieces. Arrange them on a plate in a single layer.
2 Cook for 2 to 3 minutes on full power. Set aside, covered.
3 Put the redcurrant jelly in a small bowl and heat in full power for 1 minute.

4 Serve the kebabs on a bed of brown rice and pour the sauce over.

Yvonne Coull
Sea Fish Industry Authority,
Edinburgh

PICKLED HERRINGS

Often served cut into strips and mixed with a potato salad. Delicious as a starter on their own with brown bread or rolls. Can be frozen after pickling – best to pack individual fillets with a little liquor in small containers – so it's worth making a quantity.

3 herrings
Salt

PICKLING LIQUOR
120 ml/4 fl oz white vinegar
120 ml/4 fl oz wine or tarragon vinegar
120 ml/4 fl oz water
75 g/3 oz granulated sugar
1 small onion, thinly sliced or finely chopped
Freshly ground black pepper
3 allspice berries
3 cloves
A pinch of fennel seed

1 Clean the herrings (or ask the fishmonger to do this for you) and divide fish into several fillets, removing as many bones as possible.
2 Sprinkle a layer of salt (about 1 tablespoon) into an earthenware or Pyrex casserole. Arrange a layer of fillets on top. Add another layer of salt, then fish, ending with a layer of salt. Cover and leave in a cool place (bottom of the refrigerator) for 1 to 2 days.
3 Remove the herrings from the salt and carefully peel away the skin. Leave to soak in cold water for about an hour, changing the water if very salty.
4 Prepare the pickling liquor by mixing together the remaining ingredients.
5 Lift the fillets out of the water, pat

43

dry, replace in a clean dish and pour over the pickling liquor. Cover and leave at least 48 hours in a cool place.

Margaret Heywood
Todmorden, Yorkshire

CITRUS MACKEREL
For 2; try them served hot with a green salad.

Half a small red apple, cored
   and chopped
Half a small orange, peeled and
   chopped
1 teaspoon chopped fresh tarragon
   or ½ teaspoon dried tarragon
1 tablespoon lemon juice
15 g/½ oz butter or margarine
50 g/2 oz porridge oats
Salt and black pepper
2 mackerel fillets, 225 to 275 g/8 to
   10 oz each

1 Put the apple, orange, tarragon, lemon juice and butter or margarine in a saucepan and gently heat through, until the apple has softened.
2 Stir in the oats and seasoning and divide the filling in two.
3 Place the mackerel on a board, skin side down, spread the filling over the mackerel and roll up each fish from the head end. Secure with cocktail sticks and place in a shallow dish.
4 Preheat oven to moderately hot, Gas 6, 400°F, 200°C.
5 Cover the dish and cook the mackerel for 10 to 15 minutes. Serve with salad.

Microwave

1 Put the apple, orange, tarragon, lemon juice and butter or margarine into a bowl. Cover and cook on full power for 1 minute until the apple has softened.
2 Stir in the oats and season with salt and pepper. Divide into 2 portions.

3 Place the mackerel on a board, and follow the rest of step 3 above.
4 Cover and cook on full power for 3 minutes.

Yvonne Coull
Sea Fish Industry Authority,
Edinburgh

CRISP LEMON SOLE
For 2.

2 skinned fillets of lemon sole
   or plaice, about 225 to 275 g/8 to
   10 oz each
2 rindless rashers back bacon
Salt and black pepper
Lemon juice
A knob of butter or margarine
25 g/1 oz Cheddar cheese, grated
A few potato crisps, slightly
   crushed

1 Preheat the oven to moderately hot, Gas 6, 400°F, 200°C.
2 Place each fillet on top of a rasher of bacon, season with salt and black pepper and sprinkle with a little lemon juice.
3 Roll up the fillets from head to tail and place in an ovenproof dish, ensuring that the tails are secured underneath. Dot with butter.
4 Bake in the preheated oven for 15 minutes.
5 Remove the dish from the oven, sprinkle with cheese and the crisps, then bake for a further 5 minutes until golden brown.

Yvonne Coull
Sea Fish Industry Authority,
Edinburgh

SOLE WITH CREAM AND PARMESAN
For 1 or 2. Can also be made with haddock or whiting. For one person, this simple, delicious recipe can be eaten from the dish in which it has been cooked.

44

A little butter
1 or 2 fillets of sole, haddock or
    whiting, skinned*
Salt and freshly ground black
    pepper
4 tablespoons double cream, but
    single will do
About 6 teaspoons Parmesan
    cheese

* For instructions to skin fish, see Fish
Pie in Puff Pastry, page 121, step 2.

1 Preheat grill to moderately hot.
2 Butter a shallow flameproof dish
and put in the fish. Season with salt
and pepper.
3 Spoon over the cream and sprinkle
well with Parmesan.
4 Grill slowly until fish is cooked and
the cream and cheese turn into a
lovely sauce.

Mrs J. B. Morrison
Elgin, Grampian

POACHED SALMON WITH TWO SAUCES

*Here's the main course cooked by Simon
Dunn, who won third place in the 1987
Junior Cook of the Year competition.
You'll find a liquidiser or processor is
needed for the sauces. The dish is for 2.*

250 ml/½ pint water
A quarter of a Spanish onion,
    sliced
Half a stick of celery, sliced
1 bay leaf
Juice of a lemon
Salt and pepper
2 fresh salmon steaks

FRESH TOMATO SAUCE
25 g/1 oz butter
1 small onion, finely chopped
A clove of garlic, crushed
2 large tomatoes, skinned (page
    26) and deseeded
A pinch of oregano
Salt and pepper
A pinch of sugar
1 tablespoon dry white vermouth

WATERCRESS SAUCE

Half a bunch of watercress,
  washed
2 tablespoons double cream
2 tablespoons natural yoghurt
2 twists of sliced lemon and
  sprigs of watercress to
  garnish

1 For the tomato sauce: melt butter
in a pan and cook onion and garlic
until transparent. Add remaining
ingredients and cook quickly for 4
minutes. Liquidise and set aside to
reheat when salmon is ready to serve.
2 For the watercress sauce, which is
served cold, liquidise the watercress
with the cream and yoghurt, adding
salt if necessary. Keep cool.
3 Now for the salmon. Put water,
onion, celery, bay leaf, lemon juice,
pepper and a little salt in a saucepan.
Bring to the boil, reduce heat and
simmer for 15 minutes.
4 Add the salmon, placing the steaks
carefully in the pan. Cover and
simmer for 10 minutes. Lift out
carefully so they do not break.
5 Serve the salmon on individual hot
plates with a spoonful of each sauce
alongside. Hand the rest of the sauces
in two small bowls.

Simon Dunn
Bickley, Kent

Microwave

*For microwaving, choose salmon steaks
weighing 175 g/6 oz each; substitute a
squeeze of lemon juice for the juice of a
whole lemon and disregard the rest of the
ingredients for poaching the fish. You
should need only one large tomato for
the Fresh Tomato Sauce. Otherwise, the
sauce ingredients are the same.*

1 Arrange the salmon steaks on a
plate, thickest parts to the outside.
Sprinkle with lemon juice and a good
grind of black pepper. Cover with
clear film and set aside while you
make the sauces.

2 First, make the tomato sauce: put
the butter, onion and garlic in a small
basin and heat on full power for 3
minutes. Stir in the rest of the
ingredients and heat on full power for
2 minutes. Liquidise and set aside to
reheat when the salmon is ready to
serve.
3 Make the watercress sauce,
following step 2 of the main method.
Keep it cool.
4 Cook the prepared salmon steaks on
full power for 3 to 4 minutes, then
stand for 5 minutes.
5 Meanwhile, reheat the tomato
sauce on full power for 30 seconds to
1 minute. Serve and garnish as
above.

TEIFI SALMON IN A SAUCE

(Saws Ellog Teifi)

*This main course for 2 was cooked by
Lucy Barton-Greenwood when she won
second place in the 1987 Junior Cook of
the Year competition. See page 179 for
her full menu. We suggest serving this
with new potatoes and mange-tout
peas.*

2 salmon steaks
25 g/1 oz butter
A liqueur glass of port or sweet
  sherry
A dash of tomato ketchup
1 fillet from a can of anchovies
Pepper and salt
Lemon rings and tiny hearts cut
  from tomato skins to garnish

1 Preheat oven to moderately hot,
Gas 5, 375°F, 190°C.
2 Wash and dry the salmon and put
it in an ovenproof dish.
3 Melt the butter and add the port,
ketchup and anchovy; stir over a low
heat until hot and it becomes a
smooth sauce. Season with pepper
and salt. Pour over the salmon.

4 Cover dish and bake for about 35 minutes – the time depends on the thickness of the salmon.
5 Carefully remove the skin from the salmon steaks, put them on a serving dish, and pour over the sauce. Garnish with lemon rings and tiny tomato hearts.

Lucy Barton-Greenwood
Radyr, Cardiff

 Microwave

1 Wash and dry the salmon steaks. Arrange in a shallow dish with the thickest parts to the outside.
2 Put 50 g/2 oz butter in a jug and heat on full power for 1 to 1½ minutes until melted. Stir in two 15 ml tablespoons port, 1 tablespoon tomato ketchup and the anchovy. Stir until well combined.
3 Pour the sauce over the salmon. Cover the dish with clear film and cook on full power for 4 to 5 minutes.
4 Serve with the sauce poured over, garnished as above.

SEA BASS WITH CLAMS AND HERBS

This main course was cooked by Sally Wilson, 14, when she became Junior Cook of the Year, 1987. (See page 179 for the other dishes in her 3-course menu.) This recipe is also very successful with salmon instead of sea bass and prawns instead of clams. For 2.

300 ml/½ pint hot court
   bouillon (see step 1)
275 g/10 oz clams in shells,
   washed
40 g/1½ oz butter
1 shallot, chopped
A clove of garlic, chopped
Two 150 g/6 oz fillets of sea bass
Sea salt

A bouquet garni (or small bunch of
   fresh herbs)
1 tablespoon chopped fresh
   parsley
Juice of half a lemon
1 large tomato, skinned (page 26)
   and diced

FOR THE BASIL CRUST
25 g/1 oz pine nuts, ready-
   roasted and chopped
1 tablespoon olive oil
5 leaves of fresh basil, chopped, or
   a pinch of dried basil
25 g/1 oz fresh white
   breadcrumbs
Salt and pepper

1 A simple court bouillon is made by simmering together gently for 20 minutes 300 ml/½ pint water, 1 small sliced carrot, half an onion, 1 bay leaf, a pinch or sprig of thyme, 1 or 2 sprigs of parsley, a pinch of salt, 3 peppercorns and 2 tablespoons cider or white wine vinegar. Strain and use.
2 Cook the clams by putting them into a pan of boiling, lightly salted water and cooking over moderate heat just until the shells open. Drain.
3 Melt 25 g/1 oz of the butter, put in the shallot and garlic and fry gently for 1 or 2 minutes just to soften.
4 Put the sea bass into the pan and sprinkle over the clams and a little salt. Add the hot court bouillon and bouquet garni. Bring just to boiling point, cover pan and let it simmer for 5 minutes.
5 Meanwhile prepare the basil crust. Liquidise the pine nuts (or put them through a food processor) with the olive oil; transfer to a bowl and mix in basil, breadcrumbs, pepper and salt.
6 Lift the sea bass carefully out of the pan into a heatproof dish, spread each piece with basil crust and grill until golden brown.
7 Remove the clams from pan and keep them warm. Remove the bouquet garni.

47

8 Strain the cooking liquid and then return it to the pan to boil and reduce the quantity until there is just enough to make a sauce for 2 people.
9 Add parsley and whisk in remaining butter. Add lemon juice, salt, pepper and lastly the diced tomato.
10 Spoon the tomato mixture into the hot serving dish. Carefully lift the sea bass fillets and place them on top. Serve at once with the clams arranged prettily around the dish.

Sally Wilson
Hatch End, Middlesex

![Microwave]

The only changes to the ingredients given above is that the bouquet garni is not required and the court bouillon has been adjusted.

1 To make the court bouillon put 150 ml/¼ fl oz hot water into a 1.1 litre/2 pint basin. Add 1 small sliced carrot, 1 onion, peeled and cut in half, 1 bay leaf, a pinch each of thyme and salt, 2 to 3 sprigs of parsley, 2 to 3 peppercorns and 2 tablespoons cider or wine vinegar. Heat on full power for 5 minutes then let it stand for 5 minutes. Strain into a jug and use.
2 Put 15 g/1 oz of the butter, the shallot and garlic into a shallow 20-cm/8-inch round dish. Heat on full power for 2 minutes.
3 Arrange the sea bass over the onion mixture. Put the clams on top of the sea bass. Sprinkle over four 15 ml tablespoons court bouillon and cover the dish with a piece of clear film. Cook on full power for 4 to 5 minutes. The clam shells should have opened and the sea bass should be opaque.
4 Meanwhile prepare the basil crust. Put the pine nuts and olive oil into a liquidiser or food processor and blend until smooth. Mix in the breadcrumbs

and basil and season with a little salt and pepper.
5 Carefully lift the sea bass out of the dish, leaving the clams behind. Spread each fillet with the basil crust and grill until golden brown.
6 Drain the cooking juices from the dish of clams into a 600 ml/1 pint jug, heat on full power for 3 to 5 minutes or until the juices are reduced to half. Add the parsley and whisk in the remaining butter. Add the lemon juice, diced tomato and season to taste with salt and pepper.
7 Re-cover the dish of clams and heat on full power for 30 to 45 seconds. Spoon the sauce on to a hot serving dish. Carefully lift the sea bass fillets and place them on the sauce. Arrange the clams prettily in the dish.

MUSHROOM-STUFFED PLAICE

For 2, but easy to make just for 1.

2 whole plaice, pocketed* or whole white fish, cleaned, 225 to 275 g/8 to 10 oz each

STUFFING
100 g/4 oz mushrooms, finely chopped
25 g/1 oz walnuts, finely chopped
2 teaspoons chopped parsley
25 g/1 oz butter or margarine
2 tablespoons fresh brown breadcrumbs
50 g/2 oz sweetcorn
Freshly ground black pepper
Lemon juice

* *'Pocketed' means filleted down the backbone. Ask your fishmonger to do this for you, if necessary.*

1 Preheat the oven to moderately hot, Gas 6, 400°F, 200°C.
2 Heat the mushrooms, walnuts, parsley and butter or margarine together in a saucepan. Stir in the breadcrumbs, sweetcorn and pepper.

3 Divide the mixture equally between the two whole plaice, filling the pockets. Put them in an ovenproof dish. If there is spare stuffing, put it between fish. Sprinkle with lemon juice.

4 Cover the dish and cook in the preheated oven for 15 to 20 minutes. Serve with plain boiled potatoes and green beans.

Microwave

1 Cook the mushrooms, walnuts, parsley and butter or margarine in a covered bowl for 1 minute on full power. Stir in the breadcrumbs, sweetcorn and pepper.

2 Divide the mixture equally between the two whole plaice, filling the pockets. Sprinkle with lemon juice.

3 Put each fish on a separate plate, cover and cook separately on full power for 1 to 2 minutes each.

Yvonne Coull
Sea Fish Industry Authority,
Edinburgh

BAKED GREY MULLET

For 2.

450 g/1 grey mullet, gutted and
    scaled
2 rashers smoked bacon
4 fresh sage leaves, finely
    chopped, or 1 teaspoon dried
    sage
25 g/1 oz fresh breadcrumbs
Butter
$\frac{1}{2}$ glass dry white wine or dry
    cider
60 ml/2 fl oz double cream

1 Make 4 or 5 cuts on each side of the fish.

2 Lightly grill the bacon, then chop it up finely almost to a paste.

3 Mix the bacon with the sage and put a little of this mixture into the

cuts in the fish. Add the breadcrumbs to the remaining sage and bacon. Season with salt and pepper and use it to stuff the gut cavity.

4 Put the fish into a thickly buttered dish and cook in a moderately hot oven, Gas 6, 400°F, 200°C for 15 minutes.

5 Pour over the wine or cider and cook for a further 10 to 15 minutes.

6 Pour over the cream and cook for just 2 minutes more. Serve.

David Shepperdson
Huddersfield, Yorkshire

Microwave

1 Make 4 or 5 cuts on each side of the fish.

2 Put the bacon on a rack set over a drip tray and lightly cover with a piece of kitchen paper. Cook on full power for 2 to 3 minutes until crispy – the time will vary depending on the fat content in the bacon so check after half of the cooking time.

3 Finely chop the bacon and mix it with the sage, so that it is almost a paste. Put a little of this mixture into the cuts in the fish. Mix the remainder with the breadcrumbs, season with a little salt, if needed, and black pepper. Use this to stuff the cavity of the fish.

4 Put the fish into a shallow oval dish, pour over the wine or cider and cover with clear film. Cook on full power for 5 to 6 minutes.

5 Lift the fish on to a warm serving plate. Stir the cream into the cooking juices and heat on full power for 1 minute. Stir well then pour the sauce over the fish and serve.

TROUT WITH HAZELNUTS

For 2. Rainbow or brown trout can be used.

2 trout, gutted
Seasoned flour
50 g/2 oz butter and 1 tablespoon
    oil
25 g/1 oz hazelnuts, skins
    removed,* roughly chopped
Juice of 1 lemon
2 tablespoons chopped parsley
Salt and pepper
A few lemon slices to garnish

** To remove skins from hazelnuts, put
them under the grill for 5 minutes
turning often. Then rub the skins off.*

1 Dip the prepared trout in seasoned
flour and shake off any excess.
2 Heat the butter and oil together
and gently fry the trout for about 7
minutes on each side (the time will
vary according to the size of the fish).
When cooked and nicely browned,
remove them from the pan and place
on a warmed serving dish.
3 Add the roughly chopped hazelnuts
to the frying pan and cook until
lightly browned, then scatter them
over the trout.
4 Add the lemon juice and chopped
parsley to the remaining butter in the
pan, season, warm through and pour
over the fish. Garnish with slices of
lemon.

Angela Henderson
Fleet, Hampshire

SALMON SAVOURY

*For 1 or 2. Serve hot, sliced in wedges
with mashed potato and vegetables, or
cold with salads.*

A 213 g/7½ oz can of red or
    pink salmon, drained
1 large egg
50 g/2 oz fresh breadcrumbs
Salt and pepper
A little milk
A little lemon juice (optional)
1 tomato, sliced

1 Mash salmon with a fork, adding
egg, breadcrumbs, salt and pepper. If
it is dry, moisten with a little milk or
lemon juice.
2 Spoon mixture into a greased
shallow ovenproof dish, level it and
mark the top with the fork. Decorate
with tomato slices.
3 Cook in a moderately hot oven, Gas
6, 400°F, 200°C for 20 minutes until
firm and just lightly browned.

Mrs S. Joules
Croydon, Surrey

1 In a bowl, mash the salmon with a
fork. Mix in the egg, breadcrumbs,
salt, pepper and lemon juice.
2 Spoon the mixture into 2 ramekin
dishes. Smooth over the surface and
decorate with tomato slices.
3 Cook on full power for 2 to 3
minutes until just firm to the touch.

SALMON AND POTATO BAKE

Another recipe which uses canned salmon, though tuna fish or 175 g/6 oz grated cheese can be used instead. Makes 2 helpings.

175 g/6 oz boiled or steamed
　potatoes
A good 15 g/½ oz margarine or
　butter
175 to 225 g/6 to 8 oz canned pink
　salmon
1 tablespoon chopped parsley
A squeeze of lemon juice
Salt and pepper
150 ml/¼ pint milk
2 eggs, separated

1 Preheat oven to moderately hot,
Gas 5, 375°F, 190°C.
2 First cook the potatoes and keep
them hot.
3 Meanwhile, use a little of the
margarine or butter to grease a 1.2-
litre/2-pint pie dish or soufflé dish.
4 Chop fish finely, removing any
bone, and mix in parsley, lemon juice,
salt and pepper.
5 Mash the hot potatoes until
smooth, beating in margarine or
butter and milk until light and
creamy.
6 Mix in the salmon and parsley
mixture.
7 Beat in the egg yolks.
8 Whisk egg whites until stiff and
fold them in.
9 Bake in the preheated oven until
risen and golden brown, about 35
minutes.

Mrs Powell
Enfield, Middlesex

SARDINES FOR TEA

*For 2. Easy and very tasty. See also
Sardine Pasties (page 122).*

A 120 g/4 oz can of sardines in
　oil

1 small onion, finely chopped
A small cup of rice, about 120 g/
　4 oz weighed when cooked
Pepper and salt
1 hard-boiled egg, sliced
1 tomato, sliced

1 Preheat oven to moderately hot,
Gas 6, 400°F, 200°C.
2 Pour oil off sardines and mash
them, adding onion and cooked rice.
Mix well and season to taste.
3 Divide mixture between two
individual ovenproof dishes.
4 Chop the hard-boiled egg and
spread it over. Cover with tomato
slices. Brush tomato with oil.
5 Cook in middle of preheated oven
for 30 minutes. Serve with fresh
salad.

Mrs M. Lownds
Uttoxeter, Staffordshire

*15 g/½ oz butter is needed in addition
to the ingredients given above. Cook the
sardines in two individual dishes.*

1 Put butter and onion into a bowl.
Cook, uncovered, on full power for 2
minutes to soften the onion.
2 Drain the sardines and mash them
and mix with the onion and rice.
Divide the mixture between two
dishes.
3 Chop the egg and spread it over the
sardines. Then cover with tomato
slices.
4 Cook on full power for 3 to 4
minutes.

HERB SAUCE

*Makes about 300 ml/½ pint. Serve
with the Salmon Parcels, or any
firm-fleshed white fish.*

25 g/1 oz butter
25 g/1 oz flour
300 ml/½ pint milk

51

1 teaspoon chopped chives
1 teaspoon chopped parsley
Salt and pepper
1 egg yolk
2 tablespoons cream

1 Melt the butter in a saucepan, add
the flour and cook for 1 minute.
2 Stirring all the time, gradually pour
in the milk.
3 Heat up the sauce and boil for 1
minute, then stir in the chives, parsley
and seasoning. Remove the pan from
the heat.
4 Mix together the egg yolk and
cream and stir them into the sauce, do
not re-boil or the yolk will curdle.

Dilwen Phillips
Gileston, South Glamorgan

1 Put the butter into a 600 ml/1 pint
jug. Heat on full power for 1 minute.
Stir in the flour and gradually blend
in the milk.
2 Heat on full power for 1½
minutes, then stir in the chives,
parsley and seasoning. Continue to
heat on full power for a further 30
to 60 seconds until the sauce has
thickened.
3 Mix together the egg yolk and
cream. Stir into the sauce and serve.

Reheating by microwave

If the sauce is to be made in advance
and reheated, cover the surface of the
sauce with clear film after step 2 –
this will prevent a skin forming.
Reheat the sauce on full power for 1
to 1½ minutes, stirring once, then stir
the egg yolk and cream into the hot
sauce.

If the completed sauce needs
reheating, once the egg and cream are
added to the sauce take care not to
overheat as they will curdle. Reheat
on full power in 10 second bursts,
stirring after every 10 seconds.

52

SHARP MUSTARD SAUCE

*This sauce goes very well with poached,
grilled or baked fish.*

75 g/3 oz butter
1 large egg yolk
3 dessertspoons water
1 teaspoon dry mustard
White pepper and salt
1 dessertspoon lemon juice or
   wine vinegar
1 teaspoon finely chopped fresh
   parsley

1 Put the butter in a hot bowl and
melt it over a pan of hot water. Leave
it to cool slightly.
2 Put the egg yolk into a small pan
and, using a small wire whisk, add the
water and whisk the mixture over a
gentle heat until it begins to thicken.
3 Stir the mustard into the cool
butter and season with white pepper
and a grain or two of salt.
4 Beat the buttery mixture into the
egg yolk, a little at a time, and it will
begin to thicken.
5 Add the lemon juice or vinegar and
parsley and serve as soon as possible.

Grace Mulligan

1 Heat the butter in a jug on full
power for 1 to 2 minutes till melted.
2 Put the egg yolk into a small basin
and whisk in the water with a small
wire whisk. Stir in the mustard.
3 Whisk in the butter in a steady
stream.
4 Heat the sauce on full power for 10
seconds, then whisk well. Repeat
twice until the sauce has thickened
slightly.
5 Season with salt and pepper. Add
the lemon juice or vinegar and parsley
and serve as soon as possible.

Take care not to overheat or the sauce
will curdle.

Chapter 4

Poultry
and Game

TO POACH A CHICKEN

Sometimes it makes good sense to buy more than you need particularly if there is a special offer or an exceptional bargain. Here are instructions for poaching, then recipes for using the lovely moist meat. Not only do you have the meat but also a delicious, jellied, strongly flavoured stock.

A 1½ kg/3 to 3½ lb chicken
1 small onion
A piece of carrot
1 bay leaf
4 peppercorns
Salt and pepper

1 Put the chicken into a close-fitting pan with the vegetables, bay leaf, peppercorns, salt and pepper, and add enough water to cover.
2 Cover with a lid, bring to the boil, then lower the heat and simmer for about 1½ hours or until the meat is falling from the bones.
3 Remove from the heat and allow to cool. Remove the chicken, strain the stock into a jug and put it in a cool place overnight.
4 Strip all the chicken from the bones, keeping the pieces as large as possible. Keep in the refrigerator until needed.
5 Remove the layer of solidified fat from the surface of the stock – which can then be used for making soups or sauces.
6 A little more stock can be made by returning the bones, skin etc. to a pan with more onion, carrot, herbs and seasoning and simmering as before.

Grace Mulligan

Microwave

Chicken cooked in the microwave has a delicious flavour and is exceptionally moist. It is an ideal way of cooking chicken which is then to be used in other dishes. If you allow the dripping to set you can discard the fat and underneath you will have a jelly which can be used for stocks and soups.

A 1½ kg/3 to 3½ lb chicken
15 g/½ oz butter, melted

1 Place the chicken on a microwave roasting rack (or an upturned plate) set in a shallow dish. Brush with the melted butter. Cover with a roasting-set lid or with a roaster bag, which has been split up one side and then tented over the bird. Cook on Medium for 28 minutes. Allow to stand covered, or wrapped in foil, shiny side in, for 15 minutes.

In 2-powered microwave cookers: Cook chicken on full power for 24 minutes, then stand as above.

CHICKEN MOULD

For this recipe you need a firm well-flavoured stock. If your stock hasn't set to a firm jelly, put it in a saucepan and boil it up to reduce the volume and strengthen the flavour.
For 1 or 2.

100 g/4 oz cooked chicken, diced
1 tablespoon cold cooked peas
2 tablespoons cold cooked mixed vegetables, diced
Salt and pepper
Jellied chicken stock

1 Put the chicken into a bowl or dish, add the peas and other vegetables and season.
2 Bring the jellied stock to the boil, allow to cool and then pour it over the mixture so that it just covers the ingredients.
3 Put into the refrigerator to set.
4 When chilled, serve with a salad of crisp lettuce; in winter, it is nice with hot mashed potatoes.

Grace Mulligan

CHICKEN SALAD

For 2. This salad goes well with new potatoes tossed in a French Dressing (page 106)

1 small red eating apple, cored
   and diced but not peeled
2 spring onions, chopped
1 stick of celery, chopped
100 g/4 oz cooked chicken, diced
3 tablespoons mayonnaise or
   salad cream
1 teaspoon chopped fresh
   chives
25 g/1 oz walnuts, chopped
Lettuce leaves for serving

1 Put all the ingredients, except the lettuce leaves, into a bowl and mix thoroughly.
2 Adjust the seasoning, then arrange the chicken salad on a few lettuce leaves.

Grace Mulligan

HONOLULU CHICKEN

Serves 2. A rice salad and a tomato and cucumber salad make excellent accompaniments.

20 g/¾ oz butter
50 g/2 oz whole blanched almonds
225 g/8 oz cooked chicken
2 sticks of celery
2 rings of canned pineapple
150 ml/¼ pint mayonnaise
1 teaspoon lemon juice
Salt and pepper
A pinch of sugar
Lettuce leaves to garnish

1 Melt the butter in a pan, add the nuts and cook until golden brown. Drain on kitchen paper, then sprinkle with a little salt and leave to cool.
2 Cut the chicken into bite-sized pieces and chop up the celery and pineapple.
3 Put the mayonnaise and lemon juice in a bowl and add the chicken, celery, pineapple, nuts and seasonings.

4 Toss all the ingredients together and serve in a bowl lined with lettuce.

Angela Henderson
Fleet, Hampshire

CREAMY CHICKEN AND MUSHROOMS

For 1. Known as Chicken à la King in restaurants and recipe books, this is delicious, quick and easy to make. Nice with Boiled Rice (page 88) and green peas or beans for colour, or a salad.

20 g/¾ oz margarine
15 g/½ oz flour
150 ml/¼ pint milk
50 g/2 oz button mushrooms,
   sliced
Salt and pepper
2 teaspoons sherry
150 g/5 oz cooked chicken, diced
1 tablespoon double cream
Chopped parsley to decorate

1 Melt the margarine in a saucepan, then stir in the flour and cook for 1 minute.
2 Gradually pour in the milk, stirring all the time, and heat until the sauce boils.
3 Add the mushrooms, seasoning, sherry and chicken, bring to the boil and cook gently for 3 minutes. Then stir in the cream and serve immediately, sprinkled with parsley.

⬛ Microwave ▬▬▬▬▬▬▬▬▬▬

1 Melt the margarine for 30 seconds on full power.
2 Add flour and gradually whisk in the milk. Cook on full power for 1 minute, whisk again and cook 1 minute more.
3 Add mushrooms, seasoning, sherry and chicken and cook, covered, on full power for 3 minutes.
4 Stir in the cream and serve.

Joan Tyers
Wingate, Co. Durham

CREAMED CHICKEN WITH RICE

For 1. Quick and easy!

50 g/2 oz long grain brown* or
  white rice
100 g/4 oz cooked chicken
A 295 g/10 oz can of condensed
  chicken soup
Half a 410 g/14 oz can of mixed
  vegetables*
A pinch of salt (optional)

** The exact timing for brown rice
depends on the type. Some have been
pre-fluffed and take only 12 minutes;
others may take as much as 20 minutes.
125 g/4 oz frozen mixed vegetables or
even frozen peas make an ideal and
more colourful alternative to canned.*

1 Cook rice by dropping it into 600
ml/1 pint of boiling water. Boil it
gently: brown rice for 20 to 25
minutes, white rice for 12 to 15
minutes, then drain it. (To cook
Boiled Rice by the absorption
method, see page 88.)
2 Cut chicken into fairly large pieces
and warm it carefully in the soup
with the vegetables, stirring so that it
does not stick to the pan. Add salt.
Allow the mixture to simmer for 5
minutes to be sure the chicken is
thoroughly heated through.
3 Make a ring of the rice on warm
plate and put the chicken in the
centre.

Miss M. Leafe
Wetherby, Yorkshire

*Use 125 g/4 oz frozen mixed vegetables,
cooked, instead of canned.*

1 Put the rice into an 18 cm/7 inch
soufflé-type dish with 300 ml/½ pint
water and a pinch of salt. Cover the
dish with the serving plate and cook
on full power for 8 minutes for white

long grain rice, 12 to 15 minutes for
brown rice. Brown rice will need
stirring once during cooking.
2 At the end of cooking, leave it to
stand, still covered, while you make
the sauce. The rice will continue to
absorb the water and stay hot.
3 Cut the chicken into 2.5-cm/1-inch
pieces. Put it into a basin with the
cooked vegetables and soup. Heat on
full power for 3 minutes, stirring
once.
4 Drain any excess liquid from the
rice and fluff up with a fork. Arrange
a circle of rice on the warm serving
plate and put chicken in centre.

QUICK CHICKEN IN A CREAM SAUCE

*For 1, but easy to make more. If you
do not like cream and wine, follow the
recipe to the end of step 4 and serve it
with lightly fried or steamed courgettes.*

1 chicken breast
1 teaspoon cornflour
Salt and pepper
1 tablespoon oil
50 g/2 oz mushrooms, sliced
2 tablespoons white wine or cider
75 ml/2½ fl oz whipping cream
Chopped parsley to garnish

1 Slice the chicken breast into thin
strips and toss the pieces in the
seasoned cornflour.
2 Heat the oil in a pan and fry the
chicken pieces until golden brown on
all sides, about 2 minutes.
3 Add the mushrooms and cook until
tender, about 2 minutes.
4 Remove chicken and mushrooms
and put on a warmed plate.
5 Pour the wine into the pan, bring
to the boil, add the cream and cook
for 1 to 2 minutes until the sauce is
thick and creamy. Season to taste.
6 Pour over the chicken. Sprinkle
chopped parsley over the top.

Dilwen Phillips
Gileston, South Glamorgan

This is an opportunity to use a browning dish. If you do not have one, cook this recipe on top of your stove (it will actually be just as quick). Do not cover the browning dish at any stage or the results will be soggy.

1 Put the empty browning dish in the microwave and heat on full power for 6 minutes (or according to the manufacturer's instructions).
2 Slice the chicken breast into thin strips and toss the pieces in seasoned cornflour.
3 Immediately the browning dish is ready, add the oil and chicken. Pressing the chicken well down so that it browns, cook on full power for 1 minute. Then turn the chicken, add the mushrooms and cook for a further 1 to 2 minutes on full power.
4 Stir in the wine, then add the cream. Cook on full power for 2 minutes, season and serve sprinkled with parsley.

CHICKEN FOR ONE

Almost a meal in itself. Serve with green peas or beans.

One chicken joint
Seasoned flour
25 g/1 oz butter
1 small onion, chopped
2 fresh tomatoes, skinned (page 26) and chopped
1 large potato, cut into 7-mm/ ¼-inch pieces
Salt and pepper
75 ml/2 to 3 fl oz stock
1 teaspoon chopped parsley

1 Remove the skin from the chicken, then coat the joint with the seasoned flour.
2 Melt the butter in a pan and fry the chicken to brown it well all over.

3 Take out the chicken and fry onion until soft.
4 Put back the chicken along with the tomatoes, potato, seasoning and stock if it seems dry. Cover the pan and cook over low heat until the chicken is tender, about 20 minutes.
5 Sprinkle the parsley over the chicken and serve.

1 Remove the skin from the chicken and coat the joint with seasoned flour.
2 Heat 15 g/½ oz margarine in a shallow dish on full power for 30 seconds. Put in the chicken upside down and cook for 2 minutes on full power.
3 Turn the chicken over, surround it with the onion, tomatoes, potatoes, seasoning and a little stock if it seems too dry.
4 Cover the dish and cook on full power for a further 6 minutes or until the chicken is tender.
5 Serve sprinkled with parsley.

Joan Tyers
Wingate, Co. Durham

CHICKEN FINGERS

Nice either as snacks or as a meal for 2, served with vegetables such as peas, corn or French beans, or with salad and Yoghurt Chutney (page 111) or tomato ketchup.

2 chicken breasts, skinned and boned
2 cloves of garlic, crushed
Juice of half a lemon
Salt and pepper
A pinch of cayenne pepper
1 small egg, beaten
Freshly made white or brown breadcrumbs
About 6 tablespoons oil

1 Wash and dry chicken and cut into

57

thin fingers about 8 cm/3 inches long
and 2 cm/¾ inch thick.
2 Mix crushed garlic and lemon juice
and dip the fingers in. Then
sprinkle them with salt, pepper
and cayenne.
3 Now dip the fingers into beaten
egg and coat with breadcrumbs.
Then leave in the refrigerator for
at least an hour.
4 Heat oil in frying pan and fry the
fingers on medium heat for 5
minutes on each side, until crisp
and golden brown.

Mrs Jaswant Chopra
Childwall, Liverpool

CHICKEN WITH
ORANGE AND
GINGER

For 2.

1 orange
½ teaspoon ground ginger
A pinch of salt
1 teaspoon cornflour
2 chicken joints
1 tablespoon oil
100 ml/3 fl oz dry cider
1 level dessertspoon golden syrup
1 teaspoon grated fresh root
    ginger

1 Cut the orange in half and cut a
fine slice off each half for decoration.
Squeeze the juice from the rest.
2 Cut the pith away from about a
quarter of the orange skin, then cut
the zest into fine strips.
3 Mix together the ground ginger,
salt and cornflour and rub this all
over the chicken joints.
4 Heat the oil in a pan, and brown
the chicken joints all over.
5 Add the cider, orange juice, syrup,
grated ginger and the prepared strips
of orange zest. Bring to the boil,
cover with a lid and simmer gently
for about 30 minutes, or until the
chicken is tender.
6 Remove the chicken pieces and, if

there is too much sauce, reduce it a
little by boiling over a high heat.
7 Pour the sauce over the chicken
and garnish with the orange slices.

Dilwen Phillips
Gileston, South Glamorgan

BAKED CHICKEN
WITH PINEAPPLE

For 1 or 2. Mrs Voce likes to have this
delicious dish with small jacket potatoes
which she bakes in the oven with the
chicken. Can be reheated satisfactorily
for another meal, and also works well
with turkey.

4 chicken joints or breasts
A 225 g/8 oz can of sliced
    pineapple in natural juice
25 g/1 oz margarine or butter
1 level tablespoon plain flour
2 level tablespoons tomato
    ketchup
2 teaspoons dry mustard
¼ level teaspoon salt
Pepper
1 teaspoon Worcestershire sauce
1 tablespoon vinegar

1 Skin the chicken joints and put
them in a roasting tin.
2 Strain pineapple and keep the
juice to use in another recipe. Chop
pineapple finely.
3 Heat the margarine or butter, stir
in flour and allow to sizzle for 1
minute. Stir in juice from pineapple,
bring to the boil and cook for 2
minutes.
4 Remove pan from heat and mix in
the rest of the ingredients and the
pineapple. Allow to cool.
5 Spoon the cooked sauce over the
chicken, cover tin and chill in the
refrigerator for about 4 hours, for
chicken to absorb the flavours.
6 Preheat oven to moderate, Gas 4,
350°F, 180°C.
7 Cook near top of oven, uncovered,
for 45 minutes. Baste chicken several
times during cooking, spooning sauce

over to prevent both pineapple and surface of meat from drying out.

Mrs A. M. Voce
Hampton, Worcestershire

1 Skin the chicken and arrange the portions in a single layer in a shallow 18-cm/7-inch flan dish.
2 Put the butter in a 600 ml/1 pint jug and heat on full power for 40 to 60 seconds until melted. Stir in the flour. Drain the juices of the pineapple into the flour and mix well. Heat on full power for 1 minute.
3 Mix in the ketchup, mustard, salt, pepper, Worcestershire sauce and vinegar. Heat on full power for a further 30 seconds.
4 Finely chop the pineapple and stir into the sauce. Allow to cool.
5 Pour cooled sauce over the chicken, then chill for about 4 hours, so the chicken absorbs the flavour fully.
6 Cover the dish with clear film and cook on Medium for 8 to 10 minutes. Stand for 5 minutes before serving.

MANDARIN CHICKEN

Chicken breasts coated in mildly hot spices, contrasting with the fruit and Madeira-flavoured sauce, this dish is garnished with flaked almonds and finished with cream. This recipe won Mrs Roberts a place in the semi-finals of a microwave cooking competition held by Sharp. It works well by conventional methods also. It was served with boiled rice (page 88) and carrots.
For 2.

25 g/1 oz flaked almonds
25 g/1 oz sultanas
2 tablespoons Madeira or sherry
2 skinned chicken breasts
15 g/½ oz butter
A pinch each of salt and white pepper
¼ teaspoon paprika pepper
Half a 312 g/10 oz can mandarin oranges in natural juice
A clove of garlic, finely chopped
4 tablespoons chicken stock
1 tablespoon soy sauce
¼ teaspoon ground ginger
2 level teaspoons cornflour mixed to a paste with 2 tablespoons cold water
2 tablespoons double cream

1 Put the almonds on a piece of kitchen paper and heat on full power for 2 to 3 minutes, until lightly browned. Stir or re-arrange every minute by gently shaking the paper. Set aside for garnish.
2 Heat the sultanas in the Madeira or sherry on full power for 1 minute. Leave to plump up while you cook the chicken.
3 Wash and dry chicken breasts. Arrange skinned side up in a shallow 18-cm/7-inch flan dish. Put the butter in a small basin and heat on full power for 20 to 30 seconds, until melted, then brush over the chicken breasts.
4 Mix together the salt, pepper and paprika and sprinkle liberally over the buttered chicken.
5 Drain 120 ml/4 fl oz juice from the can of mandarin oranges. Add the garlic, stock, sultanas and any remaining Madeira to the measured juice. Carefully pour this around the chicken breasts, so as not to wash off the paprika. Cover with clear film and cook on Medium for 6 minutes.

For a 2-power microwave cooker: Cook on full power for 5 minutes.

6 Uncover the dish, lift out the chicken, cover with a piece of foil, shiny side in, to keep hot. Stir the mandarins, soy sauce, ginger and cornflour paste into the sauce. Heat on full power for 2 minutes, stirring halfway through.

7 Stir the cream into the sauce. Replace the chicken breasts in the sauce, spoon some sauce over, and heat on full power for 2 minutes. Then scatter over the flaked almonds and serve.

If serving with rice and carrots, cook the rice first (page 88) and leave, covered, to stand. Next, cook the carrots, and leave them covered while you cook the chicken.

To serve: drain any excess water from the rice and fluff up with a fork. Spoon it on to a warm dish. Reheat the carrots on full power for 1 minute while you arrange the chicken on the rice.

Mrs Ann Roberts
Tarporley, Cheshire

MANDARIN CHICKEN

CONVENTIONAL METHOD
(*see previous page for ingredients*)
1 Place sultanas and Madeira in a small pan, cover and simmer for about 10 minutes until sultanas have plumped up.
2 Wash and dry skinned chicken breasts, place a little butter in the centre of the folded breast. Mix salt, pepper and paprika together and sprinkle over the chicken breasts.
3 Put chicken in a large frying pan and brown all over in a little extra butter or oil, if liked.
4 Drain the mandarin oranges, measure 120 ml/4 fl oz of the juice and add this to the pan with the garlic. Pour in the stock, cover the pan, bring to the boil and reduce heat; simmer for 20 minutes or until the chicken is tender.
5 Add the sultanas and Madeira in which they have been soaking. Cook for a further 5 minutes.
6 Remove the chicken breasts from the pan and keep warm.
7 Stir the cornflour mixture into the liquid in the pan. Bring to the boil, stirring until the mixture is thickened.
8 Add the soy sauce, ground ginger and most of the mandarin oranges (keep a few for decoration). Stir the cream into the sauce and cook for 4 to 5 minutes, stirring.
9 Place the chicken in a hot dish, pour the sauce over and garnish with flaked almonds and reserved mandarin segments.

STEAMED RICE WITH CHICKEN AND CHINESE MUSHROOMS

For this you will really need to visit a Chinese supermarket; you also need a steamer. For 2.

Half a small chicken or 2
   chicken thighs
6 Chinese mushrooms
1 cup of rice
1½ tablespoons oil
A pinch of salt
1 cup boiling water

2 tablespoons light soy sauce
2 spring onions, cut into 2.5-cm/
1-inch lengths
A little sesame oil

MARINADE
1 tablespoon finely chopped fresh
ginger
1 tablespoon light soy sauce
1 tablespoon water
1 teaspoon ginger juice
1 teaspoon rice wine or dry sherry
1 teaspoon sugar
1 teaspoon cornflour
½ teaspoon salt
A pinch of ground pepper
A pinch of Five Spice powder

1 Remove the chicken from the
bones and cut it into bite-sized
pieces.
2 Mix the marinade ingredients in a
bowl, put in the chicken and leave
to marinate for at least 30 minutes,
stirring from time to time.
3 Soak the Chinese mushrooms in
warm water until soft, about 10 to 15
minutes.
4 Wash the rice in several changes of
cold water to remove excess starch,
then put it into a large heatproof
bowl. Stir in 1 tablespoon oil and a
pinch of salt. Pour over 1 cup of
boiling water. Place the bowl in a
steamer, put on the lid and let it
steam for 15 minutes.
5 Drain mushrooms, remove stalks
and shred mushrooms finely. Mix
with ½ tablespoon oil and a little
salt.
6 Remove lid from steamer, loosen
the rice a little and put in the chicken
and marinade with the mushrooms on
top. Then let it steam for 15 to 20
minutes, or until chicken is cooked.
Turn off heat and leave it to stand
for 5 minutes.
7 Just before serving, sprinkle
chicken with the soy sauce, spring
onions and a little sesame oil.

Jennie Siew Lee Cook
York

PATTI'S CHICKEN FOR TWO

*But easy to make for one. The
remaining soups mix well together for
another meal. Use a soup can for
measuring.*

2 chicken portions or breasts
Half a 300 g/11 oz can of
mushroom soup
Half a 300 g/11 oz can of celery
soup
Half a can of grated Cheddar
cheese
Half a can of white wine

1 Place the chicken in an ovenproof
dish.
2 Mix together the soups.
3 Mix the cheese and wine into the
soup. Pour it over the chicken.
4 Bake for 1 hour in a moderately
hot oven, Gas 6, 400°F, 200°C.
During this time the mixture will
have turned into a delicious sauce.
Serve with jacket potatoes and green
beans.

TIP
The dish may also be cooked in a cool
oven, Gas 2, 300°F, 150°C for 2
hours.

Megan Mallinson
Fixby, Huddersfield

Microwave

1 Place the chicken in a single layer
in a 1.4-litre/3-pint casserole.
Follow steps 2 and 3 above.
4 Cover with a lid and cook on
Medium for 15 to 18 minutes.

For a 2-power microwave cooker: Cook
on full power for 10 minutes, stirring
once. Stand for 5 minutes at the end
of cooking.

5 Serve the chicken on warm plates
with the sauce stirred and poured
over.

NUTTY LEMON STUFFING

*For chicken or duck, this stuffing
mixture is baked separately, not inside
the bird.*

50 g/2 oz butter
Finely grated rind and juice of
    one lemon
75 g/3 oz fresh wholemeal
    breadcrumbs
40 g/1½ oz chopped walnuts
3 tablespoons chopped parsley
A pinch of thyme or marjoram
Salt and freshly ground pepper

1 Melt the butter, add lemon juice
and rind. Remove from the heat.
2 Mix all the other ingredients
together and add the melted butter
and lemon. The mixture should be
moist but not wet.
3 Pack into a buttered ovenproof
dish. Cover with foil and bake with
chicken or duck for 20 to 25 minutes.
Do not overcook.

Grace Mulligan

BACON AND PRUNE ROLLS

*An excellent accompaniment for a
festive bird, or may be served for pre-
dinner snacks or as a savoury finish to
a meal on slices of toast or fried bread.*

Pitted prunes – there will be 10
    to 12 prunes in 125 g/4 oz
Thinly sliced streaky bacon

1 Soak the prunes in hot water or hot
tea overnight. If they are not really
soft next day then cook them for 15
minutes in the liquid in which they
were soaked. Drain and pat them dry
with kitchen paper.
2 De-rind the bacon and cut into
pieces about 10 cm/4 inches long.
Stretch the pieces with the back of a
knife.
3 Wrap the bacon around the prunes
and thread on to skewers.
5 Bake in a moderate oven, Gas 4,
350°F, 180°C, or set under a hot grill
turning often.

Grace Mulligan

CRISP ROAST DUCK WITH GRAPEFRUIT SAUCE

*Serves 2. It has been said that there
should be only two of you when sitting
down to roast duck – you and the
duck!*

1 duckling, about 1.3 kg/3 lb
1 onion, halved
Salt
1 small grapefruit
1 tablespoon flour
200 ml/6 fl oz strong stock made
    from giblets *
Freshly ground pepper
Sprigs of parsley

* *To make giblet stock simmer the
giblets and neck from the duckling with
375 ml/¾ pint water, a bunch of herbs
or parsley and a few slices of onion for
45 minutes. Then strain.*

1 After removing the giblets, dry the
bird inside and out with kitchen
paper. Prick the skin all over with a
skewer or sharp scissors. Put the
peeled onion inside the bird. Rub
salt over the outer skin – this helps to
make it crisp.
2 Set the bird on a wire rack or
trivet inside a roasting tin so the fat
runs out easily as it cooks.
3 Preheat the oven to moderate, Gas
4, 350°F, 180°C, then cook the duck

uncovered and without basting for 30 minutes per 450 g/1 lb. When the time is up, pierce the thickest part of the thigh with a skewer. If juice is clear the bird is done; if still pink, leave it for 15 minutes more.

4 Cut grapefruit in half and cut off a slice for decorating. Finely grate the zest and squeeze out all the juice.

5 Remove the duck to a heated dish and keep warm.

6 Pour off all but 1 to 2 tablespoons of fat from the roasting tin, keeping as much as possible of the juices underneath. Sprinkle in the flour and stir over a low heat. Add the giblet stock a little at a time, stirring as it thickens. Boil for a minute or two and add the grapefruit juice and rind. (Add a spot of gravy browning or gravy salt if it is too pale.)

7 Pour the sauce into a heated jug and keep warm. Decorate the bird with one or two slices of grapefruit and lots of parsley.

Grace Mulligan

TURKEY OR CHICKEN IN A CIDER SAUCE

For 1 or 2. This reheats well. The addition of cream makes it a special occasion dish.

200 g/½ lb apples (Bramley's are ideal), peeled and cored
2 turkey or chicken pieces (leg joints are best)
1 small onion, finely chopped
1 tablespoon finely chopped fresh parsley
150 ml/¼ pint dry cider
Salt and pepper
1 teaspoon brown sugar
2 tablespoons cream (optional)

1 Cut the apples into slices and put them in a casserole.

2 Remove skin from the chicken pieces and put them on top of the apples.

3 Scatter the onion and half the parsley over the chicken, then pour in the cider.

4 Cover with a lid and cook in a preheated oven, Gas 4, 350°F, 180°C, for 1 hour, or cook on top of the stove, just letting it simmer until chicken is tender – 30 to 45 minutes.

5 Remove the chicken pieces to a warmed serving dish. Sprinkle sugar over apples and spoon both apples and sauce on top of chicken. Sprinkle with the remaining parsley.

6 To make the sauce extra rich, stir in cream at the last minute.

Reheat on top of stove, 5 to 8 minutes in a covered pan over low heat. To reheat in oven, preheat to moderately hot, Gas 5 to 6, 375° to 400°F, 190° to 200°C and heat for 20 minutes in a covered dish on the middle shelf.

Grace Mulligan

Microwave

1 Slice the apples and put them into a 1.5-litre/3-pint ceramic casserole. Cut each chicken quarter in half at the leg joint and arrange the pieces on top of the apple.

2 Scatter onion and half the parsley over the chicken, then pour over the cider. Cover the dish with a lid or clear film and cook on Medium for 15 minutes. Allow to stand for 5 minutes.

3 Lift the chicken portions out on to a warm serving plate.

4 *For a smooth sauce*, put the apples and cider into a processor or liquidiser and blend until smooth. Sweeten with the sugar and add 1 level (5 ml) teaspoon cornflour mixed with 1 tablespoon water. Return sauce to the cleaned dish. Reheat on full power for 2 to 3 minutes to thicken. Then pour it over the chicken. Sprinkle with the remaining parsley.

TURKEY KEBABS

Makes about 6 kebabs. This recipe is useful for leftover cooked turkey. The kebabs freeze well before they are fried and can be cooked straight from the freezer. Chicken can be used instead. If you have no food processor, then it is a matter of chopping or mincing by hand.

2 cloves of garlic
Half a green chilli, seeds removed
A 7 mm/¼ inch cube of fresh
   ginger
325 g/¾ lb cooked turkey meat,
   skin and bones removed
1 small egg
½ teaspoon garam masala
½ teaspoon cumin powder
¼ teaspoon ground nutmeg
½ teaspoon salt
Oil for deep frying

1 Put the garlic, chilli and ginger into a food processor and process until it is finely chopped.
2 Add the turkey, egg, spices and salt and process until everything is smooth and well mixed.
3 Brush your hands with a little oil and form shapes with the turkey mixture about 1 cm/½ inch thick. Put them on an oiled tray in the refrigerator for 2 hours. They are easier to fry when very cold.
4 Deep-fry the turkey kebabs in hot oil for a few minutes each side, then drain them on kitchen paper. Serve them hot with Tangy Tomato Sauce, (page 95) and salad, or as a snack with Yoghurt Chutney (page 111).

Nirmal Singh
Nuneaton, Warwickshire

GAUDY RABBIT

For 1 or 2. This delicious dish reheats well. By adding mushrooms and red pepper at the last minute along with a second lot of wine or cider, the flavours of all the ingredients are refreshed and distinct.

2 tablespoons oil, preferably
   olive oil
1 clove of garlic, finely chopped
450 g/1 lb rabbit joints
A wineglass of dry white wine or
   dry cider
1 tablespoon tomato paste
250 ml/8 fl oz light stock (a
   chicken stock cube will do)
125 g/4 oz button mushrooms
Half a red pepper or a green one
   which is beginning to colour
15 g/½ oz butter

1 Heat oil, add garlic and rabbit and cook over medium heat until rabbit is browned all over.
2 Add half the wine or cider, turn up heat and let it bubble to evaporate a little.
3 Stir in half the tomato paste with half the stock. Cover and cook over medium heat for 15 minutes.
4 Now turn the rabbit pieces over. Replace the lid and cook over low heat for 20 to 25 minutes – the sauce will be very much reduced.
5 Take pan off heat, lift out rabbit pieces and, when cool enough to handle, strip flesh from bones.
6 Meanwhile, cut mushrooms into thin slices and chop the pepper. Cook together very gently in the butter in another pan for 3 to 4 minutes, then add remaining wine or cider and simmer until pepper is tender.
7 Stir rabbit carefully back into sauce in pan in which it cooked. Mix in remaining tomato paste and stock.
8 Stir in mushroom mixture. Reheat gently and serve.

Dr Doug McEachern
Stirling, South Australia

Chapter 5

Main Course Meats

BACON RIBS

These can be bought at most butchers' who bone their own bacon. One sheet (half a rib cage) weighs approximately 1.1 kg/2½ lb. This should give about 350 g/¾ lb of meat and a good 1.2 litres/2 pints of stock. Very economical – very satisfying.

1 Cut ribs into 3 to 4 pieces and put them in a large pan. Cover with cold water, bring to the boil and then pour off the water. This gets rid of any excess salt.
2 Cover again with cold water and bring to the boil. Cover pan and cook gently until tender – about 1 hour.

Alternatively in a pressure cooker, it will take about 20 minutes. The result will be less quantity but a stronger stock which can be diluted for use.

3 Drain the stock into a bowl; leave until quite cold, then skim off the fat.
4 Strip the meat from the bones.

To use the Stock:

LENTIL SOUP WITH SAUSAGE

100 g/4 oz lentils
2 sticks celery, finely chopped
1 onion, finely chopped
A small piece of swede, or 1 turnip, finely chopped
1 potato, peeled and chopped
1 small cooking apple, peeled and chopped
1 bay leaf
1.2 litres/2 pints stock from bacon ribs
225 g/8 oz smoked Continental sausage

1 Put all ingredients except the sausage into a large pan and cook gently for about ¾ to 1 hour (20 minutes in pressure cooker) or until vegetables are tender and lentils soft.
2 Liquidise the soup if you prefer it smooth. At this stage it can be cooled and frozen if you're keeping some for another day.
3 Chop the sausage, add to the soup and heat to warm the sausage through.

To use the Bacon Meat:

1 BACON MOULD

This turns out nicely on to a plate and looks attractive.

225 g/8 oz meat from bacon ribs
150 ml/¼ pint stock from ribs
2 level teaspoons gelatine
Pepper

1 Mince the meat or put it through a food processor.
2 Heat stock and sprinkle on the gelatine. Stir until dissolved.
3 Stir gelatine mixture into meat, seasoning if desired, but no extra salt should be required.
4 Pour into a wetted mould or basin and leave to set. Turn it out on to a plate to serve.

2 BACON CAKES

100 to 150 g/4 to 6 oz meat from bacon ribs
100 g/4 oz cooked potato, mashed
Pepper and salt, if necessary
1 small egg, beaten
2 tablespoons fresh or dried breadcrumbs
25 g/1 oz fat or 1 tablespoon oil for frying

1 Mince the bacon meat, or put it through a food processor.
2 Mix it into the potato, seasoning to taste. Shape into 4 round cakes.
3 Coat in egg, then in crumbs.
4 Heat fat or oil and fry the bacon cakes until crisp and golden on the outside and nicely warmed through, about 3 minutes on each side. Serve with carrots, parsnips or beans.

Margaret Heywood
Todmorden, Yorkshire

HAM SHANK

A ham shank is a cheap cut, but rewarding if you are prepared to go to a little trouble. It can be cooked in two ways — conventionally simmered in a good-sized pan until the meat is falling off the bone, or in a pressure cooker. If using a pressure cooker, it will take barely half an hour but follow the manufacturer's instruction and never fill the cooker more than half-full of liquid.

1 ham shank, about 1 kg/2 to
   2½ lb in weight, plain or
   smoked
About 1½ litres/3 pints water
1 small onion
1 piece of carrot
1 bay leaf
4 peppercorns

1 Put everything into a large pan. Bring to the boil and skim off any grey scum which rises to the surface. At this point, taste the water and if it is very salty, pour it away and add fresh water, otherwise you will have very salty stock.
2 Cook the shank for about 1½ hours, or until the meat is falling from the bone. Remove pan from heat and allow everything to cool until you can handle it easily.
3 Strain off the stock and leave in a cool place, preferably overnight. Remove the top layer of fat before using.
4 To prepare the ham meat: remove all fat and gristle while it is still hot. Allow to cool and store in refrigerator until needed.

Grace Mulligan

SAVOURY HOT POT

*This is very good made with cooked ham from a shank or bacon ribs. Also good for cold beef, pork or lamb.
For 1.*

2 medium potatoes
A little butter
1 medium onion, finely chopped
1 large tomato, sliced
100 g/4 oz cooked meat,* sliced or
   minced
Pepper and salt
50 g/2 oz grated cheese
150 ml/¼ pint milk or stock

* *If using ham, make the dish without the cheese and use stock instead of milk.*

1 Preheat the oven to moderate, Gas 4, 350°F, 180°C.
2 Boil potatoes until nearly cooked, then slice them thinly.
3 Butter an ovenproof dish and put in layers of potato, onion, tomato and meat. Season with pepper and a little salt.
4 Repeat layers, finishing with potato.
5 Cover with cheese. If not using cheese, dot with butter. Pour in milk or stock.
6 Cook in preheated oven for 40 to 45 minutes.

Mrs Catherine Sangster
Aberdeen

SWEET-AND-SOUR PORK CHOP

For 1.

1 tablespoon oil
1 pork chop
1 small onion, chopped
2 teaspoons brown sugar
1 teaspoon finely chopped fresh
   ginger or a pinch of dry ginger
1 tablespoon light soy sauce
4 tablespoons cider
Salt and pepper

1 Heat the oil in a small frying pan with a good lid. Quickly brown the chop on both sides.
2 Remove the chop for a moment and fry the onion for 2 minutes. Then mix and add the rest of the ingredients and reduce the heat to the lowest possible.

3 Replace the pork chop, cover with
a lid and simmer slowly for 15 to 20
minutes, or until the chop is cooked.

Grace Mulligan

SHERRIED PORK CHOPS

Creamed potatoes and courgettes,
lightly fried with sliced green and red
peppers, go well with this dish. For 2.

15 g/½ oz butter
2 pork chops
1 small onion, finely chopped
150 ml/5 fl oz apple juice
3 tablespoons dry sherry
1 teaspoon dried thyme or 2
    teaspoons chopped fresh thyme
Salt and pepper
A pinch of sugar
100 g/4 oz mushrooms, wiped and
    thinly sliced

1 Melt the butter in a frying pan and
brown the chops on both sides, then
remove from the pan and set aside.
2 Add the onion to the remaining
butter and fry for a few minutes,
then pour in the apple juice, 2
tablespoons of the sherry, the thyme
and seasonings.
3 Replace the pork chops and scatter
the mushrooms over.
4 Bring to the boil, cover with a lid
and cook for 25 minutes, or until the
pork chops are tender.
5 Just before serving, stir in the
remaining tablespoon of sherry and
transfer the chops and sauce to a
warmed serving dish.

Angela Henderson
Fleet, Hampshire

PORK STIR-FRY

For 2, but easy to make just enough for
1 person. Serve with Boiled Rice (page
88) or Vegetable Rice (page 90).

175 to 225 g/6 to 8 oz pork fillet,
    cut into thin strips

1 tablespoon cornflour, seasoned
    with salt and pepper
1 to 2 tablespoons oil
A clove of garlic, crushed
75 to 100 g/3 to 4 oz red cabbage,
    finely shredded
50 g/2 oz mushrooms, wiped and
    sliced
Half a green pepper, thinly sliced
    in strips
1 to 2 tablespoons soy sauce

1 Toss the meat in the seasoned
cornflour.
2 Heat the oil in a large frying pan
or a wok and cook the garlic for a
minute, then stir-fry the meat until it
is well browned, about 2 minutes.
3 Add the cabbage, mushrooms and
green pepper and continue to stir-fry
until the meat is cooked, about 5 to 8
minutes.
4 Stir in the soy sauce and serve at
once.

Dilwen Phillips
Gileston, South Glamorgan

CELERY PORK STEAKS

This is delicious and a very easy recipe,
ideal if you have a 'slow cooker'; simply
cook on the low setting for 6 to 7 hours.
Makes 2 helpings.

2 pork steaks
A can of condensed celery soup
1 tablespoon cold water
Chopped celery leaves or parsley
    (optional)

1 Put the pork steaks into a pan with
a tight-fitting lid and pour the soup
over. Add 1 tablespoon cold water to
the empty soup tin to rinse it out,
then pour this over too. Put on the
lid.
2 Put the pan on a low heat and let
it slowly simmer for 40 minutes.

Alternatively arrange the pork and
soup in an ovenproof dish, put on a

tight-fitting lid and cook in a
moderately hot oven, Gas 6, 400°F,
200°C, for 40 to 45 minutes.

3 Garnishing with celery leaves or
parsley makes the dish look as nice as
it tastes. Serve with rice and green
vegetables.

Mrs A. M. Anderson
Stamford, Lincolnshire

Microwave

1 Arrange the pork steaks in a single
layer in a small ceramic casserole.
Pour over the soup. Add cold water
to rinse out the can, then pour this
over the soup.
2 Cover the casserole with a lid or
clear film and cook on Low for 20
minutes. Allow to stand for 5
minutes.

For a 2-power microwave cooker:
Cook on Defrost.

3 Serve sprinkled with parsley.

PORK WITH CHESTNUTS

*For 2, but as this dish freezes and
reheats well it would make two
substantial meals for one person.
Remember to start this recipe the day
before you plan to eat the dish.*

125 g/4 oz chestnuts, whole or
    broken pieces
225 g/8 oz pork fillet or tenderloin
1 to 2 tablespoons oil
1 medium onion, chopped
1 medium apple, peeled, cored
    and chopped
300 ml/½ pint apple juice
300 ml/½ pint light stock
½ to 1 teaspoon dried marjoram
25 g/1 oz millet-flakes *
50 g/2 oz mushrooms, sliced
15 g/½ oz butter
25 g/1 oz raisins

* *Millet flakes can be bought from good
wholefood or health food shops.*

1 Soak the chestnuts in water
overnight; next day, pick out all the
brown flakes of skin that may still
adhere.
2 Trim the pork and cut it
into 2-cm/¾-inch cubes.
3 Heat a little of the oil and fry pork
briskly for only 2 to 3 minutes,
turning and stirring it so that all sides
are sealed. Then transfer to a
casserole.
4 Fry onion in remaining oil until
just turning golden. Add to casserole
with apple and chestnuts.
5 Stir in the apple juice and stock,
marjoram and millet.
6 Cover and cook in a moderately hot
oven, Gas 6, 400°F, 200°C, for 45
minutes.
7 Ten minutes before the end of
cooking time, lightly fry the
mushrooms in butter and stir them
into casserole with the raisins.
8 Serve with a green vegetable and
boiled potatoes.

Catriona Mulligan
Leatherhead, Surrey

Microwave

*This dish turns out rather pale and
needs a bright-coloured vegetable to
accompany it.*

*See below for the microwave way to
peel chestnuts.*

You need no oil and only half the
stock, but increase the butter to
25 g/1 oz.
Follow steps 1 and 2 from the
previous method.
3 Put 25 g/1 oz butter into a 2.1
litre/4 pint casserole with the onions
and mushrooms and heat on full
power for 3 minutes.
4 Stir in the pork, apple, chestnuts,
raisins, apple juice, 150 ml/¼ pint
stock, the marjoram and millet. Cover
the casserole with a lid or clear film

69

and cook on Low for 30 minutes, stirring once.

For a 2-power microwave cooker: Cook on full power for 5 minutes, then on Defrost for 25 to 30 minutes.

5 Let it stand for 10 minutes, then stir well and season to taste before serving.

A Microwave Tip

TO PEEL CHESTNUTS
Cut a cross in the top of each chestnut and place 8 at a time, in a circle, on kitchen paper in the microwave. Cook on full power for 1 minute. Cool slightly, then peel.

Yvonne Hamlett
Haddenham, Buckinghamshire

SWEET AND SOUR PORK

This is especially delicious if you can buy fresh ginger. Chicken, fish fillets or king prawns can be used instead of pork. Makes enough for 2.

225 g/8 oz pork, cut into 1-cm/
$\frac{1}{2}$-inch cubes
1 egg, beaten
2 tablespoons self raising flour mixed with salt, pepper and 1 teaspoon cornflour
Oil for deep frying

SAUCE
1½ tablespoons oil
1 large onion, chopped roughly
1 clove of garlic, crushed
2.5 cm/1 inch fresh ginger, peeled and grated, or 1½ teaspoons ground ginger
2 tablespoons tomato ketchup *
1½ teaspoons cornflour mixed with 8 tablespoons water
2 tablespoons sugar
Salt and pepper
½ teaspoon vinegar

2 tomatoes, skinned (page 26) and cut into wedges
Sliced pickled cucumber and carrot shreds to garnish

* *Pineapple juice can be used as an alternative and gives a delicate and slightly richer flavour.*

1 Start by making the sauce: heat the oil in a saucepan and cook the onion until soft, then add the garlic and ginger and cook for a few minutes.
2 Mix in all the remaining ingredients, except the fresh tomatoes, and cook until the sauce thickens.
3 Now coat the pork in beaten egg, then roll the pieces in the seasoned flour and cornflour mixture.
4 Heat the oil and deep-fry the pork until golden brown. Drain well on kitchen paper.
5 Reheat the sauce, mix in the tomato wedges and pour the sauce over the cooked pork. Serve at once, garnished with pickled cucumber and carrot shreds.

Jennie Siew Lee Cook
York

BARBECUE SPARE RIBS
For 2.

450 g/1 lb pork spare ribs
½ tablespoon honey, warmed
1 teaspoon cornflour mixed with 1 tablespoon water

MARINADE
1 small onion, chopped
1 clove of garlic, crushed
1 tablespoon light soy sauce
1 tablespoon dark soy sauce
1 tablespoon dry sherry
1 tablespoon golden syrup, or sugar
1 dessertspoon chilli sauce, or Worcestershire sauce
1 dessertspoon tomato ketchup, or Hoisin sauce

¼ teaspoon salt
A pinch of Five Spice powder

1 First mix together the marinade ingredients and put the pork ribs to marinate in this mixture for at least 2 hours. Turn them every now and then.
2 Remove the ribs and brush them lightly with the warmed honey.
3 Grill the chops, turning them frequently, until cooked – 15 to 20 minutes. Alternatively, they may be cooked on a barbecue or in a hot oven, Gas 7, 425°F, 210°C for about 20 minutes.
4 Put the remaining marinade into a pan with the cornflour and water and heat until it thickens. Add more water if necessary to make a tasty sauce to serve with the ribs.

Jennie Siew Lee Cook
York

BARBECUE SAUCE

This sauce will keep well in the refrigerator for about 2 weeks. Use with hot and cold food as a dip; good also hot with sausages or chops. Makes about 300 ml/½ pint.

300 ml/½ pint dry cider or dry
   home-made wine
1 dessertspoon cornflour
1 large teaspoon dry mustard
1 tablespoon soy sauce
1 level tablespoon brown sugar
125 g/4 oz canned pineapple
   pieces, drained and diced

1 Put all the ingredients into a saucepan and, stirring all the time, bring slowly up to the boil.
2 Cook for 3 minutes. The sauce is then ready to use.

Grace Mulligan

Microwave

1 Put the cornflour in a 600-ml/1-pint jug. Mix to a smooth paste with a little of the cider.
2 Stir in the mustard, sugar and soy sauce. Blend in the remaining cider.
3 Stir in the pineapple pieces and cook on full power for 3 to 4 minutes, stirring once, halfway through cooking.

BELLY PORK WITH APPLE AND SAGE COATING

One hot plus one cold meal for two people. Ask the butcher for a single piece of belly pork.

A 675 g/1½ lb piece of belly
   pork
A little fat or oil

STUFFING
1 small onion, finely chopped
1 small dessert apple, grated
50 to 75 g/2 to 3 oz fresh
   wholemeal breadcrumbs
1 small egg

71

2 teaspoons chopped fresh sage or
  ½ teaspoon dried sage
½ teaspoon salt
Freshly ground black pepper

1 Preheat the oven to moderate,
Gas 3, 325°F, 160°C.
2 Prepare the pork, removing rind,
excess fat, bones and gristle. Lay the
piece of meat rough side up on a
board or plate.
3 Mix the stuffing ingredients
together, then pile it neatly on top of
pork, pressing it down gently.
4 Grease or oil a small roasting tin
and place the prepared pork in it.
Cover with a piece of greased foil.
5 Put it above the middle of the
preheated oven and cook it for 45
minutes.
6 Take it out and increase oven
temperature to Gas 4, 350°F, 180°C.
Remove foil, baste top of stuffing all
over with the dripping from the meat
and return it, uncovered, to the top
shelf of the oven for 30 minutes. The
stuffing will be nicely browned and
just crisp and firm, and the meat well
done, tender and moist.
7 Serve with plain boiled potatoes
and lightly steamed vegetables, such
as carrot and cabbage.

Mary Watts

Microwave

1 Trim the pork, removing the rind,
excess fat, bone and any gristle. Lay
the meat on an upturned plate in the
base of a 20-cm/8-inch pie dish.
2 Mix the stuffing ingredients
together and pile neatly on top of the
pork, pressing it down gently. Cover
with clear film and cook on Low for
35 minutes or until tender.
3 Remove the film, drain off any
excess fat, slide out the upturned
plate and then put the dish under a
moderate grill until the top is crisp
and brown.

ALL-IN-ONE SAUSAGE SUPPER
For 2, but easy to reduce for one.

4 to 6 sausages
15 g/½ oz fat, lard or dripping
1 onion, peeled and sliced
125 g/4 oz cabbage, finely
  chopped
225 g/8 oz potatoes, peeled and
  diced
A pinch of dried mixed herbs
1 carrot, peeled and sliced
A 230 g/8 oz can of tomatoes
Salt and pepper

1 Cut the sausages into chunks and
fry them in the fat until browned.
2 Remove sausages and all but 2
tablespoons of the fat. Fry the onion
until soft.
3 Add all the remaining ingredients,
mix well together and cook for 2 to 3
minutes.
4 Put the sausages back on top of the
vegetables, put on the lid and simmer
gently for 30 minutes, or until
potatoes and carrots are soft.

Miss Pauline Eddowes
Heworth, York

CIDER WITH SAUSAGES
For 2, but easy to make for 1.

225 g/8 oz pork sausages
50 g/2 oz streaky bacon, cut small
100 g/4 oz tiny onions or 1 small
  onion cut in 4 pieces
1 level tablespoon plain flour
225 ml/8 fl oz dry cider
½ teaspoon dried thyme
1 bay leaf
A small clove of garlic, peeled and
  crushed
Half a beef stock cube

1 In a frying pan, lightly brown the
sausages, bacon and onions.
2 Sprinkle in the flour and gradually

add the cider, stirring as it thickens.
Add the thyme, bay leaf, garlic and
stock cube and simmer, covered with
a lid, for 20 minutes.
3 Remove the bay leaf before serving
with potatoes and vegetables.

The June Hulbert Cookbook

SCOTCH EGGS

For 1 or 2. Hot one day, cold the next.
Bake or deep-fry them. Nice with
freshly made Tomato Sauce (page 175).

2 large sausages
A generous pinch of dried sage
2 small hard-boiled eggs, shelled
1 egg, beaten
Dried breadcrumbs
Oil

1 Skin the sausages, then work the
dried sage into the sausagemeat.
2 Divide the sausagemeat in half and
flatten each piece into a large circle.
Mould the circles around the eggs,
pressing firmly to ensure that there
are no holes.
3 Chill the eggs for about 1 hour,
then dip each one into the beaten egg
and coat in breadcrumbs.
4 Heat the oil to 350° to 360°F, 180°
to 185°C, and deep fry the Scotch
Eggs for about 5 minutes, turning
them frequently.
5 Drain well and serve hot or cold.

To bake the Scotch Eggs: leave out
steps 3 to 5 above and simply put the
sausage-coated eggs straight on to a
greased baking tray. Preheat the oven
to moderately hot, Gas 6, 400°F,
200°C, and bake for 20 minutes.

Grace Mulligan

CRISPY NOODLES WITH BEEF

For 2. This recipe is a meal in itself as
it contains meat, noodles and
vegetables.

175 g/6 oz rump steak
75 to 100 g/3 to 4 oz egg noodles
150 g/5 oz whole green beans,
    topped, tailed and cut into
    5-cm/2-inch pieces
250 ml/8 fl oz oil
1 clove of garlic
150 ml/¼ pint beef stock
1 teaspoon cornflour mixed with
    1 tablespoon water
2 spring onions, cut in small
    pieces

MARINADE
1 teaspoon dark soy sauce
½ teaspoon sugar
½ teaspoon rice wine or dry
    sherry
½ teaspoon cornflour
Freshly ground pepper
90 ml/3 fl oz water
2 tablespoons oil

1 Cut the beef into thin strips. Mix
the marinade, put in the beef and
leave it for 30 minutes.
2 Plunge the noodles into boiling
water for a short time to soften them,
then rinse thoroughly and drain
them.
3 Unless you like very crisp beans,
put them in a pan with a little water
and steam them for 2 or 3 minutes;
otherwise add them at step 5.
4 Heat the oil in a wok or large deep
frying pan and deep-fry the noodles,
half at a time, until crisp on both
sides. Transfer to 2 heated plates and
keep warm.
5 Remove all but 3 tablespoons of oil
from the wok. Add the garlic. Drain
and add the beef. Fry over a high
heat for about 30 seconds, then add
the beans and mix well.
6 Pour in the stock and bring to the
boil.
7 Stir in the cornflour mixture to
thicken the sauce and lastly put in the
spring onions.
8 Spoon the mixture evenly over the
2 plates of noodles and serve.

Jennie Siew Lee Cook
York

BEEF IN A TOMATO AND CREAM SAUCE

Nice with rice or potatoes and a green vegetable. For 2.

175 g/6 oz stewing beef
A little seasoned flour
1 to 2 tablespoons dripping or oil
Half a 300 g/10 oz can of
  condensed tomato soup
6 small pickling onions, or 1 small
  onion cut into 6 pieces
Half a red or green pepper,
  deseeded and sliced
150 ml/¼ pint beef stock
50 g/2 oz mushrooms, sliced
2 tablespoons soured cream *

* See page 111 for another recipe using soured cream.

1 Cut the beef into 1-cm/½-inch strips, toss in seasoned flour, then fry them in hot fat until browned.
2 Drain off the excess fat, add all the rest of the ingredients, except the mushrooms and cream, and bring gently to the boil. Cover with a lid and cook very slowly for 1 hour, or until the meat is tender.
4 Add the mushrooms and cook for a further 10 minutes, then remove from the heat and stir in the soured cream just before serving.

Mrs Jill Gouldstone
Wokingham, Berkshire

Microwave ▰▰▰▰▰▰▰▰▰▰

This works well by microwave using rump steak but you do need a browning dish.

A 15 ml tablespoon oil
1 onion, sliced
Half a red or green pepper,
  deseeded and sliced
50 g/2 oz mushrooms, sliced
175 g/6 oz rump steak
Half a 300 g/10 oz can condensed
  tomato soup

Half a beef stock cube dissolved
  in 2 tablespoons boiling water
2 tablespoons soured cream

1 Put the oil, onion, peppers and mushrooms into a small basin; cook on full power for 3 minutes.
2 Cut the beef into 1-cm/½-inch strips and stir into the onion mixture so that it is well coated in oil.
3 Heat the empty browning dish on full power for 6 minutes (or according to manufacturer's instructions). Immediately tip in the onion and beef mixture, stirring quickly so the beef is seared.
4 Cook on full power for 2 minutes, then stir in the soup and beef stock. Cook on full power for a further 2 to 3 minutes, stirring once.
5 Lastly, stir in the cream and serve.

A RICH BEEF STEW

For 1, 2 or more. This stew has a lovely flavour. It keeps for a day or two in the refrigerator, and freezes and reheats well.

450 g/1 lb braising steak
1 tablespoon cooking oil
1 medium onion, sliced
1 clove of garlic, crushed
1 medium carrot, peeled and cut
  in thick strips
4 or 5 lovage or celery leaves, cut
  up
Freshly ground black pepper
2 teaspoons tomato purée
150 ml/¼ pint best bitter beer
2 tablespoons chopped parsley

1 Cut the meat into 1-cm/½-inch cubes, trimming off excess fat and gristle.
2 Heat oil and gently fry onion and garlic until soft – about 5 minutes. Then add carrot and cook for another 5 minutes. Stir in lovage or celery leaves.

3 Add meat and keep stirring so it browns all over.

4 Stir in pepper, tomato purée and the beer, which will froth up at first, and stir occasionally as it comes to the boil. Turn heat very low, cover and let it simmer, stirring occasionally, for 1 to 1¼ hours until the meat is tender.

5 For the last quarter of an hour, remove the lid so that a little of the liquid evaporates and the meat is served in a rich sauce.

6 Check seasoning before serving and add the parsley at the last minute.

Mrs Charmaine McEachern
Hawes, North Yorkshire

***

Microwave ~~~~~~~~~~~~~~~~~~

In addition to the above ingredients you need:

300 ml/½ pint hot beef stock
Two 15 ml tablespoons cornflour
Two 15 ml tablespoons cold water

1 Cut the meat into 1-cm/½-inch cubes. Trim away any excess fat and gristle.

2 Put the oil, onion and garlic into a 2-litre/4-pint casserole and heat on full power for 3 to 5 minutes until soft.

3 Add the meat, carrots and lovage or celery leaves. Stir well. Add the tomato purée, black pepper, stock and beer. Invert a small tea plate on top of the meat. This keeps the meat and vegetables under the stock and stops them dehydrating during cooking. It also means that the stew will not need stirring.

4 Cover the casserole dish with its own lid or with clear film. Cook on full power for 10 minutes to bring to the boil and then turn the power to Simmer for 60 minutes. This slow cooking will allow the meat to tenderise.

For a 2-power microwave cooker:
Cook the casserole on full power for

10 minutes and then on Defrost for 60 minutes.

5 At the end of cooking, remove the lid and lift out the plate. Blend the cornflour and water to a smooth paste and stir into the stew. Heat on full power for 5 minutes, stirring once. The stew should have thickened nicely.

6 Check seasoning and stir in parsley before serving.

STEAK AND KIDNEY PIE FILLING

This filling stores perfectly in a freezer and, if packed in small amounts, is ideal for turning into individual pies. Alternatively, the filling can be covered with mashed potatoes or just served by itself with boiled rice.

900 g/2 lb stewing steak
225 g/8 oz ox kidney
2 tablespoons oil
1 large onion, chopped
2 tablespoons wholemeal flour
450 ml/¾ pint beef stock
2 large teaspoons horseradish
**   sauce or mustard**
Salt, pepper and gravy browning

1 Prepare the steak and kidney, trimming it carefully and cutting into pieces as small as you like. Keep the trimmings (see Tip, below).

2 In a large pan, heat the oil and quickly brown the steak and kidney pieces. Remove from the pan and set aside.

3 If necessary, add more oil to the pan and cook the onion until soft.

4 Sprinkle in the flour, then add the stock and horseradish sauce, or mustard, and replace the meat.

5 Heat until the sauce boils, then cover and simmer very slowly, or transfer to a cool oven, Gas 2, 300°F, 150°C, for about 2 hours, or until the meat is tender.

6 Adjust the seasoning and add a little gravy browning if necessary.
7 Allow to cool, then pack in plastic bags in the freezer.

Grace Mulligan

TIP

The steak and kidney trimmings can be covered with water and cooked in a covered pan on top of the stove or in a covered ovenproof dish in the oven. Strain, leave the stock to go cold, lift off any fat and you have a good meat stock.

Margaret Heywood
Todmorden, Yorkshire

Use the same ingredients as above, omitting the oil and flour, but increasing the stock to 1 litre/1½ pints and using it hot. Add gravy browning, if necessary, when reheating after defrosting to serve.

1 Prepare the steak and kidney, trimming off any excess fat and gristle. Cut into even-sized pieces about 2 cm/¾ inch in size. Put into a deep 2.5-litre/4-pint casserole dish, with the onion.
2 Mix together the hot stock and the horseradish or mustard. Season with a little salt and plenty of ground black pepper. Pour the stock over the meat. Invert a small tea plate over the meat, pressing it down so that it keeps the meat under the stock. Cover the dish with a lid. Cook on full power for 10 minutes then on Simmer for 60 minutes, or longer. If the meat is not tender enough, allow up to an extra 30 minutes at Simmer. However do check and top up the liquid with HOT stock if required.

For a 2-power microwave cooker:
Use the Defrost setting instead of Simmer. Times will be the same.

3 Allow to cool, skim off any excess fat, then pack into plastic bags and freeze.

To defrost the pie filling:

Tip the frozen pie filling into a basin, heat on full power for 6 to 8 minutes, stirring and breaking up the block every 2 minutes. As the filling is already cooked, it is quite safe to defrost on full power as it is going to be fully reheated in any case.

Do not try to cook Steak and Kidney Pies in the microwave as the pastry stays soggy. However, the filling can be topped with mashed potato and reheated on full power for 5 minutes. Or it can be used as a casserole to serve with vegetables.

BEEF GOULASH

For 1, but easy to make more and larger quantities take no longer to cook. Freezes well before yoghurt is added.

1 tablespoon oil
1 onion, chopped
½ green pepper, deseeded and diced
110 g/4 oz chuck steak, cut into 1 cm/½ inch cubes
1 tablespoon tomato purée
2 fresh tomatoes, skinned (page 26) and chopped
1 small potato, diced
1 teaspoon paprika
Salt and pepper
300 ml/½ pint beef stock
1 teaspoon cornflour mixed with 1 tablespoon water
4 tablespoons natural yoghurt

1 Heat the oil and fry the onion and pepper until soft. Remove them from the pan and set aside.
2 Add the meat to the juices remaining in the pan. Seal the meat so that it is well browned, then stir in the tomato purée, fresh tomatoes, potato, paprika, salt and pepper. Return the onion and pepper to the

pan and pour in the stock.

3 Heat the goulash until it boils, then cover with a tightly fitting lid and simmer very gently for about 1 hour or until the meat is tender.

4 Stir in the cornflour mixture and cook until the sauce thickens, then mix in the yoghurt and serve at once.

Joan Tyers
Wingate, Co. Durham

BERKSHIRE MOUSSAKA

For 2.

225 g/8 oz potatoes, thinly sliced
1 small aubergine, sliced into rounds
225 g/8 oz raw minced beef or lamb
1 small onion, sliced
A 397 g/14 oz can of tomatoes
Salt and pepper
150 ml/¼ pint beef stock
150 ml/¼ pint Cheese Sauce (see below)

1 Place one third of the potatoes in an ovenproof dish, cover with half of the aubergine slices, then put half each of the mince, onion and tomatoes on top. Season with salt and pepper.

2 Cover with some of the remaining potato slices, then repeat the layers, ending with potato. Season again.

3 Pour over the stock, cover with a lid or foil and cook in a hot oven, Gas 6, 400°F, 200°C, for 1 hour.

4 Make the cheese sauce, pour it over the cooked dish and return to the oven, uncovered, for about 15 minutes or until the top is browned.

Mrs Jill Gouldstone
Wokingham, Berkshire

CHEESE SAUCE

Half quantity is suitable for Berkshire Moussaka. (Makes 300 ml/½ pint.)

25 g/1 oz butter
25 g/1 oz flour
300 ml/½ pint milk
Salt and freshly ground black pepper
½ teaspoon made mustard
¼ teaspoon freshly ground nutmeg
75 g/3 oz well-flavoured Cheddar cheese, grated

1 Melt butter over gentle heat. Stir in flour and cook for a minute.

2 Gradually blend in milk and bring to the boil, stirring until smooth and thickened.

3 Add seasoning, mustard, nutmeg and cheese. Stir well until cheese has melted. Serve straightaway.

Debbie Woolhead
Boston Spa, West Yorkshire

All-in-one method

1 Whisk the butter, flour, milk and seasonings together in a large jug. It does not matter if the butter does not combine at this stage.

2 Cook on full power for three 2-minute bursts, whisking thoroughly after each burst.

3 Stir the cheese in immediately. The sauce is so hot at this stage that the cheese will melt and the sauce will be ready to use without further cooking.

THREE-IN-ONE SAVOURY MINCE

Three meals for one person. Lee-anne Patterson lives alone and from the following recipe she prepares three separate meals: Spaghetti Bolognese for the first day, Cottage Pie the next, then there's a Savoury Crumble for the third meal.

3 tablespoons oil
2 onions, chopped
1 clove of garlic, crushed

450 g/1 lb minced beef
A 397 g/14 oz can of tomatoes
A pinch of dried oregano
100 g/4 oz mushrooms, sliced
1 green pepper, deseeded and cut
   into chunks
1 red pepper, deseeded and cut
   into chunks
Salt and pepper

1 Heat the oil in a large saucepan and
cook the onion until soft.
2 Add the garlic and mince and cook
over a moderate heat until the meat is
lightly browned.
3 Pour in the tomatoes and add the
oregano. Bring to the boil and simmer
gently for 20 minutes.
4 Mix the mushrooms and peppers
into the mince and cook for a further
15 minutes. If the meat looks a bit
dry, add a little water. Season to taste
with salt and pepper.

Lee-anne Patterson
Lockleaze, Bristol

*You may like to add 1 crumbled beef
stock cube to the ingredients listed
above.*

1 Put the oil, onions and garlic into a
2 litre/4 pint casserole with the green
and red peppers. Heat on full power
for 5 minutes.
2 Stir in the minced beef, tomatoes,
oregano, mushrooms and stock cube
and season with a little salt and
pepper. Mix, so that all the
ingredients are well combined.
3 Cover the casserole with a lid or
with film and cook on Medium for 15
minutes. Let it stand for 5 minutes
before serving.

For a 2-power microwave cooker:
Cook on full power for 10 to 12
minutes, stirring once after 6 minutes.
Stand for 5 minutes.

4 Stir and adjust seasoning before
serving.

SPAGHETTI BOLOGNESE

Make sure the spaghetti is not boiled
too long. A tablespoon of oil cooked
with it prevents the strands from
sticking together when drained. Serve
at once with 1 helping cooked
Savoury Mince on top and a
sprinkling of finely grated cheese.

This dish reheats well by microwave.
Put the prepared mince on top of the
cooked spaghetti. Cover and heat on
full power for 2 to 3 minutes.

COTTAGE PIE

1 helping cooked Savoury
   Mince
125 g/5 oz cooked mashed potatoes
25 g/1 oz cooked peas or beans

1 The dish can be assembled from
hot ingredients, in which case, put the
Savoury Mince in a small ovenproof
dish, sprinkle over it a layer of peas
or beans and cover with mashed
potato.
2 Fork up the top and brown it
under a hot grill.

For assembly from cold, the dish can
be reheated in a moderate oven, Gas
4, 350°F, 180°C, for 15 minutes. For
a change, cover the potatoes with a
layer of grated cheese.

*The potato for mashing can be cooked
by microwave –see page 117.*

1 To assemble: put the Savoury
Mince in a heatproof dish and put in
a layer of peas or beans. Cover with
a layer of potato, marking the top
with a fork.

2 If the ingredients are hot, simply brown the potato under the grill. If the ingredients are cold, reheat, covered, on full power for 3 minutes, then brown the potato under the grill as above.

SAVOURY MINCE CRUMBLE

It makes a change to have a crumble topping, and this good idea came from Mrs Susan Hersee of Hayling Island, Hampshire. Make more of the topping than you need for one meal, as it keeps well in the fridge. For 2 helpings:

100 g/4 oz plain flour, white or
    wholemeal
50 g/2 oz margarine
50 g/2 oz Edam cheese, grated
A pinch of cayenne pepper

1 Put the flour into a bowl and rub in the margarine until the mixture resembles breadcrumbs. Mix in the grated cheese and cayenne pepper.

2 Make a layer of cooked Savoury Mince in an ovenproof dish, cover with the crumble topping.
3 Cook in a preheated moderately hot oven, Gas 6, 400°F, 200°C, for 15 to 20 minutes. Serve with a good Onion Gravy (see below).

Microwave ■■■■■■■■■■■■■■■■■■

For 1.

1 Sprinkle crumble topping over one helping of cooked Savoury Mince arranged in a layer in a heatproof dish.
2 Cover and cook on full power for 3 to 4 minutes, then finish under a hot grill to brown the top for 5 to 6 minutes. Serve with a good Onion Gravy (see below).

GOOD ONION GRAVY
Makes 300 ml/½ pint.

100 g/4 oz onion, finely
    chopped
20 g/¾ oz butter
20 g/¾ oz flour
300 ml/½ pint stock
Pepper and salt

1 Fry the onion in the butter until soft and lightly brown.
2 Add the flour and cook for one minute.
3 Add the stock and stir as it comes to the boil. Simmer for 5 minutes.
4 Season to taste. (Gravy browning can be added if too light in colour.)

Judith Adshead
Porth Colmon, Gwynedd

CHILLI CON CARNE
Serves 1 or 2 – freezes well. Serve with brown rice or a jacket potato.

100 g/4 oz lean minced beef
1 medium onion, finely chopped

79

A small clove of garlic, chopped
Half a 5 ml teaspoon chilli
  powder
Salt and pepper to taste
A 227 g/8 oz can of tomatoes
A 15 ml tablespoon tomato purée
A 213 g/7½ oz can of red kidney
  beans, drained

1 Brown the minced beef for 5
minutes in a large pan without added
fat. There is always enough fat even
in lean mince and no extra is needed.
2 Drain off any excess fat, then add
the onion, garlic, chilli and other
seasoning to taste.
3 Pour in tomatoes, add tomato purée
and bring to the boil. Cover and
simmer gently for 20 minutes. If the
mince looks a little dry, add a little
water.
4 Add the kidney beans and cook for
a further 5 minutes.

Jill Myers
The British Diabetic Association,
London

---

1 Put all the ingredients in a small
(1.5-litre/3-pint) casserole. Mix so
they are well combined. Cover with a
lid or with film.
2 Cook on Medium for 7 minutes.

For a 2-power microwave cooker:
Cook on full power for 3 to 4
minutes, stirring once.

Let it stand for 5 minutes, covered,
before you eat it.

QUICK PIZZA ROLLS

*A crusty wholemeal roll is sliced open to
form the pizza-type base to this tasty
dish. Enough for 2, but easy to make for
1. Serve with salad.*

1 long crusty wholemeal roll
50 g/2 oz reduced-fat Cheddar
  cheese, grated

80

---

75 g/3 oz lean minced beef
Half an onion, chopped
A 10 ml dessertspoon of tomato
  purée
A pinch of mixed herbs
Salt and pepper

1 Cut the roll in half lengthways.
2 Save half the grated cheese and
sprinkle the rest over the halved roll.
3 Cook the minced beef and onion
gently in a saucepan until the meat is
brown. It is not necessary to add fat
if you stir it carefully.
4 Add the tomato purée, mixed herbs
and seasoning and continue to cook
gently for 5 minutes. If the mixture
is too dry, add 1 to 2 tablespoons of
water.
5 Spread the minced meat on top of
the cheese rolls and cover with the
remaining cheese.
6 Grill until the cheese melts.

Jill Myers
The British Diabetic Association,
London

Follow steps 1 and 2 above.
3 Put the onion in a basin with one
(5 ml) teaspoon of water. Heat on
full power for 1 minute. Stir in the
minced beef, tomato purée, mixed
herbs and seasoning. Cook on full
power for 2 to 3 minutes, stirring
once.
4 Spread the mince on top of the
rolls and sprinkle with the remaining
cheese. Put under a hot grill until the
cheese bubbles and melts.

MEAT ROLLS

*For 2, but easy to make just for one
person.*

50 g/2 oz fresh breadcrumbs
½ teaspoon dried mixed herbs
1 tablespoon chives, chopped
1 egg
Salt and pepper

4 slices cold beef, or any cold
  meat
125 g/1 oz butter

1 Put the breadcrumbs, herbs, chives,
egg and seasoning into a bowl and
mix well.
2 Spread a quarter of the mixture
on each slice of meat, then roll up
and tie securely with thread or thin
string.
3 Melt the butter in a pan and fry
the rolls, turning them frequently,
until lightly browned. Serve with hot
vegetables and gravy. (See page 79
for Good Onion Gravy.)

Mrs Mary Potts
Bedlington, Northumberland

BAKED LAMB CHOPS WITH COURGETTES

*A complete main course for 2, served
with plain boiled potatoes or rice.*

2 lamb chops or lamb steaks
1 tablespoon oil
1 onion, chopped
225 g/8 oz courgettes, topped,
  tailed, and cut into slices
A 227 g/8 oz can of tomatoes
1 teaspoon finely chopped fresh
  rosemary or ½ teaspoon dried
  rosemary
A clove of garlic, crushed
A pinch of sugar
Salt and freshly ground black
  pepper

1 Trim off any fat from the chops,
leaving only a small amount around
the edges. Brush them with a little
oil.
2 Heat the oil in a flameproof
casserole and fry the onion quickly
for 1 minute. Then add the
courgettes, tomatoes, rosemary, garlic
and sugar.
3 Reduce the heat, mix well and
season with salt and freshly ground

black pepper. Make 2 hollows and
add the lamb, but make sure the meat
is not completely covered.
4 Put on the lid and cook in a
moderately hot oven, Gas 5, 375°F,
190°C for 20 minutes. Then remove
the lid and cook for a further 15
minutes.

Grace Mulligan

HONEY LAMB CHOPS

*For 1. Easy to make more. Nice served
with rice and peas.*

2 lamb chops
1 tablespoon thick honey
1 tablespoon oil
1 teaspoon lemon juice
½ teaspoon dried mixed herbs

1 Place the chops in an ovenproof
dish.
2 Put the honey, oil, lemon juice and
herbs into a small saucepan and stir
over a low heat until the honey has
melted. Pour this over the chops and
leave in a cool place for 30 minutes.
3 Preheat the oven to moderate, Gas
4, 350°F, 180°C and cook the chops
until tender, about 20 to 25 minutes.

Mrs A. Chapman
Hammersmith, London

LAMB KOFTA CURRY

*Serves 2. If you don't have a food
processor you can still make this, but it
will be a matter of grating the onion,
crushing the garlic and mixing it all by
hand. This curry can also be made with
minced beef.*

50 g/2 oz onions
2 cloves of garlic
225 g/8 oz minced lamb
¾ teaspoon salt
½ teaspoon cumin powder
¼ teaspoon chilli powder
¼ teaspoon garam masala
A pinch of ground nutmeg

SAUCE

3 tablespoons oil
125 g/4 oz onions, peeled and
    sliced
2 to 3 cloves of garlic, peeled and
    crushed
125 g/4 oz canned tomatoes,
    roughly chopped
¾ teaspoon turmeric powder
½ teaspoon salt
½ teaspoon coriander powder
¼ teaspoon cumin powder
¼ teaspoon chilli powder
450 ml/¾ pint water
Green coriander leaves or parsley
    to garnish

1 To prepare the meatballs, put the
onion and garlic into a food processor
and process until finely chopped. Add
the meat, salt and spices and process
again until everything is well
blended.
2 Take small pieces of meat mixture
and roll into balls about the size of a
large walnut. Set aside in a cool place
while making the sauce.
3 Heat the oil and fry the onion and
garlic until dark brown, stirring most
of the time.
4 Add tomatoes and 1 tablespoon of
the juice, then add all the remaining
ingredients. Cook, stirring, until the
oil begins to separate. Drain the oil
away. Then pour in 450 ml/¾ pint
water.
5 Bring the liquid up to boiling
point, then put in the meatballs one
at a time. Bring back to the boil,
cover, then reduce the heat so the
meatballs simmer gently for about 20
minutes.
6 Drain and place on a warmed
serving dish. If the sauce is watery,
boil it rapidly over a very high heat
until it is reduced to a syrupy
consistency. Pour over the meatballs.
7 Serve hot, sprinkled with coriander
leaves or coarsely chopped parsley.

                    Nirmal Singh
          Nuneaton, Warwickshire

SHEEKH KEBABS

*These are delicious served with a green
salad, or they may be cut into bite-sized
pieces and served on cocktail sticks as a
tasty snack with drinks. For this recipe
you will need 4 skewers each at least 15
to 18 cm/6 to 7 inches in length. Notice
also (step 3) that you need to start in
very good time.*

225 g/8 oz minced lamb or
    tender beef
½ teaspoon salt
1 dessertspoon lemon juice
1 tablespoon oil
1 small onion, finely chopped
¼ to ½ teaspoon chilli powder
¼ to ½ teaspoon garam masala
¼ teaspoon ground nutmeg
2 tablespoons natural yoghurt

1 Put the meat into a bowl and mix
in the salt and lemon juice. Leave it
in a cool place for 20 minutes.
2 Heat the oil and fry the onion until
it starts to turn a pale brown colour.
Drain it very thoroughly on kitchen
paper, then add the onion to the
meat.
3 Mix all the remaining ingredients
into the meat and leave it in the
refrigerator for at least 4 hours, better
still, for 24 hours.
4 Divide the meat into 4 pieces and
firmly press it evenly around the 4
skewers in a long sausage shape, about
15 to 18 cm/6 to 7 inches. Make sure
the meat is the same thickness
throughout.
5 Preheat the grill to maximum heat.
Pour a little water into the grill pan,
and brush the rack with oil.
6 Put the skewers of meat on to the
rack and grill on all sides until they
are a light brown colour all over.
7 Serve at once, or wrap in foil to
keep warm.

                    Nirmal Singh
          Nuneaton, Warwickshire

MEATBALL SURPRISE

For 2.

225 g/½ lb minced beef
1 tablespoon tomato ketchup
1 small onion, finely chopped
½ teaspoon dried mixed herbs
Salt and pepper
1 egg, beaten
50 g/2 oz Cheddar cheese
25 g/1 oz flour seasoned with a
    little salt and pepper
Fat or dripping
150 ml/¼ pint beef stock, a stock
    cube will do
1 dessertspoon cornflour

1 Mix together the mince, ketchup,
onion, egg and herbs, seasoning well
with salt and pepper. Make into 8
even-sized portions.
2 Cut the cheese into 8 cubes.
3 Now make a ball carefully
surrounding each piece of cheese with
a coating of mince. Wet your hands
to make this easier.
4 Roll the meatballs in seasoned
flour.
5 Heat the fat in a pan and brown
the meatballs, then pour off any
excess fat.

6 Add the beef stock, bring up to the
boil, cover with a lid and simmer for
30 minutes.
7 Remove the meatballs to a hot
serving dish.
8 Mix the cornflour with 1
tablespoon cold water and stir it into
the liquid in the pan over moderate
heat until it thickens and comes to the
boil.
9 Pour this gravy over the meatballs
and serve with potatoes.

Catherine Sangster
Aberdeen

STIR-FRIED KIDNEYS AND BACON

For 2.

4 rashers smoked rindless
    streaky bacon, cut in strips
4 fresh or frozen lambs' kidneys,
    skinned, cored (use scissors)
    and quartered
1 level dessertspoon French
    mustard
1 tablespoon vinegar
1 tablespoon chopped parsley
1 tablespoon chopped chives
Salt and pepper

1 Cook the bacon in its own fat over a moderate heat until it is crisp. You will not need to add any oil.
2 Add the kidney pieces and fry until the kidneys are browned and just cooked.
3 Stir in the mustard, vinegar, parsley, chives and seasoning and mix well together. Serve on a bed of rice or on toasted wholemeal bread.

Grace Mulligan

Microwave

1 Follow step 1 above.
2 Arrange the liver slices in a shallow 20-cm/8-inch round dish. Sprinkle over the breadcrumbs, parsley, onion, mushrooms and seasoning.
3 Pour over the stock and cover with the rashers of bacon. Cook, uncovered, on full power for 6 to 8 minutes, then let it stand for 5 minutes before serving.

LIVER AND BACON CASSEROLE
For 2.

225 g/8 oz lamb's liver
15 g/½ oz flour
1 tablespoon fresh white or wholemeal breadcrumbs
1 teaspoon chopped parsley
1 teaspoon chopped onion
25 g/1 oz mushrooms, sliced
Salt and pepper
300 ml/½ pint stock or gravy
2 rashers of bacon

1 Cut the liver into slices 7 mm/¼ inch thick and toss them in the flour.
2 Arrange in a greased ovenproof dish and sprinkle over the breadcrumbs, parsley, onion, mushrooms, salt and pepper.
3 Pour over the stock and cover with the rashers of bacon.
4 Cover with a lid and cook in a moderate oven, Gas 4, 350°F, 180°C, for 40 minutes. Before serving, put the dish under the grill to crisp the bacon.

Alternatively, this dish can be cooked on top of the stove. Assemble all the ingredients except the bacon in a saucepan and cook gently for 20 minutes. Grill the bacon at the last minute and put it on top of the liver as you serve it.

Mrs M. W. Kirk
Runcorn, Cheshire

LIVER BALLS IN TOMATO SAUCE

This is a good recipe for a food processor because of the number of ingredients that need chopping. Makes 2 helpings.

225 g/8 oz lamb's liver, skinned and chopped small
50 g/2 oz fresh breadcrumbs
1 onion, peeled and finely chopped
75 g/3 oz rindless bacon, cut in small strips
1 egg, beaten
A pinch of dried thyme
25 g/1 oz flour
25 g/1 oz dripping or 1 tablespoon oil
A 227 g/8 oz can of tomatoes, chopped

1 Mix together the liver, breadcrumbs, onion, bacon, egg and thyme. Roll the mixture into 6 balls and coat each one with flour.
2 Heat the fat in a frying pan and brown the liver balls evenly, then transfer to an ovenproof dish with a well-fitting lid.
3 Pour the tomatoes over the balls, sprinkle with a little extra dried thyme and put on the lid.
4 Cook in a moderate oven, Gas 4, 350°F, 180°C, for 20 minutes then

turn the balls over and cook for 20
minutes more.

Mrs Mary Potts
Bedlington, Northumberland

LIVER RISOTTO

*For 1. Serve with brown rice, or boiled
or baked potatoes and a green
vegetable.*

A 15 ml tablespoon of oil
1 small onion, finely chopped
100 g/4 oz lambs liver, skinned
   and thinly sliced
A 15 ml tablespoon of wholemeal
   flour seasoned with salt and
   pepper
A 227 g/8 oz can of tomatoes
60 ml/2 fl oz water
A 15 ml tablespoon of dried
   mushrooms
Half a chicken stock cube
A 15 ml tablespoon of frozen peas
   or sweetcorn
Salt and pepper

1 Heat the oil in a pan and fry the
onion until soft.
2 Toss the liver in the seasoned flour
and fry with the onion until the liver
is lightly browned.
3 Add all the remaining ingredients
to the pan, bring to the boil, stirring
continously, then reduce the heat and
let it simmer gently for 10 minutes
before serving.

Jill Myers
The British Diabetic Association,
London

HEARTS BRAISED IN AN ORANGE SAUCE

*For 2. This dish can be cooked on top
of the stove or in the oven.*

1 or 2 lamb's or pig's hearts
Salted water for soaking
15 g/½ oz butter
1 tablespoon oil
125 g/4 oz onions, chopped
A clove of garlic, chopped
1 tablespoon flour
150 ml/¼ pint meat stock
1 dessertspoon tomato purée
1 bay leaf
A sprig of thyme or a pinch of
   dried thyme
The juice and 1 fine strip of peel
   from a small orange
1 tablespoon bitter marmalade
Salt and freshly ground black
   pepper
1 teaspoon lemon juice

1 Prepare the hearts by washing
under running water. With sharp
scissors, carefully cut away the
muscular artery walls and any outside
skin.
2 Soak hearts in lightly salted water
for 30 minutes. Drain and dry.
3 Heat butter and oil in a saucepan
or flameproof casserole. Fry hearts
for several minutes until brown all
over. Remove from pan.
4 Reduce heat, add onion and garlic
and fry for about 5 minutes until
soft.
5 Sprinkle in the flour, stirring all
the time. Stir in stock, tomato purée,
bay leaf, thyme, orange juice and
rind, and marmalade. Return to heat
and bring slowly to the boil. Season
with salt and pepper.
6 Cut the hearts diagonally into quite
thick slices and return them to the
pan or casserole. Cover and simmer
gently for 1 hour. Or cook in a
moderate oven, Gas, 3, 325°F, 150°C,
for 1 to 1½ hours.
7 Lift out the slices of heart and
arrange in a serving dish. Keep
warm.
8 Lift off fat from the cooking
liquid by tilting casserole and
spooning it away.
9 Add lemon juice and boil rapidly
until liquid is reduced to a thick
sauce. Pour over the hearts and
serve.

Grace Mulligan

Chapter 6

Rice, Pulses, Eggs

and Vegetable Dishes

BOILED RICE
The absorption method

**Allow about 50 g/2 oz brown or
 white rice per person.**

1 Put the rice into a measuring jug or
cup to calculate the amount of water
required: almost twice the volume of
the rice. Heat the water until almost
boiling.
2 Meanwhile, wash the rice
thoroughly, shaking it in a sieve under
the cold water tap.
3 Put the rice on to cook in the hot
water. When it boils, stir, then let it
boil steadily without the lid until the
grains are almost breaking the
surface.
4 Now put on the lid. It should fit
tightly. Turn the heat to the lowest
possible and let the rice cook; 15
minutes for white rice, 20 minutes for
brown.
5 Turn off the heat, leave the pan
for 5 minutes. When you look inside,
the rice should be perfectly cooked,
every grain separate and no water
left.
6 Season to taste after cooking,
forking the salt and pepper very
gently through the rice.

Mary Watts

**50 g/2 oz long grain rice
 (or 3 fl oz)
300 ml/½ pint cold water
 (or 10 fl oz)
A pinch of salt**

1 Put the ingredients into an 18-
cm/7-inch soufflé-type dish. Cover
the dish with a serving plate (which
will be nice and hot by the time you
need to eat).
2 Cook on full power: 8 minutes for
white rice; 12 minutes for 'pre-
fluffed' brown * rice. Stir brown rice
once during cooking. (If you have

100 g/4 oz rice to cook, measure in
600 ml/1 pint boiling water and put 2
plates on top to cover the dish and
warm up at the same time.)
3 Leave the dish, covered, to stand
for 5 minutes – or while cooking the
accompanying food. The rice will
absorb the remaining water and stay
hot. Fluff it up with a fork before
serving.

* *If your brown rice is the ordinary
hard grain type a different procedure is
necessary.*

1 Use an 18-cm/7-inch soufflé-type
dish or casserole but it must be at
least 9 cm/3½ inches deep.
2 Cook on full power for 5 minutes.
Then cook on Medium for 12
minutes. Let it stand for 10 minutes
and then cook on Medium for 5
minutes more. Stir at once and serve.
It will stand for 5 minutes before
beginning to cool.

No time is saved and you may prefer
to follow the conventional method.
However, at least in the microwave it
will not burn if you forget it!

Yvonne Hamlett
Haddenham, Buckinghamshire

GARLIC RICE
*For 1 or 2. Delicious on its own, or
with cold meat. Reheats well.*

**125 g/4 oz long grain white or
 brown rice
2 medium to small potatoes,
 quartered
2 cloves of garlic, finely chopped
50 g/2 oz butter
25 g/1 oz Parmesan or finely
 grated Cheddar cheese mixed
 with a little Parmesan
 (Parmesan on its own is better)**

1 Boil rice with potato. If using
brown rice, cut potato into 2.5-cm/
1-inch cubes and add to rice for 10

minutes before end of cooking time. (Brown rice normally takes 20 to 25 minutes to cook.)

2 At last minute, fry garlic in butter until just turning golden.

3 Season the rice and potato with a little salt and pepper and put them into a warm serving dish. Pour over the garlic and fork it in lightly. Sprinkle top with cheese and serve piping hot.

To reheat: melt 15 g/½ oz butter in a shallow pan (non-stick is ideal). Add the garlic rice and stir for 1 minute to break the lumps of rice. Then cover pan, reduce heat to lowest and let it all heat through. Takes 5 minutes for half the above quantity.

To reheat in the microwave: half quantity, covered, on full power for 2 minutes.

Mrs. R. Bright
Sutton, Surrey

STIR-FRIED RICE WITH PRAWNS OR HAM

For 2. This tasty dish is a meal by itself. It is cooked over quite high heat, constantly stirring with a large kitchen spoon and fork.

3 tablespoons oil
A clove of garlic, chopped
1 onion, sliced
75 to 100 g/3 to 4 oz cooked peeled prawns or diced ham
125 g/5 oz cooked rice (cold rice will do)
2 eggs, beaten
1½ tablespoons light soy sauce
½ tablespoon dark soy sauce
100 g/4 oz diced cooked mixed vegetables
Spring onion curls and cucumber wedges to garnish

1 In a wok or large frying pan, heat 2 tablespoons oil. Add the garlic and cook until slightly brown, then add the onion and cook for 2 minutes, stirring.

2 Add the prawns and allow them 2 minutes to heat through, then mix in the rice. Stir all the time.

3 Push the rice to one side of the wok or pan, add an extra tablespoon of oil and pour in the beaten eggs.

4 Scramble the eggs slightly, then cover with the rice and leave for about 1 minute until the eggs are set.

5 Pour the light and dark soy sauces into the pan, add the mixed vegetables and stir well, breaking the egg into little pieces.

6 Serve at once, garnished with spring onion curls and wedges of cucumber.

Jennie Siew Lee Cook
York

TUNA RISOTTO

A substantial dish for 2, this is pleasant either hot or cold.

1 tablespoon oil
2 rashers of bacon, finely chopped
1 large onion, chopped
50 g/2 oz mushrooms, chopped – but not too small
100 g/4 oz white or brown rice, washed
450 ml/¾ pint hot chicken stock, a cube will do
A 397 g/14 oz can of tomatoes
170 g/6 oz frozen mixed vegetables
A 200 g/7 oz can of tuna, drained
Salt and pepper
Slices of tomato, and chopped parsley, to garnish

1 Heat oil and fry bacon and onion for 2 or 3 minutes. Then add mushrooms and fry until oil is absorbed.

2 Add rice and fry for 2 minutes, stirring from time to time.

3 Add hot stock, bring to the boil and allow to simmer for 15 minutes

(20 minutes for brown rice).
4 Roughly chop the tomatoes and add with their juice and the frozen mixed vegetables.
5 Break tuna into quite large pieces and mix in gently; add salt and pepper to taste. Cook for 5 minutes more until liquid is absorbed.
6 Serve at once, garnished with tomato slices and parsley.

Miss Lisa Lant
Hazelrigg, Newcastle upon Tyne

SAVOURY VEGETABLE RICE

For 1 or 2. Eaten hot it goes well with Pork Stir-Fry (page 68). Mixed with French Dressing (page 106), it can be served cold as a salad.

75 to 100 g/3 to 4 oz long grain
    brown or white rice
½ tablespoon oil
1 small onion, diced
25 g/1 oz cucumber or courgette,
    or green or red pepper, diced
75 to 100 g/3 to 4 oz peas or
    sweetcorn, cooked
25 g/1 oz sultanas or raisins
Salt and pepper

1 Cook the rice by the absorption method (page 88).
2 Heat the oil and fry the onion until soft but not brown. Add the cucumber, courgette or pepper and stir-fry for 2 minutes.
3 Stir in the rest of the ingredients and cook to reheat, seasoning to taste.

Dilwen Phillips
Gileston, South Glamorgan

STUFFED PEPPER

For 1.

1 medium green or red pepper
50 g/2 oz lean bacon rasher

A 10 ml dessertspoon of oil
50 g/2 oz cooked brown rice
A 15 ml tablespoon of frozen peas
    or sweetcorn, cooked
A 15 ml tablespoon of raisins
Salt and pepper

1 Slice the top off the pepper and remove the seeds and any white pith.
2 Put the pepper in a saucepan of boiling water and simmer for 10 minutes, or until it is tender. Drain and keep it warm.
3 Chop the bacon and fry in the oil until crisp. Add the rice, vegetables, raisins and seasoning to taste. Heat through, then spoon the mixture into the pepper. Serve.

Jill Myers
The British Diabetic Association,
London

Microwave

1 Slice the top off the pepper, remove the seeds and any white pith. Stand the pepper in a small cereal bowl.
2 Put the bacon on a small plate, cover loosely with a piece of kitchen paper. Cook on full power for 1 to 2 minutes until crisp.
3 In a basin, mix together the rice, vegetables and raisins. Crumble in the bacon and spoon the mixture into the pepper.
4 Replace the pepper's lid, cover the dish with clear film and cook on full power for 4 to 5 minutes. Let it stand for 5 minutes before serving. The pepper softens during the standing time.

CURRIED NUT LOAF

Delicious and quite filling for 2, but nice hot or cold served with a green salad with French Dressing (page 106).

2 tablespoons oil
1 small onion, sliced

1 small green pepper, deseeded
 and chopped
175 g/6 oz tomatoes, skinned (page
 26) and finely chopped
175 g/6 oz hazelnuts or walnuts,
 finely chopped
75 g/3 oz fresh wholemeal
 breadcrumbs
1 clove of garlic, crushed
1 teaspoon dried mixed herbs
1 teaspoon curry powder
1 egg, beaten
Salt and pepper

1 Heat the oil in a pan and cook
the onion, pepper and tomato until
soft.
2 Mix together the nuts,
breadcrumbs, garlic, herbs and curry
powder. Stir in the tomato mixture
with the egg and seasoning and put
the mixture into a greased 450-g/1-lb
loaf tin.
3 Bake in a moderate oven, Gas 4,
350°F, 180°C, for 30 minutes until
golden brown.
4 Turn out and serve either hot or
cold.

The June Hulbert Cookbook

Microwave ▬▬▬▬▬▬▬▬▬▬▬▬▬▬

1 Put just 1 tablespoon of oil with
the onion and green pepper into a
mixing bowl. Heat on full power for
5 minutes until soft. Add the
tomato.
2 Stir in the nuts, breadcrumbs,
garlic, herbs and curry powder.
Season with a little salt and pepper.
Bind together with the egg.
3 Line the base of a 450-g/1-lb loaf
dish with a piece of greaseproof
paper. Tip the mixture into the dish
and smooth over the top. Cook on
full power for 8 to 10 minutes until
the centre is just firm to the touch.
Let it stand for 5 minutes before
turning out.
4 Serve hot or cold in slices with a
green salad.

SAVOURY SEMOLINA WITH PEANUTS

*The garnishes are very important for
this dish. It's nice also with grilled
tomatoes or fresh Tomato Sauce (page
175).*

150 ml/6 fl oz coarse semolina,
 available from Indian grocers *
300 ml/12 fl oz boiling water
2 tablespoons cooking or salad oil
1 small onion, chopped
1 medium potato, diced small
1 teaspoon black mustard seeds
1 tablespoon peanuts
Salt and pepper
A pinch of cayenne pepper
Garnish with lemon wedges, 1
 tablespoon lightly toasted
 desiccated coconut and chopped
 fresh coriander leaves
Natural yoghurt or Yoghurt
Chutney for serving (page 111)

* *Ordinary semolina can be used but the
coarse variety gives a crumbly texture to
the finished dish.*

1 Measure both semolina and water
separately in a measuring jug.
2 Put one tablespoon of the oil in a
pan and fry semolina on a low heat
until golden brown. Stir continuously
in case it burns.
3 In a small frying pan, fry onion
and potato in the rest of the oil with
mustard seeds and peanuts until
lightly browned and potato is cooked.
Add to semolina.
4 Add water and cook on a very low
heat, stirring continuously for 4 to 5
minutes. Season with salt, pepper and
cayenne to taste.
5 Serve on a warmed dish with lemon
wedges (or sprinkled with juice),
sprinkled with toasted coconut and
chopped coriander leaves.

Mrs Jaswant Chopra
Childwall, Liverpool

TO COOK DRIED BEANS AND PEAS

These freeze well when cooked and it makes sense to cook a substantial amount, pack into bags of suitably sized portions and freeze for another day.

1 Soak overnight.
2 Discard soaking water and cook in plenty of fresh water in a roomy pan as they often froth up and over the top.
3 Bring to the boil and always boil hard for 10 minutes before reducing heat and simmering until tender. The hard boiling is essential to eliminate either toxic or indigestible factors.

Cooking times vary enormously from soya (2½ to 3 hours) and chick peas (2 hours) to black-eye beans (40 to 45 minutes) and haricot (45 to 50 minutes). It is best to keep an eye on the pan until you are accustomed to the cooking times so that the beans are cooked until just tender. When they are beginning to overcook they will burst out of their skins and the appearance will be spoilt.

Pressure cooking saves time but always follow procedure given in the manufacturer's handbook, because you cannot see if they are ready and possibly bursting from their skins and turning to mush.

For salads it is best to have French dressing ready, well flavoured with garlic and herbs, and put the hot drained beans and peas into it to marinate.

TIP
Do not cook white beans in the same pan with red or black ones as the colours will spoil the look of the white ones.

HOT HARICOT BEANS AND HAM
Serves 2

This quick lunch or supper dish is cooked and served in a frying pan. Useful for the ham derived from cooking a Ham Shank (page 67).

15 g/½ oz butter or margarine
1 tablespoon oil
75 g/3 oz courgettes, trimmed and sliced into rounds
75 g/3 oz cooked ham, diced
50 g/2 oz cooked haricot beans *

SAUCE
15 g/½ oz butter or margarine
1 tablespoon flour
150 ml/¼ pint ham stock – chicken or vegetable stock will do
1 tablespoon chopped chives
25 g/1 oz grated cheese

* See opposite for notes on cooking dried beans and peas.

1 Heat the butter and oil in a frying pan and cook the courgettes for a short while. Stir often and do not over-cook them or they lose their crispness.
2 Stir in the diced ham and haricot beans and leave on a low heat while the sauce is prepared.
3 For the sauce, put the butter, flour and ham stock into a saucepan. Whisk well to disperse any lumps of flour. Stirring all the time, heat up the sauce until it boils, then add the chives.
4 Pour the sauce over the courgettes and scatter the grated cheese on top.
5 Place the frying pan under a hot grill until the cheese melts and browns slightly. Eat at once.

Grace Mulligan

1 Put the butter or margarine (the oil is not needed) with the courgettes into a small shallow heatproof dish – about 600 ml/1 pint size. Cover with clear film and cook on full power for 2 minutes. Stir in the ham and haricot beans.

2 For the sauce, put the butter in a 600-ml/1-pint jug and heat on full power for 30 seconds. Stir in the flour and blend in the stock. Heat on full power for 1 minute. Stir in the chives and heat for 30 seconds.

3 Pour sauce over the courgettes and scatter the grated cheese on top. Put under a hot grill until the cheese melts, bubbles and begins to brown.

POTATO AND BEAN CASSEROLE

A substantial dish for 2, best eaten hot as a main course. Green salad goes well with it. Reheats easily.

15 g/½ oz butter, or a little oil
A 213-g/7½-oz can of red kidney
    beans
225 g/8 oz potatoes
Salt and pepper
50 g/2 oz mature Cheddar cheese,
    grated
1 egg
300 ml/½ pint milk, hot but not
    boiling

TOPPING

15 g/½ oz butter
1 large tablespoon sesame seeds
1 large tablespoon sunflower
    seeds
1 tablespoon soy sauce

1 Preheat oven to moderate, Gas 4, 350°F, 180°C.

2 Use butter or oil to grease a 900-ml/1½-pint ovenproof dish lightly.

3 Drain beans and rinse them with cold water.

4 Scrub the potatoes and slice them thinly.

5 Arrange half of the potatoes in the dish, season with salt and pepper. Spread half of the cheese over the potatoes and cover with the beans. Season again and cover with remaining potatoes.

6 Beat egg into hot milk and pour this over the potatoes and beans. Top with the remaining cheese.

7 Bake in preheated oven for about 1 hour, or until potatoes are tender.

8 Meanwhile prepare the topping. Melt butter in a saucepan and fry sesame and sunflower seeds for 2 minutes, or until golden. Add soy sauce and cook for 1 minute more. Leave to cool.

9 About 15 minutes before the casserole is cooked, sprinkle with the topping.

To reheat: cover with foil and give it 15 to 20 minutes in a moderate oven, Gas 3, 325°F, 160°C.

Grace Mulligan

LENTIL AND COTTAGE CHEESE CROQUETTES

Makes about 10.

75 g/3 oz red lentils
300 ml/½ pint water
About 4 spring onions
50 g/2 oz cottage cheese
25 to 50 g/1 to 2 oz wholemeal
    breadcrumbs
1 teaspoon dried thyme
½ teaspoon lemon juice, optional
Pepper and salt
25 g/1 oz sesame seeds for coating
A little oil for frying

1 Wash and pick over lentils for sticks and stones.

2 Cook lentils in the water. Bring to the boil, cover pan and simmer for 12 to 15 minutes, stirring occasionally,

until lentils are a soft paste and little water remains.

3 Strain if necessary and mash with a fork.

4 Chop spring onions finely and combine with the other ingredients except sesame seeds. Leave mixture in a cool place to firm up, about 30 minutes.

5 Make sausage shapes and roll them in sesame seeds.

6 Heat oil and fry lightly until golden brown.

Or, put on a greased baking tray and bake at the top of a moderate oven, Gas 4, 350°F, 180°C, for 25 to 30 minutes.

7 Serve with fresh vegetables.

Janet Horsley
Headingley, Yorkshire

SPLIT PEA PATTIES

Serves 2. Nice with Tangy Tomato Sauce (see right). Remember to start the night before!

100 g/4 oz green or golden split
    peas
A small clove of garlic, crushed
    (optional)
½ teaspoon ground cumin
½ teaspoon dried basil
A pinch of ground turmeric
1 egg, beaten
Salt and pepper
Oatmeal or bran for coating
50 g/2 oz butter for frying

1 Soak the split peas overnight in cold water.

2 Drain, cover in fresh cold water and simmer for about 30 to 35 minutes or until soft.

3 Drain the peas thoroughly or the mixture may be difficult to shape. If necessary, return them to the pan and stir over a moderate heat for a few

minutes to dry them out. Remove from the heat and mash the peas with the garlic, cumin, basil, turmeric, half the beaten egg and the seasoning.

4 When the mixture is cool enough to handle, shape it into four little patties. It is easier to do this if you wet your hands first.

5 Dip the patties into the remaining beaten egg (if there is not quite enough egg, add a few teaspoons of milk).

6 Toss the patties in the dry oatmeal or bran and leave them in the refrigerator for at least 20 minutes to allow them to firm up a little.

7 Melt the butter and fry the patties until they are crisp and heated through.

Grace Mulligan

TANGY TOMATO SAUCE

Good eaten hot with grills, or as a pizza topping. Keeps well in the refrigerator for 2 weeks. A liquidiser or food processor is useful. Makes about 450 ml/¾ pint.

1 tablespoon oil
1 large onion, finely chopped
A 400 g/14 oz can of tomatoes
3 tablespoons brown sugar
1 tablespoon Worcestershire sauce
2 teaspoons lemon juice
1 teaspoon dry mustard
Salt and black pepper
4 tablespoons malt vinegar
2 tablespoons water

1 Heat the oil and fry the onion for a few minutes until soft.

2 Liquidise the tomatoes and add them, with all the other ingredients, to the onions.

3 Bring to the boil and cook gently for 3 minutes, seasoning to taste.

Grace Mulligan

95

1 Put the oil and onion into a 1.1-litre/2-pint basin. Heat on full power for 4 minutes.
2 Stir in all the remaining ingredients. Heat, uncovered, on full power for 6 to 7 minutes.

MACARONI AND TUNA LAYER

For 2.

100 g/4 oz wholewheat macaroni
25 g/1 oz low-fat spread
25 g/1 oz wholemeal flour
300 ml/½ pint skimmed milk
Salt and pepper
An 85 g/3½ oz can of tuna fish in brine, drained
25 g/1 oz reduced-fat Cheddar cheese, grated
Chopped parsley to garnish (optional)

1 Cook the macaroni in boiling water for 10 to 15 minutes.
2 Meanwhile, melt the low-fat spread in a saucepan and add the flour. Cook for 1 minute, then gradually stir in milk. Bring to the boil and cook gently for a further 3 minutes. Season to taste.
3 Drain the macaroni and mix it with the sauce.
4 Pour half of the macaroni into an ovenproof dish and sprinkle the tuna fish over it. Cover with the remaining macaroni mixture.
5 Sprinkle the grated cheese on top and bake in a moderately hot oven, Gas 6, 400°F, 200°C, for about 10 minutes. Garnish with chopped parsley, or serve with green vegetables.

Jill Myers
The British Diabetic Association, London

PASTA AND VEGETABLE CASSEROLE

Enough for 2 but easy to make for 1. Delicious!

1 tablespoon oil
1 onion, roughly chopped
Half a green and half a red pepper, diced (or 1 whole green pepper)
1 courgette, trimmed and sliced
175 g/6 oz wholemeal pasta shapes
125 g/4 oz mushrooms, sliced
A 400 g/14 oz can of ready-chopped tomatoes, or 4 fresh tomatoes
A pinch of dried mixed herbs, or 1 tablespoon chopped fresh herbs
Pepper and salt
Chopped parsley to garnish

1 Heat oil and fry onion gently with pepper and courgette for 3 to 5 minutes until onion softens.
2 Meanwhile put pasta on to cook in boiling water until tender but not soft.
3 Mix mushrooms into other vegetables and cook for 2 minutes.
4 Add tomatoes and herbs, bring to the boil, then simmer without the lid for 5 minutes. Season to taste with pepper and a little salt.
5 Drain pasta, mix it into vegetables and serve sprinkled with chopped parsley.

For a change, serve sprinkled with grated cheese.

Mrs Debbie Munton
Llanedeyrn, Cardiff

1 Put the pasta into a 1.7-litre/3-pint casserole. Cover with boiling salted water and add 1 tablespoon oil. Stir well. Cover and cook on full power

for 6 minutes. Stir, then drain.
2 Put the onion, peppers and 1
tablespoon oil into a 1.3-litre/2½-
pint basin. Heat on full power for 3
minutes. Add the courgettes and
mushrooms and cook on full power
for 2 minutes.
3 Stir the tomatoes and herbs into
the vegetables and season lightly.
Cook on full power for 2 to 3
minutes.
4 Stir in the drained pasta and heat
on full power for 1 minute. Serve
sprinkled with chopped parsley, or
sometimes with grated cheese.

OMELETTES

*An omelette makes a quick and
nourishing meal; try some of these
different fillings. For 1.*

BASIC RECIPE
2 eggs
2 teaspoons water
Salt and pepper
A tiny piece of butter
2 teaspoons oil

1 Lightly beat together the eggs,
water and seasoning with a fork; do
not use a whisk.
2 Heat the butter and oil in a small
frying pan about 15 cm/6 inches
across. Make sure the bottom and
sides are thoroughly coated with fat.
3 Pour the eggs into the hot pan and,
after a few seconds, pull the cooked
edges in towards the centre and let
the uncooked egg run out and fill the
space.
4 Cook the omelette until set
underneath and slightly golden but
still moist on top.
5 Pile the chosen filling on to one
half of the omelette, and fold the
other half over to enclose the filling.
6 Serve at once with vegetables or a
salad.

Suggested fillings:

CHICKEN AND BACON

50 g/2 oz cooked chicken, diced
1 cooked rasher of bacon, diced
1 teaspoon chopped parsley
Butter

Warm the ingredients through
thoroughly in a little butter.

HAM AND MUSHROOM

50 g/2 oz cooked ham, diced
50 g/2 oz mushrooms, wiped and
    sliced
Butter
1 teaspoon chopped parsley

Toss the ham and mushrooms in a
little butter over moderate heat until
mushrooms are cooked and ham is
hot. Stir in parsley.

COURGETTES

50 g/2 oz courgettes, trimmed
    and diced
Butter
A pinch of mixed herbs

Cook the courgettes briefly in a little
butter. Sprinkle in the herbs.

TOMATO

A little butter
1 tomato, skinned (page 26) and
    diced
1 teaspoon chopped chives
25 g/1 oz grated cheese

Melt the butter in a small pan, add
the tomato and chives and warm them
through. Spread them over half the
omelette and cover with the grated
cheese. When the omelette is folded,
there will be enough heat in the eggs
to melt the cheese.

Grace Mulligan

SAVOURY STUFFED OMELETTE

Serves 1. Delicious!

1½ tablespoons oil
½ small onion, sliced
100 g/4 oz cooked shelled
   prawns
½ red or green chilli, deseeded
   and finely chopped
A few sprigs of fresh parsley,
   chopped
50 g/2 oz beansprouts
1 teaspoon light soy sauce
Salt and pepper
1 tablespoon water
2 eggs
Sliced cucumber, spring onion
   curls or parsley to garnish

1 Heat 1 tablespoon of the oil in a
small frying pan and cook the onion,
prawns, chilli, parsley and
beansprouts for a few minutes,
until hot but not browned.
2 Add the soy sauce and salt and
pepper to taste.
3 Remove the filling from the pan,
set aside and keep warm.
4 Heat the ½ tablespoon of oil in
the pan. Beat the eggs together and
add 1 tablespoon water, salt and
pepper.
5 Pour the egg mixture into the pan
and cook quickly until the omelette
has set. As it cooks, use a fork to pull
aside the set mixture and let the
runny mixture flow underneath.

6 Place the filling on one half of the
omelette and fold over the other half.
Turn omelette on to a warmed plate.
7 Serve at once, garnished with sliced
cucumber, spring onion curls or
parsley.

Jennie Siew Lee Cook
York

CHEESY EGGS WITH SPINACH

For 2.

2 eggs
450 g/ 1 lb fresh spinach
Buttered wholemeal toast for
   serving

SAUCE
15 g/½ oz butter
1 tablespoon flour
300 ml/½ pint chicken stock
75 g/3 oz strong-flavoured cheese,
   grated

1 Cover the eggs with cold water,
bring them to the boil, then reduce
the heat and boil gently for 10
minutes. Put them in cold water and
shell them.
2 Put the spinach on to cook for 5
minutes. Then drain, chop small and
drain it again.
3 Put the spinach into a shallow
heatproof dish.
4 Meanwhile, in a small saucepan
melt the butter, add the flour and

cook for 1 minute.
5 Gradually pour in the chicken stock, stirring all the time, and bring up to the boil. Remove from the heat and stir in 50 g/2 oz of the cheese.
6 Cut the eggs in half and arrange them, yolks down, on the spinach. Pour over the cheese sauce and sprinkle with the remaining cheese.
7 Put the dish under a very hot grill to brown the top.
8 Serve with buttered wholemeal toast.

Grace Mulligan

1 Hard-boil eggs as above.
2 Wash the spinach well, drain and put it in a mixing bowl. Cover with clear film and cook on full power for 5 minutes. Drain well, then chop. Drain again, squeezing out as much water as possible.
3 Put the spinach in a shallow 18-cm/7-inch dish.
4 Put the butter in a 600-ml/1-pint jug and heat on full power for 30 seconds. Stir in the flour and gradually blend in the stock. Heat on full power for 1½ minutes, then stir in 50 g/2 oz of the cheese. Heat on full power for a further 30 seconds.
5 Finish as steps 6 and 7 above and serve with buttered toast.

EGG AND LEEK NESTS

For 2, but it's easy to halve the ingredients for 1 person.

225 g/8 oz young leeks
A knob of butter
Salt and pepper
2 eggs
2 tablespoons milk
A shake of paprika

1 Top and tail the leeks and remove any very coarse green tops. Cut in

half lengthways and wash under a running tap to remove any grit. Then slice them.
2 Cook the leeks gently in the butter over a medium heat, stirring all the time. Season lightly and keep hot.
3 Scramble the beaten eggs with the milk and take off the heat when just set. Season with salt and pepper.
4 Arrange the shredded leeks on two hot plates, making a nest.
5 Spoon the eggs into the nests, dust lightly with paprika and serve at once.

Grace Mulligan

1 Prepare the leeks as above, then slice into strips about 7 mm/¼ inch wide.
2 Put the leeks in a basin with the butter. Heat on full power for 4 to 5 minutes, stirring once.
3 In a jug, mix together the eggs and milk. Heat on full power for 1¼ to 1½ minutes, stirring once. The eggs should be creamy.
4 Arrange the leeks on two hot serving plates, making a nest. Season lightly. Spoon the eggs into the nest, dust lightly with paprika and serve at once.

SHRIMP EGG FU-YUNG

For 2. Cooked finely sliced pork, beef, chicken or turkey may all be substituted for the shrimps.

2 tablespoons oil
1 small onion, chopped
50 g/2 oz mushrooms, wiped and sliced
1 spring onion, chopped
50 g/2 oz cooked shelled shrimps
1 tablespoon light soy sauce
½ tablespoon dark soy sauce

A pinch of salt
½ teaspoon sugar
3 eggs

SAUCE
75 ml/2½ fl oz chicken stock
1 teaspoon light soy sauce
1 teaspoon cornflour mixed with 1
   tablespoon cold water
A pinch of salt

1 Heat one tablespoon of the oil in a
wok or large frying pan and cook the
onion, mushrooms and spring onion
for one minute. Stir in the shrimps,
soy sauces, salt and sugar. Mix well
and leave to cool.
2 Beat the eggs together and add the
cooled shrimp mixture to them.
3 Heat up one tablespoon oil in a
wok or frying pan and ladle in half
of the egg mixture.
4 Cook the eggs until the underside is
lightly browned, then turn over and
cook the other side. Set aside on a
hot plate and keep warm while the
remaining fu-yung mixture is cooked
in the same way. Turn this out on to
another hot plate.
5 For the sauce: put the chicken
stock, soya sauce, cornflour mixture
and salt into the wok and, stirring
continuously, heat until the sauce
thickens. Pour the sauce over the fu-
yung and serve with rice or boiled
potatoes.

Jennie Siew Lee Cook
York

CHEESE AND CAULI-FLOWER SOUFFLÉ
For 2.

Half a small cauliflower
15 g/½ oz margarine or butter
15 g/½ oz flour
150 ml/¼ pint milk
50 g/2 oz grated cheese
2 eggs, separated
Pepper and salt

100

1 Preheat oven to moderately hot,
Gas 5, 375°F, 190°C.
2 Make cuts in cauliflower stem, so
that it will cook evenly throughout.
Steam it until nearly tender. Or, put
it in a saucepan with a good, tight-
fitting lid and 1.5 cm/½ inch of
water and simmer until nearly tender,
8 to 10 minutes.
3 Break cooked cauliflower into
florets, cutting the stem into bite-
sized pieces, and put in a 1-litre/1½-
pint greased soufflé dish or casserole.
4 Melt margarine or butter in a pan,
add flour and let it sizzle for 1
minute.
5 Mix in milk, stir as it thickens and
cook for 3 minutes.
6 Take pan off heat and beat in
cheese and egg yolks.
7 Whisk egg whites to a stiff froth
and gently fold into the sauce.
8 Pour sauce over cauliflower and
put it at once into the oven to cook
for 30 minutes. (As soufflés tend to
fall when cold air reaches them, try
not to open oven door during
cooking.) Serve immediately.

Judith Adshead
Porth Colmon, Gwynedd

GLAMORGAN SAUSAGES
*For 1 or 2, to eat hot with a Tomato
Sauce (opposite) and potatoes, or cold
with a salad. Freeze well.*

75 g/3 oz mature Cheddar
   cheese, grated
75 g/3 oz fresh brown or white
   breadcrumbs
1 small onion, finely chopped
Half a large egg, beaten
½ teaspoon dried mixed herbs
½ teaspoon mustard powder
Salt and pepper

COATING
Half a large egg, beaten
50 g/2 oz fresh or dried
   breadcrumbs

Oil for frying

1 Mix together the first seven ingredients. Roll the mixture into six sausage shapes.
2 Dip each sausage in the beaten egg, then coat with the breadcrumbs.
3 Leave in a cool place for 30 minutes, then fry the sausages in hot oil for 6 to 8 minutes turning them frequently.
4 Drain on kitchen paper and serve hot.

Margaret Heywood
Todmorden, Yorkshire

QUICK TOMATO SAUCE

Goes nicely with Glamorgan Sausages (above).

1 teaspoon cornflour
1 tablespoon milk
A 220 g/8 oz can of tomatoes, drained and chopped small
1 dessertspoon tomato ketchup
A pinch of sugar
A pinch of basil, oregano or mixed herbs
Pepper and salt

1 Mix the cornflour into the milk.
2 Put all the ingredients together in a small pan over gentle heat and stir as it thickens and comes to the boil

Mary Watts

Microwave

1 Put the cornflour into a 600-ml/1-pint jug. Mix to a smooth paste with the milk.
2 Stir in the remaining ingredients. Cook on full power for 4 to 5 minutes, stirring after half of the time.
3 Stir well then serve.

POTATO, HAM AND EGG PIE

Enough for 1, but it's easy to make more. A favourite way to serve potato.

1 tablespoon oil
1 onion, finely chopped
1 tablespoon flour
1 teaspoon made mustard
Salt and pepper
A dash of Worcestershire sauce
7 tablespoons milk
Butter or margarine for greasing
200 g/7 oz boiled potatoes, sliced
1 hard-boiled egg, sliced
75 g/3 oz cooked ham or bacon, chopped
40 to 50 g/1½ to 2 oz grated cheese (optional)

1 Heat the oil in a frying pan and cook the onion until soft.
2 Add the flour and cook for 1 minute, then stir in the mustard, seasoning, Worcestershire sauce and milk. Cook until the sauce thickens.
3 Arrange half the potato slices in a well-buttered oven dish. Cover with half the sauce, then arrange the sliced egg and chopped ham on top. Cover with the remaining sauce and potato slices.
4 Bake in a hot oven, Gas 8, 450°F, 250°C for 12 to 15 minutes or until the top is lightly browned.

Variation: sprinkle the top with grated cheese before baking.

Microwave

1 Put oil and onion in a 600-ml/1-pint jug and cook on full power for 1 to 2 minutes to soften.
2 Stir in the flour, mustard, salt, pepper, Worcestershire sauce and milk. Cook, uncovered, on full power for 2 minutes or until the sauce thickens. Stir after 2 minutes.
3 Arrange the potato slices in a

buttered dish. Pour over it half the onion sauce, then arrange the egg and ham on top. Cover with remaining sauce and then the rest of the potatoes.

4 Cook, uncovered, on full power for 3 minutes.

5 Brown the top (adding grated cheese if you like it) under a hot grill.

Joan Tyers
Wingate, Co. Durham

POTATO SLICE

Serves 2. Simple, tasty and fits nicely in a 25-cm/10-inch frying pan.

2 medium potatoes, peeled
2 rashers bacon, chopped
1 onion, chopped
1 egg, beaten
2 tablespoons milk
Salt and pepper
25 g/1 oz fat

1 Grate the potatoes into a bowl and stir in the bacon, onion, egg, milk and seasoning.

2 Heat the fat in a frying pan, then press in the potato mixture.

4 Cook for 10 minutes, then turn it over and cook for a further 10 minutes.

Mrs S. E. Firth
Bradford, West Yorkshire

SAVOURY POTATO BAKE WITH FRANKFURTERS

Serves 2, but easy to make just for one. Very satisfying.

2 medium potatoes, peeled
1 small onion, roughly chopped
A knob of butter, and a little for greasing
100 g/4 oz Cheddar cheese, grated
1 egg, beaten

A 200 g/7 oz can of sweetcorn, drained
Black pepper
2 or 4 Frankfurters, depending on size
2 tomatoes, skinned (page 26) and sliced

1 Boil the potato and onion together in salted water until cooked, then drain and mash together. Add a knob of butter, half the cheese and the beaten egg. Stir in half of the sweetcorn and season with black pepper.

2 Spread the potato mixture in a buttered ovenproof dish, slice the Frankfurters and arrange them on top, then add the remaining sweetcorn and the tomatoes. Finally, sprinkle with the rest of the cheese.

3 Bake in a preheated moderately hot oven, Gas 6, 400°F, 200°C, for 20 to 25 minutes, or until the cheese is golden brown.

Miss G. J. Miles
Southend on Sea, Essex

Microwave

1 Quarter the potatoes and put them with the onion into an 18-cm/7-inch soufflé-type dish. Sprinkle with 4 measured 15 ml tablespoons cold water. Cover with clear film and cook on full power for 6 minutes. Stand for 5 minutes.

2 Then drain and mash with the butter, half the cheese and the beaten egg. Stir in half the sweetcorn and season with freshly ground black pepper.

3 Slice the Frankfurters and arrange them over the potato. Sprinkle with the remaining sweetcorn and arrange the tomato slices on top. Finally sprinkle with the remaining cheese.

4 Heat on full power for 6 to 8 minutes.

5 Then brown the top under a preheated grill.

102

HOT VEGETABLE PANCAKES

Serves 2; very filling and satisfying.

225 g/8 oz parsnips, scrubbed
   and sliced
325 g/12 oz mixed raw vegetables
   e.g. carrots, leeks, cauliflower,
   peas, whatever you have
15 g/½ oz butter
Milk
4 cooked wholemeal pancakes
   (page 139)
75 g/3 oz matured Cheddar cheese,
   grated

1 Cook the parsnips in boiling salted
water until tender.
2 In another pan, bring carrots (if
using) to the boil, add the other
chosen vegetables and cook until
tender but not soft.
3 Drain the parsnips and mash them
up with the butter and a little milk.
Add the cooked vegetables to this.
4 Place a quarter of the vegetable
mixture on each pancake and roll
them up. Place them in a lightly
buttered ovenproof dish and cover
with the grated cheese.
5 Either put the dish under a hot grill
until the cheese melts or, heat in a
moderate oven, Gas 4, 350°F,
180°C, for 10 to 15 minutes.

                      Grace Mulligan

Microwave

VEGETABLES WITH CHEESE

*A substantial dish on its own for 2.
Reheats well; can also be served with
baked jacket potatoes to accompany
grilled chops or cold meats. This recipe
won Mrs Webster a place in the semi-
finals of a microwave cooking
competition organised by Sharp. The
conventional method follows this
microwave version.*

2 medium leeks, well washed
2 medium courgettes, trimmed
   and sliced
225 g/8 oz broccoli
Two 15 ml tablespoons water
100 g/¼ lb grated cheese
1 tomato, sliced
Microwave browning or paprika
   (optional)

1 Cut the leeks into 1-cm/½-inch
pieces and put them in a shallow 18-
cm/7-inch flan dish. Arrange the
courgettes on top of the leeks.
2 Trim the broccoli stalks and divide
into 4 equal portions. Arrange these
on top of the courgettes so that the

103

stalks are pointing towards the edge of the dish. Sprinkle over the water and cover the dish completely with clear film. Cook on full power for 6 minutes.

3 Loosen the film and drain off any excess water. Remove film completely, then sprinkle over the cheese. Arrange the tomato slices on top of the cheese. Cook uncovered, for a further 2 minutes on full power.

If you wish you can sprinkle the cheese with a little microwave browning or paprika to give the cheese a 'brown' appearance. However, the dish is so colourful that this is not really necessary.

Mrs Jean Webster
Lea, Lancashire

CONVENTIONAL METHOD

1 Cut leeks into 1-cm/½-inch slices and cook them in a close-fitting pan until almost tender.

2 At the same time, cook the broccoli and courgettes separately so that they are still crunchy and keep their good green colours. Do not let them go soft and floppy.

3 Arrange leeks in a heatproof dish, then make a layer of courgettes and finally the broccoli, with the stems to the outer edge of the dish.

4 Over this spread the cheese and decorate with tomato slices.

5 Put the dish into a hot oven, Gas 6, 400°F, 200°C for 20 minutes. The cheese melts into the vegetables but it still looks attractive and there is no need for paprika – or microwave browning!

Chapter 7

Salads and Vegetables

SALAD DRESSING

An old recipe quite worth the trouble as it will keep for several weeks in the refrigerator. Makes 300 ml/½ pint.

2 eggs, lightly beaten
75 g/3 oz sugar
1 level teaspoon dry mustard
150 ml/¼ pint milk
75 ml/3 fl oz vinegar
1 level teaspoon salt
15 g/½ oz margarine

1 Put all ingredients in a double saucepan or a basin, set over a pan of simmering water. Let it slowly come to the boil, stirring about every 5 minutes, for 30 minutes. If it should curdle, whisk with an egg-beater.
2 Once mixture has boiled, take pan off heat and allow to cool a little before bottling.

Mary Hunter
Addingham, Yorkshire

FRENCH DRESSING

3 tablespoons salad oil
1 tablespoon cider or wine
   vinegar
A squeeze of lemon juice
1 teaspoon sugar (try Barbados)
¼ teaspoon salt
A knife end of mustard
Freshly grated black pepper

1 Combine all ingredients in a screwtop jar and shake up well immediately before using.

Mary Watts

SOY SAUCE DRESSING

Makes about 150 ml/¼ pint. Keeps in the refrigerator for 6 or 7 days. Goes well with Rice Salad (page 108); or try it with a salad of beansprouts, bamboo shoots and fresh mushrooms.

5 tablespoons olive oil
2 tablespoons soy sauce

1 tablespoon lemon juice
A large clove of garlic, crushed
½ teaspoon peeled and chopped,
   or grated fresh root ginger
Salt and pepper

1 Combine all ingredients together in a screwtop jar and shake up well before using.

Grace Mulligan

TOMATO DRESSING

Makes about 150 ml/¼ pint. Very nice served with Green Split Pea Salad (page 109). Eat within 3 to 4 days before the garlic goes stale.

150 ml/¼ pint canned tomato
   juice
½ level teaspoon sugar
A clove of garlic, crushed
1 tablespoon chopped chives
1 tablespoon olive oil, or good
   salad oil
2 teaspoons lemon juice
Pepper and salt

1 In a small pan, mix the tomato juice and sugar. Bring it to the boil and boil for 1 or 2 minutes. Allow to cool.
2 Mix all the other ingredients into the cooled tomato juice, adding pepper and a little salt. Put all into a screwtop jar and shake well before serving.

Grace Mulligan

 Microwave

1 Put the tomato juice and sugar into a 600-ml/1-pint jug. Heat on full power for 2 to 2½ minutes, until it is boiling, then allow to cool.
2 Mix all the other ingredients into the cooled tomato juice, adding pepper and a little salt. Pour all of it into a screwtop jar and shake well before serving.

COTTAGE CHEESE AND YOGHURT DRESSING

This low-fat dressing keeps for a week in the refrigerator. Especially nice with Savoury Stuffed Apples, Chicken and Grape Salad, Potato and Herring Salad and Pasta Salad – all in this chapter.

225 g/8 oz cottage cheese
150 ml/5 fl oz natural yoghurt
2 tablespoons salad dressing,
    salad cream or mayonnaise
1 tablespoon vinegar – cider or
    wine vinegar is best
1 tablespoon lemon juice

1 Sieve cottage cheese into a bowl.
2 Add rest of ingredients and beat well together.

To vary flavour: made mustard or horseradish sauce can be added, to taste.

Mrs Margaret Heywood
Todmorden, Yorkshire

SAVOURY STUFFED APPLES

For 2.

2 large, red, crisp apples
A little lemon juice
1 stick of celery (optional)
25 g/1 oz raisins, roughly chopped
25 g/1 oz stoned dates, chopped
25 g/1 oz chopped nuts or seeds,
    e.g. walnuts, cashews, sunflower
    seeds
Salad dressing to bind – Cottage
    Cheese and Yoghurt
    Dressing (above) is ideal
Lettuce leaves or cress for serving

1 Take a slice off the top of each apple.
2 Remove apple core and carefully take out apple flesh to leave a firm shell.
3 Brush cut surfaces of apple with lemon juice.
4 Chop apple flesh and mix with the finely sliced celery, dried fruits and nuts. Bind them together with dressing.
5 Pile mixture into apple cases, put tops back on and serve on a bed of lettuce or cress.

Mrs Margaret Heywood
Todmorden, Yorkshire

POTATO AND HERRING SALAD

For 2.

225 g/8 oz cold cooked potato
1 pickled herring (page 43) or
    rollmop
2 spring onions or 1 small onion,
    finely chopped
Cottage Cheese and Yoghurt
    Dressing (left)
Lettuce leaves and brown bread
    for serving

1 Roughly chop the potato.
2 Snip the herring into bite-sized pieces.
3 Mix all together with onions and enough dressing to bind.
4 Serve on a bed of lettuce with brown bread.

Mrs Margaret Heywood
Todmorden, Yorkshire

TUNA SALAD

A tasty snack for 2.

1 small onion or 2 to 3 spring
    onions, finely chopped
15 g/½ oz butter or margarine or
    cooking oil (optional)
A 100 g/4 oz can of tuna, or half
    of a large can, drained
1 hard-boiled egg, roughly
    chopped

Salt and pepper
2 to 3 tablespoons salad cream,
   mayonnaise, or Cottage Cheese
   and Yoghurt Dressing (page
   107)
A squeeze of lemon juice
   (optional)
Lettuce leaves or cress for serving

1 If you do not like the taste of raw
onion, cook it in butter or oil or even
in the oil from the tuna can, until
soft but not browning.
2 Break up tuna in a bowl and stir in
onion, egg, seasoning to taste and
enough salad cream to bind mixture
together.
3 Serve with a squeeze of lemon juice
in lettuce leaves, or on a bed of cress,
or on toast.

Mrs Doris Wilkinson
Hull, Humberside

CHICKEN AND GRAPE SALAD
For 2.

1 cooked, skinned chicken joint,
   or about 150 g/6 oz cooked
   chicken
100 g/4 oz seedless grapes, roughly
   chopped or halved
4 to 5 tablespoons Cottage Cheese
   and Yoghurt Dressing (page
   107)
Curry powder or paste – about $\frac{1}{2}$
   teaspoon – to taste
Lettuce leaves

1 Cut chicken into bite-sized pieces.
Add grapes.
2 Put dressing into a bowl and blend
in curry powder or paste, adding
more if you like to suit your taste.
3 Gently mix in chicken and grapes.
Serve on a bed of lettuce.

Mrs Margaret Heywood
Todmorden, Yorkshire

PASTA SALAD
*For 2. A crisp, green salad goes well
with this.*

50 g/2 oz wholemeal pasta
2 to 3 spring onions or 1 small
   onion, finely chopped
1 stick of celery, finely chopped
Pieces of red and green pepper,
   chopped
A small piece of cucumber, peeled
   and chopped
A few chopped nuts, if liked
Cottage Cheese and Yoghurt
   Dressing (page 107)

1 Cook pasta in boiling salted water
until just tender. Drain, rinse with
cold water and drain again
thoroughly.
2 When pasta is cold, put it into a
bowl with the rest of the salad
ingredients.
3 Add enough dressing to give a
creamy consistency. Wholewheat pasta
needs more dressing than the white-
flour variety.
4 Serve with a green salad.

Mrs Margaret Heywood
Todmorden, Yorkshire

RICE SALAD
*This makes a substantial and nutritious
dish. It looks attractive served in lettuce
leaves. For 1 or 2.*

75 g/3 oz round grain brown
   rice (nicest with round, but long
   grain rice can be used)
Half a red pepper, chopped
2 spring onions, finely chopped
25 g/1 oz raisins
25 g/1 oz salted peanuts
1 tablespoon chopped parsley
2 tablespoons Soy Sauce Dressing
   (page 106)
Pepper and salt

1 Cook the rice in simmering water
until just done. Drain through a sieve
and cool under running cold water.

Or cook it by the absorption method (page 88).
2 Mix all the ingredients together, seasoning to taste with pepper and salt.

Grace Mulligan

THREE BEAN SALAD

For 2. If you add the chicken, it makes a very good lunchtime snack.

75 g/3 oz red kidney beans,
    cooked weight
75 g/3 oz haricot beans, canned or
    home-cooked
2 tablespoons French Dressing
    (page 106)
75 g/3 oz fresh green beans
3 spring onions, sliced
1 tablespoon fresh parsley
50 to 75 g/2 or 3 oz cold cooked
    chicken (optional)
Salt and pepper

To cook the dried beans:

50 g/2 oz dry red kidney beans and 50 g/2 oz haricots will give 75 g/3 oz of each when cooked.

1 Remember to start the night before by soaking both red kidney and haricots in separate bowls of cold water.
2 Cook them separately in fresh cold water, bringing them to boil and then boiling hard for 10 minutes before reducing heat and simmering until tender, about 45 to 50 minutes in all. Take care not to let them crack open or go mushy. Using a pressure cooker halves the cooking time but it is hard to gauge how long to give before the beans burst.

For the salad

1 As soon as you have drained them, toss the hot beans into the French dressing. If using canned beans, drain and then rinse them under the cold tap. Toss in dressing.
2 String the green beans. Top and tail them and cut into 1-cm/½-inch pieces. Cook them in a little simmering water for 7 to 8 minutes or less so that they are cooked but still crisp. Drain well.
3 Now mix all the ingredients together, seasoning carefully with pepper and a little salt before serving.

Grace Mulligan

GREEN SPLIT PEA SALAD

For 1 or 2. The dressed peas keep for 2 days but keep the fresh salad ingredients ready to toss in at the last minute. Remember to start the night before.

75 g/ 3 oz green split peas
3 tablespoons Tomato Dressing
    (page 106)
Pepper and salt
2 spring onions, sliced
2 very firm red tomatoes,
    deseeded and chopped small
1 large crisp stick of celery,
    trimmed and sliced
Chopped parsley

1 Soak the peas in cold water overnight.
2 Drain peas and put in a saucepan; cover with fresh cold water and bring to the boil. Boil them hard for 10 minutes, then simmer until just done but not mushy, or the texture of the salad will be spoilt.
3 Drain the hot peas and mix with the dressing. Season well and leave until cold.
4 Gently toss in the other ingredients, saving the parsley to sprinkle on top.

Grace Mulligan

CORN RAITA

A pleasant accompaniment to some of the other recipes contributed to this book by Nimmi Singh: Sheekh Kebabs (page 82), Lamb Kofta Curry (page 81), Turkey Kebabs (page 64) and Potato Bhaji (page 116).

50 g/2 oz frozen sweetcorn
150 ml/¼ pint natural yoghurt
A pinch of salt
½ teaspoon cumin seed
Ground black pepper
A pinch of paprika

1 Cook the corn in boiling salted water until tender, then rinse it in cold water and drain thoroughly, patting it dry with a cloth or paper towel.
2 Add the corn to the yoghurt and season with salt.
3 Put the cumin seeds into a frying pan and cook (that is, dry-roast) over a moderate heat for about 1 minute. Crush the hot seeds with the end of a rolling pin.
4 Put the yoghurt and corn mixture into a bowl, grind a little black pepper over the top then scatter over the crushed cumin seeds and a little paprika.

Nirmal Singh
Nuneaton, Warwickshire

MINTY TOMATO SALAD

Enough for 2 as a starter with soft brown rolls or hot brown bread. Makes a good accompaniment to cold roast lamb.

225 g/8 oz tomatoes, skinned
  (page 26)
Salt and pepper
A pinch of sugar
3 or 4 teaspoons freshly chopped
  mint

DRESSING
3 tablespoons soured cream or
  natural yoghurt
¼ teaspoon grated lemon rind
1 tablespoon lemon juice
Lettuce leaves for serving
Sprigs of mint to garnish

1 Quarter the skinned tomatoes and remove the seeds. Sprinkle lightly with salt, pepper, sugar and a little chopped mint.
2 Put the soured cream or yoghurt into a bowl and mix in the lemon rind and juice and more chopped mint.
3 Arrange a few crisp lettuce leaves on 2 plates, lay the tomatoes on top and spoon the soured cream/yoghurt dressing over them. Garnish with sprigs of fresh mint.

The June Hulbert Cookbook

YOGHURT CHUTNEY or RAITA

This is a good, hot, spicy dressing. If you prefer to leave out the ginger or chilli, add more mint and freshly ground black pepper. Nice to eat with Chicken Fingers (page 57), Savoury Semolina and other Indian dishes, curries etc., see Index.

150 g/5 oz natural yoghurt
1.5-cm/½-inch cube of peeled fresh
    ginger
Half a fresh green chilli (optional)
1 tablespoon chopped fresh mint
Salt and pepper

1 Put yoghurt in a bowl.
2 Chop ginger, chilli and mint and mix into yoghurt with salt and pepper to taste.

Mrs Jaswant Chopra
Childwall, Liverpool

CABBAGE WITH SOURED CREAM SAUCE

For 2. A delicious way to serve the humble cabbage.

15 g/½ oz butter
1 teaspoon vinegar
1 tablespoon water
1 onion, finely chopped

175 g/6 oz white cabbage,
    shredded and washed

SAUCE
15 g/½ oz butter
15 g/½ oz flour
150 ml/¼ pint milk
Salt and pepper
3 tablespoons soured cream*

*See page 74 for other recipes using soured cream

1 Melt the butter in a saucepan, pour in the vinegar and water and bring to the boil. Add the onion and cook for 2 minutes.
2 Put the cabbage into the pan, cover with a tight-fitting lid and cook for about 10 minutes until the cabbage is tender. If necessary, add a little water to prevent it sticking.
3 For the sauce, melt the butter in a small pan, add the flour and cook for 1 minute. Gradually pour in the milk, stirring all the time, and heat until the sauce boils. Simmer the sauce for 1 minute then add the seasoning and soured cream.
4 Pour the sauce over the cabbage, mix well together and serve at once.

Joan Tyers
Wingate, Co. Durham

 Microwave

1 Put the butter and onion into a 15-cm/6-inch soufflé dish and cook on full power for 1 minute.
2 Add the cabbage, vinegar and 2 tablespoons water. Cover the dish and cook on full power for 5 minutes. Then leave to stand, covered, while you make the sauce.
3 Put the butter into a jug and heat on full power for 30 to 40 seconds. Stir in the flour and gradually blend in the milk. Heat on full power for 2 minutes, stirring once.
4 When the sauce has boiled, stir in the soured cream and seasoning and heat on full power for a further 30

seconds if necessary.
5 Uncover the cabbage and stir in the sauce, mixing well so that the cabbage is completely coated in the sauce. Serve at once.

GLAZED CARROTS

Accompanying Mandarin Chicken (page 59) with this dish, Mrs Roberts won a place in a national microwave cooking competition conducted by Sharp.

225 g/8 oz baby carrots
1 teaspoon sugar
One 15 ml tablespoon water
A knob of butter
Chopped parsley to garnish

1 Scrub the carrots. Put them in a dish, add sugar and water, cover and cook on full power for 3 to 4 minutes.
2 Drain, add butter, stir and garnish with chopped parsley.

Mrs Ann Roberts
Tarporley, Cheshire

CONVENTIONAL METHOD
1 Scrub the carrots and put them into a pan with the sugar and 120 ml/4 fl oz water. Bring to the boil, cover pan and simmer (making sure the pan does not boil dry) for about 6 minutes or until they are tender, slightly crisp, but not soft.
2 Drain, add butter and stir.
3 Serve sprinkled with chopped parsley.

CELERY FRITTERS

The batter is enough for 6 sticks of celery, almost too much for 2 people! The fritters are so delicious, however, that after you have eaten as many as you can, turn to page 114 for a Deep Fried Mushroom recipe using the spare batter. Serve as a first course with a dip (see below) or with grilled meats such as chops or sausages.

Sticks of celery
Boiling water

BATTER
50 g/2 oz plain flour – delicious with wholemeal
Salt and pepper
½ teaspoon baking powder
1 beaten egg
A scant 150 ml/¼ pint milk
Oil or fat for deep-frying

1 Clean celery, remove strings and cut into 10-cm/4-inch lengths. Cover with boiling water and leave for 10 minutes. Then drain and wipe dry.
2 Meanwhile, mix batter. Put flour in a bowl with salt and pepper. Mix in baking powder, make a well in centre and drop in the egg. Gradually beat in enough milk to make a smooth thick consistency.
3 Heat oil until very hot but not smoking.
4 Dip celery fingers into batter and fry until golden and crisp.
5 Drain on kitchen paper and eat at once. They are crisp and delicious.

Mrs A. M. Taylor
Boyton, Suffolk

A DIP FOR CELERY FRITTERS

2 tablespoons good thick mayonnaise
2 tablespoons natural yoghurt
A 2.5-cm/1-inch piece of cucumber, chopped
1 tablespoon freshly chopped mint
1 tablespoon freshly chopped parsley
Salt and freshly ground black pepper

1 Measure all the ingredients into a bowl.

2 Mix lightly and season to taste.
3 Serve well chilled.

Debbie Woolhead
Boston Spa, West Yorkshire

STIR-FRIED CHINESE LEAVES

For 2 – easy to make just enough for 1. Nice with chicken and other roast or grilled meats. Must be eaten the moment it is cooked or the Chinese leaves go soggy.

225 g/½ lb Chinese leaves
1 tablespoon oil
1 small onion, chopped
1 small clove of garlic, chopped
½ teaspoon grated fresh ginger,* or
    a pinch of ground ginger
A pinch of salt
½ teaspoon vinegar
½ teaspoon sugar
1 dessertspoon soy sauce

* See Soy Sauce Dressing (page 106) for another recipe using fresh ginger. Ground ginger is nothing like as good as fresh in these recipes.

1 Prepare all the ingredients before you start to cook, removing tough stalks on Chinese leaves before cutting it into manageable pieces.
2 Put a large shallow pan or wok on to a high heat.
3 Put in the oil, onion, garlic and ginger and fry for 1 minute.
4 Quickly add the chopped Chinese leaves and salt. Toss it all continuously, keeping the heat high.
5 Add the vinegar, sugar and soy sauce.
6 Lower heat and keep turning the vegetables for only one minute more. By now the liquid should be reduced to almost none and the Chinese leaves will be piping hot, brilliant green and white but still crisp. Serve at once.

Grace Mulligan

Microwave

The microwave is ideal for 'stir-frys', although really it is not frying in the true sense – it gives quick, crisp results.

1 Prepare all the ingredients before you start cooking. Remove any tough stalks from the Chinese leaves before cutting into 3.5 cm/1½ inch pieces.
2 Put the oil, garlic, ginger and onion into a large mixing bowl and heat on full power for 2 minutes.
3 Stir in the vinegar, soy sauce and sugar. Add the Chinese leaves, tossing them well so that they are coated in the sauce. Cover the dish with clear film and cook on full power for 3 minutes, stirring after 2 minutes and at the end of cooking.
4 Season with a little salt and serve immediately. The leaves will be a brilliant green and white with a crisp texture.

COURGETTES WITH TOMATOES

This versatile dish may be served cold as a starter, a salad with hot and cold meats, eaten hot as an accompanying vegetable, or tossed in freshly cooked pasta shapes. For 1 or 2 or more.

1 tablespoon oil
1 small onion, sliced
A clove of garlic, crushed
50 ml/2 fl oz dry white wine or
    dry cider
Salt and pepper
275 g/10 oz courgettes, wiped
225 g/8 oz tomatoes, skinned (page 26)
Chopped fresh parsley or chervil

1 Heat the oil in a saucepan and cook the onion until soft but not coloured. Add the garlic, wine and seasoning.
2 Top and tail the courgettes and cut into slices. Quarter the tomatoes and

remove the seeds.

3 Add the courgettes and tomatoes to the saucepan and cook slowly for 10 minutes without a lid, or longer if you prefer the courgettes softer.

4 Sprinkle with chopped parsley.

The June Hulbert Cookbook

1 Put the oil, onion and garlic into an 18-cm/7-inch soufflé-type dish. Heat on full power for 3 minutes.

2 Top and tail the courgettes and cut into slices. Cut the tomatoes into quarters and remove the seeds.

3 Stir the wine and courgettes into the onion. Cover with clear film and cook on full power for 2 minutes. Then add tomatoes and cook 2 minutes more.

4 Season with salt and pepper and sprinkle with parsley.

DEEP-FRIED MUSHROOMS

A delicious way to use up batter made for Celery Fritters (page 112). Alternatively, make these and use up the batter on the Celery Fritters! For 2 or more.

About 50 g/2 oz garlic and herb
   soft cream cheese
100 g/4 oz button mushrooms

1 Remove the stalks from the mushrooms. Sandwich two mushrooms together with a little cream cheese and secure with a cocktail stick. Repeat with remaining mushrooms.

2 Dip each pair of mushrooms into the leftover batter and deep-fry until golden brown and crisp.

3 Drain well, remove cocktail sticks and serve at once.

Debbie Woolhead
Boston Spa, West Yorkshire

114

CASSEROLED POTATOES WITH ONION AND GARLIC

For 2.

225 g/½ lb potatoes, peeled and
   thinly sliced
1 small shallot or onion, sliced
A clove of garlic, crushed
   (optional)
1 teaspoon chopped parsley
Salt and pepper (optional)
150 ml/¼ pint milk or single
   cream
25 g/1 oz butter
Salt and pepper to taste

1 Arrange half the potatoes in an ovenproof dish, cover with shallot, garlic and parsley. Season with salt and pepper.

2 Place the remaining potatoes neatly on the top and pour over the milk or cream. Season again, dot with butter and put the dish on a baking tray.

3 Bake in the centre of a moderate oven, Gas 4, 350°F, 180°C, for 1 hour.

Dilwen Phillips
Gileston, South Glamorgan

For this only half of the milk or cream is used – four 15 ml tablespoons. A little paprika is added for colour.

1 Arrange half the potato slices in a 12.5-cm/5-inch soufflé-type or casserole dish. Cover with the shallot, garlic and parsley. Season with salt and pepper.

2 Arrange the remaining potatoes overlapping neatly on the top. Pour over the 4 tablespoons milk or cream and dot with butter. Sprinkle the top with a little paprika and cover the dish with clear film.

3 Cook on full power for 5 to 6 minutes then let it stand for 5 minutes. The potatoes should be tender when pierced with a knife.

CHEESE-BAKED POTATOES

For 2. Delicious on their own or with cold meat.

2 medium potatoes
1 tablespoon milk
15 g/½ oz butter
1 egg, lightly beaten
Pepper and salt
50 g/2 oz grated Cheddar cheese
1 tablespoon chopped parsley, if
  liked

1 Scrub potatoes and bake them near top of a moderate oven, Gas 4, 350°C, 180°C, until soft to the touch, about 1¼ hours. Alternatively, they will cook in 1 hour in a moderately hot oven, Gas 6, 400°F, 200°C. To save more time, push a skewer right through the potatoes. The heat is conducted through the skewer so that the potato begins to cook from inside as well as the outside.

2 Wasting no time, cut each hot potato in half and scoop the flesh out into a basin.

3 Mash potato with milk and butter adding egg, pepper and a very little salt, the cheese and parsley.

4 Spoon the hot mixture back into the potato shells and either return them to the oven for 15 minutes or put them under the grill to brown.

Mrs S. Dislay
Newquay, Cornwall

The first way will make the skins more crisp.

1 Scrub the potatoes and dry on kitchen paper. Prick all over with a fork. Place the potatoes on a piece of

115

kitchen paper in the microwave, cook on full power for 7 to 8 minutes. Some microwave manufacturers recommend turning the potato over after half the cooking time.

2 Allow the potatoes to stand for 5 minutes, then cut them in half and carefully scoop out the potato, taking care not to tear the skin.

3 Mash the potato with the milk, butter, egg and season lightly with salt and pepper. Stir in the cheese and parsley.

4 Spoon the mixture back into the potato shells.

5 *Either* – place on a baking tray and cook in a conventional oven for 15 minutes at Gas 6, 400°F, 200°C, until crisp and brown.

Or – reheat on full power for 2 minutes then, if desired, brown under a hot grill for 2 to 3 minutes.

POTATO PUFFS

These are especially nice with bacon and peas.

225 g/8 oz firm cold boiled
    potatoes
A knob of butter
1 egg, separated
Pepper and a little salt
1 teaspoon flour, white or
    wholemeal
Oil or fat for frying (good with
    sunflower oil)

1 Mash the potatoes with a knob of butter, the egg yolk, seasoning and a little flour to make a firm mixture.

2 Beat egg white until stiff and mix it gently into potato mixture.

3 Heat fat or oil – you will need it 1 cm/½ inch deep in pan to ensure the potatoes do puff. Fry spoonfuls of the mixture until golden brown on both sides.

Mrs A. Hughes
Bethesda, Gwynedd

POTATO BHAJI

These spicy potatoes are delicious by themselves or served with a meat dish and rice or chappatis. For 2.

2 to 3 tablespoons oil
½ teaspoon cumin seeds
225 g/8 oz potatoes, peeled and cut
    into bite-sized pieces
½ teaspoon turmeric powder
¼ teaspoon chilli powder
½ teaspoon coriander powder
¼ teaspoon salt
Water
Chopped coriander or parsley
    leaves to garnish

1 Heat the oil in a shallow pan, add the cumin seeds and cook for about half a minute.

2 Add the potatoes and stir them around until they are well coated with oil. Add all the remaining spices and salt and mix well so that the spices coat the potato pieces.

3 Add about four tablespoons of water, cover the pan and cook very slowly until the potatoes are tender. Shake the pan occasionally to prevent sticking.

4 Remove the potatoes from the pan and put into a warmed serving dish. Sprinkle with the chopped coriander leaves or parsley.

Nirmal Singh
Nuneaton, Warwickshire

Microwave

1 Heat the oil in an 18 cm/7 inch shallow casserole on full power for 1 minute.

2 Add all the spices and heat for half a minute.

3 Add the potatoes, mix well to coat and stir in 2 to 3 tablespoons of water. Cover the dish and cook on full power for 5 minutes, stirring half way through.

4 Allow to stand covered for 2

minutes, then stir in salt to taste and
serve.

Nirmal Singh
Nuneaton, Warwickshire

MASHED POTATO

1 For 1: cook one 150 g/6 oz potato
in its jacket on full power for 5 to 6
minutes.
For 2: cook two 150 g/6 oz potatoes
in their jackets on full power for 7 to
9 minutes.
2 Let the potatoes stand for 2 to 3
minutes then scoop the flesh out of
the skin and mash with butter, milk,
salt and pepper to taste.

Yvonne Hamlett
Haddenham, Buckinghamshire

QUICK STIR-FRIED VEGETABLES WITH OYSTER SAUCE

*Enough for 2, but easy to do for 1. A
delicious way to cook green vegetables as
a change from boiling or steaming.
Cabbage, spring greens, Chinese leaves,
celery, crisp lettuce and watercress are
suitable. Must be served the moment it
is cooked, so it is a last-minute job.*

325 g/12 oz leafy vegetable of
   your choice
2 tablespoons oil
1 clove of garlic, chopped
1 tablespoon oyster sauce
Salt, pepper and a pinch of sugar

1 Prepare the vegetable, washing it
thoroughly, and cut or shred it into
bite-sized pieces. If it has thick stems
separate these from the rest as they
take longer to cook.
2 Heat the oil in a wok or large
frying pan and quickly fry the garlic
until lightly brown.
3 Add the stem pieces and cook for
3 to 4 minutes, tossing constantly over
quite a high heat.

4 Add the rest of the vegetable and
stir-fry only until its colour begins to
change to a more brilliant green.
5 Add the oyster sauce, a little salt,
pepper and sugar; stir and cook for 1
or 2 minutes more. Serve at once.

Jennie Siew Lee Cook
York

CHAPPATIS

*The quantity of flour you need will
depend on how many chappatis you
want to make: 100 g/4 oz flour would
make about 8 to 10, sufficient for 2
people with curries and other Indian
dishes.*

*If you cannot get chappati flour it is
possible to use finely ground strong
wholewheat flour. Put the flour into a
measure and then you can reckon that
the amount of water needed will be
approximately one third of that amount
– but it does depend on the nature of
the flour, the heat of your kitchen and
the extent of your experience!*

Chappati flour
Water
Melted butter

1 Put the flour in a bowl and mix in
sufficient water to give a dough
which is the consistency of putty.
Knead it well for 5 minutes, then
cover and put it aside for half an
hour.
2 Take a small piece of dough about
the size of a golf ball, knead it and
then roll it out on a floured surface
to a round about as thick as a 10p
piece. Prepare the rest of the dough
in the same way and keep them all
covered as you begin the cooking.
3 Heat a griddle or frying pan and
heat the grill until it is very hot.
4 Put one piece of the rolled-out
dough on to the griddle or frying pan
and reduce the heat to medium.
5 Cook for a few seconds until the
top begins to look dry. Then turn it

over and cook until brown spots
appear on the underneath.
6 Put the chappati under the grill
with the undercooked side uppermost.
It will start to blow up like a balloon
and brown spots will appear on this
side as well.
7 Put the chappati into a tea towel
and brush the top lightly with melted
butter or margarine.
8 Cook the rest of the chappatis in
the same way, stacking them buttered
sides together in the tea towel.
9 Wrap the tea towel in foil and keep
warm until needed.

It does take a time or two to get your
hand in at chappati-making. When
you are skilled, you will find you can
cook one in 30 seconds.

Nirmal Singh
Nuneaton, Warwickshire

SAVOURY PUDDING

*A well-flavoured variation on
Yorkshire Pudding, especially good with
roast pork. Rather a lot for 2 people to
eat all at once, but can be reheated
carefully in the grill pan or by
microwave, although the latter spoils the
crispness. Mrs Maxfield simply adds
sage and onion as she mixes the batter.
You may prefer to cook the onion a bit
more, as given below.*

100 g/4 oz plain flour, either
   white or an even mixture of
   white and wholemeal
1 level teaspoon dried sage or 2
   teaspoons chopped fresh sage
Salt
1 egg
300 ml/½ pint milk and water
   mixed
1 medium onion, finely chopped
A little dripping

1 Preheat oven to moderately hot,
Gas 6, 400°F, 200°C.
2 Mix flour, sage and salt in a bowl
and make a well in the centre.
3 Drop in egg and gradually beat in
the milk and water to form a batter
the consistency of pouring cream.
Beat well.
4 Put dripping from the tin in which
meat is roasting into a small roasting
tin. Add onion and cook in oven for
10 minutes.
5 Then pour in the batter and cook
at the top of the oven for 30
minutes.

Mrs A. Maxfield
Worksop, Nottingham

118

Chapter 8

Pies and Pasties Savoury and Sweet

QUICK EGG, BACON AND MUSHROOM PIE

If you like short cuts in the kitchen this recipe will appeal to you. Surprisingly, the pastry forms a golden crust all around the savoury filling and it seems like a crunchy omelette. If you use a large jug for beating the eggs, all the other ingredients can be mixed in it too. It's best served hot and fresh from the oven with a crisp green salad. Does not freeze well. Makes one 15-cm/6-inch pie.

75 g/3 oz bacon, finely chopped
75 g/3 oz mushrooms, sliced
2 eggs
120 ml/4 fl oz milk
100 g/4 oz shortcrust pastry mix, either white or wholemeal
1 tablespoon chopped parsley
25 g/1 oz grated cheese

1 Preheat oven to moderately hot, Gas 6, 400°F, 200°C, and put in a baking tray.
2 Fry bacon lightly, then toss mushrooms into the pan and fry them for 2 or 3 minutes.
3 Beat eggs and pour in the milk.
4 Mix all the ingredients together using all but 2 tablespoons of the cheese.
5 Pour the mixture into a greased flan dish, sprinkle over the reserved cheese, stand the dish on the hot baking tray and bake for 30 minutes. When cooked you will find that the pastry has formed nicely around the soft filling.

Mrs E. Jowett
Victoria, Australia

CHEESE AND LEEK FLAN
(Fflan caws a cenyn)

Serves 2, but very generously. There is enough to eat hot, then keep 2 portions

to eat cold or freeze for another day. Another recipe from Lucy Barton-Greenwood, 14, who took second place in the 1987 Junior Cook of the Year competition. This was her starter (see page 179 for the other dishes in her menu).

PASTRY
100 g/4 oz wholemeal flour
1 teaspoon baking powder
25 g/1 oz lard
25 g/1 oz butter
4 teaspoons cold water

FILLING
1 large leek
25 g/1 oz butter
A pinch of nutmeg
A pinch of cayenne pepper
Salt
3 eggs
50 ml/2 fl oz milk
2 tablespoons soured cream
175 g/6 oz grated Cheddar cheese

1 Preheat oven to moderately hot, Gas 6, 400°F, 200°C.
2 Start with the pastry. Put flour and baking powder into a bowl and rub in the lard and butter. Add sufficient water to give a soft dough.
3 Roll out the pastry and line an 18-cm/7-inch flan tin.
4 Wash and slice leek in 1 cm/½ inch slices.
5 Melt butter and cook leek slowly until tender. Add nutmeg, cayenne and a little salt.
6 Whisk eggs, milk, soured cream and a little salt together.
7 Sprinkle half of the grated cheese over bottom of flan. Spread the leek on top and cover with remaining cheese. Pour over egg mixture.
8 Bake for 20 minutes until the top is golden.

Lucy Barton-Greenwood
Radyr, Cardiff

A little paprika is used to colour the dish.
This cooks successfully on Low but if you have a 2-power microwave cooker then do not try it – the result is not satisfactory and the flan should be baked conventionally.

1 Make the pastry, as in step 1.
2 Roll out the pastry and line a 18-cm/7-inch ceramic flan dish. Cover the pastry with a piece of kitchen paper – pressing it down lightly. Cook on full power for 2 to 3 minutes. The pastry should have lost its wet and shiny look and now be dry.
3 Wash and slice the leek into 1-cm/½-inch slices. Put them in a small basin with the butter. Cook on full power for 3 to 4 minutes, stirring once. Stir in the nutmeg, cayenne and a little salt.
4 Whisk together the eggs, milk, soured cream and a little salt.
5 Sprinkle the base of the flan case with half of the cheese. Spread the leeks over the top. Cover with the remaining cheese, then pour over the egg mixture. Sprinkle a little paprika on the top for colour.
6 Cook on Low for 10 to 12 minutes until the surface is firm to the touch.

FISH PIE IN PUFF PASTRY

Start this recipe in good time so that the fish and mushroom filling can cool before it is put into the pastry. This pie freezes well. For 2.

125 g/4 oz fillet of white fish, any variety
125 g/4 oz smoked white fish – Finnan haddock or other smoked fillets are suitable
150 ml/¼ pint milk
60 g/1½ oz butter
Freshly ground black pepper
1 small onion, finely chopped
50 g/2 oz mushrooms, wiped and chopped
15 g/½ oz plain flour
1 to 2 tablespoons frozen sweetcorn
1 tablespoon chopped fresh parsley
Half a 370 g/14 oz packet of frozen puff pastry*

* *For another recipe using frozen puff pastry see Apple and Mincemeat Parcel (page 126).*

1 Preheat the oven to moderate, Gas 4, 350°F, 180°C.
2 Skin the fish by placing the fillet skin side down on a board and sliding a very sharp knife under the flesh just above the skin. This is done by just slicing the knife in at the tail end of the fillet. Then, holding the tail piece firmly to the board with the other hand, work the knife along until flesh is separated and skin remains on the board.
3 Put fish into a shallow ovenproof dish in which it neatly fits, just cover with milk, dot with 15 g/½ oz of the butter and grind on some black pepper.
4 Cover dish and cook for 15 minutes in the preheated oven. Then strain liquid into a measuring jug and, when the fish is cool, flake it in quite large pieces, carefully removing bones.
5 Meanwhile melt another 15 g/½ oz butter and fry onion until transparent. Then add mushrooms, raise heat and cook them for 2 or 3 minutes, stirring so that onion does not go brown.
6 Now for the sauce. Melt remaining 15 g/½ oz butter in a small pan, stir in the flour and cook it for 1 minute.
7 Gradually stir in all but a tablespoon of the milk strained from the fish. Stir over a low heat as it thickens. The consistency should be slightly thicker than for pouring. Simmer for 2 minutes.

121

8 Mix in the fish, onion and mushrooms, sweetcorn and nearly all of the parsley. Remove from heat and allow to cool.

9 When you are ready to cook the pie, preheat the oven to moderately hot, Gas 6, 400°F, 200°C.

10 Cut the pastry into 2 even pieces and roll out thinly, taking care to mend any holes.

11 Place a piece of pastry on to a damp baking sheet and spoon the fish mixture along the middle.

12 Dampen the edges of the pastry with water, cover with the remaining piece of pastry and press the edges to seal.

13 Crimp the edges with a fork and trim to make them tidy. Make parallel slashes across the top, but do not cut right through the pastry. Brush over with the remaining fishy milk.

14 Bake near the top of the oven for 30 minutes or until the pastry is well risen and golden.

15 Serve sprinkled with the remaining chopped parsley.

To reheat a single piece of pie wrap it in foil and put it in a warm oven, Gas 3, 325°F, 160°C for 15 minutes, then remove the foil and heat for a further few minutes to crisp up the pastry.

Mary Hunter
Addingham, West Yorkshire

SARDINE PASTIES

Makes 2: nice hot or cold; serve with a fresh Tomato Sauce (page 175).

SHORTCRUST PASTRY
100 g/4 oz plain flour, white or
    wholemeal
A pinch of salt
50 g/2 oz margarine and lard or
    butter, mixed
2 to 3 teaspoons water
A little milk

FILLING
A 120 g/4½ oz can of sardines
1 onion, finely chopped
1 medium potato, peeled and
    diced small
Salt and pepper
1 heaped teaspoon parsley, finely
    chopped
A pinch of mixed herbs
1 dessertspoon water

1 First make the pastry: mix flour and salt and rub in fat. Add water and mix to a dough, then let it rest in refrigerator for half an hour, especially if using wholemeal flour.

2 Cut pastry in half and roll out each piece to a circle 18 cm/7 inches across.

3 Preheat oven to moderately hot, Gas 6, 400°F, 200°C.

4 Now for the filling: drain oil from sardines and mash them with a fork, adding onion, potato, seasoning, parsley and herbs.

5 Mix in enough water just to moisten the filling.

6 Spoon half of the filling on to each piece of pastry.

7 Moisten edges of pastry, fold over to pasty shape, press edges together to seal and brush top with a little milk.

8 Bake near top of preheated oven for 15 minutes, then reduce heat to Gas 4, 350°F, 180°C, for 15 to 20 minutes more to cook filling through.

Mrs Anne Walton
Frome, Somerset

HAM AND LEEK FLAN

Makes 3 good helpings. Nice hot or cold. Freezes successfully. A good way to use meat from a Ham Shank (page 67).

SHORTCRUST PASTRY
125 g/4 oz plain white or
    wholewheat flour or a mixture
A pinch of salt
25 g/1 oz hard margarine

122

25 g/1 oz lard
2 to 3 teaspoons cold water

FILLING
15 g/½ oz ham fat or lard
1 small onion, finely chopped
1 small whole leek, washed and
  finely sliced
50 g/2 oz cooked ham, diced
Ground black pepper
1 egg
About 300 ml/½ pint milk
25 g/1 oz grated cheese

*Use an 18-cm/7-inch loose-bottomed
flan tin or a ring set on a small baking
sheet.*

1 Mix flour and salt in a bowl, rub
in the fats and then add enough cold
water to make a dough. Put it in a
cool place to rest for half an hour,
especially if using wholemeal flour.
2 Roll out the pastry on a floured
surface and line the flan tin. Put
aside while the filling is prepared.
3 Preheat oven to moderately hot,
Gas 6, 400°F, 200°C, and put a
baking tray on the top shelf to
preheat also.
4 Melt the ham fat or lard in a small
frying pan and gently cook the onion
and leek until soft. Set aside to cool,
then spread this mixture over the base
of the pastry case.
5 Arrange the diced ham on top of
the leeks and season generously with
ground black pepper.
6 Beat together the egg and milk and
pour this into the pastry case, then
sprinkle the grated cheese on top.
7 Put the flan on to the hot baking
tray in the oven – this ensures that
the bottom of the pastry cooks
properly. Bake for 20 minutes, then
reduce the heat to Gas 4, 350°F,
180°C, and cook for a further 20
minutes.

Grace Mulligan

CHICKEN AND MUSHROOM PIE

2 generous helpings.

SHORTCRUST PASTRY
75 g/3 oz flour, wholemeal or
  white
A pinch of salt
40 g/1½ oz lard and margarine,
  mixed
1 to 2 teaspoons cold water
A little milk or beaten egg, to
  glaze

FILLING
15 g/½ oz butter
1 small onion, chopped
175 g/6 oz cooked chicken, diced
1 Frankfurter sausage, cut into
  slices
75 g/3 oz mushrooms, wiped and
  sliced

ALL-IN-ONE SAUCE
150 ml/¼ pint milk
40 g/1½ oz butter or margarine
40 g/1½ oz plain flour
150 ml/¼ pint chicken stock
1 teaspoon lemon juice
1 tablespoon chopped fresh
  parsley

1 Make the pastry. Mix flour and salt
in a bowl and rub in the fats. Mix to
a firm dough with the water – if
using wholemeal flour, it may require
a little more. Leave it in a cool place.
2 In a small frying pan, melt
15 g/½ oz butter and cook the onion
very gently until soft.
3 Meanwhile, prepare the sauce in
another pan. Put in the milk, butter
and flour and whisk the mixture until
the flour is all dispersed. Using a
wooden spoon, stir the 'all-in-one'
sauce over a moderate heat and, when
it has thickened, gradually add the
stock. Keep stirring and add the
lemon juice and parsley.
4 Remove sauce from heat and mix
in the onion, chicken and the
Frankfurter sausage.

5 Set a pie funnel in the middle of a deep pie dish and pour the chicken mixture all round it. Cover with the sliced mushrooms. Leave until cold.
6 Roll out the pastry to about 1.5 cm/½ inch wider than needed to cover the pie. Cut off a 1.5-cm/½-inch strip round the outer edge. Moisten the rim of the pie with water, then press the strip of pastry down on this rim.
7 Moisten the top of the strip with cold water and cover with the remaining pastry. Seal very well round the outer edge. Trim off any overlapping pastry and use a fork or a spoon handle to flute the outer rim. Press the pastry gently over the pie funnel to make a small hole to allow the steam to escape.
8 Roll out the pastry trimmings and make some leaves.
9 Paint the top of the pie with a little milk or beaten egg. Arrange the pastry leaves on top and brush again.
10 Put the pie dish on a baking tray and cook near the top of a preheated, moderately hot oven, Gas 6, 400°F, 200°C, for 20 minutes, when the pastry will be crisp and golden. Eat hot.

Grace Mulligan

SAUSAGEMEAT FLAN

Will cut into six slices. Nice hot or cold. Slices of this flan will freeze very satisfactorily.

SHORTCRUST PASTRY
100 g/4 oz flour, wholemeal or white
A pinch of salt
25 g/1 oz lard
25 g/1 oz margarine
2 brimming teaspoons water

FILLING
1 dessert apple, peeled, cored and chopped
450 g/1 lb sausagemeat

124

1 large egg
1 teaspoon of mixed herbs
Freshly ground black pepper

Use either a 20-cm/8-inch flan tin with a loose base or a 20-cm/8-inch flan ring set on a baking sheet, or an 18-cm/7-inch square sandwich tin.

1 Mix flour and salt in a bowl, rub in the fats and mix to a firm dough with water. Wholemeal flour may require a little more water.
2 Roll out the pastry and line the flan tin. Then put it in a cool place until needed.
3 Preheat oven to moderately hot, Gas 5, 375°F, 190°C and put in a baking tray to heat up.
4 In a large bowl, mix together all the filling ingredients so that the herbs and pepper are well distributed. Press the mixture into the pastry case and level it off.
5 Put the flan on to the hot baking tray and cook near the top of the oven for 30 minutes.

Grace Mulligan

FRIED CURRY PUFFS

Makes 4. Good to eat hot or cold and suitable also for picnics and packed lunches. When fried they are very rich, but they can also be baked.

FILLING
2 to 3 teaspoons curry powder
2 tablespoons water
3 tablespoons oil
1 small onion, chopped
175 g/6 oz minced beef
1 large potato, diced small
Water

PASTRY
225 g/8 oz flour, white or wholemeal
A pinch of salt
50 g/2 oz margarine
50 g/2 oz lard

1 egg, lightly beaten
Oil for deep-frying
Sprigs of parsley

1 Mix the curry powder and water to make a paste.
3 Heat the oil in a pan and fry the curry paste for a minute or two until it becomes fragrant.
3 Add the onion, minced beef and potato and mix well together to coat with the curry.
4 Add about 5 tablespoons cold water, cover with a lid and cook until the potatoes are soft. Leave the filling to cool.
5 Now mix the pastry. Mix the flour and salt in a bowl and rub in margarine and lard until the mixture resembles breadcrumbs. Mix in the egg and sufficient water to bring the dough together.
6 Divide the dough into four and roll out each piece to a circle about 15 cm/6 inches across.
7 Place a quarter of the filling on each circle of pastry, dampen the edge and fold over like a pasty. Seal the edges well and flute them.
8 Deep-fry the pasties in hot oil and until golden brown, then drain well and serve garnished with sprigs of parsley.

Alternatively, bake in a moderately hot oven, Gas 6, 400°F, 200°C, for 20 minutes.

Jennie Siew Lee Cook
York

PIZZA FOR TWO

Serve this hot or cold with a green salad.

SCONE BASE
75 g/3 oz wholemeal self-raising flour *
25 g/1 oz porridge meal or rolled oats
½ teaspoon dried mixed herbs
Freshly ground pepper

50 g/2 oz polyunsaturated margarine
50 g/2 oz cottage cheese
3 tablespoons natural low-fat yoghurt

FILLING AND TOPPING
2 tablespoons tomato pickle or red tomato chutney
1 teaspoon dried mixed herbs
75 g/3 oz cottage cheese, either plain or with added sweetcorn and peppers
A 120 g/4½ oz can of sardines in oil, drained
2 tomatoes

* *If you cannot buy wholemeal self-raising flour, sift in 1 level teaspoon baking powder.*

1 Preheat oven to hot, Gas 7, 425°F, 220°C.
2 Mix flour, oats, herbs and pepper.
3 Rub in margarine.
4 Lightly mix in cheese and use enough yoghurt to make a soft dough.
5 Roll out about 1 cm/½ inch thick into a circle about 18-cm/7-inches across, and lift on to a greased baking tray. Work up a little raised edge to the dough to contain filling.
It will make a nice crusty edge when baked.
6 Now for the filling. Spread pickle over scone base, sprinkle with herbs and cover with cottage cheese.
7 For the topping, split sardines in half lengthways and arrange them cut side down like the spokes of a wheel. Cut tomatoes into enough slices to fit in the gaps between sardines. Brush over with oil from sardine can.
8 Bake for 35 minutes, just above the middle of the oven.

Mrs Powell
Enfield, Middlesex

APPLE AND MINCEMEAT PARCEL

Serves 2. Delicious with a spoonful of yoghurt or cream.

110 g/4 oz frozen puff pastry*
3 tablespoons mincemeat
1 cooking apple, peeled, cored and
    cut into thin slices
Caster sugar

* *For other recipes using bought, frozen puff pastry see Fish Pie in Puff Pastry (page 121).*

1 Preheat oven to hot, Gas 7, 425°F, 220°C.
2 Cut the pastry in half and roll out one piece to an oblong 10 to 12 cm/4 to 5 inches long.
3 Spread the mincemeat over the pastry, but leave a clear border around the edges. Cover the mincemeat with the apple slices.
4 Roll out the other piece of pastry to cover the base and, keeping a 2-cm/¾-inch border all round, make cuts across the centre 2 cm/¾ inch apart. Dampen edge of the base piece, then carefully place the top piece over the apple slices and seal the edges well.
5 Brush with water and sprinkle with a little caster sugar. Lift the parcel on to a baking tray.
6 Bake in the preheated oven for 20 to 25 minutes when it will be crisp and golden.

Joan Tyers
Wingate, Co. Durham

MARMALADE FLAN

This flan can be made with any type of thick-cut orange marmalade – preferably Seville. It freezes well either whole or in portions.

SHORTCRUST PASTRY
125 g/4 oz flour
A pinch of salt
15 g/1 oz butter
15 g/1 oz lard
1 tablespoon cold water

FILLING
25 g/1 oz sugar
25 g/1 oz margarine
1 egg, beaten
225 g/8 oz marmalade

1 Mix flour and salt and rub in the butter and lard. Mix to a firm dough with water. Leave the dough to rest for 15 minutes.
2 Roll out the pastry, and use it to line an 18-cm/7-inch flan ring.
3 Now for the filling. Cream together the sugar and margarine, then gradually stir in the beaten egg.
4 Mix in the marmalade. The mixture will curdle and look messy at this stage, but it looks fine when it is cooked.
5 Pour the filling into the pastry case and bake in the centre of a preheated moderate oven, Gas 4, 350°F, 180°C for 35 minutes.
6 Leave to cool then cut into slices and serve with cream, custard or yoghurt.

Miss Kathleen Cliff
King's Heath, Birmingham

PECAN PIE

Expensive but delicious! Makes 6 good helpings but it is good both hot and cold and can be frozen in portions for up to 3 months. A less extravagant pie can be made substituting walnuts, but it is not quite so good. Serve hot or cold with ice-cream or whipped cream.

PASTRY
50 g/2 oz plain flour, white or
    wholemeal
A pinch of salt
25 g/1 oz margarine
About 2 teaspoons water

FILLING

1 egg
25 g/1 oz butter
75 ml/2½ fl oz dark corn syrup or
   maple syrup*
25 g/1 oz muscovado sugar
½ teaspoon vanilla essence or
   flavouring
A pinch of salt
50 g/2 oz shelled pecan nuts

* Golden syrup can be used but will
produce a heavier texture.

1 Preheat oven to moderately hot,
Gas 6, 400°F, 200°C.
2 Mix flour and salt and rub in
margarine. Mix to a firm dough with
water.
3 Roll out to fit a 15-cm/6-inch flan
dish or ring set on a baking tray (2.5
cm/1 inch deep is about right for this
pie).
4 Now for the filling. Beat the egg
lightly but not to a frothy state.
5 Melt butter and mix into it all the
remaining ingredients and then the
egg.
6 Pour mixture into pastry case.
7 Bake for 15 minutes in preheated
oven, then reduce to moderate, Gas 4,
350°F, 180°C, for 20 minutes more,
when pie should be firm around
edges and soft in centre.

Mary Hunter
Addingham, West Yorkshire

ALMOND MINCE PIES

*Makes 12. These are popular all year
round and the almond topping makes a
pleasant change from the usual pastry
crust. Serve by themselves or with ice-
cream. They freeze well. Just defrost
them and warm through in a moderate
oven, Gas 3, 325°F, 160°C.*

PASTRY

50 g/2 oz margarine
110 g/4 oz plain flour, white,
   wholemeal or a mixture
2 to 3 teaspoons cold water

FILLING AND TOPPING

12 teaspoons mincemeat
50 g/2 oz margarine
40 g/1½ oz caster sugar
1 egg
50 g/2 oz ground almonds
Icing sugar for dusting

1 Rub the margarine into the flour
and add enough cold water to make a
firm dough. Let it rest for 20 minutes
before rolling out, especially if using
wholemeal flour.
2 Roll the pastry out on a floured
board and cut out 12 rounds using a
fluted biscuit cutter. Grease 12 tartlet
tins and line with the pastry rounds.

3 Preheat oven to moderately hot, Gas 6, 400°F, 200°C.
4 Put a teaspoonful of mincemeat in each tart case.
5 To make the topping, cream the margarine and sugar together, beat in the egg and ground almonds. If the mixture is too dry, add a small spoonful of milk to slacken it.
6 Spread the almond topping over the mincemeat and bake for 15 or 20 minutes.
7 Let the pies cool slightly before removing to a wire rack.
8 Dust with icing sugar when cold.

Grace Mulligan

APRICOT AND COCONUT TARTS

Makes 10 tarts. They freeze well and taste just as nice when thawed as when freshly baked.

PASTRY
50 g/2 oz plain white or wholemeal flour
50 g/2 oz self-raising white flour
A pinch of salt
25 g/1 oz hard margarine
25 g/1 oz lard
2 to 3 teaspoons cold water

FILLING
25 g/1 oz dried apricots
Apricot jam
40 g/1½ oz soft margarine
40 g/1½ oz caster sugar
40 g/1½ oz desiccated coconut
1 small egg, beaten

1 Mix the two types of flour together, add the salt and rub in the margarine and lard until the mixture resembles breadcrumbs. Add sufficient cold water to bring the pastry together. Chill for 15 minutes in the refrigerator, especially if using wholemeal flour.

2 Cut the apricots into small pieces and pour some boiling water over them. Leave them to soak for 10 minutes, then drain.
3 Roll out the pastry and line bun tins.
4 Place a teaspoonful of apricot jam in each pastry case and then prepare the filling.
5 Cream together the margarine and sugar, stir in the coconut, drained apricots and enough beaten egg to bind.
6 Put the filling over the apricot jam, smooth the top and bake in a preheated moderate oven, Gas 4, 350°F, 180°C, for about 15 minutes.

Mrs L. Johnson
York

MEGAN'S TREACLE ROLL

When making pies, utilize the small leftover pieces of pastry by making this rich, fattening and delicious dish.

Pastry
Golden syrup
Milk

1 Roll out the pastry into a square.
2 Spread golden syrup quite thickly on to the pastry, roll up quickly and loosely seal the edges.
3 Place the roll in a small milk pudding or pie dish and cover with milk until only the top of the pastry is visible.
4 Put the dish into the top part of a warm oven, Gas 3, 325°F, 160°C for about 1 hour.

During the cooking the milk will become a thick, golden sauce. The milk may curdle if the oven is too hot.

Megan Mallinson
Fixby, Huddersfield

Chapter 9

Puddings

OLD-FASHIONED MILK PUDDINGS

Despite the fact that nearly all milk puddings are available in cans these days, they do not have the same authentic flavour as home-made ones. Milk puddings are delicious by themselves or served with all kinds of stewed fruits, or just a spoonful of jam.

SEMOLINA – PEARL TAPIOCA – GROUND RICE

The old way of cooking semolina was to bring it to a boil and simmer for 3 to 4 minutes, then pour the mixture into a pie dish and finish the cooking in the oven for a very long time. I think it is easier to make it on the top of the cooker. The following method can be used for both tapioca and ground rice.

300 ml/½ pint milk*
25 g/1 oz semolina, pearl tapioca
    or ground rice
25 g/1 oz sugar

* *If you wish to make a pudding with 600 ml/1 pint milk then increase the semolina etc. and the sugar to 40 g/1½ oz each.*

1 In a small pan, heat the milk and sprinkle on the semolina (or tapioca or ground rice).
2 Stirring continuously, bring the mixture up to the boil, then simmer gently for 3 to 4 minutes.
3 Stir in the sugar. Pour the mixture into a jug or bowl, stand it in a pan of gently simmering water and continue cooking for a further 20 to 30 minutes or until the mixture is thick. Stir with a wooden spoon from time to time. (Tapioca especially needs stirring or it sinks to the bottom and glues together.)

TO MAKE A BAKED PUDDING

After adding the sugar, stir in a beaten egg, then pour the mixture into an ovenproof dish and bake in a moderate oven, Gas 4, 350°F, 180°C, for 15 to 20 minutes or until the pudding has set. It is best to use the quantities based on 600 ml/1 pint milk for this or the egg sets it too hard.

Grace Mulligan

BAKED RICE PUDDING

Too much for 2 people to eat all at once but as the oven has to be on for such a long time it makes sense to cook a substantial pudding. It is good to eat warm or cold, on its own or with stewed fruit, especially prunes and apricots. Also try Quick Peach Condé, see next recipe.

You can use any type of milk for this recipe but the richer the milk the creamier the pudding. Gold Top milk (from Channel Islands breeds of cow) is the best one, but a good substitute is Silver Top (ordinary pasteurised) or homogenised milk with a heaped tablespoon of dried milk mixed into it. Stir it around well to ensure that the milk powder dissolves.

40 g/1½ oz round pudding rice,
    well washed
600 ml/1 pint milk
40 g/1½ oz granulated sugar
15 g/½ butter

1 Put all the ingredients in a buttered pie dish and leave overnight.
2 Bake the pudding uncovered in a cool oven, Gas 2, 300°F, 150°C for about 2 hours. Stir often during the first hour until the rice begins to thicken and the skin forms. When it begins to turn golden, gently slide a knife in at the edge of the dish to stir the pudding without disturbing the lovely brown skin – the part that many people like the best.

Grace Mulligan

Rice pudding cooked in the microwave is every bit as creamy as that cooked in the conventional oven. However it will not have a skin on top – the part some people particularly like! You can transfer the pudding to the oven for 20 minutes to brown the surface if desired.

1 Put the milk into a deep 2½–litre/4–pint casserole. You need a very large dish to allow the milk to boil up – if you use too small a dish, the milk will boil over and on to the turntable. Cook on full power for 3 minutes.
2 Stir in the rice, sugar and butter. Cook on Low for 1 hour, stirring twice.

For a 2-power microwave cooker: Cook on Defrost for 50 to 60 minutes, stirring twice.

The rice should have absorbed all the milk and become creamy.

To reheat leftover rice pudding, put the rice pudding into the serving dish, heat on full power for 1 minute, then stir.

QUICK PEACH CONDÉ

For 2.

2 peach halves
150 ml/¼ pint cold rice
    pudding *
2 tablespoons raspberry jam

* *See opposite for home-made rice pudding recipes.*

1 Put the peach halves into two ramekin dishes.
2 Top with the rice pudding and level out evenly.
3 Warm the raspberry jam gently in a small pan, then pour over the top of the rice pudding.
4 Chill well before serving.

Debbie Woolhead
Boston Spa, West Yorkshire

BOILED RICE AND RAISIN MILK PUDDING

Easy to make half-quantity.

40 g/1½ oz round pudding rice
600 ml/1 pint milk
40 g/1½ oz granulated sugar
25 g/1 oz raisins

1 To burst the rice, wash it first, drain and then barely cover with cold water. Bring it to the boil and boil gently until the water has all evaporated. Shake the pan occasionally to prevent it sticking.
2 Add the milk and simmer until soft and creamy, about 15 to 20 minutes.
3 Add the sugar and raisins, reheat and serve.

Grace Mulligan

ZARDA OR SWEET SAFFRON RICE

A rich and aromatic sweet. Serves 2, but it's easy to make more.
When cooking rice, it is easier to measure it by the cupful (than by weight), then use the same cup to measure the water. Any size cup will do but for two people a teacup is ideal.

1 cup basmati rice
A few drops of orange colouring
50 g/2 oz sugar
75 ml/3 fl oz water
50 g/2 oz ghee or clarified butter,
    or unsalted butter
2 to 3 cloves
2 to 3 green cardamoms
25 g/1 oz flaked almonds
25 g/1 oz pistachio nuts

25 g/1 oz sultanas
1 dessertspoon rose water or
   Kevda water
A pinch of saffron
Lightly whipped cream for
   serving

1 Wash the rice in several changes of
cold water to remove the excess
starch. Pick out any husks or grit.
2 Put the rice into a saucepan with
1½ cups of hot water and a few
drops of orange food colouring. Bring
to the boil and let it boil quite
steadily without the lid until you can
see the grains just below the surface.
Then cover the pan lightly, reduce
the heat to a gentle simmer and cook
until all the water has been absorbed,
about 20 minutes.
3 When the rice is cooked, spread it
out on a large plate and leave it to
cool.
4 Put the sugar and 75 ml/3 fl oz
water into a saucepan and stir to
dissolve the sugar over a gentle heat.
Bring to the boil and cook for 1
minute.
5 In a large saucepan, melt the ghee
or butter and cook the cloves and
cardamom seeds for a few seconds.
Add the rice and stir it gently so that
the grains are coated.
6 Add the sugar syrup, nuts and
sultanas to the rice.
7 Warm the rose water with the
saffron and pour it over the rice.
Cover the pan with a lid and cook
over a very gentle heat until the liquid
has been absorbed. Alternatively, turn
the rice out into an ovenproof dish
and put it into a cool oven, Gas 2,
300°F, 150°C, for about 20 minutes
when the syrup will have dried out
and the rice will be hot.
8 Serve hot with lightly whipped
cream.

Nirmal Singh
Nuneaton, Warwickshire

SIMPLE CHRISTMAS PUDDING

50 g/2 oz self-raising
   wholemeal or plain flour
50 g/2 oz shredded suet
50 g/2 oz fresh breadcrumbs,
   wholemeal or white
100 g/4 oz mixed dried fruit
100 g/4 oz soft brown sugar
1 egg
90 ml/3 fl oz milk
1 tablespoon black treacle
1 teaspoon mixed spice
½ teaspoon baking powder

1 Simply put everything into a large
bowl, mix well and make a simple
wish.
2 Put into a 600-ml/1-pint pudding
basin or two smaller ones, cover with
greaseproof paper and foil and steam
in simmering water for 1½ hours.

Mrs Bernice Graham
Wirral, Merseyside

Microwave ━━━━━━━━━━━━━━━━━━━━

*This pudding is not one to cook in
advance to store like a traditional pud
– but it is ideal to make at the last
minute. It has good flavour and the
texture of a steamed pudding.*

For this method use wholemeal self-
raising flour, 50g/2 oz grated butter
instead of suet, wholemeal
breadcrumbs and dark brown sugar.
Leave out the baking powder.

Never leave the microwave cooker
unattended when cooking or reheating
Christmas puddings, especially if your
recipe contains large quantities of
spirits. Overcooking in the microwave
means dehydration and, when the
moisture has evaporated, the fats and
sugar can become hot enough to
ignite.

1 Simply put everything into a large
bowl and mix well together. Wish
carefully!

132

2 Put the mixture into a 600-ml/1-pint basin. Cover the top with clear film and cook on full power for 3 minutes, let it stand for 5 minutes and then cook on full power again for 2 minutes more.

Alternatively, 2 little puddings can be made in teacups: cover them with clear film and cook one at a time on full power for 1½ minutes, allow to stand for 2 minutes then cook again on full power for 1 minute more.

To reheat leftover pudding: pack into a clean small basin, cover with clear film and heat on full power for 1 to 1½ minutes.

To reheat portions of pudding: on a plate, covered with clear film, allow 20 to 30 seconds on full power for each portion.

BRANDY OR SHERRY SAUCE
Makes about 300 ml/½ pint.

15 g/½ oz cornflour
300 ml/½ pint milk
15 g/½ oz butter
1 level tablespoon caster sugar
1 to 2 tablespoons brandy or
   sherry

1 Mix cornflour to a smooth paste with a little of the cold milk.
2 Warm remaining milk, pour on to cornflour mixture and mix well.
3 Return to pan and cook, stirring, until sauce thickens and comes to the boil.
4 Simmer 2 minutes.
5 Remove from heat, stir in butter, sugar and brandy or sherry.

Mrs Margaret Heywood
Todmorden, Yorkshire

Microwave

1 In a 600-ml/1-pint jug, mix the cornflour to a paste with a little of the cold milk. Blend in the remaining milk. Cook on full power for 1½ minutes then stir.
2 Cook on full power for a further 30 to 60 seconds until thick.
3 Then stir in the butter, sugar and brandy or sherry.

CHRISTMAS MINCEMEAT ROLL
Light, rich and delicious!

75 g/3 oz self-raising flour
3 eggs
75 g/3 oz caster sugar
Icing sugar for dredging

FILLING
150 ml/¼ pint double cream
2 tablespoons mincemeat
1 tablespoon brandy, rum or
   sherry

1 Preheat oven to moderately hot, Gas 6, 400°F, 200°C.
2 Line a Swiss roll tin 35 by 23 cm/14 by 9 inches with greased, greaseproof paper.
3 Sieve flour three times.
4 Put eggs and caster sugar into a basin over a pan of hot water and whisk well until really thick.
5 Fold in flour with a metal spoon.
6 Pour mixture into prepared tin and put straight into oven on the top shelf for about 10 minutes, until firm to the touch.
7 Meanwhile, sprinkle a sheet of greaseproof paper generously with icing sugar from a dredger or sifter.
8 Turn the hot cake upside down on to the sugared paper. Remove the lining paper, trim edges of cake and lay over it a clean sheet of greaseproof paper. Roll up and leave to cool.

133

9 Whip the cream, mix in gently the mincemeat and brandy, rum or sherry.
10 When cake is cold, gently unroll and remove both sheets of paper. Spread inside of cake with filling. Roll up.
11 Chill the cake and dust finally with icing sugar before serving. It can be decorated with a sprig of holly.

Mrs Stella Boldy
Sykehouse, North Humberside

APPLE PUDDING

Rudin Afal is the Welsh for this delicious soufflé, which must be eaten straight out of the oven. From Lucy Barton-Greenwood, 1987 Junior Cook of the Year. For 2.

450 g/1 lb cooking apples
Sugar to taste
15 g/½ oz butter
15 g/½ oz plain white flour
150 ml/¼ pint milk
15 g/½ oz sugar
Vanilla essence
1 large egg, separated

1 Preheat oven to moderately hot, Gas 6, 400°F, 200°C.
2 Peel, core and slice the apples. Stew them in a very little water until nearly tender but still crunchy. Sweeten to taste. Put them into a buttered 1-litre/1½-pint soufflé or pie dish.
3 Melt the butter and stir in flour. Cook for 1 minute as it sizzles. Then gradually stir in the milk and bring to the boil to make a smooth sauce.
4 Mix in sugar, vanilla and egg yolk.
5 Beat the egg white until stiff and fold it into the sauce. Pour it over the prepared apples.
6 Bake immediately for 12 minutes until well risen and golden brown.

Lucy Barton-Greenwood
Radyr, Cardiff

APPLE SAUCE PUDDING

For 1 or 2 to eat hot or cold. A good way to cook apples to retain their flavour:

3 good-sized cooking apples
Demerara sugar
15 g/½ oz sultanas
½ teaspoon finely grated lemon rind

1 Wash the apples and remove the cores, then place in a saucepan which just contains them standing upright. Pour in enough cold water to cover the bottom of the pan, about 5 mm/¼ inch. Put on the lid and cook gently for about 30 minutes or until the apples are soft.
2 Remove the apples from the pan and scoop out the pulp, discarding the skins. While still hot, stir in enough sugar to sweeten, then add the sultanas and lemon rind.
3 Serve hot with custard.

Mrs Susan Hersee
Hayling Island, Hampshire

Microwave ▬▬▬▬▬▬▬▬▬▬

1 Peel, core and slice the apples. Put them in a small casserole with the sugar. Cover and cook on full power for 6 minutes.
2 Mash the apples with a fork, stir in the sultanas and lemon rind and serve.

BAKED APPLES WITH MUESLI

A good pudding to make when cooking the main course in a moderately hot oven, Gas 5, 375°F, 190°C. For 2.

2 large Bramley apples
25 g/1 oz raisins
2 heaped teaspoons golden syrup

250 ml/8 fl oz liquid (you can use
apple juice, cider or water)
2 large tablespoons muesli (see
page 16 for a recipe)

1 Wipe the apples and remove the
cores. Using a sharp knife, score
around the centre of the apples, just
cutting the skin.
2 Stand the apples upright in a small
ovenproof dish and fill the centres
with the raisins. Spoon golden syrup
over each apple and pour the liquid
into the dish.
3 Bake uncovered in a moderately hot
oven, Gas 5, 375°F, 190°C, for about
40 minutes or until the apples are
soft. About 15 minutes before they
are ready, put the muesli on to a
baking sheet and cook in the oven
until it is lightly browned.
4 Serve the apples and juice in
individual bowls with the muesli
scattered over the top.

Grace Mulligan

Microwave

1 Prepare the apples following steps
1 and 2 above, but pour only 120
ml/4 fl oz of the liquid into the
microwave dish.
2 Cook uncovered on full power for
5 to 6 minutes. Some apples may take
up to 7 minutes to cook. Allow to
stand for 5 minutes before serving.
The apples will look quite green and
shiny when they come out of the
oven; however, during the standing
time they will become dull and soft.
3 Sprinkle the muesli on to a baking
tray and grill carefully under a hot
grill for 2 to 3 minutes until lightly
browned. Shake the tray every minute
to prevent the muesli burning.
4 Serve as above.

SAVOURY BAKED APPLE

*This delicious pudding can be cooked on
top of the stove or put in the oven if
you have it on. Serve hot. For 1.*

Butter
1 cooking apple, peeled, cored and
sliced
1 tablespoon brown sugar
1 tablespoon water
25 g/1 oz seedless raisins
50 g/2 oz Cheddar cheese, grated

1 Arrange the apple slices in a
shallow, buttered, ovenproof dish.
Sprinkle the sugar, water and raisins
over the top and cover with a lid or
some foil. Bake in a moderately hot
oven, Gas 5, 375°F, 190°C, for about
25 minutes or until the apple is
tender.

Alternatively, put the apple, sugar,
water and raisins in a pan and cook
gently until tender but not mushy.
Then put it all into a heatproof dish.

2 Cover the apple with the cheese
and put the dish under a hot grill
until the cheese has melted.

Joan Tyers
Wingate, Co. Durham

Microwave

1 Arrange the apple slices in a
shallow 12-cm/5-inch round
ovenproof dish. Sprinkle the sugar
and raisins over the top and cover
with a piece of clear film. Cook on
full power for 2 minutes.
2 Remove the clear film and cover
the apple with the cheese. Grill until
the cheese has melted.

BANANA FRITTERS

Pineapple rings, apple slices or rounds of sweet potato may be used. For 2.

50 g/2 oz plain white flour
1 tablespoon rice flour
½ teaspoon baking powder
A pinch of salt
60 ml/2 fl oz milk
1 to 2 tablespoons water
Oil for deep frying
2 bananas, skinned and cut in half lengthways*
Golden syrup for serving

* *To keep sliced bananas from going brown, see below.*

1 Sieve the flour, rice flour, baking powder and salt into a bowl. Make a well in the centre; pour in the milk.
2 Stir to make a smooth batter, gradually adding the water if necessary to achieve a coating consistency. (If any lumps develop, use a whisk to disperse them.)
3 Heat the oil until hot, then dip the banana halves in the batter and fry them until golden brown.
4 Drain the fritters on kitchen paper.
5 Serve on hot plates with a little golden syrup dribbled over them.

Jennie Siew Lee Cook
York

TO KEEP SLICED BANANAS FROM GOING BROWN

Put unpeeled bananas in cold water for 5 to 10 minutes. They may then be peeled, sliced and left for some time without going brown.

Miss M. Owen
Elworth, Cheshire

In our test, with firm bananas, there was only slight discolouration after 4 hours. It was 8 hours before they were brown and soft. Very ripe bananas and a warm kitchen could give less good results. This useful tip was given to Farmhouse Kitchen in 1977 and has appeared in our books ever since.

Mary Watts

CHERRY SPONGE PUDDING

This recipe is known to Mrs Jackson's family as 'Queen Mum's Hat'! Can be eaten warm or cold. For 2.

2 trifle sponge cakes
1 to 2 tablespoons sherry or rum
A 220 g/7½ oz can of black cherries, drained and stoned
75 ml/2½ fl oz stiffly whipped cream
1 egg white
50 g/2 oz caster sugar

1 Place the sponge cakes on a heatproof plate and sprinkle with the sherry or rum.
2 Arrange the cherries on top then cover with the stiffly whipped cream. Put the dish in the refrigerator for one hour.
3 Whisk the egg white until stiff then gradually whisk in the sugar. Spread this meringue mixture over the cream to cover it completely.
4 Bake in a preheated moderately hot oven, Gas 6, 400°F, 200°C, for 5 minutes until the meringue is slightly brown.

Mrs Joan Jackson
Swinton, Manchester

OATY RHUBARB CRUMBLE

For 1 or 2. Nice hot or cold. Mrs Knight makes this without sugar, which is useful for diabetics. You may prefer to use the small amounts of sugar given below, or try it without and simply sprinkle with sugar or sweetener on serving. The topping is delicious.

225 g/8 oz rhubarb, cut into 2.5-cm/1-inch pieces
Two 15 ml tablespoons soft brown sugar
Juice of 1 orange
25 g/1 oz margarine
25 g/1 oz wholemeal flour

25 g/1 oz rolled oats
25 g/1 oz bran flakes, crushed
   slightly

1 Preheat oven to moderately hot,
Gas 5, 375°F, 190°C.
2 Put the rhubarb into an ovenproof
dish, sprinkle with 1 tablespoon of
the sugar, and pour orange juice over
the top.
3 Rub margarine into flour until the
mixture resembles breadcrumbs, then
lightly mix in the rolled oats, crushed
bran flakes and remaining sugar.
4 Sprinkle the crumble topping over
the rhubarb and bake for 30 to 40
minutes. Serve with custard or
cream.

Mrs Knight
Belvedere, Kent

1 Put the rhubarb into a 12.5-cm/5-
inch soufflé-type dish or small
casserole. Sprinkle with 1 tablespoon
sugar and pour over the orange juice.
2 Rub the margarine into the flour
until the mixture resembles fine
breadcrumbs. Mix in the remaining
sugar, oats and bran flakes.
3 Spread the crumble over the
rhubarb and cook on full power for
7 minutes. Let it stand for 5 minutes
before serving.

OATY APPLE CRUNCH

*Nice hot or cold. Makes 2 helpings.
Serve with fresh cream, custard,
yoghurt or top of the milk. This crumble
topping can be used over any fruits.*

25 g/1 oz butter
25 g/1 oz demerara sugar
25 g/1 oz wholemeal flour
25 g/1 oz rolled oats
1 large eating apple
1 tablespoon lemon juice

A generous pinch of cinnamon
25 g/1 oz sultanas

1 Preheat oven to moderately hot,
Gas 5, 375°F, 190°C.
2 Melt butter and mix into it the
sugar, flour and oats.
3 Peel, core and slice the apple thinly
into a small ovenproof dish. Sprinkle
with lemon juice, cinnamon and
sultanas.
3 Cover with crumble mixture,
pressing down lightly.
5 Bake in preheated oven for 20 to 25
minutes until apple is tender.

Mrs Patrick
Motherwell, Scotland

*The crumble topping used for this
delicious pudding is ideal for
microwave cooking. If you are fond of
coconut, add 1 tablespoon along with
the oats.*

1 Rub the butter into the flour until
it is like fresh breadcrumbs, mix in
the sugar and oats.
2 Peel, core and slice the apple into a
450 ml/¾ pint casserole. Sprinkle
with lemon juice, cinnamon and
sultanas.
3 Cover with the crumble mixture,
pressing down lightly. Cook on full
power for 5 minutes. Let it stand for
5 minutes before serving.

STEAMED PUDDING

Makes 2 small puddings.

50 g/2 oz margarine
50 g/2 oz caster sugar
50 g/2 oz self-raising flour
1 size 4 egg
1 to 2 tablespoons water

SOME TOPPINGS:
Lemon curd, golden syrup or jam,
apple sauce or fruit purées

**Cream, top-of-the-milk or custard
for serving**

1 Combine all the ingredients and
beat until smooth. The mixture
should drop off the spoon to the
count of 3. This can be quickly done
in a food processor.
2 Divide the mixture between two
greased cups and cover them with
greaseproof paper and foil.
3 Steam the puddings for 45
minutes. If you have no steamer, put
a bread and butter plate upside down
in a suitable saucepan, stand the cups
on it and pour in 2.5 cm/1 inch of
boiling water. Put on the lid and let
the puddings steam for 45 minutes,
taking care not to let the water go off
the boil, nor to let the pan boil dry.
4 Turn the puddings out on to hot
plates and pour the topping over.

*This is where the microwave cooker
really excels.*

1 Proceed up to step 2 above.
2 Put the mixture in two greased
cups, cover loosely with clear film
and cook on full power for 2
minutes.
3 Leave to stand for 1 minute.
During the standing time warm the
chosen topping for one minute on full
power.
4 Turn out the puddings and pour
topping over.

Joan Tyers
Wingate, Co. Durham

138

WHOLEMEAL PANCAKES

When making pancakes, it is much easier to make at least a dozen at one time and keep the rest either in the refrigerator for a few days, or store them in the freezer. It is not necessary to pack the pancakes with a sheet of paper or film between each one. It is quite safe to thaw and refreeze these pancakes. Makes about 12.

125 g/4 oz fine plain wholemeal
   flour
1 egg
360 ml/12 fl oz semi-skimmed
   milk, or whole milk and water
   mixed
A pinch of salt
Oil

1 Put all the ingredients, except the oil, into a liquidiser or food processor and mix until the batter is smooth. Pour the batter into a large jug.
2 Put a little oil into a small heavy-based frying pan (about 15 cm/6 inch in size). Heat it up and tilt the pan until the inside is well coated, then pour off any excess oil.
3 Pour a little batter into the hot pan and tip the pan from side to side so that the base is covered. Do be careful not to pour in too much batter or the pancakes will be too thick.
4 Cook the pancake until the surface looks dry (about 1 minute) then flip it over and cook the other side for about 30 seconds.
5 Tip the pancake out, if necessary add a little more oil and cook the remaining pancakes in the same way. It is a good idea to stir the batter in between cooking each pancake.

Instead of using oil to grease the frying pan, you can tie up a piece of beef suet in a circle of muslin or fine cloth and use this to rub over the frying pan.

Grace Mulligan

SWEET PANCAKES

A variety of fillings and an orange sauce in which to heat the pancakes. (See previous recipe for Grace Mulligan's pancakes.)

**Wholemeal Pancakes as in
   previous recipe**

FILLINGS
Stewed apples and raisins
Canned fruit pie fillings
Mincemeat
Banana halves warmed in the
   Orange Sauce (below)

Warm the filling before putting it into the pancakes.

ORANGE SAUCE
75 ml/3 fl oz orange juice
10 g/$\frac{1}{4}$ oz butter
10 g/$\frac{1}{4}$ oz brown sugar
1 tablespoon cream

1 Put the orange juice, butter, sugar and cream into a frying pan and heat it gently.
2 Place the pancakes in, one at a time, and warm them through, then fill the pancakes with your chosen filling and if any sauce is left, pour it over the pancakes.

Dilwen Phillips
Gileston, South Glamorgan

Microwave

Pancakes are not very suitable for microwave cooking, but to reheat 4 cold pancakes in the cold sauce will take 1 to 1$\frac{1}{2}$ minutes on full power.

BUTTERSCOTCH CUSTARD

This is very quick, easy and delicious. When turned out it seems a bit spotty; however, the sprinkling of nutmeg hides this effectively. For 1.

139

Butterscotch Custard continued
1 large egg
1 teaspoon dark soft brown sugar
120 ml/4 fl oz milk
A grating of nutmeg (optional)

1 Whisk egg and sugar into milk.
2 Pour the mixture into a small,
buttered, heatproof dish or cup and
cover the top – foil will do.
3 Put the dish on to a saucer placed
inside a small saucepan. Pour in just
enough boiling water to come to the
rim of the saucer. Put the lid on the
saucepan and let the water only just
simmer for 15 minutes.
4 Leave the custard inside the closed
pan until it is cool.
5 Turn it out to serve and sprinkle
with nutmeg, or more dark brown
sugar, or both, just before you eat it.

Grace Mulligan

Microwave

1 Whisk the egg and sugar into the
milk.
2 Pour the mixture into a small
ramekin dish or teacup. Cook on Low
for 3 to 5 minutes until just set.

For 2-power microwave cookers: Use
Defrost setting for 5 to 7 minutes.

3 Leave the custard to cool, then turn
out and serve sprinkled with nutmeg,
or a little dark brown sugar, or both.

QUICK FRUIT PUDDINGS

*For 1 or more, this is lovely made with
soft fruits but is perfectly suitable for
stewed fruit, or any fruit you like.*

**Soft fruit, blackcurrants,
blackberries, raspberries etc.**
Sugar
Double cream
Natural yoghurt
Demerara sugar

1 Cook the fruit with some sugar and
a very little water, just to soften, then
put it into a small heatproof dish.
2 Whisk equal amounts of cream and
yoghurt and spread it over the fruit.
3 Sprinkle with demerara sugar and
put the dish immediately under a very
hot grill until the sugar melts
slightly.
4 Serve immediately, or chill the
pudding for a few hours.

Dilwen Phillips
Gileston, South Glamorgan

GRAPES WITH MUSCOVADO SUGAR AND SOURED CREAM

*An unusual, simple and delicious dessert
to make in any quantities. Apart from
the time it takes to de-pip the grapes,
this is a delightful sweet for a dinner
party. Of course, you could use seedless
grapes.*

**Large white grapes of the
muscatel type**
Dark muscovado sugar
Soured cream,* chilled

** See Smoked Mackerel and Lemon
Dip (page 28) for another recipe to use
up the soured cream.*

1 Cut each grape in half and take out
the pips. This can be done 2 or 3
hours in advance. Leave the
prepared grapes in a bowl in a cool
place until you are ready to eat
the sweet course.
2 Sprinkle with sugar and smother
with soured cream.
3 Serve at once while the sugar is still
crunchy.

Jane Temperley
London

GOOSEBERRY FOOL

*For 1 or 2. No need to top and tail the
gooseberries as these bits go when the
fruit is sieved.*

225 g/8 oz fresh or frozen
  gooseberries
2 tablespoons water
50 g/2 oz granulated sugar
150 ml/¼ pint thick custard or
  whipped cream

1 Cook the gooseberries gently with
the water and sugar for about 15
minutes until soft and pulpy.
2 Sieve the fruit and leave it to cool.
3 Stir the custard or cream into the
purée and pour into individual
glasses. Chill for several hours.

Mrs Butler
Sheffield

 ■■■■■■■■■■■■■■■■■

1 Put the fresh gooseberries and
water into an 18-cm/7-inch round
dish. Cover and cook on full power
for 3 to 5 minutes. (If you are using
frozen fruit, omit the water. Cook the
frozen gooseberries for 6 to 7 minutes
on full power, stirring once.) Leave to
stand for 5 minutes. Then sieve the
fruit and leave to cool.
2 Stir the custard or cream into the
purée and pour into individual
glasses. Chill for several hours before
serving.

ORANGES AND NECTARINES IN CARAMEL SAUCE

*The caramel sauce and orange segments
may be prepared in advance, but do not
cut up the nectarines more than a few
hours before serving or they may
discolour. Makes 2 helpings.*

3 oranges
50 g/2 oz granulated sugar
1 teaspoon lemon juice
2 nectarines
1 to 2 tablespoons Grand Marnier
  or Cointreau

1 Squeeze the juice from one orange,
strain it into a measuring jug, and if
necessary add cold water to make 60
ml/2 fl oz of liquid. Set aside while
you prepare the caramel.
2 Put the sugar, lemon juice and 4
tablespoons of cold water into a
saucepan and stir over gentle heat.
Once the sugar has dissolved, increase
the heat and let the liquid boil
fiercely until it turns a brown caramel
colour. Pour the prepared orange juice
into the saucepan – be careful to
cover your hand as it will bubble up
and spit. Stir over the heat until all
the caramel has dissolved. Leave
sauce to cool.
3 Peel the oranges and cut into
segments, making sure all the pith
and membrane are removed. Wash
the nectarines and cut into segments.
4 Mix the nectarine and orange
segments together in a serving bowl
and pour over them the caramel
sauce. Stir in the liqueur and chill
slightly before serving.

Angela Henderson
Fleet, Hampshire

FRESH PEACHES WITH RASPBERRY SAUCE

*For 2. This makes a light and
refreshing finish to a meal, quick and
easy to prepare, especially if the sauce
is made beforehand. The peaches should
not be peeled and prepared more than a
few hours before serving or they may
discolour. The raspberry sauce may be
frozen.*

175 g/6 oz fresh or frozen
  raspberries
A few drops of lemon juice
Icing sugar to taste
3 ripe peaches
Whipped cream or natural
  yoghurt to serve separately
  (optional)

1 Purée the raspberries and pass them through a fine nylon sieve to remove all the pips. Add the lemon juice and sufficient icing sugar to sweeten.
2 To peel the peaches, plunge them into boiling water for about 15 seconds, then remove and place immediately in cold water. The skins should now be easy to peel away.
3 Cut the peaches into segments and add them to the raspberry purée. Ensure that all the segments are well coated with the sauce.
4 Serve slightly chilled in sundae dishes and hand the whipped cream or yoghurt separately.

Angela Henderson
Fleet, Hampshire

STRAWBERRIES AND KIWI FRUIT IN A CREAM-FILLED SPONGE

This 'roulade' was the dessert prepared by Simon Dunn, aged 14, when he won third place in the 1987 Junior Cook of the Year competition. For a less extravagant occasion, or when strawberries are out of season, replace them with diced fresh orange which goes perfectly with Grand Marnier.

3 eggs, separated
50 g/2 oz caster sugar, plus a little more
A few drops of vanilla essence
2 tablespoons white flour, sifted
100 g/4 oz strawberries
1 kiwi fruit
Icing sugar
1 tablespoon Grand Marnier
75 ml/2½ fl oz double cream

1 Oil a 27 by 18-cm/11 by 7-inch Swiss roll tin and line it with oiled greaseproof paper or non-stick silicone paper.

2 Preheat oven to moderate, Gas 5, 350°F, 180°C.
3 Whisk the egg whites until they are stiff but not dry.
4 Beat the egg yolks with 500 g/2 oz of the caster sugar until very thick and pale yellow.
5 Add vanilla and carefully fold in flour and whisked egg whites.
6 Spread the mixture evenly in the prepared tin and bake for about 12 minutes or until the sponge is firm.
7 Remove from the oven, and turn the cake out upside-down on to a sheet of greaseproof paper which has been lightly dusted with caster sugar. Peel off the baking paper and leave the cake to cool.
8 Prepare the fruits, keeping 2 or 3 small strawberries and 2 or 3 thin slices of kiwi fruit for decorating later. Roughly chop the rest and put it in a bowl with 1 tablespoon icing sugar and the Grand Marnier. Leave to soften for 20 minutes, turning fruit gently from time to time.
9 Beat the cream until it is thick.
10 Drain Grand Marnier from fruit and whisk it into the cream, along with a little sieved icing sugar to taste.
11 Fold the fruit and cream together and spread it over the cake. Roll it up and lift carefully on to a pretty plate.
12 Sieve a little extra caster sugar over the cake and decorate with the reserved fruit. Serve within 2 hours.

Simon Dunn
Bickley, Kent

BANANA ALASKA

This is a good recipe to make when the oven has been on for other cooking as it requires only a few minutes at a high temperature. For 1; easy to make more.

1 trifle sponge
1 tablespoon sherry
1 large egg white
25 g/1 oz caster sugar

1 individual block of ice cream –
   store in the freezer until
   needed
1 small banana*

* To prevent sliced banana from going
brown, see page 136.

1 Cut the trifle sponge in half
horizontally and lay the pieces side by
side on a heatproof plate.
2 Dribble the sherry over the
sponges.
3 Whisk the egg white until very
stiff, then gradually whisk in the
sugar until the meringue is firm and
glossy.
4 Take the ice cream out of the
freezer and lay it on top of the
sponge.
5 Quickly peel and slice the banana
horizontally and cut each piece to fit
neatly on top of the ice cream.
6 Spread or pipe the meringue neatly
over the ice cream and the banana,
making absolutely sure the ice cream
and banana are completely covered.
7 Place near the top of a preheated
hot oven, Gas 7, 425°F, 220°C, for
about 3 to 4 minutes until the
meringue is slightly brown. Serve at
once.

Grace Mulligan

ICE CREAM CHRISTMAS PUD

*It is worthwhile making up the whole
quantity, then dividing the mixture
between a variety of small basins or old
teacups. Once frozen, the puddings can
be released from their containers by
dipping momentarily into hot water.
Then refreeze them on a tray and in
polythene bags for storage. The full
quantity fits a 1-litre/1½-pint pudding
basin. Easy to make less.*

A 495 ml/17½ fl oz carton of
   vanilla ice cream*
75 g/3 oz each of raisins, sultanas
   and currants

2 tablespoons sherry or brandy
40 g/1½ oz broken walnuts
50 g/2 oz glacé cherries, red, green
   and yellow

* Use chocolate ice cream if you want
the pud to look dark.

1 Overnight soak the raisins, sultanas,
and currants in the sherry or brandy.
2 Turn out the ice cream to soften
very slightly. Chop the walnuts and
cherries.
3 Mix everything together very
swiftly. Pack into pudding basins or
teacups.
4 To serve, allow to soften slightly
and turn out into a deep dish and top
with a sprig of holly.

Grace Mulligan

COFFEE ICE CREAM

For 2. Very nice with brandy snaps.

75 ml/2½ fl oz double cream
1 egg, separated
1 tablespoon instant coffee,
   dissolved in 1 teaspoon boiling
   water
25 g/1 oz icing sugar
1 tablespoon Tia Maria (optional)
Chopped walnuts or hazelnuts to
   decorate, if desired

1 Whip the cream until stiff, then
stir in the egg yolk and dissolved
coffee.
2 In a separate bowl, whip the egg
white until stiff, then gradually whisk
in the sieved icing sugar.
3 Fold the egg white into the coffee-
cream mixture and add the liqueur, if
desired.
4 Pour into 2 ramekin dishes, cover
with clear film and freeze. Decorate
just before serving.

Angela Henderson
Fleet, Hampshire

CHOCOLATE MOUSSE

A really light and delicious sweet to which you could add a dessertspoon of Brandy or Cointreau for a treat. For 1.

25 g/1 oz plain chocolate
1 egg, separated

1 Melt the chocolate in a bowl set over a pan of hot water.
2 Remove the bowl from the heat and mix in the egg yolk.
3 Whisk the egg white until stiff, then fold it into the chocolate mixture.
4 Pour into a dish and chill for about one hour.

Caroline Hyde
Maltby, Rotherham

CHOCOLATE MOULDS

Makes 2.

1 packet miniature chocolate
 Swiss rolls
1 teaspoon gelatine
25 g/1 oz plain chocolate
120 ml/4 fl oz milk
1 egg yolk
25 g/1 oz caster sugar
¼ teaspoon instant coffee
 powder
1 teaspoon cocoa powder
1 teaspoon ground arrowroot
75 ml/2½ fl oz double cream

1 Cut the Swiss rolls into round slices and carefully line the inside of two cups or small bowls with the slices (dishes with sloping sides are easiest). Make sure the Swiss roll pieces are well pushed together so that there are no gaps.
2 Now prepare the filling: put 2 tablespoons of cold water into a small saucepan and sprinkle over the gelatine. Put to one side.
3 Break up the chocolate, put it into another saucepan with the milk and heat gently until the chocolate melts.
4 Beat together the egg yolk, sugar, coffee powder, cocoa and arrowroot, then gently stir in the warmed chocolate and milk. Mix well, pour into a clean saucepan and heat slowly without boiling until the liquid thickens slightly. It is ready when the custard will coat the back of a spoon.
5 Gently warm the gelatine over a low heat until it is clear and runny. Do not let it boil. Then pour it on to the chocolate custard. Strain the custard into a clean bowl and allow to cool. (To speed up the cooling, stand the bowl in a basin of cold water.)
6 When the mixture is cold and just starting to set, lightly whip the cream and fold it into the custard.
7 Pour into the prepared mould and leave in the refrigerator for several hours until completely set and well chilled.
8 When serving turn the moulds upside down on to the serving plates. Give them a shake to help them out.

Angela Henderson
Fleet, Hampshire

CHOCOLATE BRANDY CAKE

A very rich and exotic pudding for a special dinner, or to serve in small slices with coffee afterwards. It can be made a couple of days before it is needed and also freezes well.

100 g/4 oz butter
100 g/4 oz good-quality dessert
 chocolate
1 egg
40 g/1½ oz caster sugar
100 g/4 oz digestive biscuits,
 coarsely crushed
25 g/1 oz walnuts, chopped
25 g/1 oz glacé cherries, chopped

1 tablespoon brandy or sherry
Walnut halves and glacé cherries
   to decorate

1 Put the butter and chocolate into a
bowl set over a pan of hot water and
leave until both have melted.
2 Beat the egg and sugar together
until light and fluffy, then stir in the
melted chocolate and butter.
3 Fold in the biscuits, nuts and
cherries and lastly add the brandy or
sherry.
4 Spread the mixture into a loose-
bottomed 18-cm/7-inch round cake
tin (or you could use an 18-cm/7-inch
square tin lined with non-stick paper)
and press on the walnuts and cherries.
Put into the refrigerator to set and
keep it there until you serve it.

Mary Hunter
Addingham, Yorkshire

MANDARIN SURPRISE

For 2, twice! Use 2 small, shallow
margarine or yoghurt tubs as moulds,
each of which will make 2 adequate
helpings. You also need a liquidiser.
Tangerines, clementines, satsumas can
also be used for this dish – but choose
large fruits.

MANDARIN FILLING
100 g/4 oz large fresh mandarin
   oranges plus 2 more for
   decorating

1 small cooking apple
1 tablespoon lemon juice
50 g/2 oz caster sugar
Orange food colouring
1 egg white

ICE CREAM
25 g/1 oz meringue shells
150 ml/¼ pint double cream
25 g/1 oz caster sugar

1 Chill the moulds you plan to use in
the freezer or refrigerator ice-making
compartment.
2 Peel the 100 g/4 oz mandarins and
keep half of the rind. Using a sharp
knife, remove the white pith from the
rind, then put this scraped rind into
a saucepan. Divide the mandarins into
segments, removing pith, and add
them to the pan.
3 Peel, core and slice the apple, add
it to the mandarins in the pan,
along with lemon juice and
25 g/1 oz of the sugar. Cook over a
low heat until the fruit is soft and
pulpy. Allow to cool slightly.
4 Pour mixture into a liquidiser with
1 or 2 drops of orange food
colouring, switch on until mixture
is smooth. Allow to cool.
5 Put the egg white in a clean,
grease-free bowl and whisk until stiff
but not dry. Whisk in 25 g/1 oz caster
sugar and the mandarin purée.
6 Now prepare the ice cream. Crush
the meringue shells. Whisk cream
until it just holds its shape, then fold
   the meringue and sugar into
   the cream.

7 Place this mixture in the iced moulds. Using the back of a spoon, smooth the cream up the sides of the moulds to make a hollow in the centre.
8 Fill the hollows with mandarin mixture.
9 Cover with foil and freeze for at least 3 hours.
10 To serve, dip the mould in hand-hot water for a few seconds. Place a chilled plate on top, invert and shake. Decorate with fresh mandarin segments.

Grace Mulligan

PEACH MOUSSE

A very light pudding for 1 or 2.

4 peach halves from a can of
     peaches in natural juice
1 egg, separated
Two 15 ml tablespoons low-fat
     natural yoghurt
Half a sachet of powdered
     gelatine

1 Put the peach halves, egg yolk and yoghurt into a food processor or liquidiser and process until smooth.
2 Put 2 tablespoons cold water into a small saucepan; sprinkle over the gelatine. Leave it for a few minutes, then warm it over a gentle heat until it is runny and looks clear.
3 Add the gelatine to the peach purée. Then whisk the egg white until stiff but not dry, and fold it into the purée.
4 Pour the mousse into a bowl or sundae dishes and leave in the refrigerator until set.
5 Decorate the mousse with a few sliced peaches.

Jill Myers
The British Diabetic Association,
London

RASPBERRY CLOUD

For 2.

1 orange
Half a lemon
2 trifle sponges
1 tablespoon Cointreau
15 g/½ caster sugar
120 ml/4 fl oz double cream
125 g/4 oz frozen or fresh
     raspberries

1 Grate rind from half of the orange and the half lemon. Squeeze juice.
2 Cut up sponges and divide between two sundae glasses or dishes.
3 Put half of the rind and half of the juice on top of sponges.
4 Put remaining rind, juice and liqueur into a bowl. Stir in sugar and cream.
5 Whisk until it forms a soft peak. Fold in raspberries.
6 Pile mixture into the dishes and chill in refrigerator for at least 3 hours before serving.

Judith Adshead
Porth Colman, Gwynedd

APPLE SOUFFLÉ CHEESECAKE

This cheesecake freezes well (before decorating). Cut individual slices and open-freeze them before wrapping to store. Allow 2 hours to thaw at rooom temperature.

BISCUIT BASE
50 g/2 oz butter
75 g/3 oz ginger biscuits, crushed

FILLING
225 g/8 oz cooking apples, peeled,
     cored and sliced
5 tablespoons cold water
2 teaspoons gelatine

100 g/4 oz cottage cheese, sieved
75 ml/2 fl oz soured cream*
75 g/3 oz caster sugar
1 egg, separated
A drop of green vegetable
    colouring (optional)
Apple slices, lemon juice and
    whipped cream (optional) to
    decorate

* *See Grapes with Muscovado sugar
page 140 for another recipe using soured
cream*

1 Melt the butter in a pan, then
pour it over the biscuit crumbs and
mix well together. Press this mixture
into the base of a loose-bottomed
flat tin, about 15 cm/6 inches
across.
2 Now for the filling. Cook the
apples with 3 tablespoons of cold
water until they are tender, then sieve
or blend them to a purée. Set aside to
cool.
3 Put 2 tablespoons water into
a small pan and sprinkle over
the gelatine. Leave it to soak for
5 minutes then, without letting
it boil, melt the gelatine over a
gentle heat until it is clear and
runny.
4 Mix together the apple purée,
gelatine, cottage cheese, soured cream,
sugar and egg yolk. This can quickly
be done in a food processor. If you
want to colour the filling a little, add
one or two drops of green food
colouring, but take great care not to
put in too much.
5 Whisk the egg white until
stiff then fold it into the apple
mixture.
6 Pour the filling into the biscuit case
and leave in the refrigerator for
several hours until set.
7 Decorate the top at the last minute
with slices of apple dipped in lemon
juice and also with whipped cream if
you like it, but the cake is already
very rich.

Mrs Jean McKean,
Lifford, Co. Donegal

CUSTARD SAUCE

*It's simple to make custard in a
microwave cooker. Here's enough for 2.*

300 ml/½ pint milk
1 slightly rounded dessertspoon
    custard powder
1 dessertspoon of sugar
A spoonful of cream, for a special
    occasion

1 In a 600 ml/1 pint jug blend the
custard powder, sugar and a little of
the milk to a paste. Stir in the rest
of the milk.
2 Heat, uncovered, on full power for
2 to 2½ minutes, stirring once after 1½
minutes.
3 Stir the custard before serving and
mix in the cream.

CONVENTIONAL METHOD
1 Pour the milk into a small pan and
whisk in the custard powder and
sugar.
2 Stirring continuously, heat the
mixture until it boils and thickens.
Remove from the heat and stir in the
cream.

Grace Mulligan

CRYSTALLISED LEAVES, FLOWERS, PETALS

**Violets, Primroses, Mint Leaves,
Geranium Petals**

All the above flowers and leaves can
be painted with beaten egg white,
dipped in caster sugar to preserve
their colour and flavour, and used to
decorate food. Make sure they are
dry, free from dew or rain drops.

1 Brush flowers and leaves clean.

147

2 Beat egg white until frothy.

3 Using a fine camel paint brush, coat each leaf back and front with egg white and while still wet dip in caster sugar. Shake off surplus sugar and leave to dry and crisp.

FROSTED FRUITS

The above method also applies to fruit like grapes, damsons, cherries.

1 Dip them in egg white in little bundles of two or three.

2 Drop them in a plastic bag with a little caster sugar, shake a little and then lay out carefully to dry.

TO DECORATE GLASS BOWLS AND TUMBLERS FOR PARTY DRINKS

1 Colour some caster sugar by rubbing a few drops of food colouring into dry sugar using the same movement as you would for rubbing fat into flour. Put the sugar into a flat dish about 5-cm/$\frac{1}{4}$-inch deep.

2 Whip egg white as usual and dip inverted bowl into the egg white, then into the coloured sugar.

3 Leave to dry. Be careful to keep colours very pale.

Grace Mulligan

148

Chapter 10

Breads, Scones
and Bakes

A NOTE ON 'EASY' YEASTS

The bread dough recipes in this chapter are all made using the 'Easy' dried yeasts which come in sachets called 'Easy Blend', 'Easy Bake', etc. It is wise to read the labels carefully to be certain which type it is.

1 The main feature is that you do not have to ferment these yeasts in water before starting. You mix them directly with the dry ingredients. In some cases if you do not mix them in dry they will not work.
2 The next feature is that some packets have a label such as 'Fast Action'. These contain a variety of improvers, sometimes Vitamin C (ascorbic acid) and with these it is not necessary to leave the bread to rise more than once.

It is important to note this detail because in some of the 'Easy'-labelled sachets, the contents are simply yeast granules in a pulverised form and, apart from being suitable to mix in with dry ingredients, this type works just like fresh yeast and the older forms of dried yeast, and the dough will mostly require two risings.

WHITE BREAD

Makes two 450-g/1-lb loaves or 12 medium-sized rolls or 18 dainty rolls. All freeze well.

675 g/1½ lb strong white bread flour
1 teaspoon salt
25 g/1 oz lard
1 sachet of 'easy blend' yeast *
450 ml/¾ pint warm water
Beaten egg and water to glaze (optional)

* *See above for a note about the 'easy' yeasts.*

150

1 Sieve the flour and salt into a warm bowl. Rub in lard and then stir in the dry yeast. Mix well.
2 Stir in the warm water with a wooden fork or spoon. When the dough has formed, use your hand to knead until it is soft and elastic. Finally turn out on to a slightly floured board and knead again for 5 minutes.
3 Return the dough to a clean greased bowl, cover and leave in a warm place to rise until doubled in size.
4 Knock back the dough by kneading the air out of it for a minute or two. Then cut it into two, knead briefly and shape to fit into the two, greased 450-g/1-lb tins.
5 Brush with the glaze if wanted.
6 Set loaves aside, covered loosely (a piece of oiled polythene is ideal) to prove until the dough rises to just above the top of the tins.
7 Preheat oven to hot, Gas 8, 450°F, 230°C, and bake for 30 to 40 minutes until brown and sounding hollow when removed from tin and tapped on the bottom. Cool on a wire rack.

BREAD ROLLS OR DINNER BUNS
Makes 12 to 18 rolls.

For a crusty top to the rolls, brush with a salt glaze: 5 ml/1 teaspoon salt dissolved in 30 ml/2 tablespoons water.

1 Use the above recipe for White Bread and proceed up to step 4.
2 Divide the risen dough into 12 or 18 pieces. Knead each piece to form either round buns or fancy shapes.
3 Place buns, not too close together, on greased baking sheets. Brush with the glaze if wanted and cover lightly until puffed up again – about 15 minutes.

4 Preheat oven to hot, Gas 8, 450°F, 230°C, and bake for 10 to 15 minutes according to the size of rolls. Cool on a wire rack.

Grace Mulligan

WHOLEMEAL BREAD

Makes two 450 g/1 lb loaves. Easy to make, excellent results. Freezes well.

675 g/1½ lb wholemeal plain
    flour
2 teaspoons salt
25 g/1 oz lard
1 sachet of 'easy blend' or 'easy
    bake' yeast *
1 tablespoon soft brown sugar
450 ml/¾ pint warm water
5 ml/1 teaspoon salt dissolved in
    30 ml/2 tablespoons water to
    glaze

* *For a note on 'easy' yeasts, see opposite page.*

For loaves with a lighter texture, use one third white flour to two thirds wholemeal. Wheatmeal flour also gives a good light result but does not have the flavour of wholemeal.

1 Mix flour and salt in a warm bowl and rub in lard. Stir in dry yeast.
2 Stir the sugar into the warm water and add to the dry ingredients.
3 Stir first of all, then knead in the bowl and then turn the dough out on to a lightly floured board. Knead briefly until smooth and elastic. If using a fast-action type of yeast you can leave out steps 4 and 5 and go straight to step 6.
4 Return the dough to a clean, greased bowl. Cover lightly and leave to rise in a warm place until the dough has doubled in size.
5 Knock back the dough, by kneading the air out of it for a minute or two.
6 Cut dough into 2 pieces and shape them to fit the greased bread tins, making sure that there is a smooth surface on top. Brush with the glaze.

7 Cover the tins loosely (a piece of oiled polythene is useful) and prove for 15 minutes or until the dough rises just above the rim of the tins.
8 Preheat oven to hot, Gas 8, 450°F, 230°C, and bake the loaves for 10 minutes. Then reduce the heat to moderately hot, Gas 6, 400°F, 200°C, for a further 10 minutes. Turn out and cool on wire racks.

Grace Mulligan

MILK BREAD

This is an enriched dough. Both loaves and rolls keep and freeze well. Makes two 450 g/1 lb loaves or 12 medium-sized rolls or 16 smaller ones.

450 g/1 lb strong white flour
1 teaspoon salt
50 g/2 oz lard or butter
1 sachet 'easy blend' yeast *
300 ml/½ pint warm milk
1 large egg, beaten
A little extra milk

* *See opposite page for a note about the 'easy' yeasts.*

1 Sieve the flour and salt into a warm bowl. Rub in the fat. Add the dried yeast. Mix well.
2 Mix the warm milk and all but one teaspoon of the beaten egg into the dry ingredients.
3 Mix and knead to a soft elastic dough, about 5 to 6 minutes. If using a fast-action type of yeast you can leave out steps 4 and 5 and go straight on to step 6.
4 Return the dough to a clean greased bowl. Cover lightly and leave to rise in a warm place for about 30 minutes or until the dough is almost doubled in size.
5 Knock back the risen dough by kneading the air out of it for a minute or two.
6 Cut dough in 2. Knead and shape to fit 2 well-greased 450 g/1 lb loaf tins.

7 Mix the leftover egg and about one tablespoon milk and glaze the 2 loaves. Set aside to prove, that is, let the dough rise, for about 15 minutes until it reaches to just above the top of tins.

8 Bake in a hot oven, Gas 8, 450°F, 230°C, for about 30 minutes.

POPPY SEED PLAIT

Milk Bread dough as above
25 g/1 oz poppy seeds

1 Make up the milk bread recipe then, starting at step 6, cut the dough in half.

2 Using a lightly floured surface, roll out the dough into a long oblong. Take a sharp knife and make two long cuts in the dough, making 3 fairly even strips. Squeeze together one end, plait the 3 pieces and squeeze the other end.

3 Brush with the glaze, see step 7 above, and cover with poppy seeds.

4 Set the plait on a greased baking sheet. Cover lightly – a sheet of oiled polythene is ideal –and let it rise in a warm place for 10 to 15 minutes until puffy.

5 Preheat oven to hot, Gas 8, 450°F, 230°C, and bake for about 30 minutes until golden and crisp on top and underneath. Cool on a wire rack.

BRIDGE ROLLS OR BATCH ROLLS

1 Use the milk bread recipe up to step 6 above. Then divide the dough into 16 pieces.

2 Roll each piece into a fat cigar shape. Try not to use too much flour on the board while you do this or you will get a streaky finish.

3 Place the long rolls close together on a greased baking sheet. Brush with the egg and milk glaze. Set aside, covered loosely, to puff up.

4 Bake in a preheated hot oven, Gas 8, 450°F, 230°C, for about 15 minutes. The rolls will join up during baking giving soft sides when they are pulled apart. Cool on a wire rack.

Grace Mulligan

HOT CROSS BUNS

Makes 12 buns which will freeze well for up to 2 months. Using dried yeast with added Vitamin C, one rising only is necessary.

450 g/1 lb plain wholemeal flour
1 sachet 'easy bake' yeast*
1 level teaspoon salt
25 g/1 oz soft brown sugar
2 level teaspoons mixed spice
25 g/1 oz lard
25 g/1 oz currants
25 g/1 oz sultanas
1 medium egg, size 3 or 4
200 ml/7 fl oz warm milk and water, mixed

BATTER FOR CROSSES
50 g/2 oz plain white flour
60 ml/2 fl oz cold water

GLAZE
2 level tablespoons sugar
2 tablespoons water

* For a note on 'easy' yeasts, see page 150.

1 In a roomy bowl, mix flour, dry yeast, salt, sugar and spice. Rub in lard and then mix in the fruit.

2 Beat the egg in a measuring jug, then add to it enough of the warm milk and water to make about 250 ml/8 fl oz.

3 Stir the liquid into the dry ingredients. Stir and mix until the dough comes together as a soft mixture. You may need to add a little more warm water.

4 Turn the dough on to a lightly floured surface and knead for 6 to 7 minutes until smooth and pliable.

5 Leave the dough covered for about
5 minutes to rest.
6 Divide the dough into 75 g/3 oz
pieces and shape into buns. Place on
greased baking sheets.
7 Leave lightly covered in a warm
place to rise. In 45 minutes to 1 hour
they should have doubled in size.
8 Preheat oven to moderately hot,
Gas 6, 400°F, 200°C.
9 For the crosses, mix together the
flour and water to achieve a thick
batter. Put this into a small icing bag
with a thick writing nozzle in it. Pipe
a neat cross gently on each bun.
10 Bake the buns for about 10
minutes when they will sound hollow
when tapped underneath.
11 Meanwhile, prepare the glaze. In a
small saucepan dissolve the sugar and
water and then boil it for just 2 or 3
minutes. Brush the warm glaze on the
hot buns as they come out of the
oven. Cool on wire trays.

Grace Mulligan

HONEY AND MALT FRUIT LOAF

*This loaf can be eaten plain, or in
buttered slices. Delicious, easy, and
quick!*

225 g/8 oz self-raising fine
    wholemeal flour
2 large tablespoons powdered
    malt drink
100 g/4 oz mixed dried fruit
2 tablespoons of runny honey
240 ml/8 fl oz milk or semi-
    skimmed milk

1 Mix all the ingredients together
very thoroughly.
2 Grease a 450-g/1-lb loaf tin and
line the base with a piece of
greaseproof paper.
3 Pour the mixture into the tin and
bake in the centre of a moderate
oven, Gas 4, 350°F, 180°C, for about
1 hour or until a skewer inserted into
the centre of the loaf comes out clean.

Grace Mulligan

DUMPLING LOAF

*Don't be put off by the name; this isn't
at all heavy and is delicious by itself,
or sliced and buttered. It freezes well.
Cut it into slices and wrap individually
in film, then put into the freezer.*

100 g/4 oz margarine
175 g/6 oz sugar
150 ml/¼ pint water
1 teaspoon bicarbonate of soda
225 g/8 oz sultanas
2 eggs
225 g/8 oz self-raising white or
    wholemeal flour, or a mixture
    of each
1 teaspoon mixed spice

1 Put the margarine, sugar, water,
bicarbonate of soda and sultanas into
a saucepan. Heat up, then boil for 5
minutes. Leave to cool for 10
minutes.
2 Beat in the eggs, flour and spice.
Turn the mixture into a greased and
lined 1-kg/2-lb loaf tin.
3 Bake in a warm oven, Gas 3,
325°F, 160°C, for 1¼ hours. Leave
in the tin for 5 minutes, then turn out
on to a wire rack to cool.

Mrs Oswald
Dalwhinnie, Inverness-shire

SPICED CARROT TEABREAD

*This rather unusual teabread is very
tasty, sliced and spread with butter or
cream cheese. It is moist and keeps well
lightly wrapped in foil, or it can be
frozen. Makes two 450 g/1 lb loaves.*

100 g/4 oz margarine
100 g/4 oz soft brown sugar
2 eggs, beaten
Finely grated rind of 1 orange
225 g/8 oz plain flour
1 teaspoon bicarbonate of soda
1 teaspoon salt
1 teaspoon ground cinnamon
1 teaspoon ground nutmeg

175 g/6 oz carrots, peeled and
   grated
50 g/2 oz candied mixed peel, very
   finely chopped
4 tablespoons orange juice
2 tablespoons water

1 Grease two 450–g/1–lb loaf tins and
line the bases with greaseproof paper.
2 Cream together the margarine and
sugar, then beat in the eggs and
orange rind.
3 Sieve in the flour, bicarbonate of
soda, salt and spices and carefully mix
everything together.
4 Stir in the grated carrot, mixed
peel, orange juice and water.
5 Put the mixture into the loaf tins
and bake in the middle of a moderate
oven, Gas 4, 350°F, 180°C, for about
50 minutes or until they are firm to
the touch.
6 Leave in the tins for 5 minutes
then turn out on to a cooling rack.

Margaret Heywood
Todmorden, Yorkshire

SPICY APPLE LOAF

*Makes 2 tasty, moist, small loaves.
Serve sliced and spread with butter,
margarine, or cream cheese. Freeze
well.*

1 size 2 egg
4 tablespoons oil
150 g/6 oz white or brown sugar
150 g/6 oz flour
¼ teaspoon bicarbonate of soda
½ teaspoon baking powder
½ teaspoon salt
1 teaspoon cinnamon
25 g/1 oz chopped nuts
50 g/2 oz sultanas
2 dessert apples (about 250 g/9 oz)
   peeled, cored and grated

1 Grease two 450–g/1–lb loaf tins and
line the bases with greaseproof paper.
2 Whisk the egg and oil together
until foamy, then whisk in the sugar.

3 Fold in the sieved flour,
bicarbonate of soda, baking powder,
salt and cinnamon.
4 Lastly, stir in the nuts, sultanas and
grated apples and ensure that
everything is well mixed.
5 Put the mixture into the prepared
tins and bake in the middle of a
moderate oven preheated to Gas 4,
350°F, 180°C, for about 50 minutes,
or until firm to the touch.

Margaret Heywood
Todmorden, Yorkshire

BRAN MUFFINS

*Delicious served with a cup of mid-
morning coffee. Makes 12 to 14. Freeze
well.*

50 g/2 oz All-Bran
150 ml/¼ pint milk
50 g/2 oz soft margarine
50 g/2 oz soft brown sugar
3 tablespoons lemon curd
25 g/1 oz chopped nuts
1 egg, beaten
1 tablespoon baking powder
100 g/4 oz plain flour, white or
   wholemeal

1 Soak the All-Bran in the milk until
it is soft.
2 In another bowl, beat together the
margarine, sugar and lemon curd. Stir
in the nuts, beaten egg and the milk
and All-Bran.
3 Sift the baking powder into the
flour and fold in.
4 Set 14 paper bun cases in a bun
tray and spoon the mixture into the
cases.
5 Bake in a moderately hot oven, Gas
6, 400°F, 200°C, for about 15
minutes.

Grace Mulligan

Microwave

*In the microwave this mixture comes
out better as a loaf than as muffins.*

Use 100 g/4 oz wholemeal self-raising flour and leave out the baking powder. Thick-cut marmalade, honey or ginger preserve can be used instead of lemon curd. Delicious sliced and buttered.

1 Line the base of a 450-g/1-lb loaf dish with a piece of greaseproof paper.
2 Put the All-Bran and milk into a bowl, heat on full power for 2 minutes then stir well and leave to cool for 5 minutes.
3 In another bowl, cream together the margarine, sugar and lemon curd. Stir in the nuts, egg and All-Bran mixture. Lastly fold in the flour.
4 Tip the mixture into the prepared dish, smooth over the top and cook on full power for 5 to 7 minutes. Shield the ends with small pieces of foil after 3 minutes, making sure the foil does not touch the sides of the cooker cavity. At the end of cooking the top may be sticky to the touch, but it should not have any uncooked batter on it. A cocktail stick inserted near the centre should come out clean when the loaf is cooked. Any stickiness should dry out while the loaf is standing.
5 Cool in the dish for 5 minutes, then turn on to a wire cooling rack.

COCONUT SCONES

These scones are delicious with butter or cream and black cherry jam. Easy to make half quantity, but they also freeze successfully. Makes about 12.

225 g/8 oz self-raising flour
½ teaspoon salt
50 g/2 oz lard or butter
50 g/2 oz caster sugar
50 g/2 oz desiccated coconut
About 150 ml/¼ pint milk

1 Preheat oven to hot, Gas 7, 425°F, 220°C.
2 Sieve the flour and salt into a bowl, then rub in the lard or butter until the mixture resembles fine breadcrumbs.
3 Stir in the sugar and coconut.
4 Pour in sufficient milk to make a stiff dough, then knead it lightly.
5 Roll out dough about 2 cm/¾ inch thick.
6 Cut out the scones using a 5-cm/2-inch cutter and re-roll the trimmings until all the dough is used up.
7 Put the scones on a greased baking sheet and cook towards the top of the preheated oven, for 10 to 15 minutes.
8 Cool on a wire rack.

Michelle Watkin
Thorngumbald, Hull

155

OATCAKES

Delicious hot or cold with butter and cheese or honey. Keep well in a tin for about 10 days; freeze well. Makes 10.

175 g/6 oz medium oatmeal,
    plus a little extra
A pinch of salt
A pinch of bicarbonate of soda
1 tablespoon melted butter
4 tablespoons hot water
A knob of suet or a *very* little lard
    to grease girdle

1 Mix 175 g/6 oz oatmeal with other ingredients to a workable dough.
2 Form a round lump, sprinkle with oatmeal and roll out almost paper thin.
3 Cut a large circle, using a dinner plate for guidance. Then cut this into triangles. You can get about 10 triangles.
4 Heat girdle and grease it. Cook oatcakes, turning carefully until they are crisp but not brown.

Grace Mulligan

TOM'S VANCOUVER CARROT CAKE

A lovely moist cake with a delicious topping. It freezes well with its topping and the nuts. Either freeze it in a piece, or in individual slices. These are best frozen on a tray, then transferred to a freezer box.

100 g/4 oz caster sugar
75 g/3 oz self-raising flour
A pinch of salt
½ teaspoon cinnamon
½ teaspoon bicarbonate of soda
60 ml/2 fl oz oil
1 egg
75 g/3 oz carrots, grated

TOPPING
100 g/4 oz cream cheese
50 g/2 oz butter

50 g/2 oz icing sugar
A few drops of vanilla essence
Chopped nuts

1 Grease an 18 cm/7 inch square cake tin and line the base with greaseproof paper.
2 Preheat the oven to moderate, Gas 4, 345°F, 180°C.
3 Sift the first five ingredients into a bowl, then beat in the oil and egg.
4 Mix in the grated carrots.
5 Put the mixture into the prepared tin and bake in the middle of the preheated oven, for 45 minutes or until firm.
6 Turn the cake out on to a wire rack to cool. When cold, slice it carefully through the middle ready for the filling and topping.
7 Cream together all the topping ingredients except the nuts. Divide the mixture and sandwich the two pieces of cake together with half of it. Spread the rest over the top and sprinkle with chopped nuts.

Tom Stephenson
Highgate, London

QUICK LEMON CAKE

Makes 2 very light cakes – one to eat, one to freeze for another day. For a change this cake can be made with orange rind and juice.

175 g/6 oz caster sugar
175 g/6 oz curd cheese or cottage
    cheese, sieved
Grated rind and juice of 1 lemon
2 beaten eggs
225 g/8 oz self-raising white flour,
    sieved
Milk

1 Preheat oven to moderate, Gas 3, 325°F, 160°C.
2 Mix together the caster sugar, curd cheese, lemon rind, lemon juice and beaten eggs.
3 Fold in the sieved flour and, if

necessary, add a little milk to make a dropping consistency.

4 Put the cake mixture into 2 greased and lined 250-g/1-lb loaf tins and bake in the middle of the oven for 40 to 45 minutes, until well-risen, firm to touch and golden brown.

4 When the cakes are cooked, leave them in the tins for 5 minutes then turn them on to a wire rack to cool.

Mrs Anne Walton
Frome, Somerset

GRANDMOTHER'S GINGER FRUIT CAKE

This recipe makes an 18-cm/7-inch cake, but it keeps well or can be cut into slices and frozen.

175 g/6 oz margarine
175 g/6 oz caster sugar
2 eggs, beaten
275 g/10 oz self-raising flour
2 teaspoons ground ginger
40 g/1½ oz glacé cherries, chopped
40 g/1½ oz sultanas
40 g/1½ oz raisins
100 g/4 oz crystallised ginger, chopped
Milk
1 to 2 tablespoons caster sugar

1 Cream together the margarine and sugar, then gradually stir in the beaten eggs.
2 Sieve together the flour and ground ginger and fold into the mixture.
3 Add the dried fruit and half of the crystallised ginger and pour in sufficient milk to make a dropping consistency.
4 Turn into a greased and lined 18-cm/7-inch cake tin and scatter the remaining crystallised ginger on top.
5 Sprinkle the top of the cake with caster sugar and bake in a moderate oven, Gas 4, 350°F, 180°C, for 1¼ hours.

Mrs Dawn Brown
Darlington, Co. Durham

HAROLD'S FRUIT CAKE

Simple and quick. Freezes well. Makes a 15-cm/6-inch sponge.

150 ml/¼ pint milk
100 g/4 oz dried mixed fruit
100 g/4 oz dark soft brown sugar
100 g/4 oz margarine
1 size 3 egg, beaten
150 g/5 oz wholemeal self-raising flour

1 Put the milk, dried fruit, sugar and margarine into a saucepan and boil for 5 minutes. Leave it to cool.
2 Stir the egg and flour into the saucepan.
3 Grease a 15-cm/6-inch sponge tin and line the base with a circle of greaseproof paper.
4 Pour the cake mixture into the prepared tin and level the top.
5 Preheat oven to moderately hot, Gas 5, 375°F, 190°C.
6 Bake in the centre of the oven for 25 minutes.
7 Leave in tin for 10 minutes and then turn out on to a wire rack to cool.

Mrs Winifred Bulstrode,
Waterlooville, Hampshire

Microwave

This comes out very moist and has a good dark colour if it is made with dark soft brown sugar.

1 Put the milk, dried fruit, sugar and margarine into a mixing bowl, heat on full power for 4 minutes then stir. Leave to cool.
2 Stir the egg and flour into the cooled fruit mixture.
3 Line the base of an 18-cm/7-inch round cake dish with a circle of greaseproof paper. Tip the cake mixture into the prepared dish and smooth over the top.

4 Cook on full power for 3½ to 4 minutes. Test the cake with a wooden cocktail stick. It should come out clean when the cake is cooked. If you need to add extra time, continue to cook on full power, checking every 10 to 20 seconds. Let it cool in the dish for 5 minutes before turning on to a cooling rack.

5 Preheat oven to moderate, Gas 3, 325°F, 160°C, bake for 1 hour, then reduce the temperature to cool, Gas 2, 300°F, 150°C and cook for a further 1 to 1½ hours. To test to see if it is cooked insert a fine skewer into the middle of the cake; if it comes out clean, the cake is ready.

Mrs F. E. Thompson
Crossgate Moor, Durham

SHERRY CAKE

This recipe uses quite a lot of sherry, but it makes the fruit very moist and gives the cake a special taste. It also keeps well and can be frozen in slices. Makes an 18-cm/7-inch square cake.

175 g/6 oz sultanas
175 g/6 oz raisins
100 g/4 oz currants
75 g/3 oz glacé cherries, chopped
75 g/3 oz mixed peel, chopped
150 ml/¼ pint sherry
175 g/6 oz butter or margarine
175 g/6 oz dark brown sugar
3 eggs
100 g/4 oz white or wholemeal
    plain flour
100 g/4 oz white or wholemeal
    self-raising flour
½ teaspoon mixed spice
A pinch of salt
25 g/1 oz ground almonds

1 Put the dried fruits, glacé cherries and mixed peel into a bowl and pour over the sherry. Leave overnight covered with a damp cloth.
2 Next day, cream together the butter or margarine and sugar until light and fluffy, then gradually stir in the eggs.
  Sieve the flours, mixed spice and ... d mix with ground almonds, ... into the cake mixture.
  ... in the fruit and any ... ins at the bottom of ... to a lined 18- ... in.

1 Put the dried fruits, glacé cherries and mixed peel into a bowl and pour over the sherry. Cover with clear film and heat on full power for 5 minutes. Leave to stand until cold, stirring from time to time. Alternatively leave the mixture overnight to absorb the sherry.
2 Use margarine rather than butter and cream it with the sugar until light and fluffy, then gradually stir in the eggs, beating well after each addition.
3 Fold in the flour, mixed spices, almonds and salt. Lastly stir in the fruit and any remaining sherry.
4 Line the base of a 20–cm/8-inch round cake dish with a circle of greaseproof paper. Tip the cake mixture into the prepared dish, smooth over the top and cook on Low for 18 to 20 minutes. To test if the cake is cooked, insert a fine skewer into the centre of the cake. If it is cooked it will come out clean. The top of the cake will have lost its glossy appearance and look dry and it should pull away from the sides easily if it is properly cooked. If the cake needs extra time continue cooking on Low, checking every 30 to 60 seconds.

For a 2-power microwave cooker: Cook on Defrost for 25 to 30 minutes, testing as above.

PLAIN SPONGE

The quantity of mixture will make one small sponge cake, four currant buns AND two small steamed puddings. They all freeze well. Also see the Chocolate Sponge recipe for the same idea.

BASIC ALL-IN-ONE MIXTURE

175 g/6 oz soft margarine
175 g/6 oz caster sugar
175 g/6 oz self-raising flour
1 teaspoon baking powder
3 eggs
2 to 3 drops vanilla flavouring

Put all the ingredients into a large bowl and mix well together. Alternatively, use a food processor.

1 Grease a small (18-cm/7-inch) round sandwich tin and line the base with a circle of greaseproof paper.
2 Three-quarters fill the tin with the cake mixture and level off the surface.
3 Bake in a moderate oven, Gas 4, 350°F, 180°C, for 20 to 25 minutes or until the cake is firm and just shrinking away from the sides of the tin.
4 Turn it out on to a wire rack. When cold, decorate the top with either of the following toppings:

CRUNCHY LEMON TOPPING

1 tablespoon lemon juice
1 tablespoon granulated sugar

Quickly stir together the juice and the sugar and spread this over the top of the cake. The idea is to spread it over before the sugar melts to achieve a crunchy surface.

RASPBERRY AND COCONUT TOPPING

1 tablespoon raspberry jam
1 dessertspoon coarse desiccated coconut

Spread the jam over the top of the cake and scatter the coconut on top.

STEAMED PUDDINGS

1 Grease two small cups and put a little lemon curd or plum jam into each.
2 Half-fill the cups with the sponge mixture, then cover each cup with foil and steam for 45 minutes until firm to the touch. (It is a good idea to cook something else in the simmering water under the steamer e.g. rice, or pasta.) If you haven't got a steamer, stand the cups on an upturned saucer (or on 2 jam-pot lids) in a saucepan with a well-fitting lid. Pour in boiling water to come halfway up the sides of the cups, put on the lid and keep the water simmering for 45 minutes until firm to the touch.
3 Leave for a few moments before turning out.

CURRANT BUNS

1 Stir 1 tablespoon of currants into the remaining sponge mixture.
2 Set 4 paper bun cases in a metal bun tray and half-fill them with the bun mixture.
3 Bake in a moderate oven, Gas 4, 350°F, 180°C, for 15 to 20 minutes or until the buns are risen and firm to the touch.

Grace Mulligan

Microwave

The 2 steamed puddings cook perfectly.

1 Put a little lemon curd or plum jam into 2 small tea cups and half fill them with sponge mixture.
2 Cover with clear film and cook both together on full power for 2 to 3 minutes. Allow to stand for a minute before turning out.

One pudding cooks in 1 to 1½ minutes.

CHOCOLATE SPONGE

This recipe quantity will make one small sponge cake, four cherry or walnut buns AND two small steamed puddings. They all freeze well. Also see Plain Sponge for the same idea.

BASIC ALL-IN-ONE MIXTURE

175 g/6 oz soft margarine
175 g/6 oz caster sugar
175 g/6 oz self-raising flour
1 level tablespoon cocoa
2 tablespoons warm water
1½ teaspoons baking powder
3 eggs

Mix all the ingredients together in a large bowl or in a food processor.

SPONGE CAKE

1 Grease a small (18-cm/7-inch) round sandwich tin and line the base with a circle of greaseproof paper.
2 Three-quarters fill the tin with the cake mixture and level off the surface.
3 Bake in a moderate oven, Gas 4, 350°F, 170°C, for about 20 to 25 minutes, or until the cake is firm and just shrinking away from the sides of the tin.
4 Turn it out on to a wire rack. When cold, decorate with one of Debbie's toppings suggested below:

CHOCOLATE FUDGE TOPPING

40 g/1½ oz butter
25 g/1 oz cocoa
2 tablespoons milk
100 g/4 oz icing sugar, sieved

1 Melt the butter in a small pan, add the cocoa and cook for a minute.
2 Remove from the heat and stir in the milk and icing sugar. Beat well until smooth then leave it, stirring from time to time until it thickens to a spreading consistency. Spread thickly and evenly over the top of the cake.

GINGER TOPPING

50 g/2 oz crystallised ginger, chopped
50 g/2 oz icing sugar, sieved
About 2 teaspoons water

1 Scatter the ginger on top of the cake.
2 Measure the icing sugar into a bowl and work in sufficient water to give a smooth glacé icing.
3 Spoon into a small polythene bag, snip off the corner of the bag with a pair of scissors and drizzle the icing over the ginger. Allow to set.

STEAMED PUDDINGS

1 Grease two small cups and put a little marmalade or apricot jam into each.
2 Half-fill the cups with sponge mixture, then cover each cup with foil and steam for 45 minutes until firm to the touch. (It is a good idea to cook something else in the simmering water under the steamer e.g. rice or pasta.) If you haven't got a steamer stand the cups on an upturned saucer (or even on 2 jam-pot lids) in a saucepan with a well-fitting lid. Pour in boiling water to come halfway up the sides of the cups, put on the lid and keep the water simmering for 45 minutes until the puddings are firm to the touch. Leave to stand for a few moments before turning out.

CHERRY BUNS

1 Chop up 4 glacé cherries or 2 or 3 walnuts quite small and stir them into the remaining sponge mixture.
2 Set 4 paper bun cases in a metal bun tray and half-fill them with the mixture.
3 Bake in a moderate oven, Gas 4, 350°F, 180°C, for 15 to 20 minutes or until the buns are risen and firm to the touch.

Grace Mulligan and
Debbie Woolhead

160

The 2 steamed puddings cook perfectly.

1 Put a little marmalade or apricot jam into 2 small teacups and half-fill them with the sponge mixture.
2 Cover with clear film and cook both together on full power for 2 to 3 minutes. Allow to stand for a minute before turning out.

One pudding cooks in 1 to 1½ minutes.

WHOLEMEAL CHOCOLATE CAKE

A moist cake, not too sweet, with a nutty feel given by the wholemeal flour. Freezes well with or without icing.

120 ml/4 fl oz boiling water
25 g/1 oz cocoa
175 g/6 oz caster sugar
60 ml/2 fl oz oil
A pinch of salt
60 ml/2 fl oz milk – sour milk can be used
1 egg, beaten lightly
½ teaspoon vanilla essence
175 g/6 oz wholemeal flour
1 teaspoon baking powder

1 Put the boiling water, cocoa, sugar, oil and salt into a bowl; mix well and leave until cool.
2 Stir in the milk, egg and vanilla.
3 Mix the flour and baking powder together, then fold into the cake.
4 Pour the mixture into a greased and lined round cake tin about 18 cm/7 inches in diameter, or an 18-cm/7-inch square tin.
5 Bake the cake in the middle of a warm oven, Gas 3, 325°F, 160°C, for about 45 minutes or until a fine skewer inserted into the centre of the cake comes out clean.

6 Leave the cake in the tin for 15 minutes, then turn out on to a cooling rack.
7 When the cake is cool either dust the top with icing sugar, or cover the top and sides with chocolate butter icing.

CHOCOLATE BUTTER ICING

50 g/2 oz butter or margarine or a mixture, softened
75 g/3 oz icing sugar
1 dessertspoon cocoa powder

Beat butter or margarine until soft, sift in the icing sugar and cocoa and mix to a paste. Spread over the top and sides of the cake and put it in a cool place to firm up.

Olive Robin
Abbeytown, Carlisle

Yvonne Hamlett, who did all the microwave conversions for this book, says this is one of the nicest microwave cakes she has made and has now used it as a base for a gâteau filled with fresh fruit and cream.

For this you should use self-raising wholemeal flour to obtain the best results and leave out the baking powder.

1 Put the boiling water, cocoa, sugar, oil and salt into a mixing bowl, and beat well so that the mixture is smooth like batter. Leave to cool.
2 Stir in the milk, eggs and vanilla flavouring. Fold in the flour.
3 Line the base of 20-cm/8-inch round cake dish with a circle of greaseproof paper. Tip the cake mixture into the dish and smooth over the top.
4 Cook on full power for 4 to 4½ minutes. When the cake is cooked, it should just pull away from the sides of the dish; the top may look a little

wet but there should be no raw batter. A wooden cocktail stick inserted into the centre should come out clean.
5 Let it cool in the dish for 5 minutes then turn on to a wire cooling rack.

Decorate with a dusting of icing sugar or with Chocolate Butter Icing, (above).

WHOLEMEAL GINGERBREAD

This bakes best in a 18-cm/7-inch square tin. It improves with keeping in a tin for 2 days before eating. Freezes well in the piece or cut into individual slices.

100 g/4 oz block margarine
100 g/4 oz black treacle
100 g/4 oz golden syrup
50 g/2 oz Demerara sugar
125 ml/¼ pint milk
225 g/8 oz wholemeal flour
2 teaspoons ground ginger
2 level teaspoons mixed spice
2 level teaspoons bicarbonate of soda
1 beaten egg

1 In a large saucepan, warm together margarine, treacle, syrup, and sugar until the fat has melted.
2 Stir in the milk and allow to cool.
3 Mix the dry ingredients, sieving the spices and bicarbonate of soda to break up any lumps.
4 Add the beaten egg to the cooled syrup mixture and pour it into the bowl of dry ingredients. Mix well.
5 Grease an 18-cm/7-inch square tin and line the bottom with greaseproof paper. Pour in the gingerbread mixture.
6 Bake in a cool oven, Gas 2, 300°F, 150°C, for 1 to 1¼ hours or until well risen and firm to the touch.
7 Cool on a wire rack.

Grace Mulligan

Microwave

Gingerbreads cook well in the microwave – but you must have the correct size of dish. If the dish is too small, the mixture will either erupt out of the dish like a volcano or cook very unevenly.

Microwave gingerbreads tend to be slightly less deep, as they cook better in a shallow, wider dish than is used when baking conventionally.
They keep well – and the flavour, as always, improves if they are wrapped in foil and stored for 2 to 3 days before cutting.
The above ingredients give too much mixture, so halve them as follows:

50 g/2 oz margarine
50 g/2 oz black treacle
50 g/2 oz golden syrup
25 g/1 oz Demerara sugar
4 tablespoons milk
1 egg, beaten
100 g/4 oz wholemeal flour
1 teaspoon ground ginger
1 teaspoon mixed spice
1 teaspoon bicarbonate of soda

1 Put the margarine, treacle, syrup and sugar into a mixing bowl. Heat on full power for 3 minutes, then stir in the milk and leave to cool.
2 Add the beaten egg to the cooled syrup mixture. Then fold in the dry ingredients.
3 Line the base of a 20-cm/8-inch round cake dish with a circle of greaseproof paper. Pour the cake mixture into the prepared dish and smooth over the top.
4 Cook on full power for 4½ to 5 minutes. The top might look a little shiny, but the sides should pull away from the dish easily and a wooden cocktail stick inserted in the centre should come out clean.
5 Let the cake cool in the dish for 5 minutes then turn it on to a cooling rack.

6 When cold, wrap in foil and store for 2 to 3 days before slicing.

YOGHURT CAKE

A very easy cake to make because nearly all the ingredients are measured in the 150 ml/5 fl oz carton in which the yoghurt comes. Makes a moist 18-cm/7-inch cake, not rich; freezes well.

1 carton (150 ml/5 fl oz) of
   orange or mandarin yoghurt
1 carton of oil
1 carton of caster sugar
3 cartons of self-raising flour
3 eggs
Finely grated rind of 1 orange
   (optional)
1 pinch of salt

1 Preheat oven to moderately hot, Gas 5, 375°F, 190°C.
2 Stir all the ingredients together and put the mixture into a greased 18-cm/7-inch cake tin, or a 900-g/2-lb loaf tin, or two 450-g/1-lb loaf tins. It is wise to line the bottom with greaseproof paper.
3 Bake the cake in the centre of the preheated oven for about 45 minutes, or until firm to the touch.

4 Leave cake in tin for about 15 minutes, then turn it out on to a wire rack to cool.

Mrs Doreen Wright
Forthampton, Gloucestershire

AUSTRALIAN CAKES

Delicious. Like cookies, they are crisp on the outside and soft inside.

75 g/3 oz margarine
75 g/3 oz caster sugar
1 egg
75 g/3 oz self-raising flour, sieved
½ teaspoon baking powder
Cornflakes, crushed slightly

1 Preheat oven to moderately hot, Gas 6, 400°F, 200°C.
2 Cream together the margarine and caster sugar, then stir in the egg.
3 Fold in the sieved flour and baking powder.
4 Take teaspoonfuls of the mixture and roll them in the crushed cornflakes.
5 Space them well apart on a greased baking sheet and bake in preheated oven for 15 minutes.
6 Transfer to a wire rack and allow to cool.

Mrs Hunter
Hessle, N. Humberside

CHERRY AND ALMOND SLICE

Can be made in an electric mixer or processor. Freezes well.

125 g/5 oz soft margarine
125 g/5 oz caster sugar
3 eggs
125 g/5 oz self-raising flour
50 g/2 oz ground almonds
75 g/3 oz chopped glacé cherries
A few drops of almond essence
A sprinkle of caster sugar to finish

1 Cream margarine and sugar until light and fluffy.
2 Mix in eggs one at a time alternately with flour.
3 Mix in almonds, cherries and essence.
4 Grease a Swiss roll tin and line it with greased and floured paper. Spread mixture evenly in tin.
5 Preheat the oven to moderately hot, Gas 5, 375°F, 190°C, and bake in the middle for 30 minutes.
6 Carefully remove cake from tin as soon as it is baked and sprinkle with caster sugar. Cut into slices when cold.

Anne Wallace
Stewarton, Ayrshire

LUCY CAKE

This nicely fits an 18-cm/7-inch square shallow tin. If you double the quantities it fits a small Swiss roll tin. Keeps well for a week.

50 g/2 oz block margarine
25 g/1 oz caster sugar
1 egg yolk
85 g/3½ oz self-raising flour
Jam, raspberry or apricot are both nice

TOPPING
1 egg white
50 g/2 oz caster sugar
25 g/1 oz desiccated coconut

1 Grease the tin.
2 Preheat oven to moderately hot, Gas 5, 375°F, 190°C.
3 Cream together the margarine and sugar until light and fluffy, then stir in the egg yolk and fold in the flour.
4 Press this mixture into the tin and spread some jam over the top of it.
5 Whisk the egg white until stiff, then gradually whisk in the sugar. Fold in the coconut.
6 Spread the meringue mixture on top of the jam and bake the cake in the middle of the oven for 35 to 40 minutes.
7 Cut the cake into portions in the tin while it is still warm.

Mrs Joyce Beresford
Bolton, Lancashire

QUICK HONEY SQUARES

Very easy to make; very bad for the figure.

225 g/8 oz Marie biscuits (or any plain sweet biscuit)
75 g/3 oz butter or margarine
3 tablespoons set honey
3 tablespoons crunchy peanut butter

1 Crush the biscuits in a food processor or put them in a strong plastic bag and crush with a rolling pin.
2 In a medium-sized pan, melt the butter and the honey very gently, then stir in the peanut butter.
3 Mix in the biscuit crumbs and stir very well together.
4 Press into a greased 18-cm/7-inch square tin. Level off the top and allow to cool. Then cut into small squares.

Grace Mulligan

WALNUT FLAT CAKE

Easy to mix – all in one saucepan.

1 tablespoon golden syrup or
    black treacle
50 g/2 oz margarine
100 g /4 oz brown sugar
100 g/4 oz self-raising flour
50 g/2 oz broken walnuts, roughly
    chopped
1 egg, beaten

1 Preheat oven to moderate, Gas 4,
350°F, 180°C. Grease and line a 15 to
18 cm/6 to 7 inch square tin with
greaseproof paper.
2 Put the syrup or treacle, margarine
and sugar into a saucepan and stir
until the margarine melts.
3 Let it cool slightly, then stir in the
flour and walnuts.
4 Mix in the beaten egg then put the
mixture into the prepared tin.
5 Bake in the middle of the oven, for
25 to 30 minutes.
6 Leave the cake in the tin until
completely cold, then cut it into
squares.

Mrs M. Boon
Stockton, Cleveland

ANZACS

*These large crisp biscuits are well-
known all over Australia. They will
keep very well in an airtight container.
You will get about 24 biscuits. Easy to
mix – all in one large saucepan.*

150 g/5 oz butter or margarine
1 tablespoon golden syrup
2 tablespoons water
1 teaspoon bicarbonate of soda
100 g/4 oz plain flour
75 g/3 oz porridge oats
50 g/2 oz desiccated coconut
100 g/4 oz caster sugar

1 Melt the butter gently with the
syrup in a large saucepan. Remove
from heat.
2 Stir in the water and bicarbonate of
soda, then all the remaining
ingredients.
3 Put teaspoonfuls of the mixture on
to greased baking sheets. Leave plenty
of room between the biscuits as they
spread as they cook.
4 Bake in a cool oven, Gas 3, 325°F,
160°C, for about 20 minutes until just
golden brown.
5 Leave the biscuits on the baking
sheets for a few minutes to harden up
slightly, then put them on a wire rack
to cool.

Mrs Eunice Heath
Thirsk, North Yorkshire

BRAN BISCUITS

*Yields about 30 light crisp biscuits
which are very 'more-ish'. Keep well in
an airtight container for at least 2
weeks.*

100 g/4 oz butter or block
    margarine
75 g/3 oz caster sugar
1 egg, beaten
Grated rind of 1 orange
50 g/2 oz bran
100 g/4 oz plain flour

1 Preheat oven to moderate, Gas 4,
350°F, 180°C.
2 Cream together the butter or
margarine and sugar until light and
fluffy.
3 Stir in the egg, orange rind, bran
and flour.
4 Form into a ball and roll out on a
well-floured board. Cut out the
biscuits with a 5-cm/2-inch cutter and
place them on a well-greased baking
tray.
5 Bake for about 25 minutes.

Variation: add a few chopped
walnuts or raisins to the recipe at
step 2.

Sylvia McBeth
Coventry, Warwickshire

165

CUMBERLAND SHORTBREAD

Keeps for weeks in an airtight container.

150 g/5 oz butter
25 g/1 oz margarine
75 g/3 oz caster sugar
200 g/7 oz plain flour
25 g/1 oz self-raising flour
A pinch of salt
Extra caster sugar

1 Cream together the butter, margarine and sugar. Work in the flour and salt then put the mixture into an ungreased 20–cm/8-inch tin and prick all over.
2 Bake at the top of a cool oven, Gas 2, 300°F, 150°C, for 45 minutes or until golden brown.
3 Remove from the oven and, while still warm, mark the shortbread into portions and sprinkle with caster sugar.
4 When cold, remove from the tin and cut up. Store in an airtight container.

Mrs E. M. Brunt
Keepers Corner, Surrey

MUESLI BARS

Makes 6 pieces. Keep well in an airtight tin. (See page 16 for a home-made muesli mix.)

3 tablespoons golden syrup
75 g/3 oz margarine
50 g/2 oz rolled porridge oats
50 g/2 oz plain peanuts, roughly chopped
100 g/4 oz muesli

1 In a large pan, melt the syrup and margarine, then stir in the rest of the ingredients.
2 Line the base of an 18–cm/7-inch square tin with non-stick paper and pour in the mixture.
3 Level it off and bake at Gas 4, 350°F, 180°C for about 20 minutes.
4 Mark into bars while still warm and leave to cool in the tin.

Grace Mulligan

Chapter 11

Preserves and Chutneys

plus Home-made Sweets

TESTING JAMS AND JELLIES FOR SETTING POINT

1 **Volume test** If you know the expected yield of your fruit – e.g. the recipe says you will get, say 2.5 kg/5 lb of jam, then measure out that amount in water. Take a 450 g/1 lb jam jar (not a 325g/12 oz jar), fill it 5 times and pour this into your pan. Use a wooden spoon handle, stand it upright in the water and mark this level with a pencil. Keep the spoon handy. Then, when you are testing for a set, draw pan off heat, wait until bubbling subsides and stand spoon in the jam. When the volume has returned to the level of the pencil mark, the jam is ready to pot.

2 **Cold plate test** Have some plates cooling in the refrigerator, and take a teaspoon of jam and drop it on a cold plate. Wait a minute and, if it wrinkles when pushed, the jam is ready. If not, go on boiling a little longer.

3 **Flake test** Dip a clean wooden spoon in boiling jam. Allow the cooling jam to drop from the spoon. If the drops run together and form a flake or curtain it is ready to pot.

4 **Temperature test** Use a sugar thermometer. It is important to dip the thermometer in hot water immediately before using it in the jam. Submerge the bulb fully in the boiling jam, but do not let it touch bottom of pan. When the thermometer registers 220°F or 106°C the jam is ready to pot.

TIPS FOR MAKING PRESERVES IN THE MICROWAVE

It is best to make small batches to avoid the mixture boiling over.
Use the biggest bowl that will fit into your microwave cooker: 4 to 5-litre/7 to 8-pint size. Pyrex bowls are ideal. If you have a large plastic dome from a roasting dish this is ideal *providing* it is made from a plastic called Polysulphane. Check the manufacturer's instructions, as some plastics will not withstand the high temperatures of boiling sugar mixtures.
There is no need to turn the oven off each time you stir – as soon as the door is opened the oven switches off, so you can set the time at the beginning rather than keep on resetting every 2 to 3 minutes.
Take care always to lift the dish using oven gloves, as the preserve will transfer its heat to the cooking container so it will be very hot.
Don't be tempted to leave the wooden spoon in the mixture – it will absorb the microwave energy and become too hot to handle.
Start checking the setting of jams etc. in the usual way after 8 to 10 minutes, then check every minute until the correct setting point is reached.

Yvonne Hamlett
Haddenham, Buckinghamshire

MATRIMONIAL JAM
Makes 1.8 to 2.2. kg/4 to 5 lb.

This recipe was given to us once before and was called High Dumpsie-Dearie Jam. Please let us know if you have ever been told any of the origins of these quaint old names.

450 g/1 lb plums
450 g/1 lb pears
450 g/1 lb cooking apples
Finely grated rind and juice
  of 1 lemon
1.3 kg/3 lb sugar

1 Cut the plums in half and remove the stones. Peel and core the pears and apples and cut into chunks.
2 Put all the fruit into a large

saucepan and add the lemon rind and lemon juice. Put on the lid.
3 Cook slowly until the fruit is soft.
4 Meanwhile put sugar and clean jam jars to warm in a very cool oven, Gas $\frac{1}{4}$, 225°F, 110°C.
5 Add the warm sugar and bring slowly up to the boil, stirring all the time. Boil the mixture until setting point is reached (see left).
6 While jam is hot, fill the warmed jars to the brim. Put on waxed paper discs, waxed side down. Either put the jam pot covers on at once or leave till jam is quite cold. Never put covers on while jam is between hot and cold or condensation could occur which might lead to mould forming on top of the jam.

Mrs Heather Wade
Leyburn, North Yorkshire

Microwave ━━━━━━━━━━━━━━

See opposite page for a few tips on making preserves by microwave.

225 g/8 oz plums
225g/8 oz pears
225 g/8 oz cooking apples
Finely grated rind and juice of
**   one lemon**
750 g/1½ lb sugar

Jam in the microwave has to be made in fairly small quantities. These ingredients will be safe if your bowl is big enough and will yield two 450–g/1–lb jars plus enough for a ramekin or small jar.

1 Cut the plums in half and remove the stones. Peel and core the pears and apples and cut into chunks.
2 Put all the fruit, lemon rind and peel into a 5–litre/8–pint Pyrex mixing bowl. Heat on full power for 8 to 10 minutes until the fruit is soft.
3 Stir in the sugar, heat on full power for 3 to 5 minutes. Stir every minute until the sugar has dissolved.

4 Continue cooking on full power for 15 to 20 minutes, stirring every 3 to 5 minutes as the jam boils up. Start testing for correct setting point after 12 minutes. (See testing notes on opposite page).
5 Cool in the bowl for 10 minutes, then pot, seal and label as in step 6 above.

QUINCE JAM

Makes about 600 g/1¼ lb of quite tart jam which has good colour and consistency.

450 g/1 lb quinces
A good 150 ml/¼ pint water
450 g/1 lb sugar, warmed
Juice of half a lemon

1 Peel and core the quinces. Put the peel and cores into a saucepan with the water and simmer until soft and pulpy.
2 Sieve the mixture and discard the peel and cores.
3 Grate (or chop and mince) the quinces and put them into a saucepan with the purée. If necessary add a very little more water. Heat to boiling point, cover the pan and simmer until soft.
4 Add the sugar and lemon juice to the pan and heat slowly, uncovered, until the mixture boils.
5 Boil the jam steadily until setting point is reached, about 15 minutes. Then bottle in clean warm jam jars.
6 Put on waxed paper discs immediately, waxed side down. Put on jam jar covers either at once or when jam is quite cold. This is to avoid condensation which can lead to mould on top of jam.

John H. J. Slater
Fareham, Hampshire

See page 168 for a few tips on making preserves by microwave.

Yields about 675 g/1½ lb

1 Peel and core the quinces. Put the peel and cores into a large Pyrex mixing bowl (use the largest one that will fit in your microwave cooker). Heat uncovered on full power for 10 minutes.

2 Sieve the mixture, reserve the liquid, and discard the cores and peel.

3 Grate the quinces into the bowl. Add the watery purée. Heat on full power for 5 minutes.

4 Add the sugar and lemon juice, stirring well. Heat on full power for 5 minutes, stirring twice. The sugar should by now have melted.

5 Heat the mixture on full power for 8 to 10 minutes until boiling, then continue heating on full power, stirring every minute until setting point is reached. Once the mixture boils it will take about 5 to 9 minutes to reach setting point. (See page 168 for testing for setting notes.) Always use a wooden spoon for stirring and stir every minute or the mixture will boil over. Do not leave the wooden spoon in the jam as this will absorb the microwave energy and get too hot to handle. It will also prolong the cooking time.

6 Allow the jam to cool for 5 minutes, then pot it in warm jars. Put on waxed paper discs at once to seal the surface. Then either put on jam pot covers immediately or else wait until the jam is quite cold. This is to avoid condensation inside the covers which can turn to mould.

RASPBERRY JAM
Yields 2.25 kg/5 lb. Easy to make less.

1½ kg/3 lb freshly picked ripe raspberries
1½ kg/3 lb granulated sugar

1 Avoid over-ripe fruit or the jam may not set. Pick over the raspberries. Do not wash unless absolutely necessary. Put in a roomy pan with the lid on.

2 Put sugar to warm in a slow oven, Gas ¼, 225°F, 110°C' Put clean jars to warm at same time.

3 Simmer fruit gently until juice begins to run. Mash it down with a potato masher to speed the process.

4 Take lid off pan and continue cooking until the fruit is tender and the contents of the pan have reduced slightly.

5 Make a pectin test: remove pan from heat. Take out a teaspoonful of the juice into a glass and let it cool. Then add 3 teaspoons methylated spirits to the sample, swirl it around gently. If plenty of pectin is present, a clear jelly clot will form. If a medium amount of pectin is present, several small clots will form. If a poor amount of pectin is present, no real clot will be found. If a reasonable clot does not occur, cook fruit in pan a little longer to reduce liquid. *Do not on any account return the test sample to the pan.*

6 Now add the warmed sugar and stir over low heat until it is dissolved.

7 Raise the heat and bring to a full rolling boil until setting point is reached. (See page 168.)

8 Pot in warmed jars, put on waxed paper discs at once and either put on jam pot covers immediately, or wait until the jam is quite cold – never in between. This is to avoid condensation inside the cover which can lead to mould on the jam. Label and store in a cool dark place.

Grace Mulligan

See page 168 for a few tips on making preserves by microwave.

It is best to make small batches of the jam in the microwave, to prevent the mixture boiling over. The amounts given below are safe if you use a large enough bowl. Any soft fruit can be substituted for the raspberries.

450 g/1 lb raspberries, fresh or frozen*
450 g/1 lb sugar
Two 5 ml teaspoons lemon juice

* *Put the frozen fruit into the bowl and heat on full power for 4 minutes, then mix in the sugar and continue as follows.*

1 Put all the ingredients in a large Pyrex mixing bowl. Use the largest that will fit in your microwave cooker, a 4-litre/7-pint size is ideal.

Heat, uncovered, on full power for 5 minutes, stirring twice. The sugar should now have melted; if not, continue to heat on full power for a further 1 to 2 minutes.
2 Once the sugar has dissolved, heat the jam on full power for 10 to 16 minutes, stirring occasionally. Start testing for setting point after 8 minutes and every 2 minutes thereafter. (See page 168 for testing notes.)
3 Finish the jam as given in step 8 above.

RHUBARB MARMALADE

This recipe came originally to Mrs Hopkins from a Canadian cousin. It's easy to make more than the 2.25 kg/5 lb this yields. Although rhubarb does not have a high pectin content, the orange makes up for this and there are no problems at all if you use the 'sugar-with-pectin' now available in shops.

Rhubarb Marmalade continued

4 oranges
1.35 kg/3 lb rhubarb, washed and
    cut into 5-cm/2-inch pieces
1.35 kg/3 lb sugar, warmed
100 g/4 oz walnuts, roughly
    chopped

1 Squeeze the juice from the oranges
and put it into a large pan with the
rhubarb.
2 Scrape away and discard the pith
from some of the orange rind. Cut
rind into fine shreds. Cook these
in boiling water until tender, then
drain and add to the rhubarb.
3 Cook the rhubarb over a low heat
with a lid on the pan until the juice
starts to run out. Then mash it down
and cook until soft.
4 Meanwhile, put the sugar to warm
in a very cool oven, Gas $\frac{1}{4}$, 225°F,
110°C. Put clean jam jars to warm at
the same time.
5 Add the warmed sugar and stir
until dissolved. Add the walnuts.
6 Increase the heat to obtain a rolling
boil and boil until setting point is
reached. (See page 168 for notes
about testing for a set.)
7 Pot the hot marmalade into the
warmed jars and immediately put on
waxed paper discs to seal the surface.
Either put on jam pot covers at once
or else wait until it is quite cold –
never in-between. (Condensation can
occur and the marmalade could go
mouldy.) Label and store in a cool
dark place.

Mrs H. Hopkins
West Midlands

*See page 168 for a few tips on making
preserves by microwave.*

1 Use the largest Pyrex bowl that will
fit into your microwave cooker. If
your microwave has only a small
cavity, make half the quantity given.

2 Squeeze the juice from the oranges
and put it with the rhubarb into the
bowl.
3 Scrape away and discard the pith
from some of the orange rind and cut
it into fine shreds. Put these in a
basin with 150 ml/$\frac{1}{4}$ pint hot water.
Cook on full power for 5 minutes,
then let it stand for 5 minutes so that
they become tender. Drain and then
add to the rhubarb.
4 Cook the rhubarb on full power for
10 minutes, stirring twice. Tip in the
sugar and stir well. Continue cooking
on full power for 5 minutes, stirring
every minute until all the sugar has
dissolved. Then continue cooking on
full power for 8 to 10 minutes,
stirring every 2 to 3 minutes – or as
the mixture boils up to the top of the
dish. For half quantities, cook on full
power for 5 to 7 minutes. (See page
168 for some notes on testing for
setting.)
5 When the correct setting point is
reached, stir in the walnuts. Allow to
cool slightly so that the walnuts don't
all float to the top, then pot, cover
and label as in step 7 above.

A JAR OF
LEMON CURD
FOR ONE

*Makes one 225 g/8 oz jar. The addition
of custard powder helps to speed the
thickening process.*

1 egg
$\frac{1}{2}$ teaspoon custard powder
75 g/3 oz sugar
25 g/1 oz butter
Finely grated rind and juice
    of 1 lemon

1 Use a basin that will fit nicely over
a pan of simmering water. Do not let
basin touch the water.
2 Beat the egg with custard powder.
Then add sugar, butter, lemon rind
and juice.

172

3 Set basin over pan of simmering water and stir mixture from time to time until it thickens. It will take about 15 to 20 minutes.
4 Fill a small jar and leave it to cool.

Keep in refrigerator and use within 4 weeks.

Mrs M. Alderson
Leeds, Yorkshire

 Microwave ━━━━━━━━━━━

1 Use a 1.1-litre/2-pint basin. Melt the butter on full power for 10 seconds. Then whisk in all the other ingredients (except the custard powder).
2 Heat on full power for 30 seconds. Stir well. Continue to cook in 10-second bursts, whisking well, until the mixture thickens. In total the lemon curd will take 60 to 90 seconds.
3 Pour it into a small jar and leave to cool.
4 Keep refrigerated and use within 4 weeks.

ELDERBERRY AND APPLE JELLY

This jelly is delicious with meat or poultry and it makes a pleasant change from the cranberry sauce traditionally served with turkey. Can be made at any time of the year, using dried elderberries available at home-brewing shops. With these it is necessary to start the night before.

450 g/1 lb elderberries or
225 g/½ lb dried elderberries
150 ml/¼ pint vinegar
1 small onion, peeled and spiked with 6 cloves
2 large cooking apples, peeled, cored and sliced
Sugar or 'sugar-with-pectin'

1 With dried elderberries just cover with boiling water and leave overnight to plump up. Then strain them.

2 Put the elderberries, vinegar and onion into a pan and boil for 20 minutes then strain, keeping the juices.
3 Cook the apples with a very little water until soft.
4 Add the strained elderberry juice.
5 Measure the amount of purée you now have and add 450 g/1 lb sugar for each 600 ml/1 pint of purée.
6 Bring the mixture to the boil, stirring to help the sugar dissolve. Then keep it at a rolling boil until setting point is reached. Using 'sugar-with-pectin', this will take only 4 minutes. (See page 168 for notes on testing for setting.)
7 Pot the jelly into small warmed jars while very hot. Put on waxed paper discs at once and either put jam pot covers on straight away, or else leave until the jelly is quite cold.

Mrs Joyce Beresford
Bromley Cross, Bolton

Microwave ━━━━━━━━━━━

'Sugar-with-pectin' is recommended for this method.

Plumping the dried elderberries by microwave was not found satisfactory; it is better if you soak them overnight as recommended in the recipe.

1 With dried elderberries, just cover with boiling water and leave overnight to plump up. Then strain them.
2 Put the elderberries, vinegar and onion into a 4-litre/7-pint mixing bowl, cover with clear film and cook on full power for 6 to 8 minutes. Then leave to stand while you cook the apple.
3 Put the apple and two 15 ml tablespoons water in a basin, cover with clear film and heat on full power for 5 minutes. Mash with a fork or a potato masher.
4 Strain the elderberry juice into the apple purée. Rinse out the large mixing bowl and measure the purée

into it. Add 450 g/1 lb 'sugar-with-pectin' for each 600 ml/1 pint purée.

5 Heat the mixture on full power for 5 to 6 minutes, stirring occasionally with a wooden spoon, to help the sugar dissolve. Once the sugar has dissolved, continue heating on full power for 4 to 5 minutes until setting point is reached.

6 Put the jelly immediately into small warm jars, cover the surface with waxed paper discs and put on the jam pot cover straight away.

7 Label and store in a cool dark place.

SWEET CHUTNEY

This recipe involves no cooking. Makes 1 kg/2½ lb —easy to make more.

225 g/½ lb cooking apples, peeled and grated
225 g/½ lb onions, finely chopped
225 g/½ lb dates, stoned and finely chopped
¼ teaspoon salt
¼ teaspoon freshly ground pepper
¼ teaspoon pickling spice
225 g/½ lb sultanas
225 g/½ lb light brown sugar
150 ml/¼ pint vinegar

1 Mix all the ingredients together and leave them for 48 hours.

2 If the chutney looks a bit dry, stir in some extra vinegar. Bottle the chutney in jars with vinegar-proof lids and store in a cool, dark place.

Mrs M. Robinson,
Hexham, Northumberland

RED TOMATO CHUTNEY

Yields 2½ to 3 kg/5 to 6 lb. Can be made with green tomatoes.

1 kg/2 lb red tomatoes
500 g/1 lb onions or shallots
500 g/1 lb cooking apples
375 g/12 oz sultanas
500 g/1 lb brown sugar
1 slightly rounded teaspoon ground cloves
1 teaspoon ground ginger
1 teaspoon dry mustard
½ teaspoon cayenne pepper
1 tablespoon salt
½ litre/1 pint vinegar

1 Skin tomatoes (see page 26) and cut them up.

2 Peel and chop onions finely.

3 Peel, core and chop apples finely.

4 Put all the ingredients into a large pan and cook slowly, stirring, until sugar has dissolved.

5 Turn heat down and let chutney

just simmer gently for about 1½ to 2 hours, stirring occasionally, until it is thick and smooth. Draw a wooden spoon through it. If the trail of the spoon holds without immediately filling with liquid the chutney is ready.

6 Meanwhile prepare clean jars with vinegar-proof lids. (Coffee jars with plastic lids are ideal.) Put jars to warm in a very slow oven, Gas ¼, 225°F, 110°C.

7 Pour hot chutney into jars and at once put on a waxed paper disc, waxed side down. Then leave until cold.

8 When jars of chutney are quite cold, put on the vinegar-proof lids. Label jars and store in a cool, dry, dark cupboard.

Always allow chutney to mature for at least three months as the flavour improves the longer it is kept.

Mrs A. I. McBain
Hull, N. Humberside

___

Microwave ∿∿∿∿∿∿∿∿∿∿∿∿∿∿∿∿∿∿

See page 168 for some notes on making preserves by microwave.

Only 450 ml/¾ pint vinegar is needed, otherwise the ingredients are as given above.

1 Prepare tomatoes, onion and apple, following steps 1 to 3 above.
2 Put onion and apple in a large 3-litre/5-pint casserole. Cook on full power for 5 to 7 minutes to soften the onion.
3 Mix in all the rest of the ingredients. Cook uncovered on full power for 15 minutes, stirring every 3 to 5 minutes.
4 When the mixture is thick, so that a spoon drawn through it leaves its mark without instantly filling with liquid, the chutney is done.
5 Pot it into warm jars, put on the waxed paper discs to seal the surface while it is still hot. Then leave to cool. Put on vinegar-proof lids for storage. Label and store in a cool dark place.

The flavour will mature if the chutney is kept for 2 to 3 months.

TOMATO SAUCE
Makes 1.2 litres/2 pints.

1.75 kg/4 lb ripe tomatoes, chopped
2 medium onions, chopped
1 clove of garlic, crushed
¼ teaspoon cayenne pepper
225 g/½ lb white sugar
225 g/½ lb muscovado sugar
25 g/1 oz salt
15 g/½ oz whole cloves
175 ml/7 fl oz vinegar

1 Put all ingredients together in a large pan and boil steadily for about 3 hours until a sauce-like consistency is reached. Stir from time to time to stop it burning and mash it down with a potato masher.
2 Liquidise the mixture and then sieve it if you prefer the pips removed.
3 Allow to cool and then bottle using vinegar-proof lids.
4 Keep bottles in a cool dark place.

Mary Hunter
Addingham, Yorkshire

___

Microwave ∿∿∿∿∿∿∿∿∿∿∿∿∿∿∿∿∿∿

Makes 600 to 750 ml/1 to 1¼ pints.

900 g/2 lb ripe tomatoes, quartered
1 onion, sliced
1 clove of garlic, crushed
100 g/4 oz granulated sugar
100 g/4 oz muscovado sugar
1 teaspoon salt
6 tablespoons vinegar
4 whole cloves
A pinch of cayenne pepper

1 Put the tomatoes in a 4 litre/7 pint mixing bowl with the onion, garlic and sugar. Heat on full power for 5 minutes, then stir well, mashing down the tomatoes.
2 Add the remaining ingredients and cook on full power for 10 minutes, stirring twice. Cool slightly. Cook longer for a thicker sauce.
3 Liquidise the mixture and then sieve to remove the pips.
4 Allow to cool completely and then bottle, using vinegar-proof lids.
5 Store in a cool dark place.

RICH RUM TRUFFLES

These are so easy to prepare, and to make them look special, put them in little paper sweet cases. Makes 12.

75 g/3 oz plain chocolate
1 egg yolk
15 g/½ oz butter
1 to 2 teaspoons rum
1 teaspoon cream
2 teaspoons ground almonds or cake crumbs
Chocolate vermicelli

1 Put the chocolate into a bowl set over a pan of hot water and leave until it has melted. Stir in egg yolk.
2 Remove from the heat and stir in butter, rum, cream and ground almonds or cake crumbs.
3 Leave the bowl in a cool place for 10 minutes or so, then beat the mixture until it is quite thick. Shape into balls and roll them in chocolate vermicelli.

Miss R. Cawson
Fareham, Hampshire.

Microwave

1 Put the chocolate and butter in a small basin and heat on full power for 1½ minutes, until melted.

2 Stir in the egg yolk, rum, cream and the ground almonds or cake crumbs.
 Leave the bowl in a cool place for 10 minutes or so. Then, when the mixture is quite thick, shape into 12 balls. Finish as above.

Another Idea!
These can also be made substituting white chocolate for plain, and using desiccated coconut instead of ground almonds. Roll them in icing sugar, grated white chocolate or coconut.

Yvonne Hamlett
Haddenham, Buckinghamshire

FRUIT AND NUT SWEETS FOR CHRISTMAS

Children may enjoy helping to make these, because there is no actual cooking involved.

50 g/2 oz blanched almonds, finely chopped
50 g/2 oz dried apricots, finely chopped
50 g/2 oz dried figs, finely chopped
50 g/2 oz glacé cherries – red and green, finely chopped
2 teaspoons brandy
75 g/3 oz marzipan

1 Mix together the nuts, fruit and brandy.
2 Divide the mixture into two and roll each into a long thin sausage shape. Chill well.
3 Roll out the marzipan thinly into two strips just big enough to wrap around the fruit and nut rolls.
4 Press the marzipan around the rolls and seal the join with a little water. Return to the refrigerator until firm.
5 Cut into small pieces and put each sweet into a small paper case.

Grace Mulligan

ALL IN THE OVEN

These lists are to help you choose
a variety of recipes to cook in the oven at the
same time. It is one of the most popular features
of the television programmes when,
with careful juggling of dishes and cake tins,
we cook a main course, vegetables, pudding and a
cake all together.

GAS 8, 450°F, 230°C

Potato, Ham and Egg Pie

White Bread
Wholemeal Bread
Milk Bread
Poppy Seed Plait
Bridge Rolls or Batch Rolls

GAS 7, 425°F, 210°C

Salmon Parcel

Barbecue Spare Ribs

Pizza for 2
Apple and Mincemeat Parcel

Banana Alaska

Coconut Scones

GAS 6, 400°F, 200°C

Cod with Sweetcorn
Citrus Mackerel
Baked Grey Mullet
Mushroom-Stuffed Plaice
Crisp Lemon Sole
Salmon Savoury
Macaroni and Tuna Layer

Tasty Fish Pie
Sardines for Tea

Patti's Chicken for Two

Celery Pork Steaks
Pork with Chestnuts
Berkshire Moussaka

Scotch Eggs
Savoury Potato Bake with
    Frankfurters
Vegetables with Cheese
Cheese-Baked Potatoes
Savoury Pudding

Cheese and Leek Flan
Quick Egg, Bacon and Mushroom
    Pie
Sardine Pasties
Ham and Leek Flan
Chicken and Mushroom Pie
Fried Curry Puffs
Pecan Pie
Almond Mince Pies

Christmas Mincemeat Roll
Apple Pudding
Cherry Sponge Pudding

Hot Cross Buns
Bran Muffins
Australian Cakes

GAS 5, 375°F, 190°C

Teifi Salmon in a Sauce
Salmon and Potato Bake

Baked Lamb Chop with
   Courgettes

Cheese and Cauliflower Soufflé

Sausagemeat Flan

Baked Apple with Muesli
Savoury Baked Apple
Oaty Rhubarb Crumble
Oaty Apple Crunch

Harold's Fruit Cake
Yoghurt Cake
Cherry and Almond Slice
Lucy Cake

GAS 4, 350°F, 180°C

Bacon and Prune Rolls
Smoked Fish Soufflé
Chicken Pieces in a Cider Sauce
Baked Chicken with Pineapple
Nutty Lemon Stuffing

Savoury Hot Pot
Savoury Lamb Chops
Liver and Bacon Casserole
Liver Balls

Curried Meat Loaf
Potato and Bean Casserole
Hot Vegetable Pancakes

Casseroled Potatoes with Onions
   and Garlic
Cheese-Baked Potatoes

Fish Pie in Puff Pastry
Marmalade Flan
Apricot and Coconut Tarts

Old-fashioned Milk Puddings
Strawberries and Kiwi Fruit in a
   Cream-Filled Sponge

Honey and Malt Fruit Loaf
Spiced Carrot Tea Bread
Spicy Apple Loaf
Tom's Vancouver Carrot Cake
Grandmother's Ginger Fruit Cake
Walnut Flat Cake
Bran Biscuits
Muesli Bars

GAS 3, 325°F, 160°C

Belly Pork with Apple and Sage
   Coating
Hearts Braised in an Orange Sauce

Megan's Treacle Roll

Dumpling Loaf
Quick Lemon Cake
Wholemeal Chocolate Cake
Anzacs

GAS 2, 300°F, 150°C

Patti's Chicken for Two

Steak and Kidney Pie Filling

Baked Rice Pudding
Zarda or Sweet Saffron Rice

Wholemeal Gingerbread
Cumberland Shortbread

SPECIAL OCCASION MENUS

Stuffed Mushrooms
Chicken with Orange and Ginger
Chocolate Moulds

Celery Fritters with a Dip
Pork with Chestnuts
Chocolate Brandy Cake

Tuna Fish Pâté
Sherried Pork Chops
Fresh Peaches in Raspberry Sauce

Pear with Stilton Sauce
A Rich Beef Stew
Grapes with Muscovado and
Soured Cream

Pea and Mint Soup
Honolulu Chicken
Coffee Ice Cream

Quick Liver Pâté
Pork Stir Fry
Quick Fruit Puddings

Eggs in a Forest
Sea Bass with Clams and Herbs
Mandarin Surprise
*(Sally Wilson's winning menu – for the
title of 1987 Junior Cook of the Year)*

Quick Chilled Tomato Soup
Squid with Green Peppers
in a Black Bean Sauce
Chocolate Brandy Cake

Cheese and Leek Flan
Teifi Salmon in a Sauce
Apple Pudding
*(Lucy Barton-Greenwood's menu won her
second place in the competition)*

Smoked Fish Soufflé
Chicken Pieces in Cider Sauce
Banana Alaska

Minted Cucumber Mousse
Poached Salmon with Two Sauces
Strawberries and Kiwi Fruit in a
Cream-Filled Sponge
(Simon Dunn's menu won him third place)

Watercress Soup
Crisp Roast Duck with
Grapefruit Sauce
Christmas Mincemeat Roll
Ice Cream Christmas Pud

INDEX

(M) *indicates that a recipe also has a microwave method.*

181

188